Teeline for Journalists

Dawn Johnston

www.heinemann.co.uk
✓ Free online support
✓ Useful weblinks
✓ 24 hour online ordering

01865 888058

Heinemann
Inspiring generations

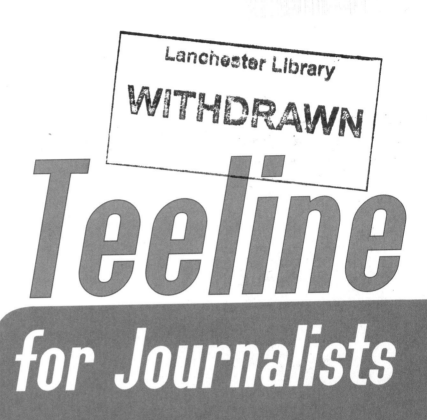

Heinemann Educational Publishers
Halley Court, Jordan Hill, Oxford OX2 8EJ
Part of Harcourt Education

Heinemann is the registered trademark of
Harcourt Education Limited

First published by Darlington College of Technology July 2004
Reprinted November 2004; February 2005; July 2005; September 2005
This edition 2006

10 09 08 07 06
10 9 8 7 6 5 4 3 2

British Library Cataloguing in Publication Data is available
from the British Library on request.

10-digit ISBN: 0 43547160 0
13-digit ISBN: 978 0 435471 60 6

Typeset by Saxon Graphics Ltd, Derby
Original illustrations © Harcourt Education Limited, 2005

Cover design by Wooden Ark Studio

Printed by CPI Bath Press Ltd

Cover photo: © royalty free/Corbis

Acknowledgements
Every effort has been made to contact copyright holders of material reproduced in this book. Any omissions will be rectified in subsequent printings if notice is given to the publishers.

The author would like to thank past students for their encouragement to embark on this venture; colleagues at Darlington College of Technology for their support; and special thanks to her husband for his patience and technical assistance.

About the author
Dawn Johnston is currently employed as a Shorthand Tutor within the School of Journalism, Media and the Arts at Darlington College of Technology. She joined the College in 1998, having previously worked part-time at various Colleges of Further Education within the Cleveland area, teaching secretarial and IT subjects. She has been responsible for training students employed by the Newsquest publishing group and the Johnston Press, as well as other NCTJ pre-entry students, since 1998. Many of the students completed their training with successful examination passes in excess of the NCTJ's 100 wpm requirement.

The Teeline outlines in this book have been written by Dawn Johnston.

Contents

Introduction

Teeline shorthand was developed in the 1960s by its inventor, James Hill, who, faced with the problem of training journalists to write at high speeds in the shortest time possible, applied method-study techniques to normal handwriting. As he said, 'If you can write, you can write Teeline'. Sadly he died in 1971 leaving a widow and son to keep his work alive.

As well as the speed at which the system can be mastered, its flexibility is to be admired – it is possible to write one word by using a number of different, yet equally correct, Teeline outlines. The only 'correct' outline is the one that you can quickly and accurately read back from your own Teeline note. Ensure that you have thoroughly grasped the theory principles before attempting to adapt your own frequently used outlines – remember 'accuracy' is the key word when transcribing your notes.

How to use this book

It is important that each Unit in this book is studied in sequence, as the theory principles have been written to ensure logical progression of your learning. Many examples of words are given in each Unit in order to illustrate a particular new theory principle and give the opportunity to revise previously learned principles – these examples are not an exhaustive vocabulary list to be learned. The principle should be learned and applied to similar words dictated/heard or read.

You will require a number of spiral-bound notebooks in which to write your Teeline notes. Choose notebooks with good quality, non-absorbent paper. The books should have ruled horizontal lines which are not too close together. The front cover of each notebook should be dated when first used, and should also show the owner's name and possibly a contact telephone number in case the notebook is inadvertently mislaid. A journalist's Teeline notes may be required as evidence in a court of law, and notebooks must be retained for three years for this purpose.

Each page of your notebook should have a ruled margin of 2–3cm. Right-handed writers will rule their margin on the left of the page and left-handed writers will use the right side of the page. The margin will be used for writing an amended Teeline outline after the original 'poor' outline has been circled. No longhand is permissible in Teeline notes for exam purposes. However, working journalists will also use the margin to spell in longhand any proper names. They will also mark the margin to indicate any significant quotes or to draw their attention to any exceptional material needed when transcribing their notes. Date the bottom of the page at the beginning of each day – this will make the location of a particular day's work much easier.

If writing Teeline whilst sitting at a desk, open the notebook and write on each page consecutively before turning the book round and working back through it. It is useful to use a

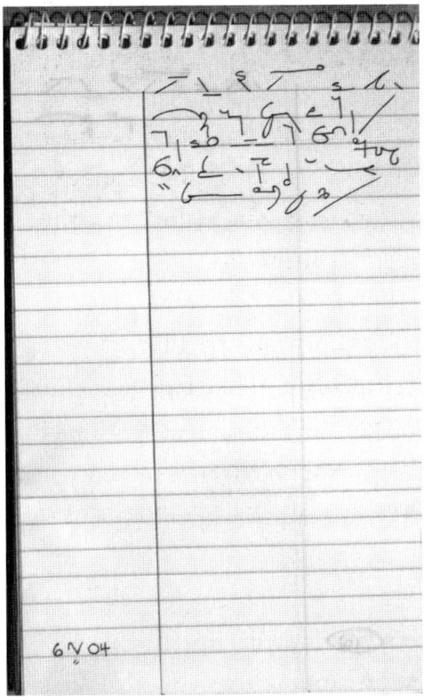

Shorthand notebook for a right-handed writer

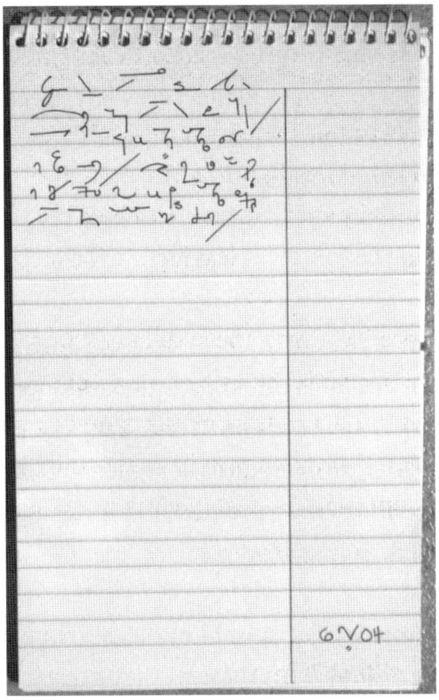

Shorthand notebook for a left-handed writer

rubber band to hold the worked pages and thereby easily locate the next clean page.

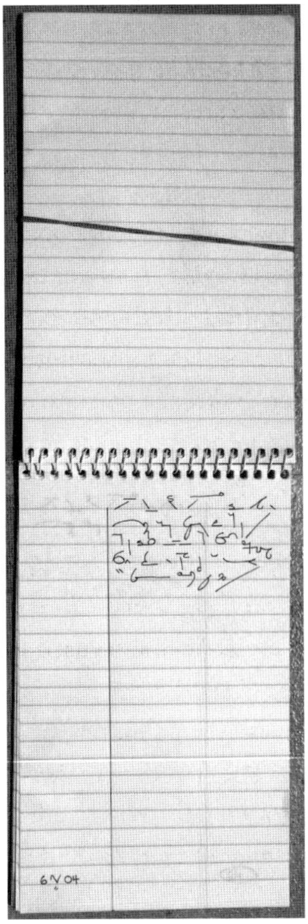

Use a rubber band to easily find clean pages in your notebook

Teeline may be written by using a pen or a pencil. Experiment with both before deciding which you prefer. Choose a fine-nibbed pen which does not leave messy blotches as these may smudge as you write across the page. If using a pencil, choose a good quality HB grade, and keep it sharpened. You should always have at least one spare pen/pencil to hand when taking dictation. Surely nothing could be worse than a pen 'running out' half-way through a piece of examination dictation, especially if you were taking it down accurately!

When you have prepared your Teeline 'equipment', you will be ready to learn the alphabet and make swift progress to master a wonderful skill which is vital for a journalist. When learning any skill subject, it is important to practise until that skill becomes automatic.

Journalists write shorthand notes, most often, to record the spoken words of a person being interviewed or whilst listening to a speech. A CD-ROM of MP3 files accompanies this book; this will enable you to practise the skill of writing Teeline whilst listening to the spoken word. With practice you will develop this skill. Your automatic response to the spoken word will be to write Teeline without a great deal of conscious thought about the formation of the outlines. A symbol to denote which tasks have accompanying dictation material is shown in the book. You will require Windows Media Player, or equivalent, on your computer in order to listen to the dictation material.

Learning

It is best to learn Teeline by doing a little and often, rather than doing nothing for days and then trying to study for hours at a time. Vary the tasks as you learn. In addition to listening to the MP3 files, perhaps you could ask someone to read the Teeline alphabet letters to you when you have learned them, then progress to words. Ask your helper to read slowly at first and then increase the speed, as you progress.

If you are able to write the 'special outlines' without hesitation, your writing speed will increase, so it is vital to learn these as they appear in each Unit. A comprehensive list of 'special outlines', 'distinguishing outlines' and 'word groupings' may be found in the Appendices. Eventually, write from dictation of longer passages – in addition to using the MP3 files, the keys to these tasks are in the back of the book – and when most of the theory has been learned, try writing notes as you listen to your favourite television or radio programme, or perhaps a piece of music from a favourite singer or band.

As you begin to study this shorthand system, I sincerely hope that you will have fun as you learn – stay positive and determined and you will succeed. You will certainly impress and be admired by those who watch you write their spoken words **accurately**!

Dawn Johnston

Unit 1
The Teeline alphabet

It has been said that 'if you can write, you can write Teeline'. Letters of the Teeline alphabet are formed by simplifying the known longhand letters of the alphabet. Some Teeline letters are derived from capital letters and others from lower case letters. The position of Teeline letters generally take the position of their longhand equivalent – many letters sit on the writing line, the letter T takes the horizontal stroke and is written above the line, and letters **G, J, P,** and **Q** cut through the writing line.

The alphabet

Vowels have two forms – full vowels and indicators. The reason for this will be explained later. **Vowels are always written smaller than consonants** – generally about one third of the size of consonants. Teeline letters are known as 'outlines'.

Although each individual's Teeline may take on the character of their longhand writing style, try to keep your Teeline outlines small, neat and written with a light touch. Remember, above all, that your Teeline outlines are the means to you quickly and accurately producing copy to meet your paper's deadline. Teeline notes are admissible, in a court of law, as evidence. Teeline is simply a means to an end, but a most valuable skill and tool for your trade.

The Teeline letters of the alphabet A–M

LONGHAND LETTER	TEELINE LETTER			EXPLANATION
	FULL VOWEL	VOWEL INDICATOR	CONSONANT	
A				Full vowel taken from the top of a capital **A**. Vowel indicator is the downstroke of that letter. Occasionally also written upwards.
B				A streamlined **b**, written from top to bottom with a large circle.
C				As a longhand **C**. Start and finish at the same vertical point. **C also represents CK** in words, e.g. back, deck, etc.

LONGHAND LETTER	TEELINE LETTER			EXPLANATION
	FULL VOWEL	VOWEL INDICATOR	CONSONANT	
D				A short dash from left to right **d**own on the line. Remember **D**own for **D**.
E	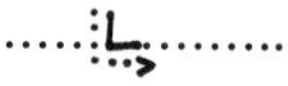	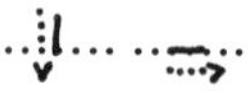		The bottom part of capital **E**, a 90° angle. The indicator has 2 forms, but the horizontal one is rarely used.
F			 or 	Part of a handwritten . It can be written upwards or downwards. **F** is written for words with the sound of **F**, e.g. **ph**one, **ph**ysical, **ph**armacy, enou**gh**, tou**gh**, gra**ph**ic, etc.
G				Curved at the start and slopes through the writing line. Letter **G** used in words with the sound of **dge**, e.g. he**dge**, fri**dge**, we**dge**, bu**dge**t, etc.
H			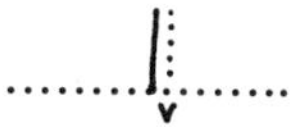	The downstroke of longhand letter **H**. Must always be written downwards.
I				A handwritten  small, sharply angled, without a dot. Vowel indicator generally written downwards, but occasionally written upwards.
J				Sloping through the writing line, without a dot.
K				The 'kicking' part of capital **K**. Written in one sharply angled stroke.

LONGHAND LETTER	TEELINE LETTER			EXPLANATION
	FULL VOWEL	VOWEL INDICATOR	CONSONANT	
L			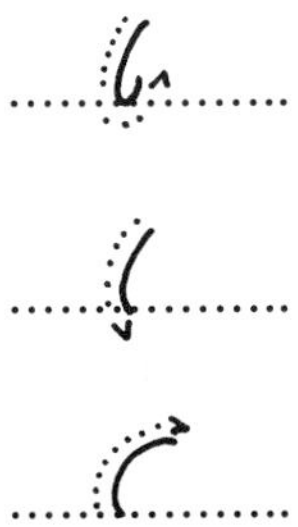	3 forms of this letter. The most commonly written is the downward form with a curl; secondly, the downward form without a curl so that it joins easily to other letters; finally, occasionally written upwards after particular letters.
M				Streamlined **m** to form an arch written from left to right.

Task 1.1

Memorise letters A–M of the alphabet by using a 'drill sheet'

MP3

To prepare a 'drill sheet', write the ***longhand letters*** **A–M** in the margin of an A4 ruled sheet. Write one letter per line down the page. Paying particular attention to the size, shape and direction of writing, copy the ***Teeline letters*** of the alphabet **A–M**. Say the letters as you write them. This will help you to memorise their name and shape. Fold the A4 sheet, concertina style, so that only the longhand letters are visible and then write the Teeline letters **A–M** again from memory. Continue folding the paper in this way until the Teeline letters **A–M** can be written without any hesitation.

This method is useful for memorising other outlines which need to be written without hesitation.

Listen to your MP3 file and write Teeline letters **A–M** accurately and without hesitation.

The Teeline letters of the alphabet N–Z

LONGHAND LETTER	TEELINE LETTER			EXPLANATION
	FULL VOWEL	VOWEL INDICATOR	CONSONANT	
N			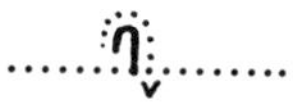	The hook and downstroke of a handwritten . Take care to keep the outline small.
O				The full vowel is used rarely. The indicator is the shallow under-section of **O** written from left to right.
P			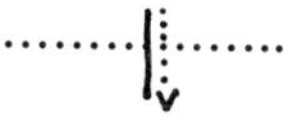	The downstroke of lower case **P**. Always written downwards and through the line when it begins a word.
Q				The loop which joins **Q** to **U** in all English words. Written through the line.
R				A straight line written from left to right and always written upwards.
S				A small circle, written in the most convenient direction. Although a consonant, it is smaller than the full vowel **O**.
T				The horizontal stroke of letter **T/t**. When standing alone, preceded by a vowel or letter **S**, letter **T** is written above the writing line. This is known as the **T** position. Remember, as letter **D** was Down, **T** is Top.

LONGHAND LETTER	TEELINE LETTER			EXPLANATION
	FULL VOWEL	VOWEL INDICATOR	CONSONANT	
U				The full vowel is a small, deep outline. Great care must be taken not to confuse this with the **O** indicator or the letter **W**. The indicator for letter **U** is the side stroke of letter **U**. Note that it is exactly the same as the indicator for letter **E**, but will never be confused.
V				Written as the longhand letter. Take care to write it upright with a sharp angle so that it cannot be confused with full vowel **I**.
W				Streamlined letter **W** which curves from left to right. Think of this as an inverted letter **M**.
X			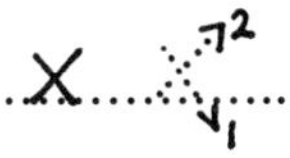	Written as a longhand **X**. Write the first stroke from left to right downwards, take the pen/pencil off and write the second stroke from left to right upwards. 
Y				Unlike its longhand partner, letter 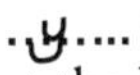 is written without the loop passing through the writing line. **Y** is represented by letter **I** at the end of words because **Y** sounds like **I** or **i**, e.g. buy, why, lady, busy.
Z				A small outline written as Teeline letter **S** with a small curled tail. The letter **Z** changes to **S** in the middle of a word.

Task 1.2

Memorise letters N–Z of the alphabet by using a drill sheet

MP3

Listen to your MP3 file and write Teeline letters **N–Z** accurately and without hesitation.

Everything you write in Teeline will require you to write the letters of the alphabet. Ensure that you know the complete alphabet of full vowels, indicators and consonants before moving on.

Common words

Many letters of the alphabet represent commonly occurring words. These words must be learnt so that they can be recalled instantly and written quickly. Learn these by preparing 'drill sheets'. When you feel that you can write these words from memory, ask someone to read them to you in random order and write them from dictation. You may find them easier to learn in two parts – **A–M** and **N–Z**.

Common words represented by the letters A–M

LONGHAND LETTER	TEELINE LETTER	COMMON WORDS
A		**able, able to, ability, after**
		**a** (written on the line)
		**at** (written in the **T** position)
B		**be, been**
C		**once, offence**
		**local** (hanging from the writing line)
D		**do, day**
E		**electric**
	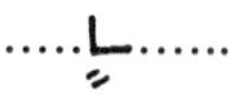	**England** (2 small lines written **upwards** under an outline indicates a capital letter)

E		**ever, every**
F		**from** (the upward form of letter **F**)
G		**go, gentleman, guilt**
		**guilty** (the **I** indicator is attached and written upwards)
H		**he**
I		**I, eye, intelligent**
		**Ireland** (letter **I** with capitals mark underneath)
K		**kind, knowledge**
		**King** (letter **K** with capitals mark underneath)
		**like** (letter **K** hanging from the writing line)
L		**letter**
		**a lot, a lot of** (letter **L** hanging from the writing line)
M		**me**
		**time** (letter **M** written in the **T** position)
		**million** (letter **M** hanging from the writing line)

Task 1.3

Memorise common words represented by the letters A–M

MP3

Listen to your MP3 file and write common words represented by Teeline letters **A–M** accurately and without hesitation.

Task 1.4

Transcribe the following words represented by the letters A–M

MP3

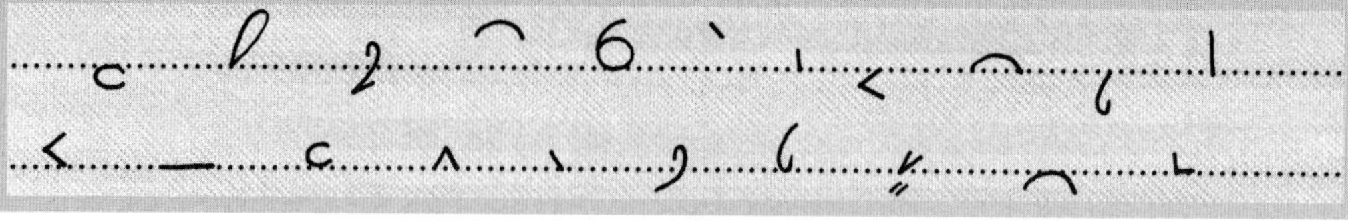

Common words represented by the letters N–Z

LONGHAND LETTER	TEELINE LETTER	COMMON WORDS
N	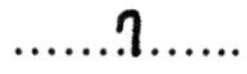	**and, new, knew**
	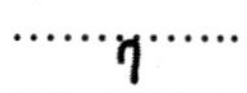	**begin** (letter **N** hanging from the writing line)
		**began, begun** (indicators **A** and **U** are written next to letter **N** to differentiate the words)
O		**or** (full **O** vowel written through the writing line)
		**of** (indicator **O** written in the **T** position)
P	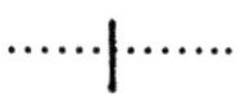	**page, pence, police**
Q		**equal, question**
	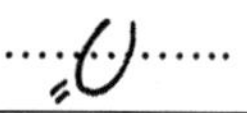	**Queen** (letter **Q** with capitals mark underneath)
R		**are, authority** (always written upwards from the writing line)
S	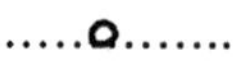	**south**
		**Scotland** (letter **S** with capitals mark underneath)
T		**to**
U	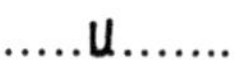	**you**
V		**very, have, versus**

LONGHAND LETTER	TEELINE LETTER	COMMON WORDS
V		**evidence** (letter V hanging from the writing line)
		**above** (letter V in the **T** position)
W		**we**
		**Wales** (letter **W** with capitals mark underneath)
X		**accident, cross**
		**accident black spot** (the same outline as accident followed by a spot written with the pen/pencil)
Y		**your**

Task 1.5

Memorise common words represented by the letters N–Z

MP3

Listen to your MP3 file and write common words represented by Teeline letters N–Z accurately and without hesitation.

Task 1.6

Transcribe the following words represented by the letters N–Z

MP3

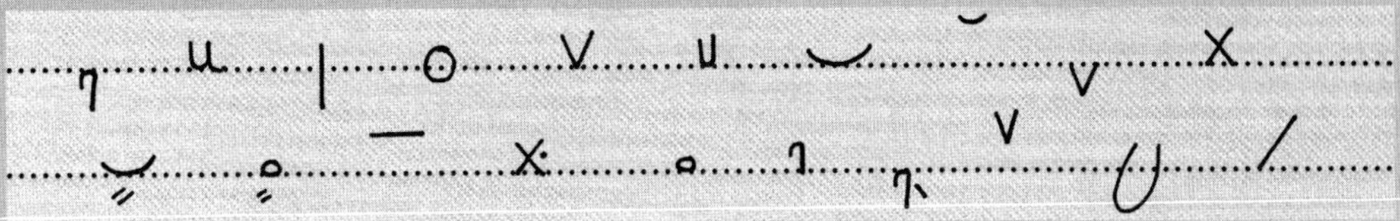

Essential punctuation marks

It has already been explained that a capital letter is indicated by writing two small **upward** strokes under an outline, for example. It is not necessary to use the capitals mark at the beginning of each sentence.

It is **essential** to indicate a full stop in one's Teeline notes. For exam purposes, the reader should indicate the presence of a full stop by inflexion of the voice. A full stop is written through the writing line as a long sloping line. It must **always be written upwards from left to right.**

Take great care to listen for full stops in dictation. Marks may be lost in exam work if a full stop is omitted, thereby changing the sense of a sentence. For example, think how misplacing the word 'however' at the end of a sentence, or at the beginning of the next sentence will alter the meaning of that sentence. For example:

'I no longer report on rugby matches however. I must confess I still like to watch the game.'

Or

'I no longer report on rugby matches. However, I must confess I still like to watch the game.'

Other punctuation marks

During transcription all punctuation marks should be included. In reality, Teeline writers rarely have time to indicate them in their Teeline notes. However, suggestions for punctuation marks are shown below:

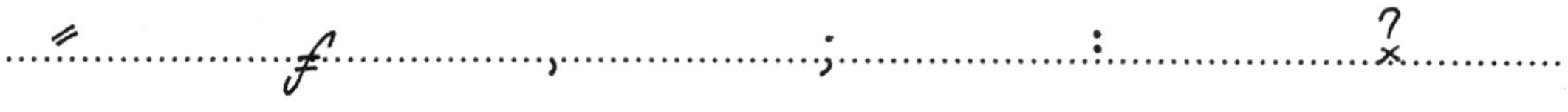

dash hyphen comma semi-colon colon question mark

Task 1.7

Write the Teeline outlines for the following sentences

MP3

Remember to write the essential punctuation marks and capital letters.

1 Do you like England?
2 I like England, Ireland, Scotland and Wales.
3 Have you ever been to Wales?
4 I have been once to Wales and once to Scotland.
5 Are you a local gentleman?
6 You are very kind, intelligent and have a lot of knowledge and ability.
7 Police have your new evidence and are able to begin to question a local gentleman.
8 From time to time we like to go to South Wales.
9 We are very cross after your accident to your eye.
10 I do like a new day and a new time to begin.

Task 1.8

Join letters of the alphabet as shown

MP3

Letters of the alphabet are joined together in order to form words. Write the vowel indicator followed by the next letter in one movement. Do not take your pen/pencil off the page as you write the two letters which form simple words. Remember that vowel indicators are written smaller than consonants. Copy the outlines below.

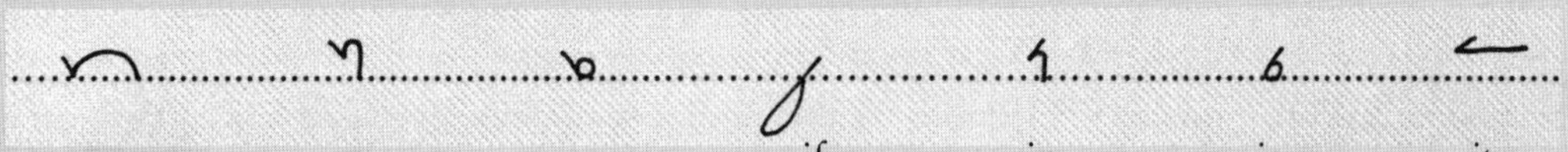

am an as if in is it

Task 1.9

Copy the outlines below

MP3

The outlines comprise vowel indicators, full vowels and consonants which have been joined together. Pay particular attention to the size, shape and direction of writing for these outlines. Note that the letters are joined together without taking the pen/pencil from the page, except for the letter X and the letter K when it is joined to H, J or P. Write the longhand letters represented by these outlines.

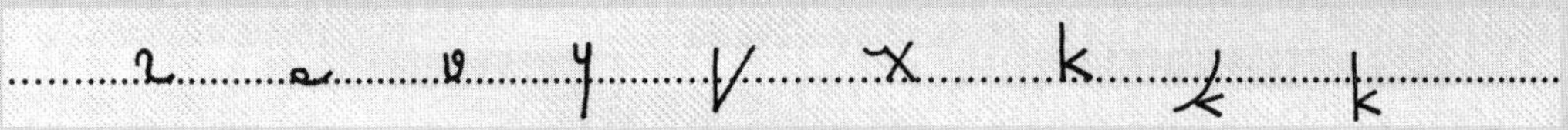

Unit 2
The basic principles of writing Teeline

Having learned the Teeline alphabet and how to join letters together, it would now be possible to write any longhand word in Teeline. However, our aim is to write words in a much faster way by reducing the amount written.

This reduction will be achieved by removing all unnecessary letters, thus leaving a skeleton word.

When read in the **context of a sentence**, these skeleton words will make sense. When reading Teeline it is advisable to 'read on' to gain the sense (or context) of the sentence because the same Teeline outline could represent more than one word.

If one thinks of vowels as being flesh and consonants as the bones of the skeleton this will help one to understand this basic principle. For example, it would be impossible to make sense of the following sentence if only the vowels were written:

Oo i e aia o Ea.

However, the same sentence makes perfect sense if consonants and only essential vowels are written:

Lndn is th cptl o Englnd.

Essential vowels are those written at the **beginning of a word** and those **sounded at the end of a word.** For example:

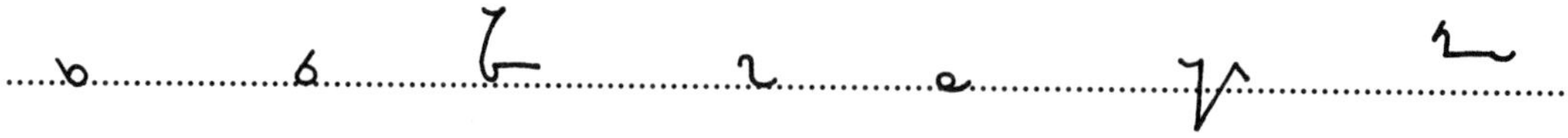

as is old no so opera into

Removal of unnecessary letters

1 Remove vowels in the middle of words

hear	remove **E** and **A** and the skeleton is **HR**	
paid	remove **A** and **I** and the skeleton is **PD**	

pour remove O and U and the skeleton is **PR** 

quit remove **U** and **I** and the skeleton is QT 

rob remove O and the skeleton is **RB** 

rock remove O and the skeleton is **RC**
(remember words ending **CK** write letter **C**) 

However, sometimes it is difficult to join two letters together without a medial vowel. Try to join **B** to **N**, **B** to **G** and **J** to **C**! Whilst not impossible, it is easier to join these letters with a vowel indicator.

Now write the following words by joining the letters with a vowel indicator:

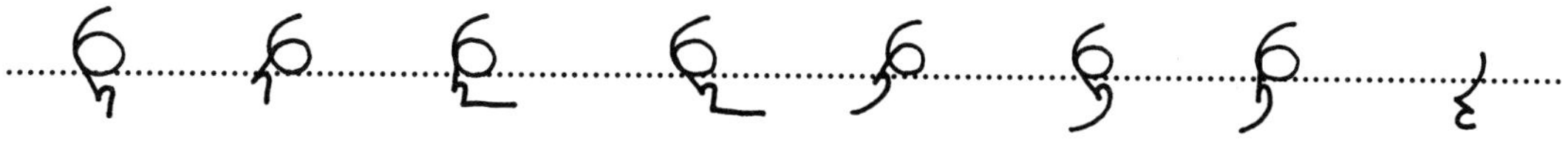

ban bin bend band big bag bug jack

Occasionally it is better to insert a vowel indicator in order to distinguish between two outlines which would otherwise be the same and may lead to confusion in transcription:

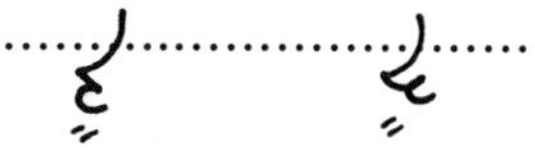

Jack Jock

2 Remove all silent letters

Letters which are not sounded are omitted:

take middle vowel omitted and the **E** is silent, so the skeleton is written as **TK** 

light middle vowel omitted and the **GH** are silent, so the skeleton is written as **LT** 

numb middle vowel omitted and **B** is silent, so the skeleton is written as **NM** 

walk	middle vowel omitted and the **L** is silent, so the skeleton is written as **WK** (note how the pen slides back down W to form letter K)	

3 Remove one of doubled letters

When double letters occur in a word it is necessary to write only one of those letters:

ball	middle vowel omitted and only one **L** is necessary, so the skeleton is written as **BL**	
tell	middle vowel omitted and only one **L** is necessary, so the skeleton is written as **TL**	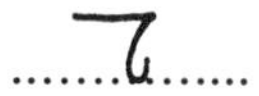
little	middle vowel omitted, only one **T** is necessary, the vowel **E** is silent, so the skeleton is written as **LTL**	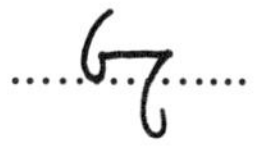
add	vowel at the beginning is always written, only one **D** is necessary, so the skeleton is written as **AD**	

Task 2.1

Read the following paragraph

MP3

All unnecessary letters have been removed. Note that some single letters represent common words which have already been learned in Unit 1 (for example u for you, n for and, etc.).

As a jrnlst u wl nd to rt fst n acrt Tln nts so tht u r abl t rt tht mmrbl qt fr yr nwsppr. Spnd prt o ech d lrnng th cmn wrds n othr otlns whch wl hlp t incrs yr rtng spd. Tln is a skl sbjct n tht skl wl bcm autmtc wth dly prctc. Gd lck n enjy yr lrnng.

Position of outlines in relation to the writing line

At the beginning of a word the first letter is usually written in its normal position. When a word starts with a vowel or a small letter which is followed by a longer letter it is sensible to start writing so that the second letter takes its normal writing position. For example:

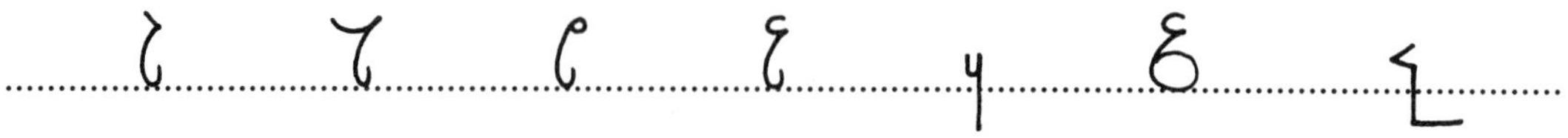

all will sail cell up cab kept

Note also that MN is easier to read if N is allowed to sit on the writing line: 
main

Task 2.2

Remove the unnecessary letters in the following words to reveal the Teeline skeleton

MP3

bold	....	peer	....	love	....	man	......	year	....
level	....	pass	....	dome	....	voice	......	accept	....
rail	....	rise	....	tough	......	give	......	manage	....

Task 2.3

Read the following Teeline outlines

MP3

Write the skeleton word for each outline. How many words can be represented by each outline? Copy each Teeline outline. Say the words each outline might represent as you copy them.

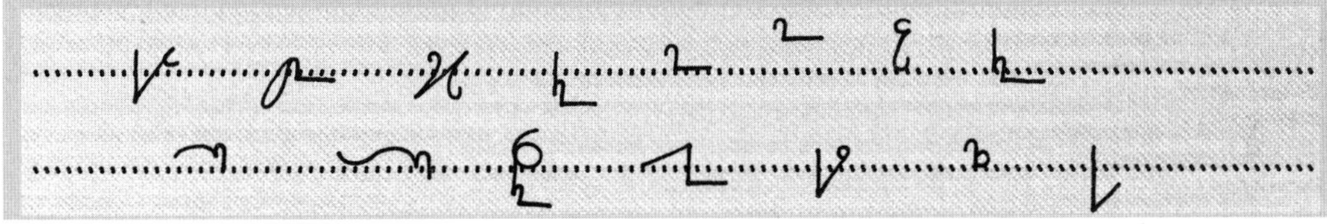

Special outlines

In Unit 1 commonly occurring words were represented by individual letters of the alphabet. In order to further speed up the writing of frequently used words **special outlines** have been devised. These also need to be committed to memory so that when that word is heard it can be written down without any real conscious thought. Special outlines occur within each unit of this book and should be practised as they appear. Gradually a memory bank of useful outlines will be built.

Special outlines – Unit 2

account  *a/c*
written on the line

o'clock  *oc*
means 'of the clock' written above the line where 'of' would be written

opportunity  *opr*

they  *the*
note the use of the horizontal E indicator

with  *wi*
written in the T position

Many special outlines are derived from longhand abbreviations already in use:

company  *Co.*

represent/ative  *rep.*
slope R slightly more than usual, so P can cut through the writing line

etcetera  *etc.*

because  *cos*
hanging from the line as B not written  would be the full outline

Many other words will occur to you, for example, days of the week, months of the year and frequently used place names may safely be reduced:

MONday  **Mn**

TUESday  **Ts**

WEDnesday  **Wd**

THURsday  **Thr**

FRIday  **Fri** (a blend of letters F and R)

SATurday  **St**

SUNday  **Sn**

JANuar**Y**		**Jni***
JUN**E**		**Jn***
SEPTember		**Spt**
DECember		**Dc**
Birmingham		**Bam**
Coventry		**CV**

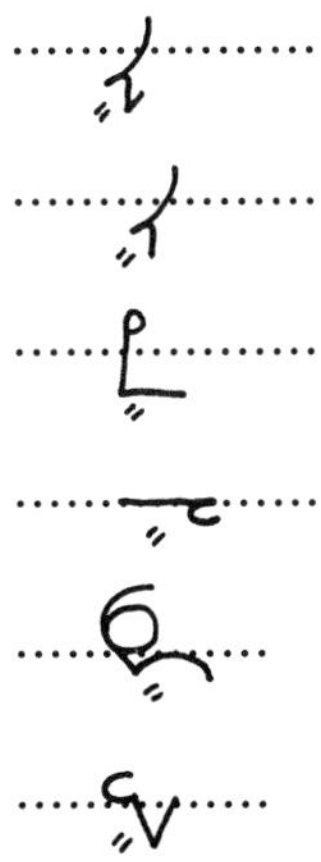

*compare these outlines – they must not be confused

Numbers

Numbers between 1 and 99 may be written as figures in your Teeline notes, but they should be circled to avoid the possibility of trying to read them back as Teeline outlines. For example number **6** ...... may be confused with Teeline letter **B** ...... number **1** ...... with Teeline letter **H** ...... or, if sloping slightly, with letter **A** ...... number **2** ...... may be confused with Teeline letters **GT** ...... Therefore:

one............ **two** .... **six**............ **seven** .... etc.

When transcribing large numbers they should be written as figures, e.g. 4,599, but numbers one to ten should be transcribed as words. If a sentence begins with a number, it should be written as a word.

Abbreviations and acronyms

If a word is dictated that word must be transcribed verbatim. However, you may abbreviate the Teeline outline and indicate by a squiggly line below that the outline must be transcribed in full:

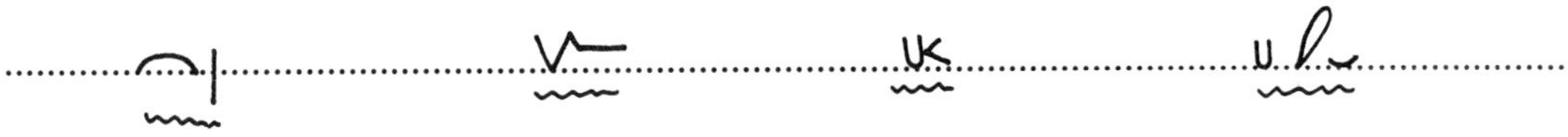

Member of Parliament Valued Added Tax United Kingdom Unidentified Flying Object

Task 2.4

Read and then neatly copy the following sentences

MP3

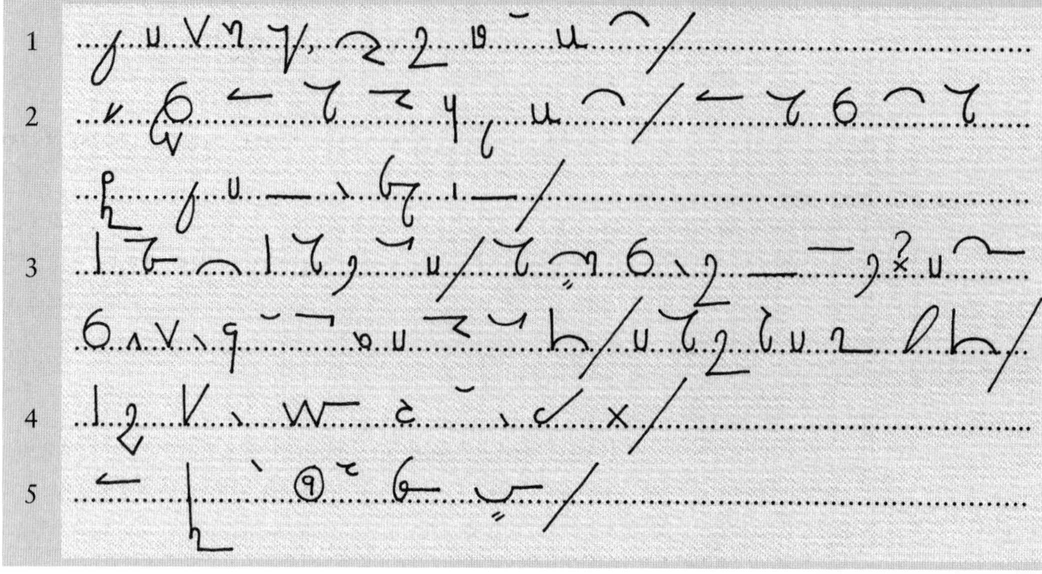

Task 2.5

Write the following sentences in neat Teeline outlines

MP3

1 I will have to go and see her at 6 o'clock because of her good news.
2 I will put her piece in if I am able to do it at 2 pm.
3 If an accident happens, it happens!
4 Let us hope it will be a good piece of evidence and he will represent you.
5 Do you have to be here? I am able to cope if you need to go home because he is not well.

Additional Teeline characters

In addition to individual letters of the alphabet, there are combinations of two letters which form additional Teeline characters.

Revision:

.... represents **once**, **offence** and .... **local** when hanging from the line.

.... represents **he.**

CH ....

C is joined to **H** and the outline is written so that **H** is in its usual position on the writing line. This combination also represents words spelled **TCH**.

CH represents the special outline **chairman** ....

If a word does not start with **CH**, then it simply follows those other letters in the outline, for example **pitch** .... **Dutch** ....

Task 3.1

Read and copy the following words

MP3

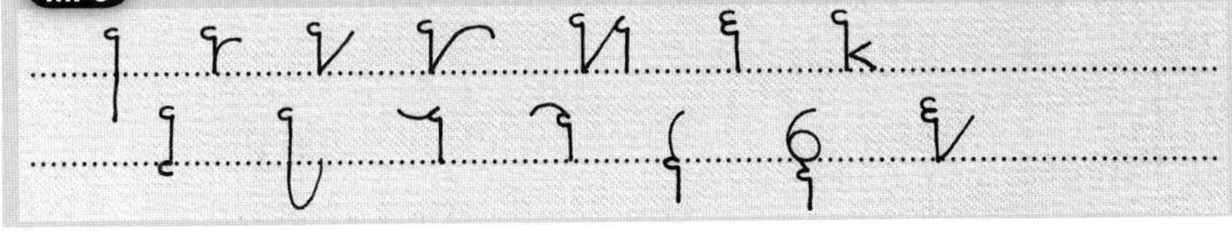

Revision:

... represents **we** and ...... represents **Wales.**

..... represents **he.**

WH ....

W is joined to **H** and the outline is written so that **H** is in its usual position on the writing line.

The letter **W** is written slightly more than double in length and above the line to represent special outline **where** ....

Special outline **what** .... does not require letter **H**.

Task 3.2

Read and copy the following words

MP3

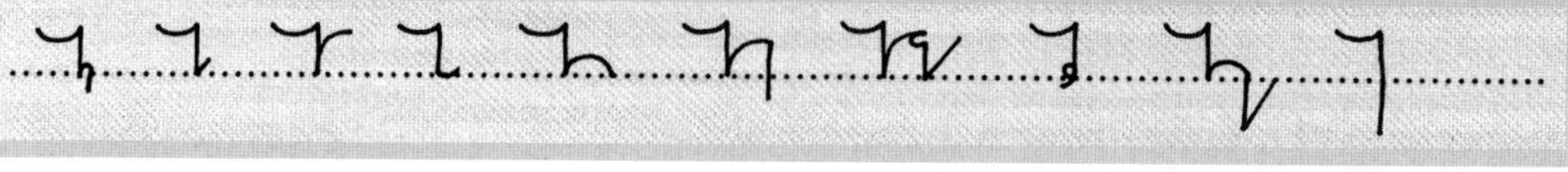

Revision:

..o.. represents **south** and ..o.. **Scotland.**

The following words are all written with a small circle **S** 

SH ..S.. Teeline letter ..S.. is used to represent the sound of SH.

It represents special outline **shall** ..S..

Task 3.3

Read and copy the following words

MP3

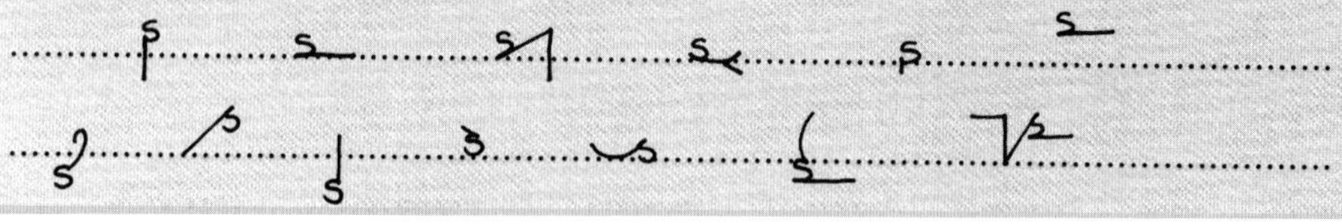

Revision:

...... represents **to.**

...|.. represents **he.**

TH..... T is written above the line in its usual position and H is joined to it so that it takes its usual position on the writing line. This combination is used to represent the sound of TH.

It represents the most commonly used word in the English language special outline **the** .....

This combination has already been used for special outline **they** ....

If a word does not start with **TH**, then it simply follows the other letters in the outline, for example **path** ....

Task 3.4

Read and copy the following words

MP3

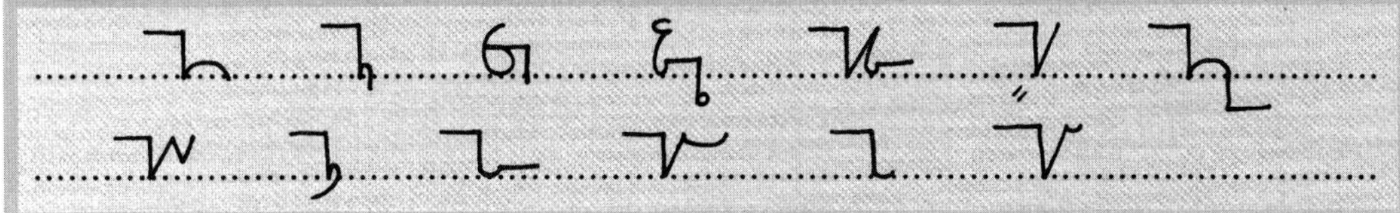

The **TH** combination is extremely useful when writing the following commonly used words. There must be no hesitation when transcribing these words. **It is essential that they are written as follows:**

this	....	The letter **H** is sloping in the direction of **I**
these	....	The **S** is written on the left hand side of **H**
those	....	The indicator **O** is written to the right hand side of **H** followed by **S**
that	....	Letter **T** is written through **TH**
there/their	....	Letter **T** written slightly more than double its usual length.

Vowels

Revision:
Vowels are written smaller than consonants. The indicator is more commonly used.

A .... normally written downwards, from left to right, but occasionally needs to be written upwards so it can be seen easily when joined to letters **V, W, X, Q** and **P.**

Task 3.5

Read and copy the following words

MP3

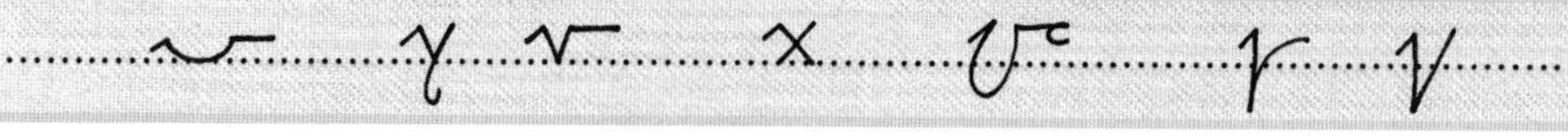

E .... written downwards, except in **they** ....
Exactly the same outline as **U** indicator, but never confused.
Remember special outline **ever/every** ....

I .... normally written downwards from right to left, but occasionally needs to be written upwards from left to right to give a sharp angle, for example **high** ...., **my** ...., **pie** ....

O .... small and fairly flat, so that it cannot be confused with **W**........, **U** .... and **V** ....

U .... always written downwards. Exactly the same outline as **E** indicator, but never confused.

If there is likely to be confusion when reading back, full vowels or indicators may be added. They are written next to the stroke to which they relate. It is very rarely necessary to include a vowel, as the context of the sentence will normally suggest the correct word to transcribe. Heavy sounds are shown by writing a full vowel, whereas light sounds use the vowel indicator.

Task 3.6

Read and copy the following words

MP3

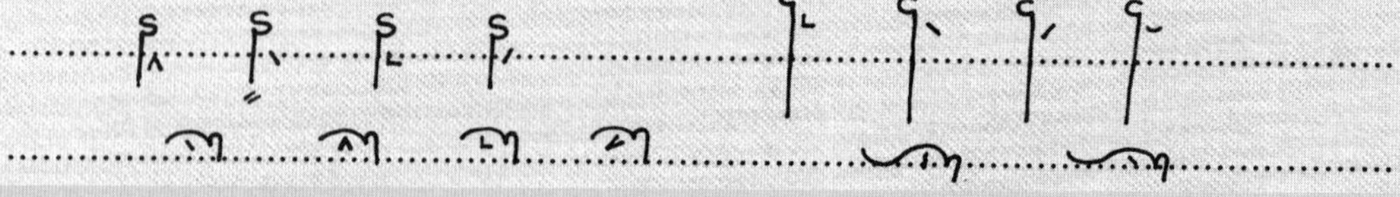

When a word begins or ends with a double vowel, either the first or more strongly sounded vowel is written:

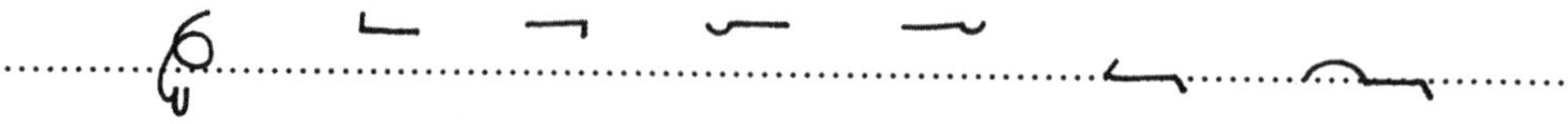

blue eat tea out too idea media

Task 3.7

Write the following words in Teeline

MP3

Asia .... die .... toe .... shoe ....

oak .... clue .... tie ....

Special outlines – Unit 3

Chairman where what shall the

to do/day to do today that there/their English

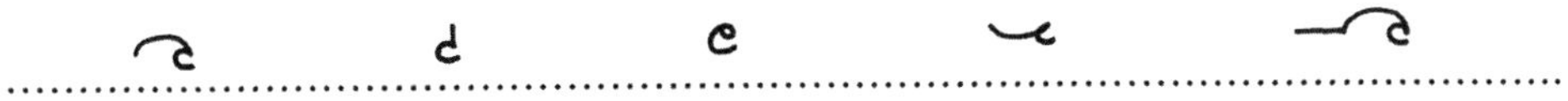

much each such which too much

(notice the **H** *is not written on these common words which end in* **CH** *)*

Distinguishing outlines

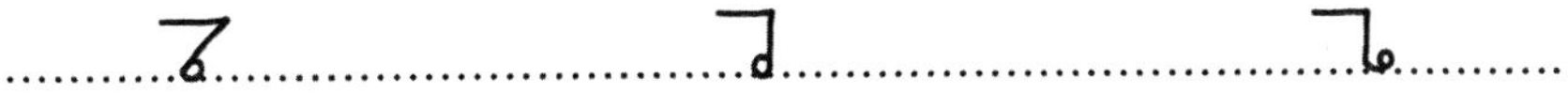

this these those

Task 3.8

Read the following sentences and write from dictation

MP3

1
2
3

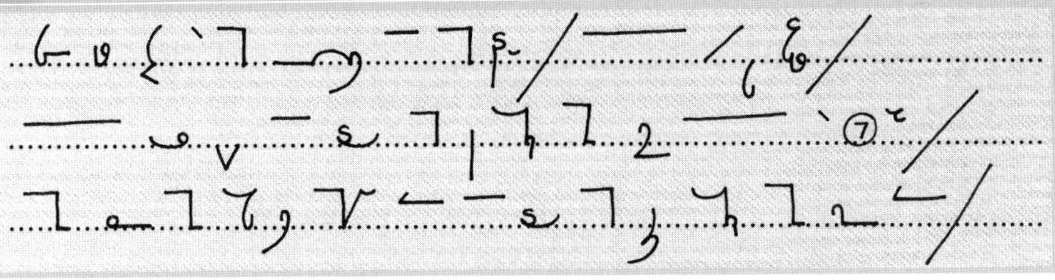

Unit 4
S and plurals

Revision:
Teeline letter **S** is written as a small circle. It can be written clockwise or anti-clockwise. .... represents **south** .... and **Scotland** ....

The letter S is written first if it is read first:

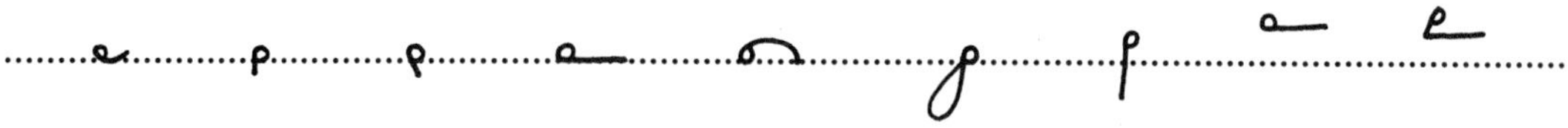

so see say said some safe sip sit site*

*(always include the vowel as part of the outline **site** as it is often confused with similar outlines)

The letter S is written last if it occurs at the end of a word:

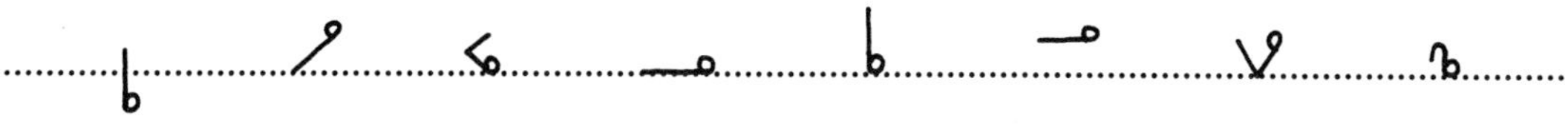

pass raise kiss does house tease vase nose

There are **two** simple rules to remember about the letter **S:**

1 S is written <u>inside</u> curved strokes

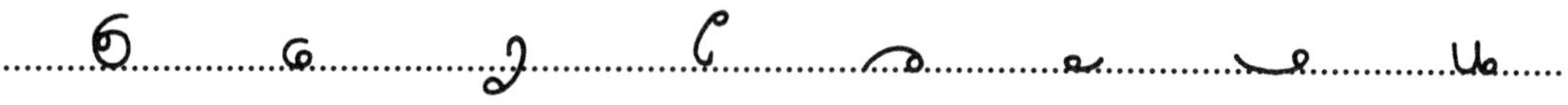

bus case goes sail miss so was yes

By tucking S inside the curved stroke you are ready to write any other letter which follows:

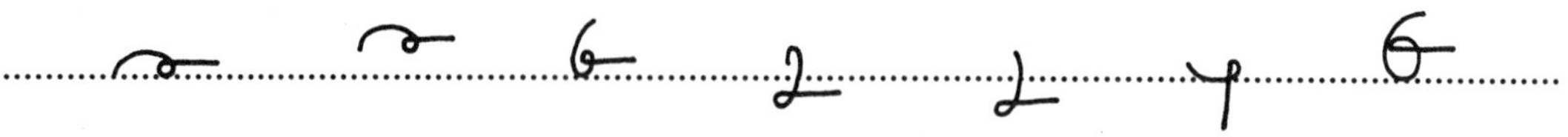

missed mist last guest/guessed just wisp best

2 S is written outside the angle of two straight strokes

'The angle of two straight strokes': 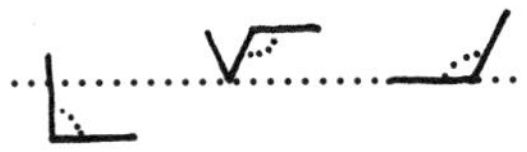 remember to write **S outside** the angle.

past rest visit hostel esteem asset desire

Plurals

To write simple plural words, add an S:

days weeks sales kinds swims allows questions

The 'SES' circle

Words which **end** in **S VOWEL S** (**sas, ses, sis, sos, sus**) are written using the circle S disjoined, but close to the first part of the outline:

guesses roses cases possess emphasis

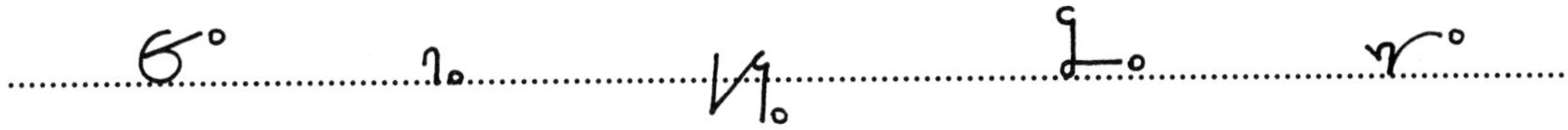

bruises noses purchases chastises analysis

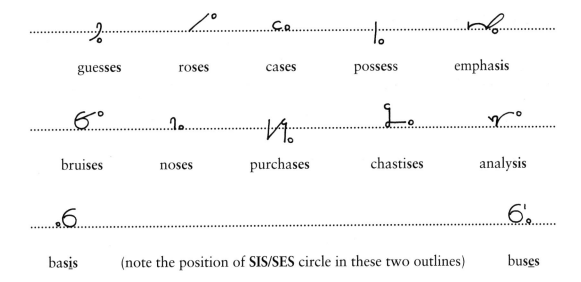

basis (note the position of **SIS/SES** circle in these two outlines) buses

Note: this theory is not used for words ending **-CES, nor at the beginning or in the middle of words:**

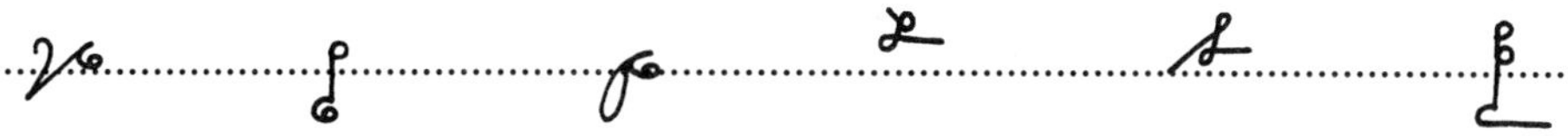

graces spaces faces assist resist suspect

Letter S may be written on **either side of a straight stroke.** Practise both ways, decide which you prefer, and then always use that form:

stiff stiff series series

taste taste stops stops

S and Z

When Z starts a word, use a Z:

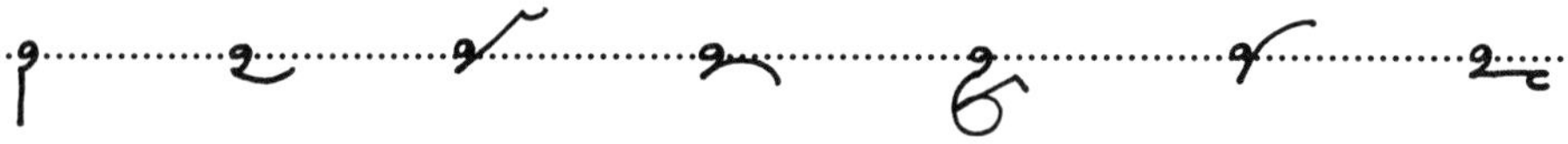

zip zoo zero zoom zebra zeal zodiac

When Z occurs in the middle of a word, use S because it sounds like S and is quicker and easier to write:

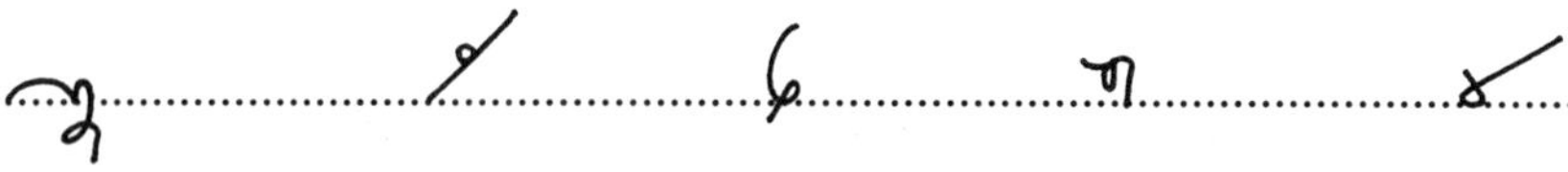

magazine razor lazy ozone azure

Note that **city** may be reduced to , therefore **citizen** 

Special outlines – Unit 4

business | businesses | success | access | city | also | always

witnesses | services *(written close to the previous word)* | these services

(but **never** use for the singular word **service**  which must be **written in full**)

Distinguishing outlines

When two or more frequently occurring words have the same outline it is necessary to write each outline differently. This will avoid errors being made in transcription, and possibly upsetting your readers! This has been shown already in the following *distinguishing outlines*:

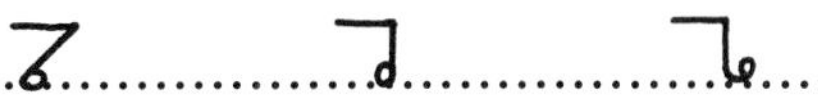

this | these | those

Here are some others:

has  Letter **H** is sloping in the direction of letter **A**

his  Letter **H** is sloping in the direction of letter **I**

amused  Written with **S** as per the spelling

amazed  Written with **Z** as per the spelling

purpose  Second letter **P** is written straight down

perhaps  Second letter **P** is sloping in the direction of letter **A** (pronounced peraps)

Task 4.1

Read and then practise the outlines written in the following passage

MP3

Practise writing from dictation at increasing speeds. Remember to include full stops in your notes.

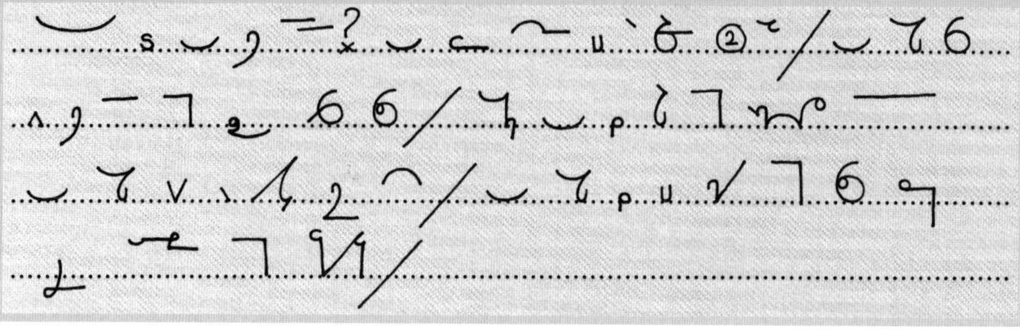

Word groupings and G or J

In speech, words and phrases are linked together. We are able to group such words in Teeline. The spaces left between Teeline outlines may be thought of as time, and any time saved means writing at a higher speed. The first word in a **word grouping** is written in its normal position and the rest of the outline(s) simply follows. The criteria for joining words should be: is the grouping easy to write and, just as importantly, is it easy to read? You will tend to write the groupings as you hear them spoken, but a few examples of commonly used word groupings are given below:

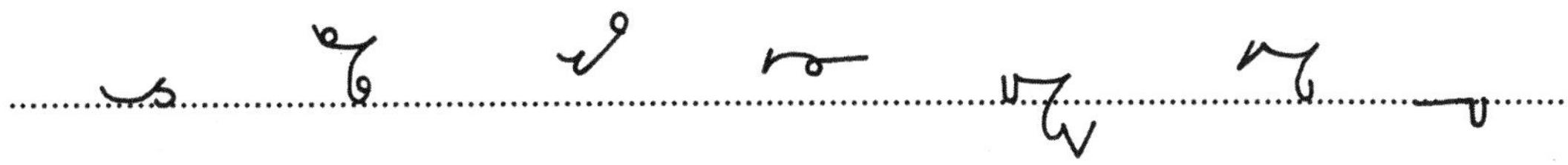

we shall as well as of course I must you will have I will do you

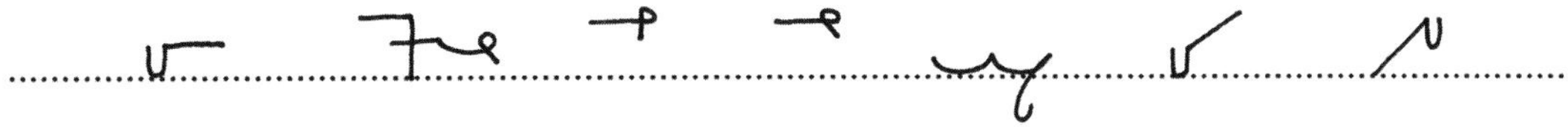

you do that was a to see to say we will you are are you

You may **leave out** or **add letters** within a word grouping:

I am sure as soon as we are it is they are will be

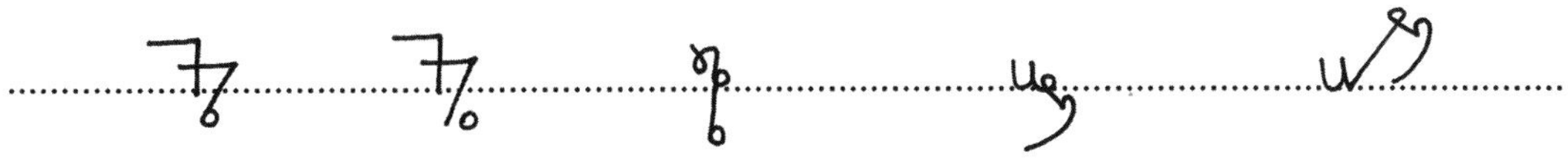

that this that this is as soon as possible years ago *but* years of age

Task 5.1

Read and write the following sentences

MP3

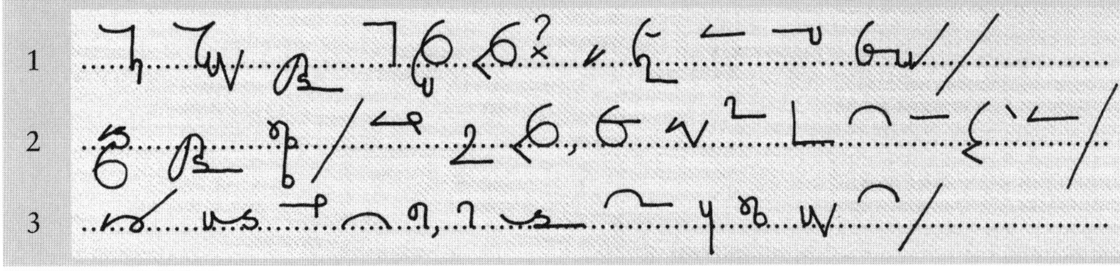

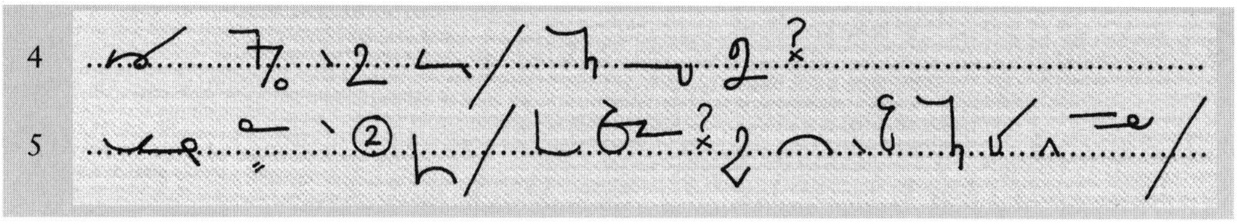

ABLE or ABLE TO in word groupings

Write the outline disjoined, but close to the last consonant in the grouping:

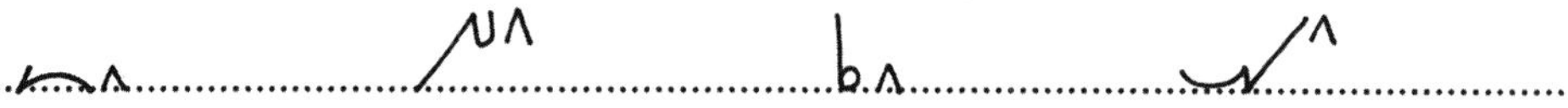

I am **able to**   are you **able to**   he is **able to**   we are **able to**

BE or BEEN in word groupings

Teeline letter  represents **be** or **been** when it stands alone. However, in some word groupings a large circle (written larger than full **O** vowel, and much bigger than the small **S** circle) can safely be used:

to **be**   should **be**   should have **been**   may **be**   could have **been**   will have **been**

I have **been** able to   we should **be** able to   had **been**   has **been**   is to **be** able to

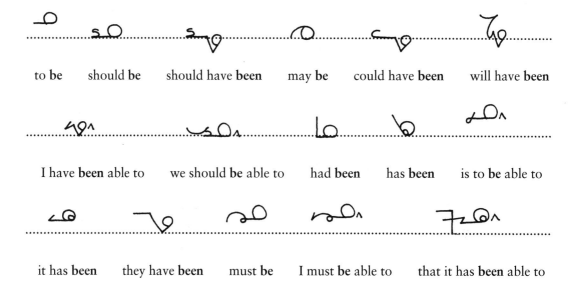

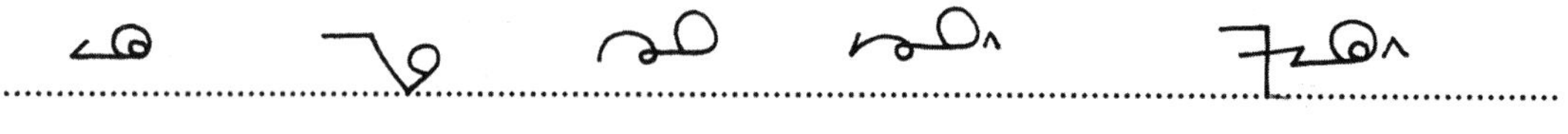

it has **been**   they have **been**   must **be**   I must **be** able to   that it has **been** able to

THERE/THEIR in word groupings

A Teeline letter T written slightly more than **double in length** represents **their/there** and may be used in word groupings:

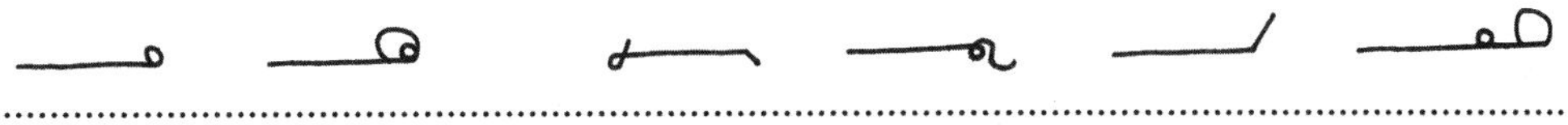

there is | **there** has been | is **there** a | **there** is no | **there** are | **there** is to be

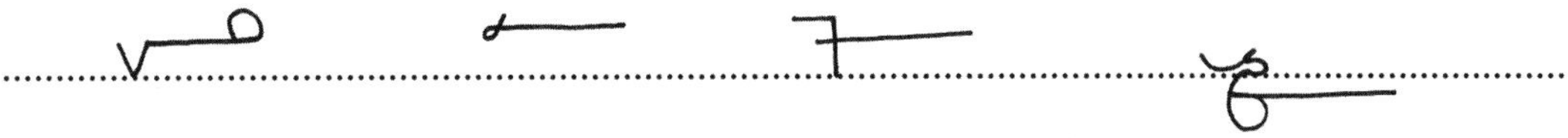

have **there** been | is **there/their** | that **there/their** | we shall be **there/their**

Take care during transcription to use the correct spelling of the appropriate word **there** or **their**.

Task 5.2

Read and write the following paragraph

MP3

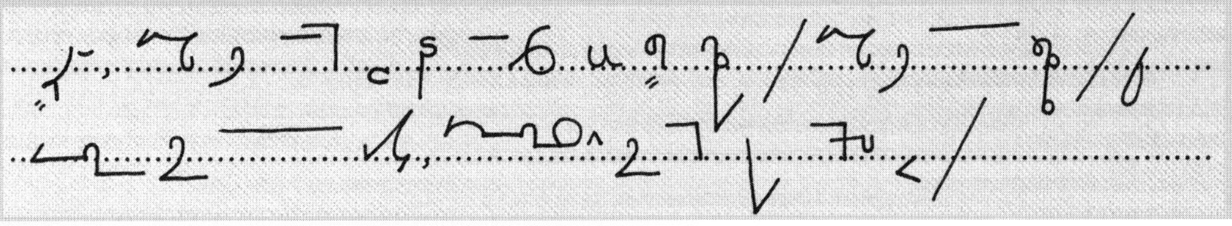

THE in word groupings

The word **THE** may, in some cases, be reduced to Teeline letter **H** when joined to other words, but the full outline is always used at the beginning of a word grouping or if it will make an outline clearer:

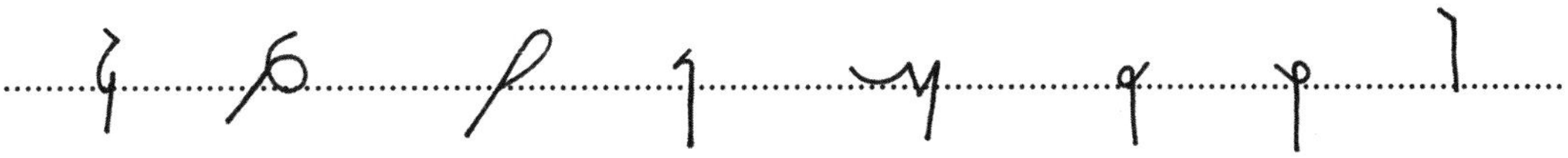

all **the** | by **the** | from **the** | in **the** | we have **the** | is **the** | as **the** | at **the**

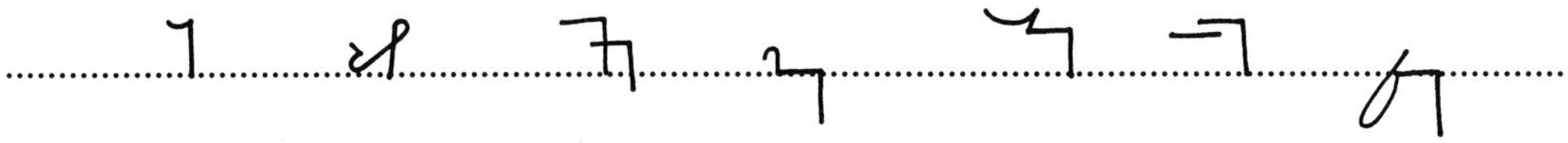

of **the** across **the** that **the** and **the** with **the** to **the** if **the**

be **the** as soon as **the** at **the** same time was **the** will have **the**

Word groupings using the <u>SES</u> circle

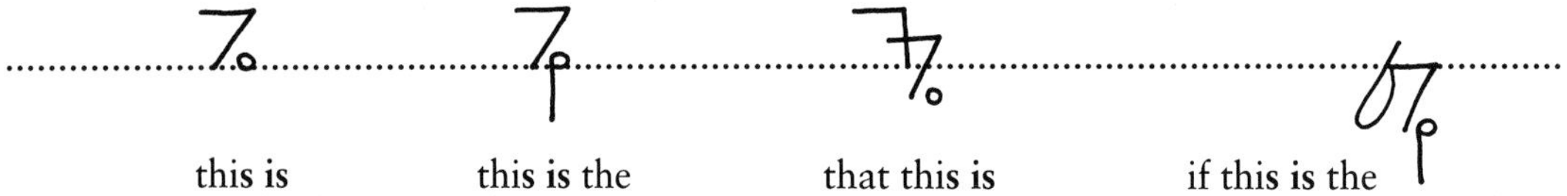

this **is** this **is** the that this **is** if this **is** the

High speed forms

1 Use Teeline letter **C** through the **centre** of any outline for the word **centre**:

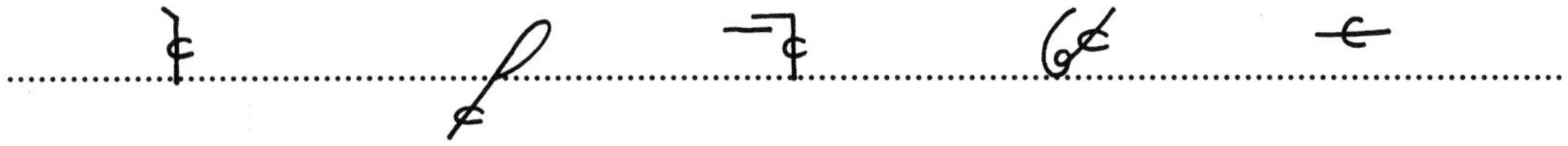

at the **centre** from the **centre** to the **centre** leisure **centre** town **centre**

2 Use Teeline letter **M** through the **middle** of any outline for the word **middle**:

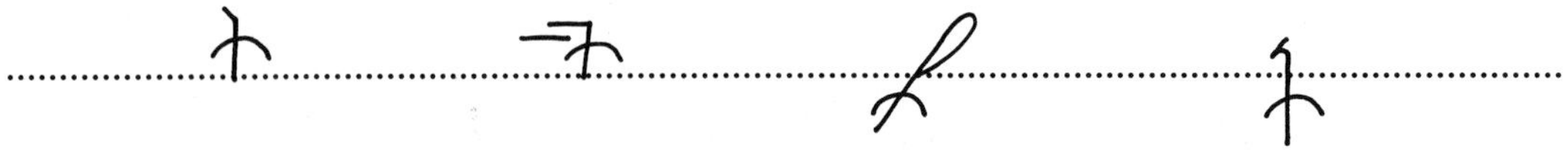

at the **middle** to the **middle** from the **middle** in the **middle**

3 Use Teeline letter **D** at the **end** of any outline for the word **end**:

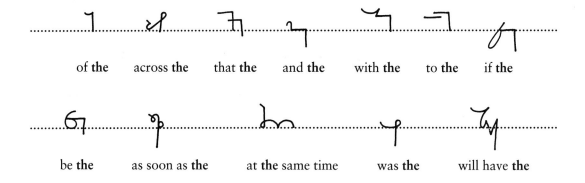

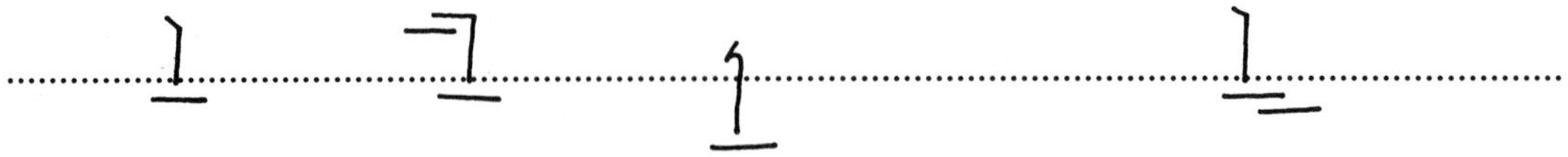

at the **end** to the **end** in the **end** *also* at the **end** of the day

4 The word **receive(d)** may be reduced in word groupings only to **SVD**:

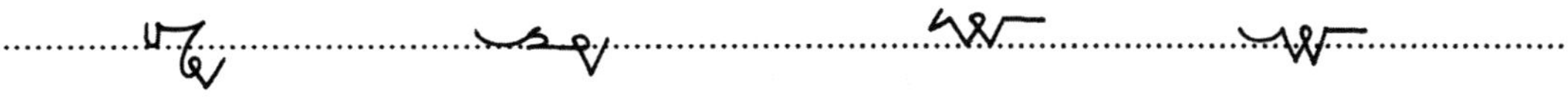

you will **receive** we should **receive** I have **received** we have **received**

G or J

To give a clearer outline you may find it easier to write letter **G** rather than **J** after **M** and **N**:

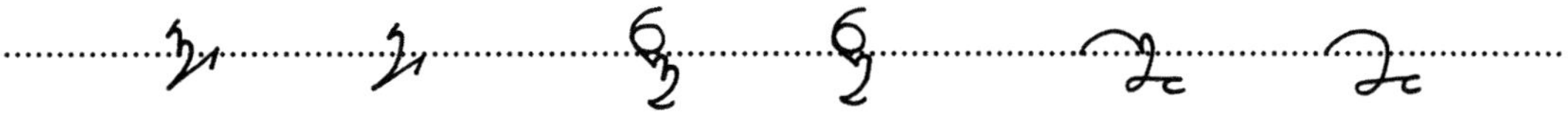

injury *or* injury banjo *or* banjo majestic *or* majestic

Special outlines – Unit 5

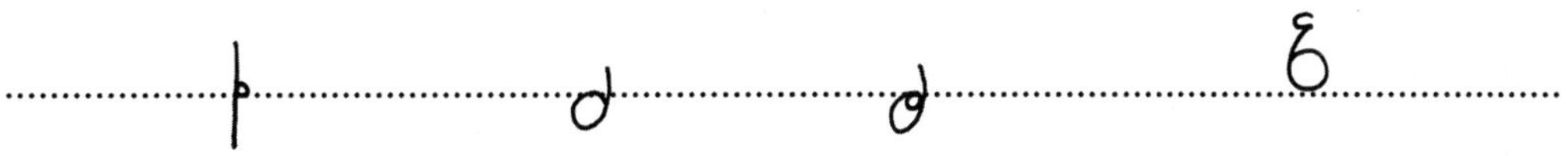

hospital job jobs club

Task 5.3

Read and write 'Accident at the bus stop'

MP3

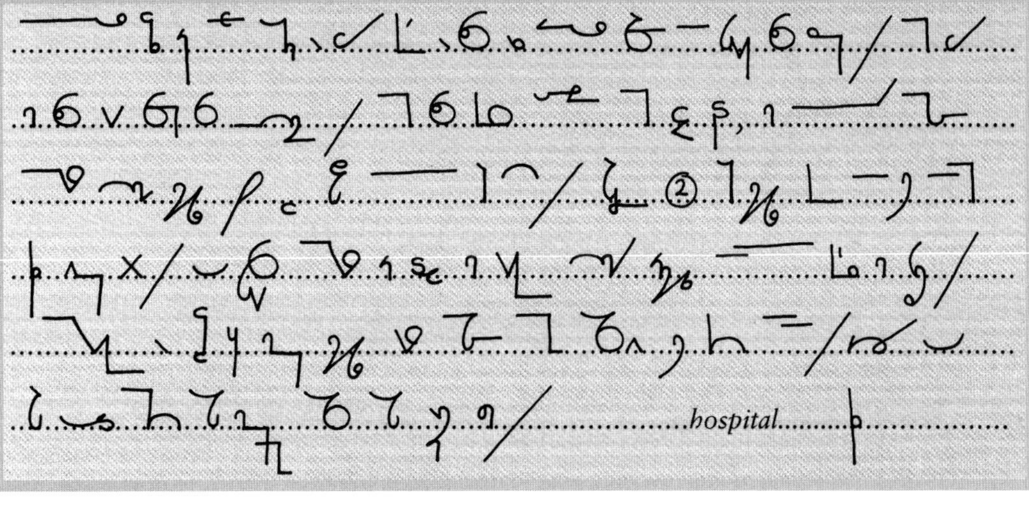

Task 5.4

Read and write 'New shop to open in June'

MP3

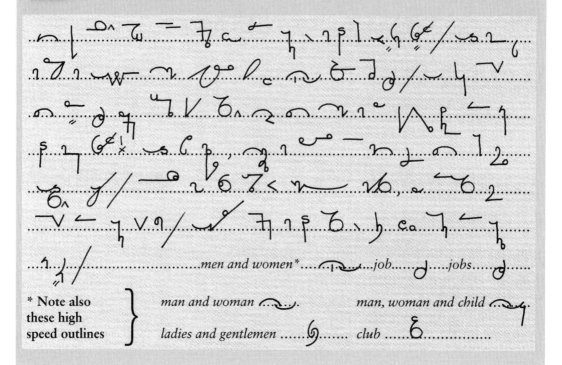

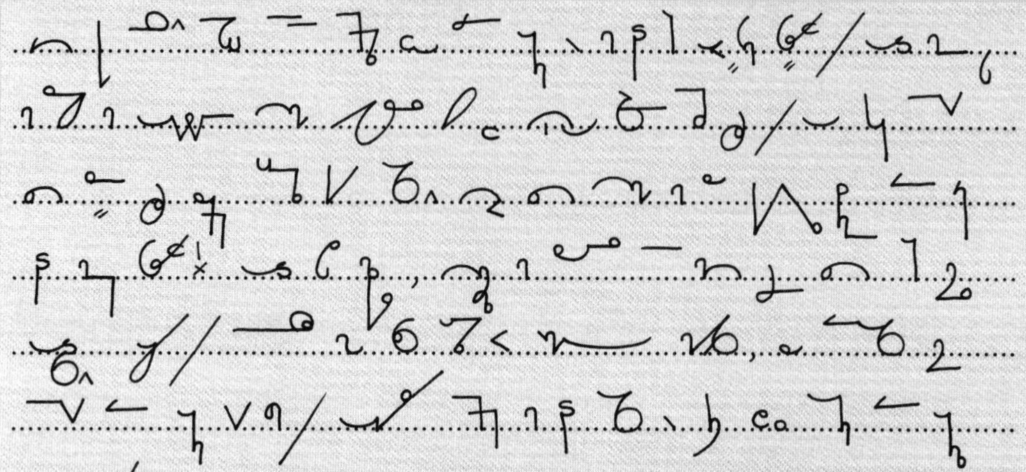

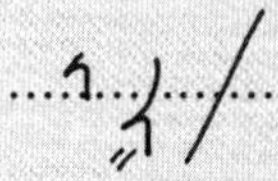

*men and women** …… *job* …… *jobs* ……

* **Note also these high speed outlines**

man and woman ……

man, woman and child ……

ladies and gentlemen ……

club ……

Unit 6
Word groupings, word endings and more new Teeline characters

WOULD in word groupings

The word **would** is written in full when it stands as a word alone or when it starts a word grouping:

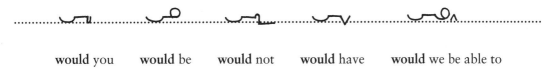

would you **would** be **would** not **would** have **would** we be able to

When **would** follows another word, it may be reduced to a smaller than normal sized **W** written **below** the preceding word in the D position

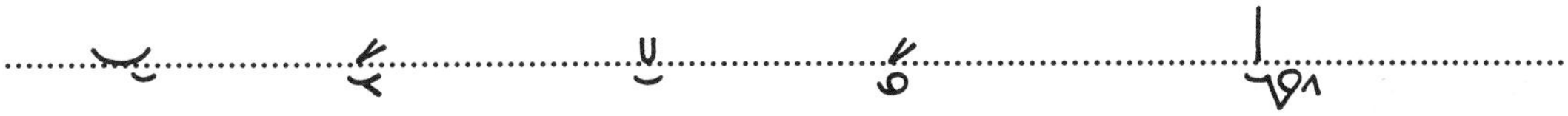

we **would** I **would** like you **would** I **would** be he **would** have been able to

compare:

it **would** be *and* it will be

If you always write these groupings as shown above you will not have any hesitation in transcribing them correctly.

Small W used as a word ending for -ward, -word, -wood, -wide

The smaller than normal sized **W** is used as a **word ending**. It is written underneath and close up to the previous part of the outline:

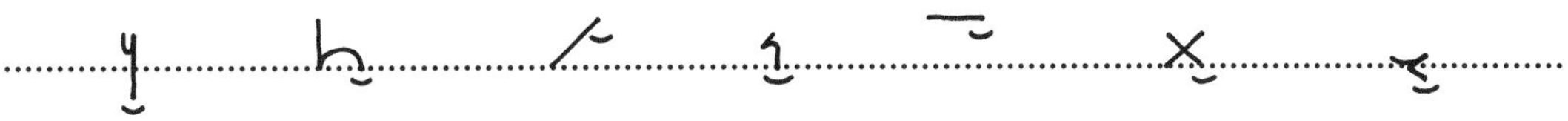

up**ward** home**ward** re**ward** in**ward** to**ward** cross**word** oak**wood**

Other letters can be added to extend the word ending:

towards rewarded

In word groupings the smaller than normal sized **W** is a good time saving device:

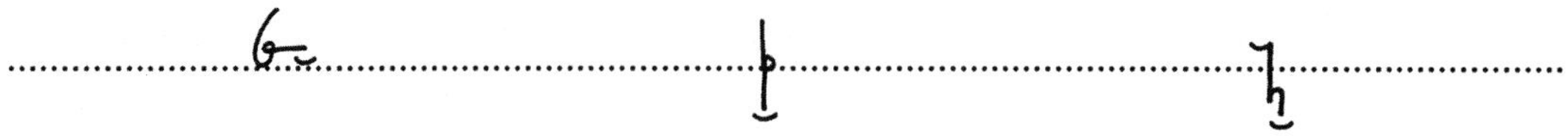

last **word** hospital **ward** open **wide**

Use the smaller than normal sized **W** for the word **forward** in word groupings:

look **forward** put **forward** go **forward** push **forward**

Task 6.1

Read and write the following sentences

MP3

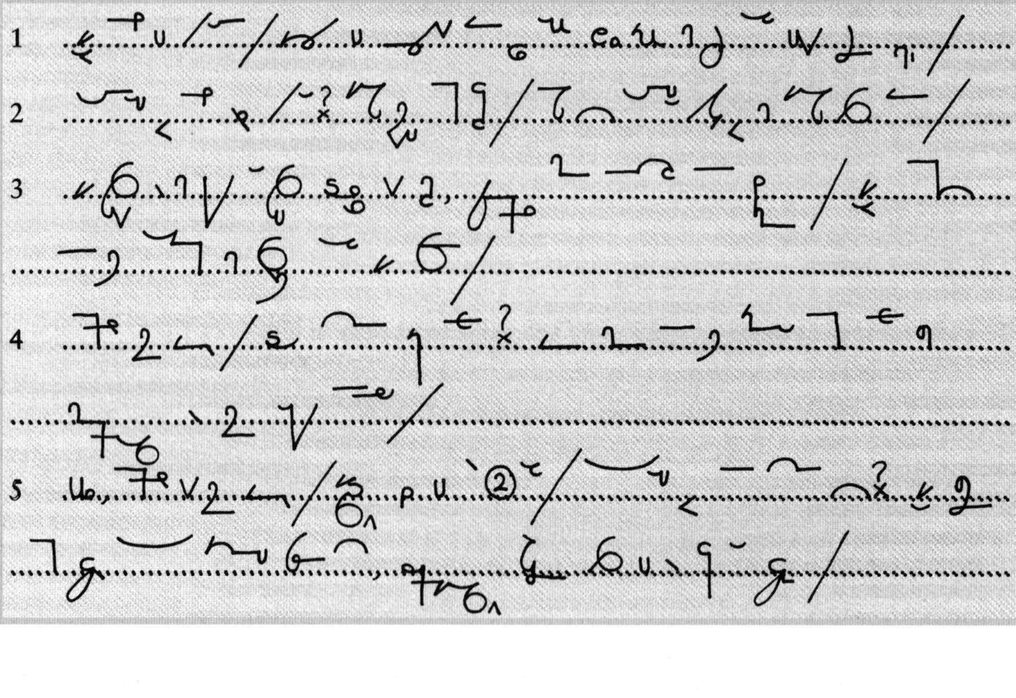

Large N

A large loop  representing two letter **N**s – shaped rather like an arch – can be written for words beginning or ending **nation** or **non**:

nation **nation**al **nation**alise **nation**alism **nation**wide nomi**nation**

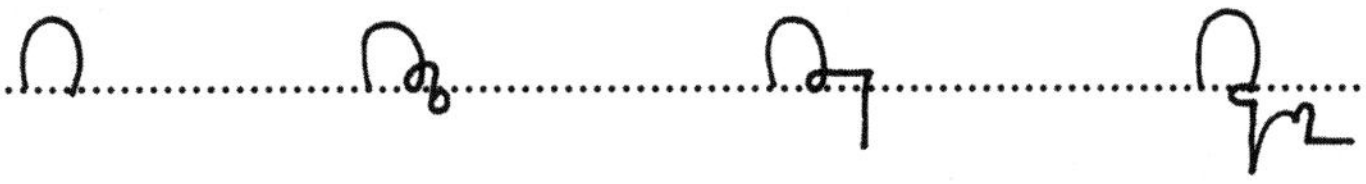

none **non**sense **non**-stop **non**chalant

Task 6.2

Read and write the following sentences

MP3

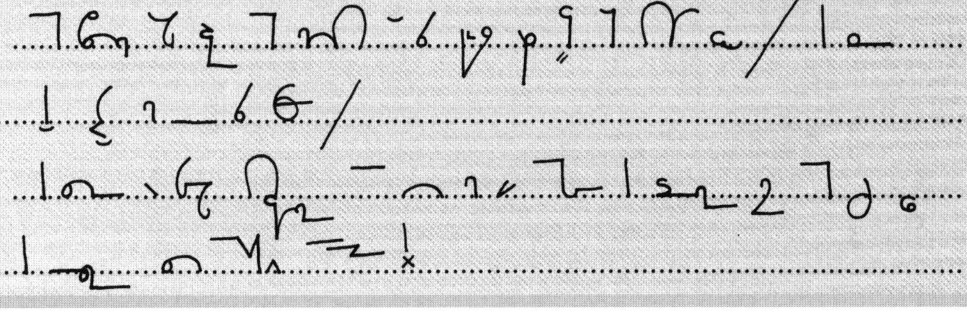

1

2

NTH blend

To represent the letters **NTH** in words, write Teeline letters **NH** and omit letter **T**. The letter **H** should be written so that it can take its normal position, sitting on the line. Therefore, start writing the **N** high above the writing line:

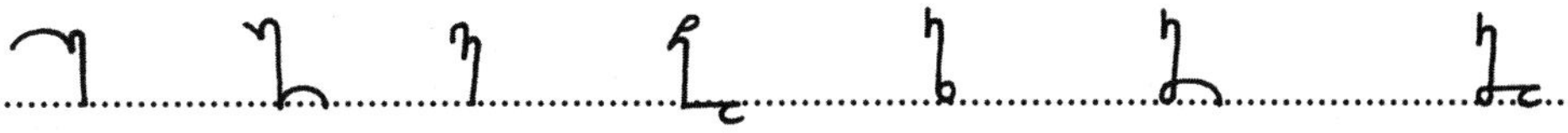

mo**nth** a**nth**em **n**i**nth** sy**nth**etic e**nth**use e**nth**usiasm e**nth**usiastic

Note that the words **enthusiasm** and **enthusiastic** have been reduced in order to make a simpler outline. In full they would be written as follows: 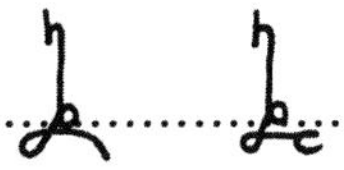

NTH in word groupings

Letter **H** is used to represent the word **the** in word groupings and **in the** is written ....

By writing **in** in its usual position and the **H** through the writing line you will not confuse **in** .... and **in the** .... when transcribing.

NTH is applied in the following groupings:

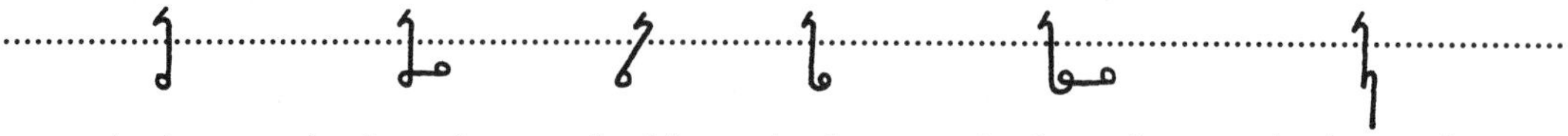

in **th**ese — in **th**ese days — in **th**is — in **th**ose — in **th**ose days — in **th**e north

Never group the words **in his** .... These words must not be confused with **in this** ....

Circle B on M and M on B

A large circle has been used already to represent the words **be** or **been** in word groupings. It can also be used with the Teeline letter **M** in order to shorten an outline:

bomb — **bum**per — **bomb**shell — su**bm**it — **bem**used — **bomb**astic — **bam**boo

mobile — ju**mb**le — sy**mb**ol — e**mb**assy — stu**mb**le — a**mb**le — e**mb**lem

Special outlines – Unit 6

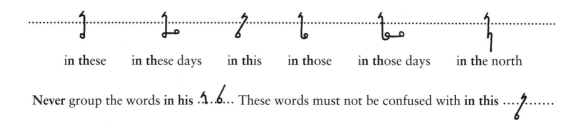

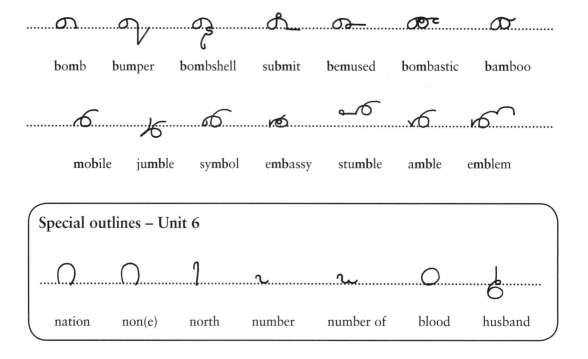

nation — non(e) — north — number — number of — blood — husband

Task 6.3

Read and write the following sentences

MP3

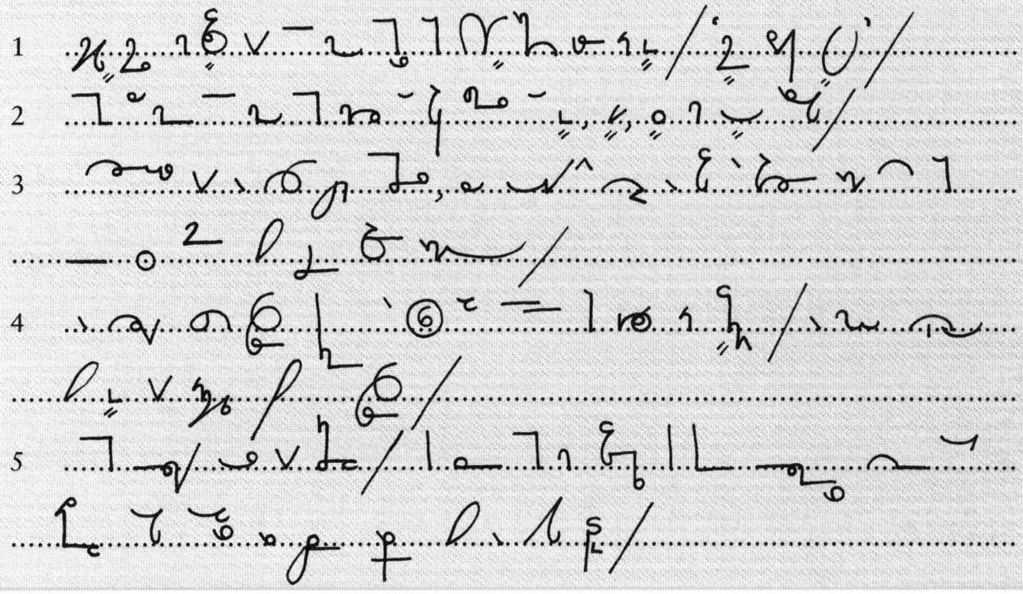

Task 6.4

Read and write 'Magazines with puzzles'

MP3

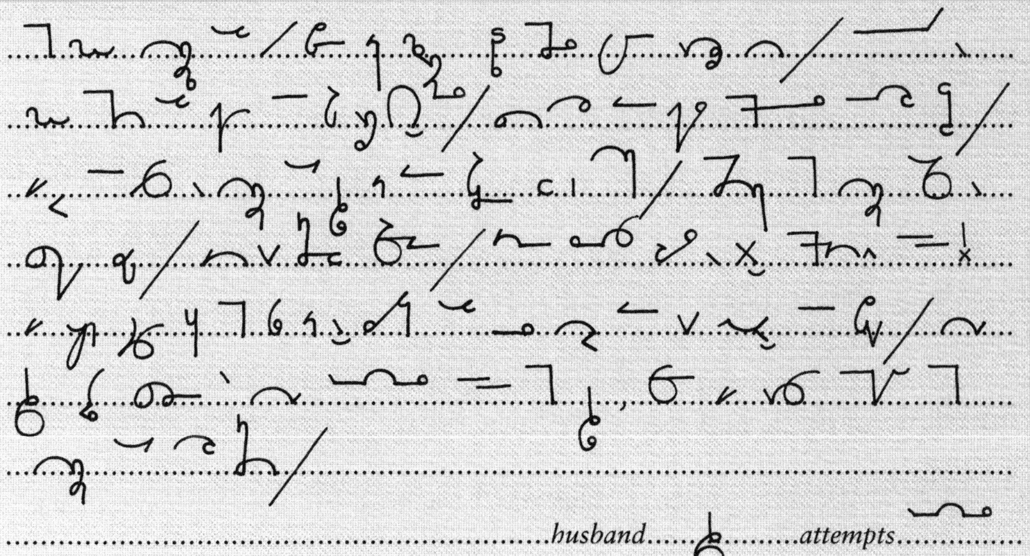

Unit 7
Letters T (top) and D (down)

T is always written above the line **in the T position** when standing alone, when beginning a word or when it is preceded by letter **S**, or a vowel:

to too tow tie tax tease test towel tomato

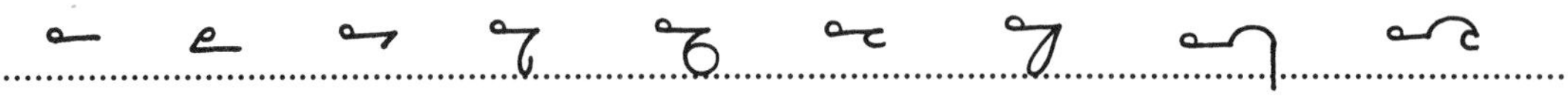

sit site sty stole stub stock stiff stamp stomach

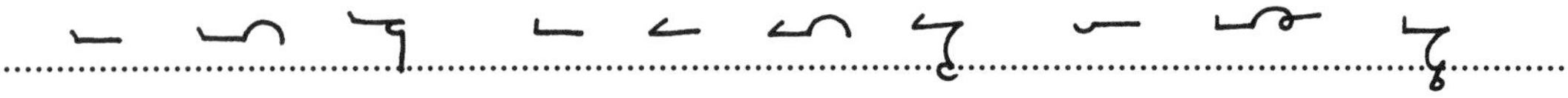

ate atom attach eat it item italic out utmost utilize

When **T** is followed by **P** or **G** start writing the outline nearer to the line, but still above it, so that **P** or **G** can cut through the writing line and take their usual position:

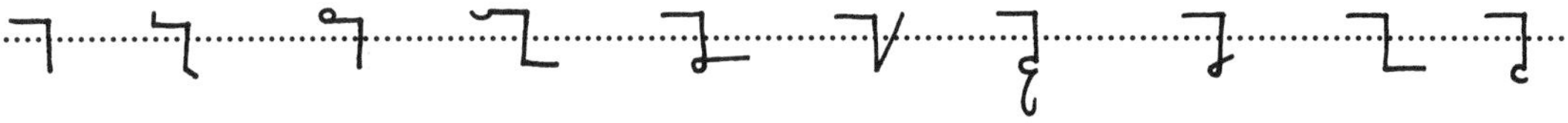

top utopia stop output typist taper typical tipsy tepid topic

tug tagged tiger stag stagger toga toggle

In order to show whether a word ends in **T** or **D**, and to help to transcribe a word quickly and accurately, write the whole word in the **T** or **D** position:

most missed out odd net need might made

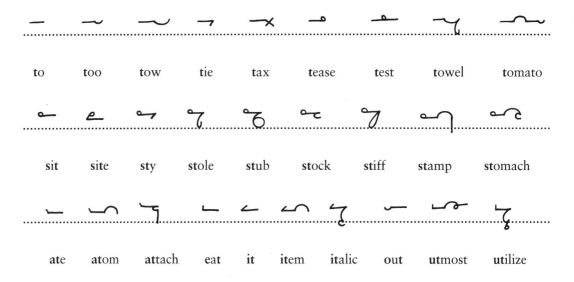

wait wade sent send cost caused site side

D is always written on the line **in the D position** when standing alone, when beginning a word or when it is preceded by letter S, or a vowel:

do deal damage said side sadistic idle aids edify

Letters T and D are **never joined together**. This has been seen in **to do** and **today** ....

The letter **T** is shown by writing the stroke slightly above and to the right of the preceding letter.

The letter **D** is shown by writing the stroke slightly below and to the right of the preceding letter.

T followed by T: tight .... title .... teeth .... toothache .... titillate ....

T followed by D: tide .... quoted .... waited .... tadpoles .... tidy ....

D followed by D: did .... divided .... deduce .... midday .... daddy ....

D followed by T: debt .... detail .... dated .... detach .... detest ....

Task 7.1

Write the following words in Teeline

MP3

duty .... dilapidated .... elated .... headed .... oddity ....

data .... destitute .... elevated .... jaded .... stadium ....

deadline .... aptitude .... escalated .... altitude .... statute ....

death .... additives .... gutted .... nonentity .... statistical ....

status .... statuesque .... studio .... tattoo .... tedious ....

When letter **B** is followed by **T** or **D**, simply follow the rule **T** – Top and **D** – Down:

but robot debated bottle both bought bottom about

bed robbed body abide abdomen bedazzle bedside bedsit

Task 7.2

Read and write the following sentences

MP3

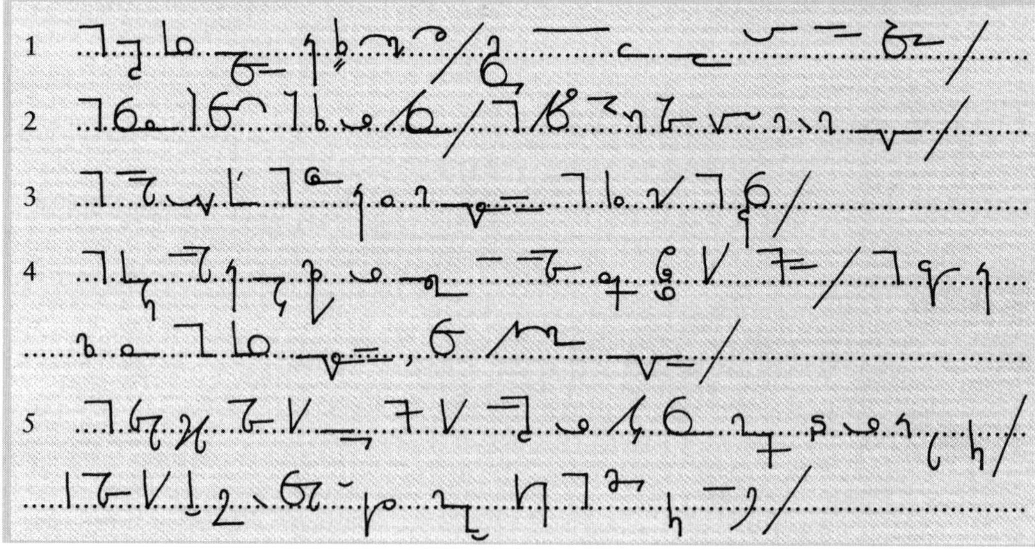

Task 7.3

Read and write 'The robot'

MP3

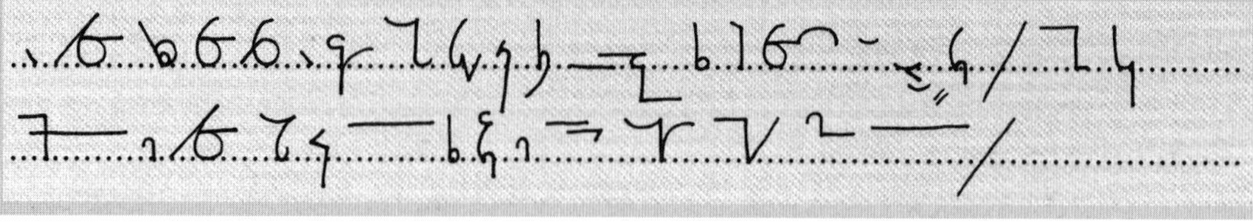

C and K

If a word begins with the letter **C** write a letter **C**:

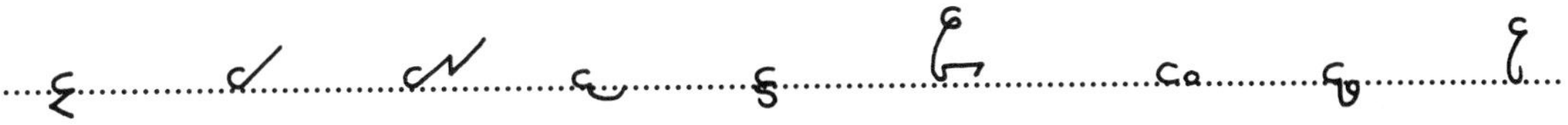

cook care career cow cash casualty cases cause cell

If a word begins with the letter **K** write a letter **K**:

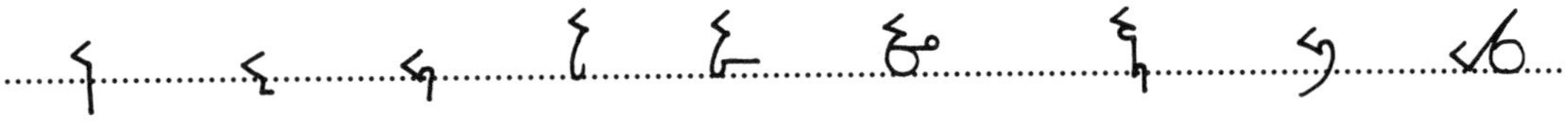

keep key keen kill kilt kibbutz kitchen keg kerb

It is not always essential but occasionally in the middle or at the end of an outline the letter **C** may be written instead of **K** in order to give a better outline:

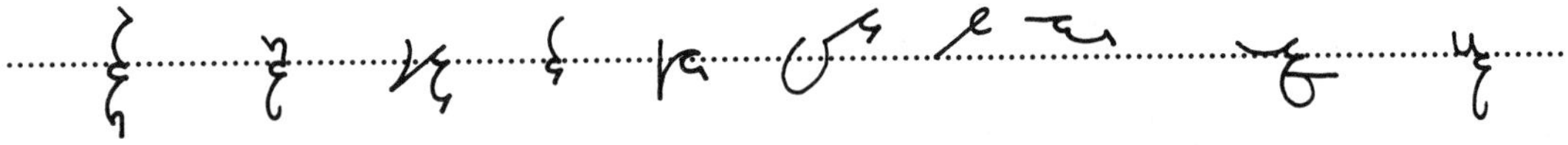

alkaline ankle jerkily leaky polka quirky risk takeaway walkabout yokel

CT and CD

When letters **T** or **D** or **R** follow **C**, blend them together:

ask *but* asked bake *but* baked *and* baker cook *but* cooked *and* cooker

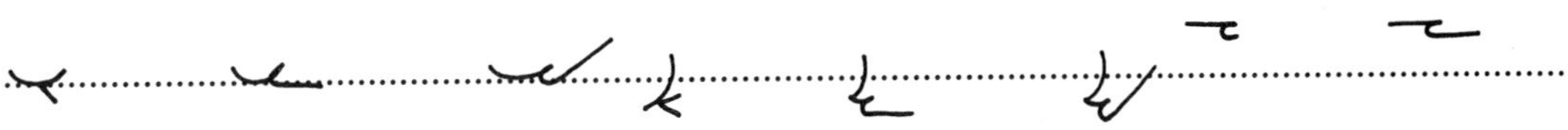

walk *but* walked *and* walker joke *but* joked *and* joker tick *but* ticket/ticked

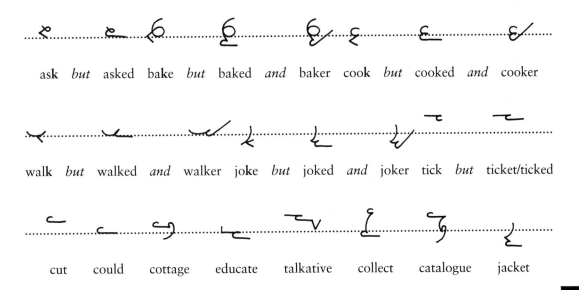

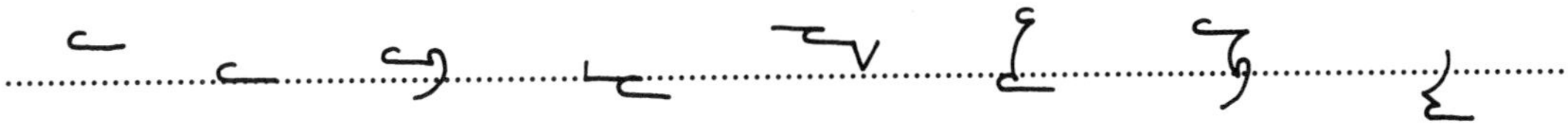

cut could cottage educate talkative collect catalogue jacket

K followed by T or D

T and D should be disjoined from K and written in the T or D position:

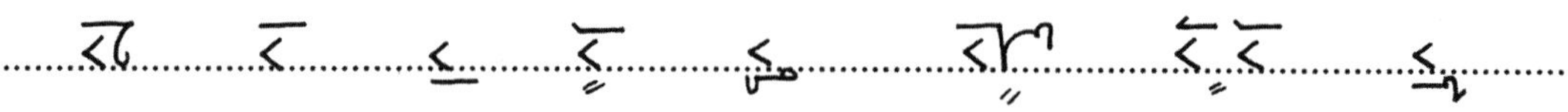

kettle kite kid Kate kudos Kathleen Kit Kat kidney

Task 7.4

Read and write 'Jobs for food lovers'

MP3

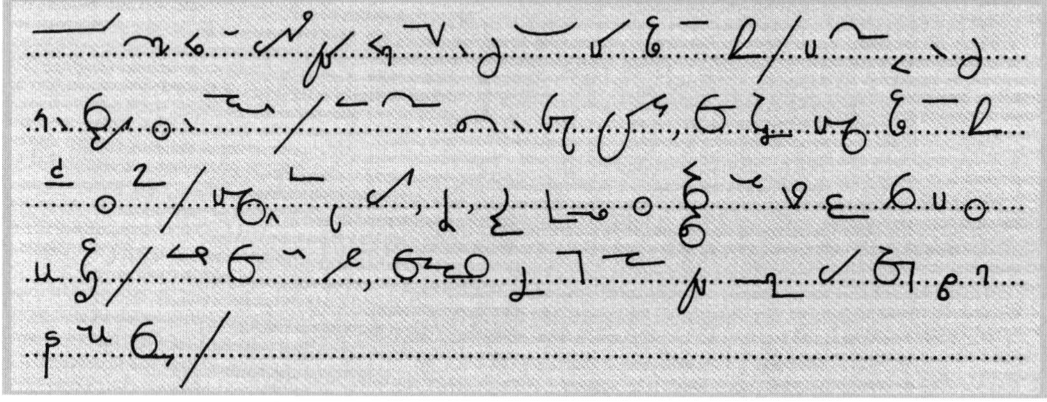

Special outlines – Unit 7

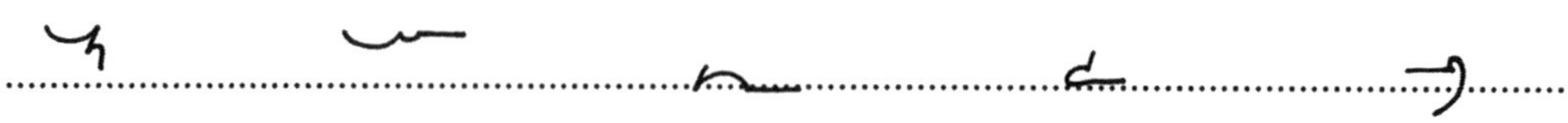

within without immediate incident together

Word groupings

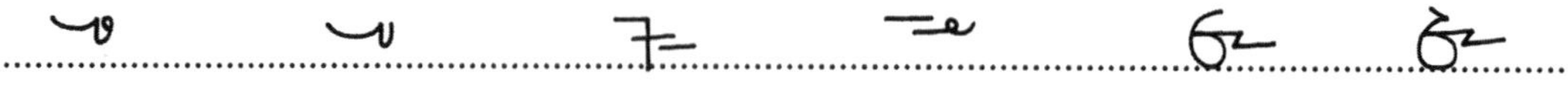

with us with you that day to do so but it about it

In word groupings the word **fact**  may be reduced to **CT**:

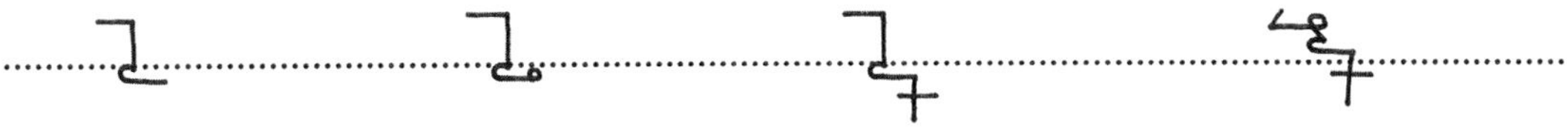

the fact — the facts — the fact that — it is a fact that

Distinguishing outlines

in fact — in effect

Task 7.5

Read and write 'Attack on eighty-three year-old woman'

MP3

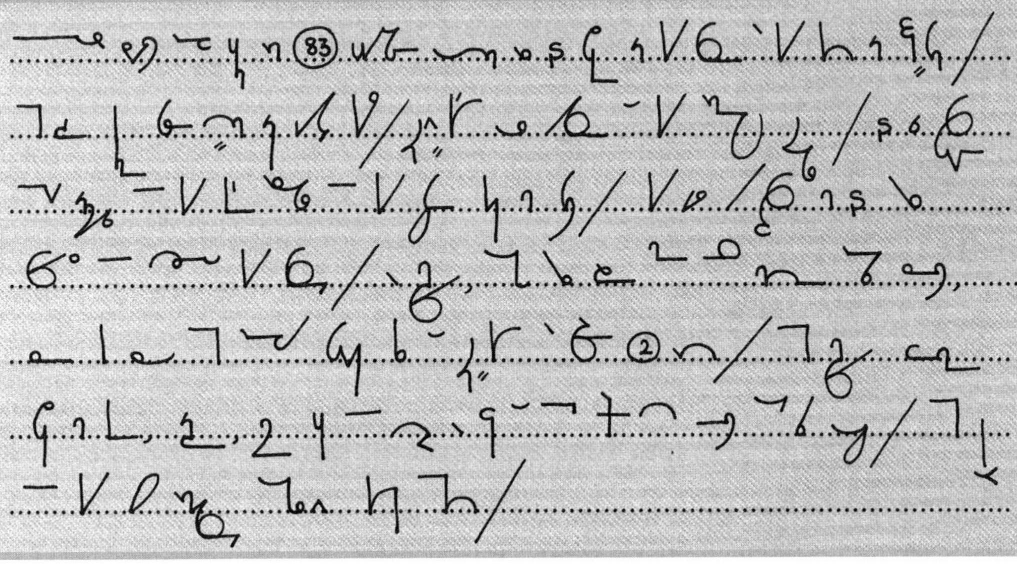

–AY at the end of a word

Words which end in the spelling **–AY** are written by omitting the letter **Y**: *Remember – if it **sounds** like an **A** write an **A***

In these examples notice that the indicator is used at the end of the word:

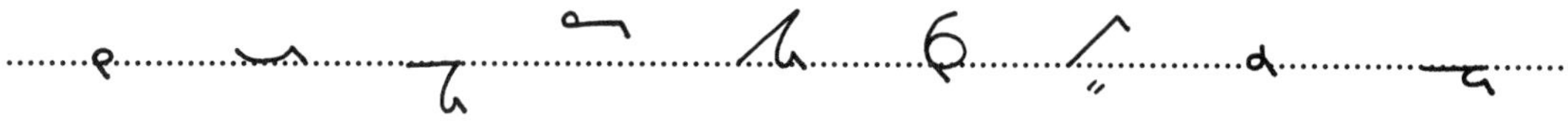

say way delay stay relay bay Ray essay decay

To give a definite shape, a sharp angle to the outline, and to help you when reading back, it is better to use a full vowel **A** after **H, M** and **P**:

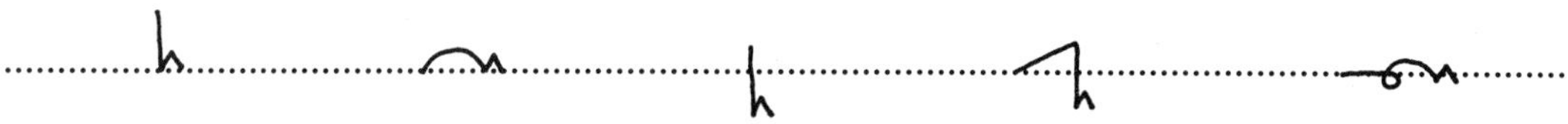

hay may pay repay dismay

Words which are not spelt with **-AY**, but have that sound may be written with the indicator **A**:

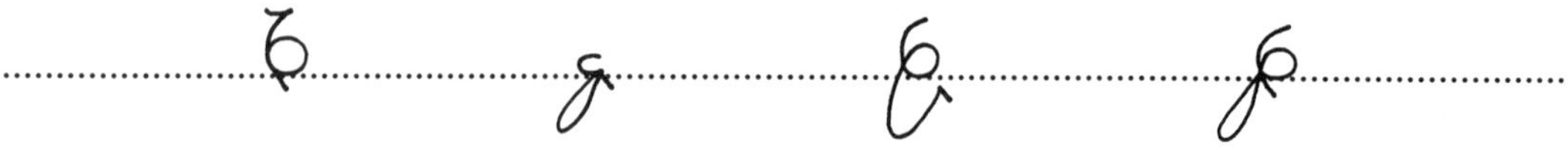

obey café bouquet buffet

Similarly, if a word ends -**EY** but sounds like **E** use an **E**. For example, **key** 

I and Y at the end of a word

Omit the silent letters in words which end in the spelling -**IE**, -**IGH** and -**Y** and simply write indicator **I**. The indicator should be written either upwards or downwards so that the sharpest angle between two letters is achieved: *Remember – if it **sounds** like an **I** write an **I***

high pie my guy buy shy sty lie why

The examples above all have a long sound of **I**, whereas the next group of examples have a short sound of **i**, but all use the indicator which gives the sharpest angle:

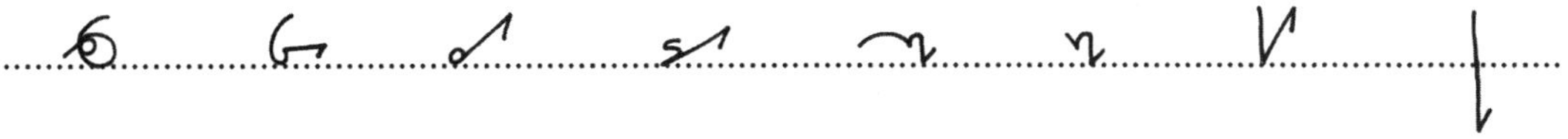

busy lady sorry sherry many any hurry happy

Task 8.1

Read and write the following sentences

MP3

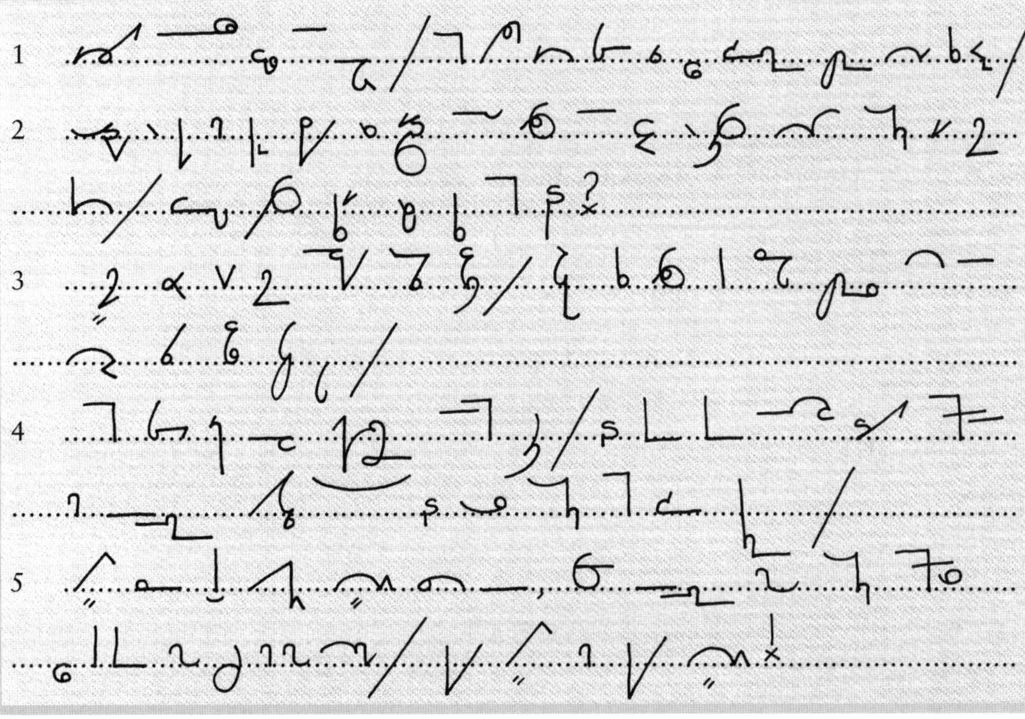

-OY in a word

Write a Teeline **Y** if -OY occurs in the middle or at the end of a word:

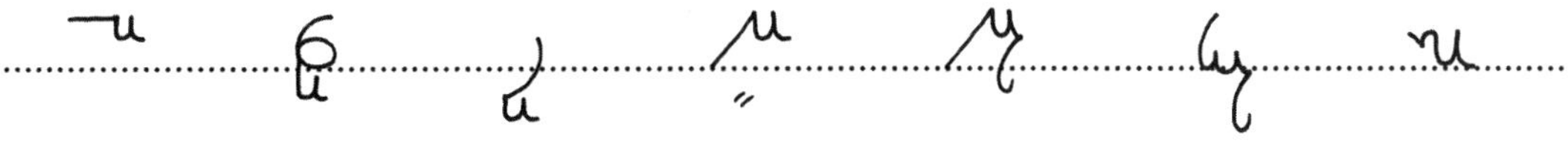

toy boy joy Roy royal loyal annoy

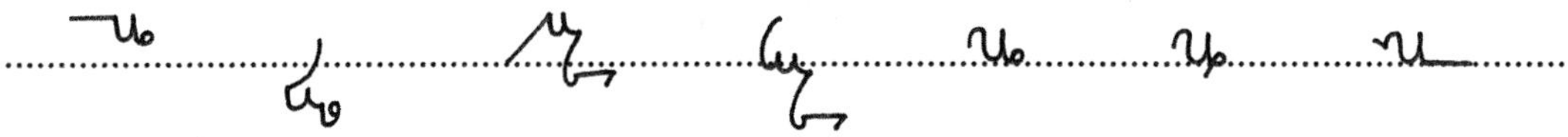

toys joyous royalty loyalty noise noisy annoyed

Y in the middle of a word

Y is not usually written when it occurs in the middle of a word. As with vowels in the middle of words, you may leave the **Y** out when it sounds like an **I**. However, very occasionally it is easier to write an outline if the **I** is written, for example: system 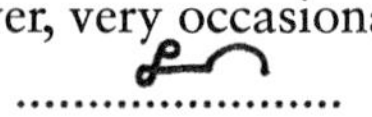

Where **Y** has a definite sound, the **Y** must be shown: lawyer 

Compare these words and outlines and apply the rules given above:

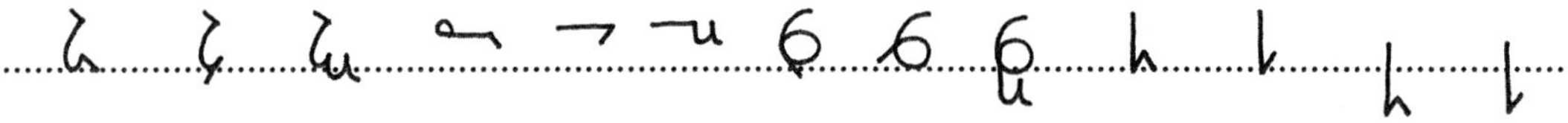

allay ally alloy stay tie toy bay by boy hay high pay pie

Task 8.2

Read and write the following sentences

MP3

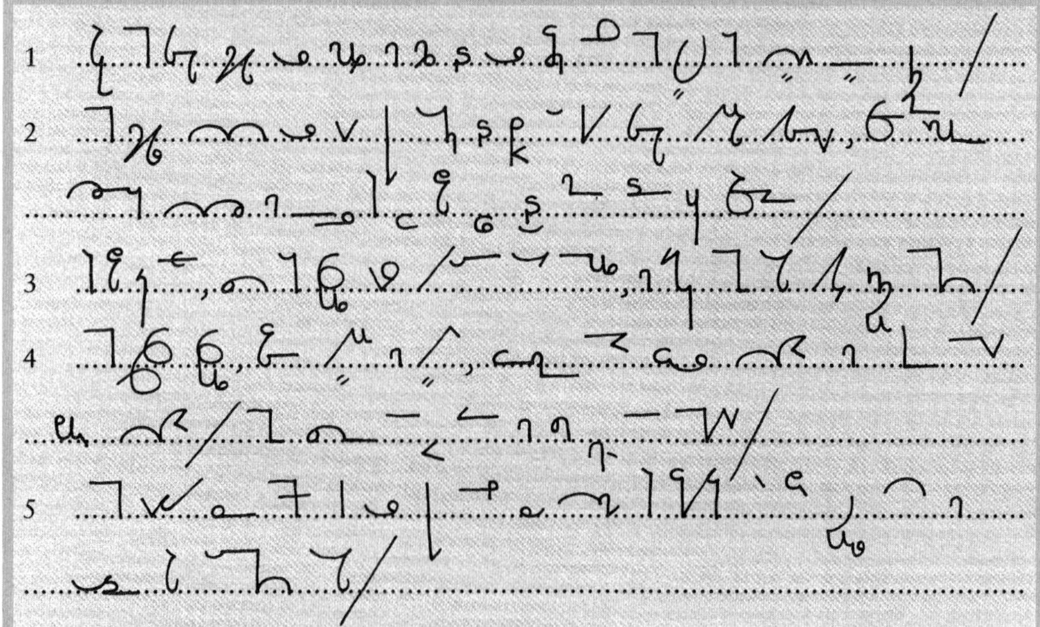

-LY at the end of a word

In most words which end **-LY**, the **L** may safely be omitted and the **I** indicator written, as the sense of the sentence usually makes transcription of the outline obvious. However, if there is likely to be any doubt, write the outline in full:

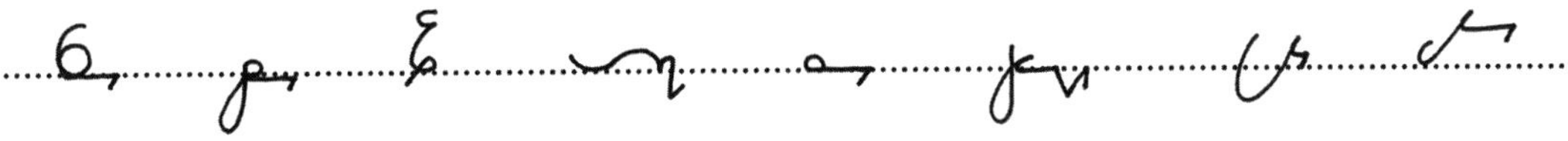

badly | softly | closely | womanly | sadly | effectively | quickly | correctly

Task 8.3

Read and write the following sentences

MP3

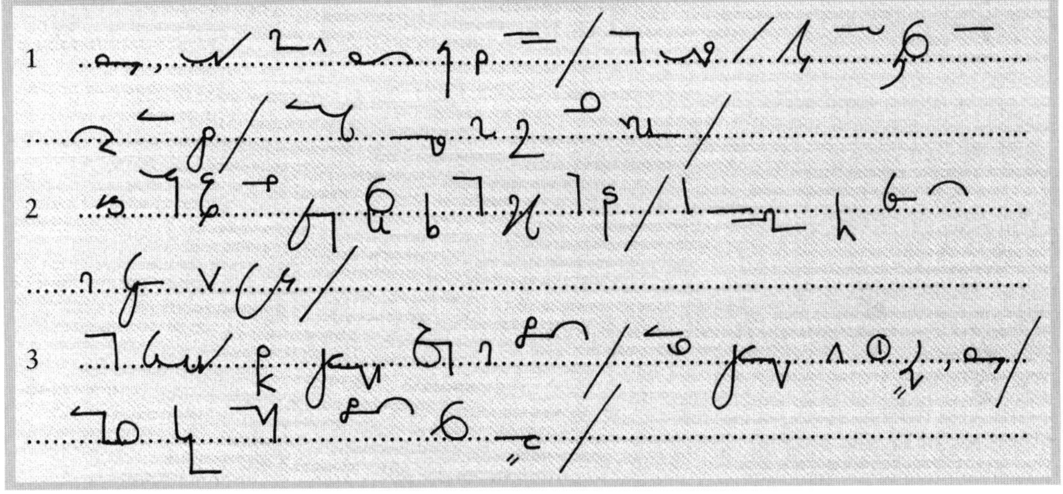

Special outlines – Unit 8

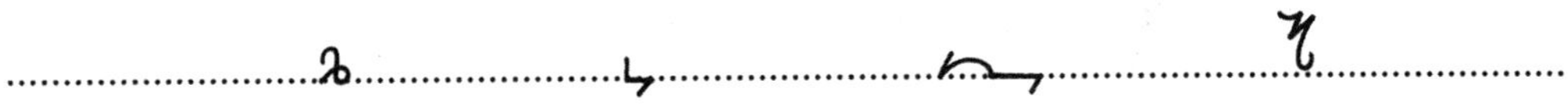

necessary | electricity | immediately | oil

absolute | absolutely | obvious | obviously

Word groupings

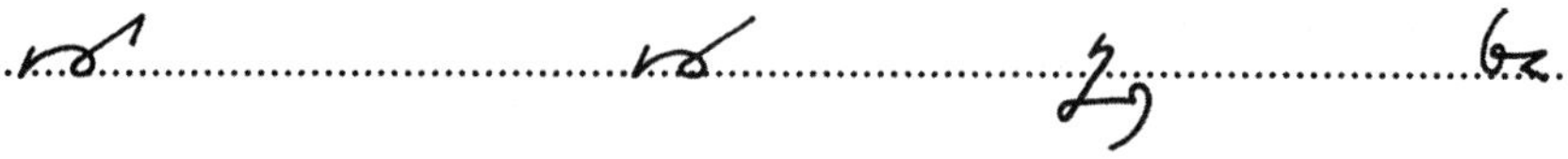

I am sorry (*compare with:* I am sure) in this day and age last week

Distinguishing outlines

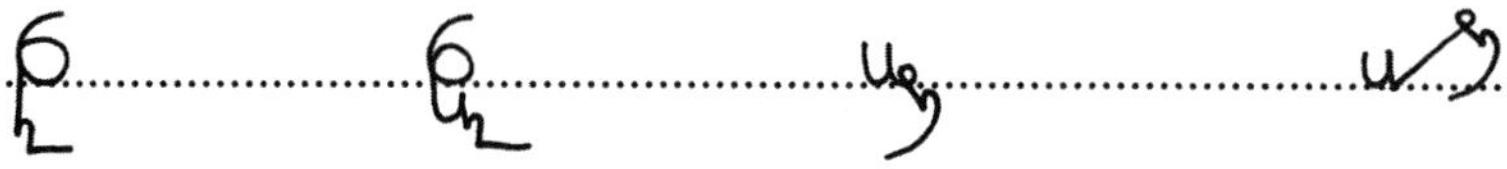

behind beyond years ago years of age

Task 8.4

Read and write 'Destitute old lady'

MP3

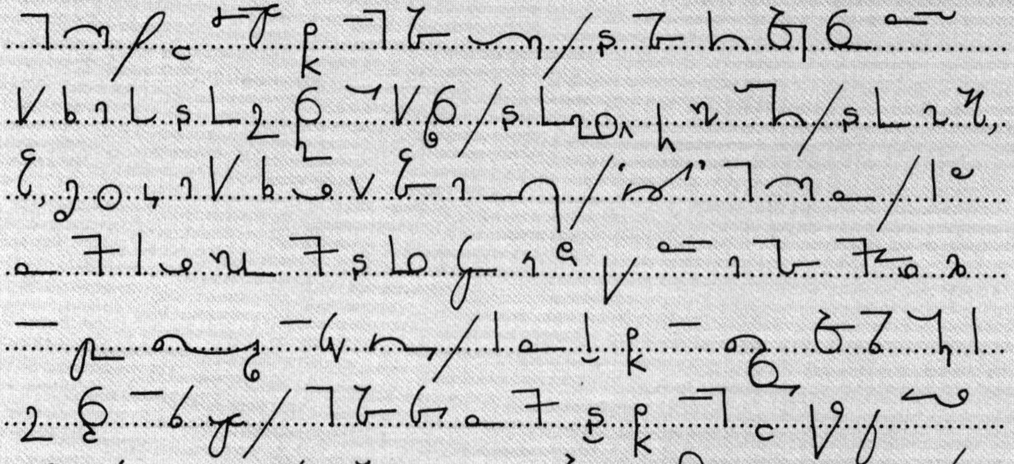

somewhere else 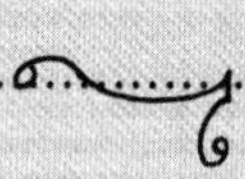 *estate office** 

* NOTE ALSO: 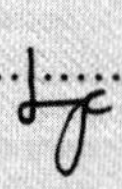 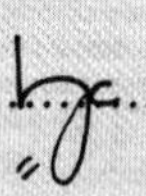

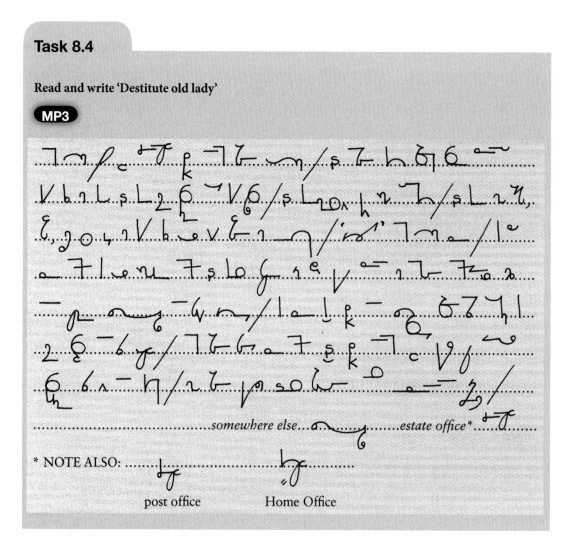

post office Home Office

Task 8.5

Read and write 'Help for destitute old lady'

MP3

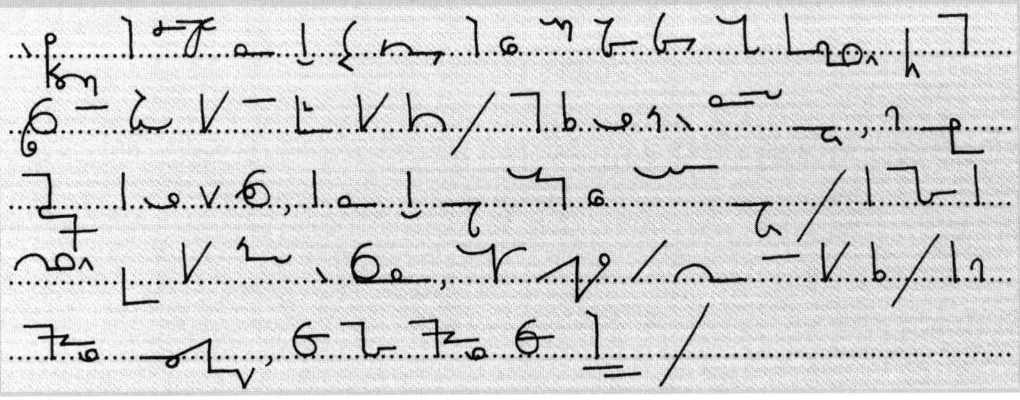

Task 8.6

Read and write 'A happy ending!'

MP3

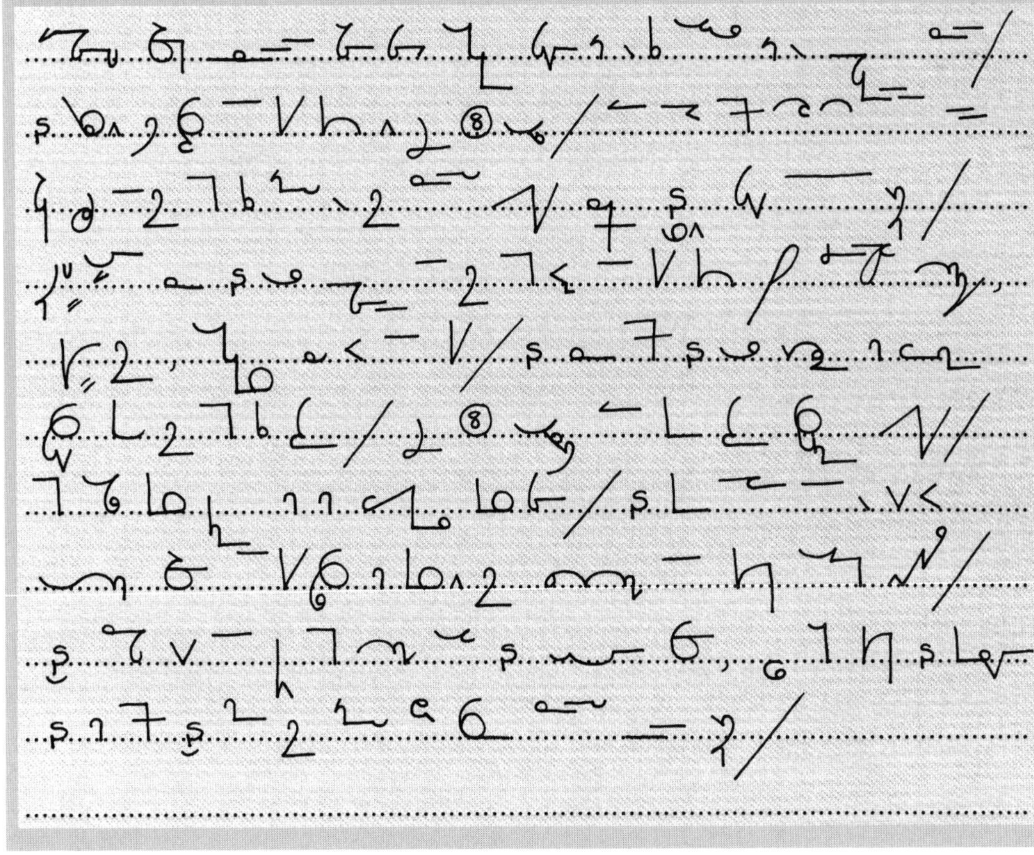

Unit 9
Use of vowels

Revision:
Vowels are written smaller than consonants.
Vowels have two forms – full vowels and indicators. The indicator is more commonly used.
(Revise theory at Unit 3)

When words **begin** with a vowel, the vowel is always written. The indicator is more commonly used:

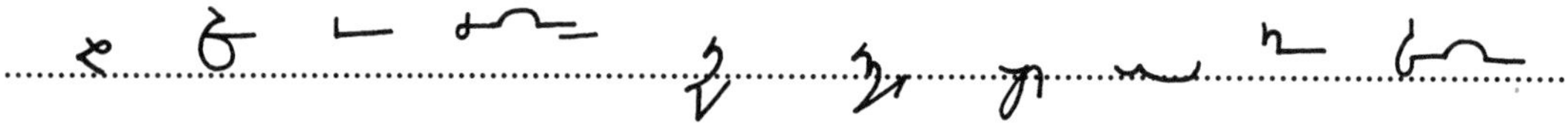

ask about eat estimated ignore injury often owe unit ultimate

When words **end** with a **sounded** vowel, the vowel is always written. The indicator is more commonly used:

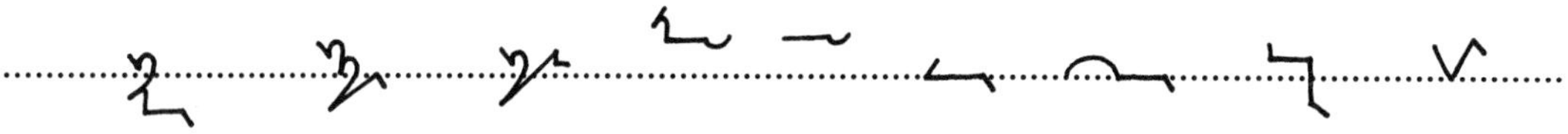

agenda angora agree into too idea media utopia via

Letter A

Revision:
Indicator **A** represents the word **a** ..\... and **at** when written above the line ..\.....
Indicator **A** is written upwards before **V**, **W**, **X**, **Q** and **P**.

avoid away axe acquit aptitude appear appeal

Full vowel **A** represents common words: **able**, **able to**, **ability** and **after** ...Λ.....

Words which begin with the prefix **AFTER**:

afternoon **after**thought **after**wards **after**math

Full vowel A is written before **R** to avoid confusion in reading back words which begin **AR** or **VR**:

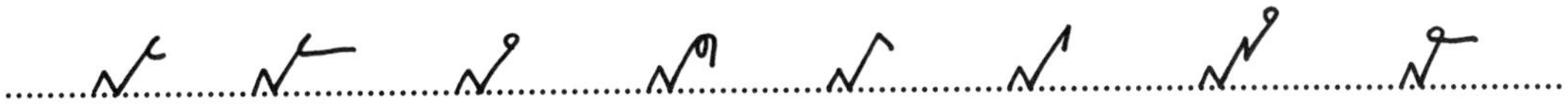

arc arcade arise arisen array awry arrears arrest

An extra large full vowel A is used to represent words which begin **AIR, AER** or **ARCH**:

air **air**y **air**liner **aer**ial **aer**osol **arch** **archi**tect **arch**ery **archi**ves

AU is represented by full vowel **A** at the beginning of a word:

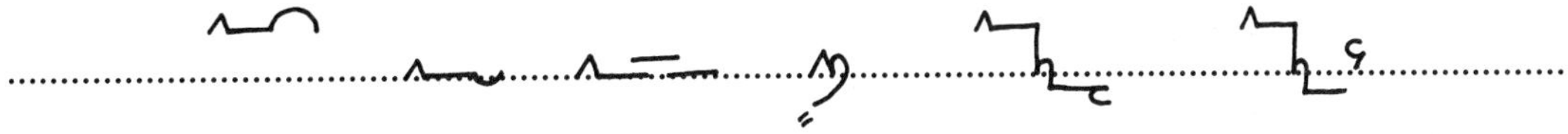

autumn **au**dio **au**dited **Au**gust **au**thentic **au**thenticity

Revision:

Authority .... is letter **R** written from the writing line, upwards.

Words which begin with the prefix **AUTO**- are written as a full vowel **A** in the **T** position ....:

automatic **auto**mobile **auto**mated **auto**nomy **auto**nomous **auto**graph*

* Note the blend of letters **G** and **F** for words ending **-GRAPH**

Task 9.1

Read and write the following sentences

MP3

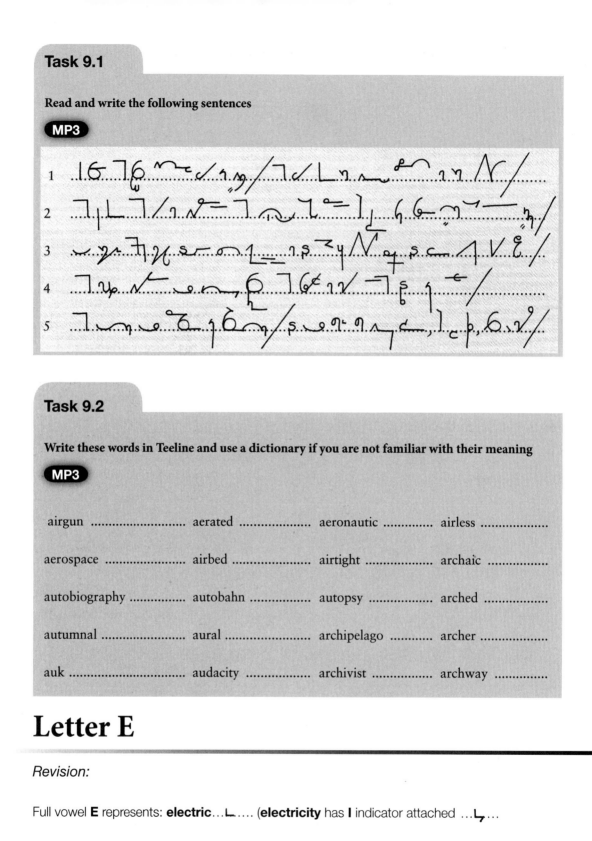

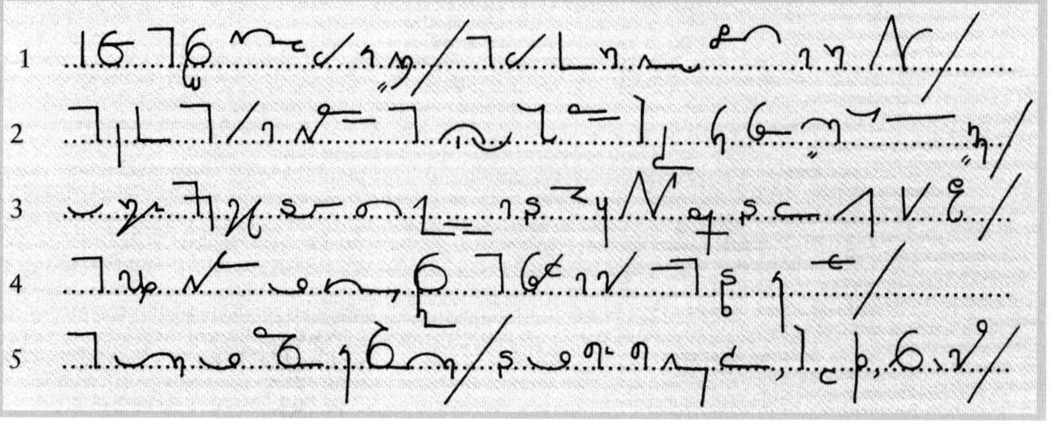

Task 9.2

Write these words in Teeline and use a dictionary if you are not familiar with their meaning

MP3

airgun	aerated	aeronautic	airless ....
aerospace	airbed	airtight	archaic ....
autobiography	autobahn	autopsy	arched ....
autumnal	aural	archipelago	archer ....
auk	audacity	archivist	archway ....

Letter E

Revision:

Full vowel **E** represents: **electric**.......... (**electricity** has **I** indicator attached ....

England .... and **English** ....

Indicator **E** represents the words **ever** and **every** ....

Full vowel **E** must be used before the letters **P** and **Q** as the indicator would be lost in the outline:

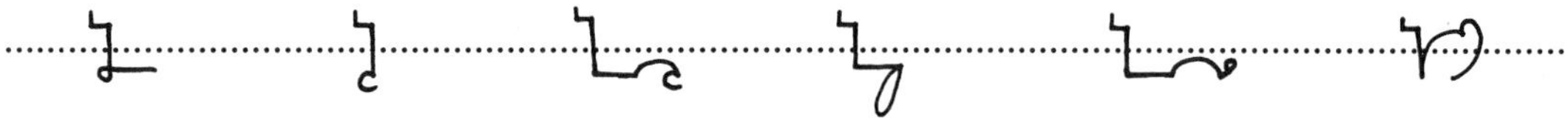

episode epic epidemic epitaph epitomize epilogue

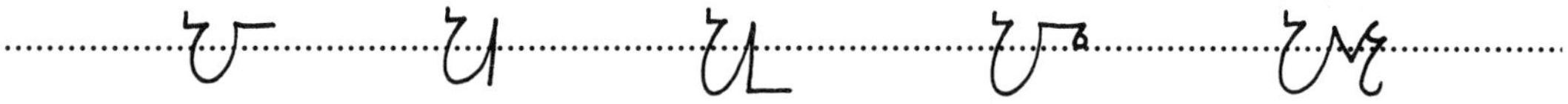

equate equip equipped equities equivocal

Letter U

Revision:

Full vowel **U** represents: **you** ....U....

Full vowel **U** must be used before the letter **P** as the indicator would be lost in the outline:

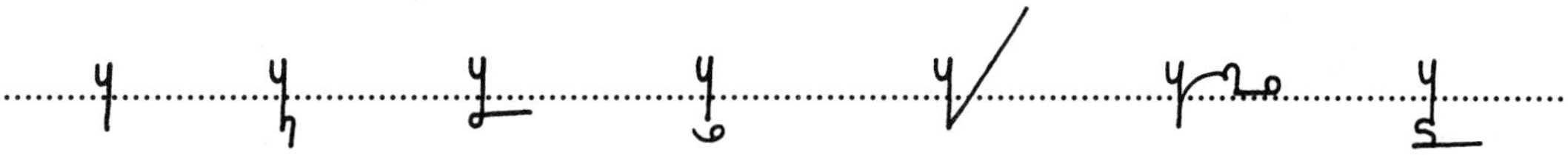

up **up**on **up**set **up**wards **up**roar **up**lands **up**shot

Full vowel **U** represents the heavy sound of **U** at the end of words:

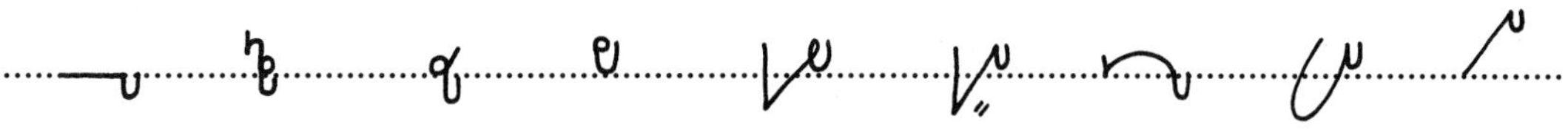

d**ue** ens**ue** iss**ue** s**ue** purs**ue** Per**u** em**u** qu**eue** r**ue**

Full vowel **U** represents the prefix **UPPER-** when disjoined and written in the **T** position:

upper-most **upper**-class **upper**-cut **upper**-case **upper**-hand*

*Note the use of a sloping letter **H** in the direction of **A** for the word **hand**. This is useful when writing: **hand**bag ......... **hand**yman ....... etc.

Full vowel **U** represents the prefix **ULTRA-** when disjoined and written on the line:

ultrasonic   **ultra**-violet

Distinguishing outlines

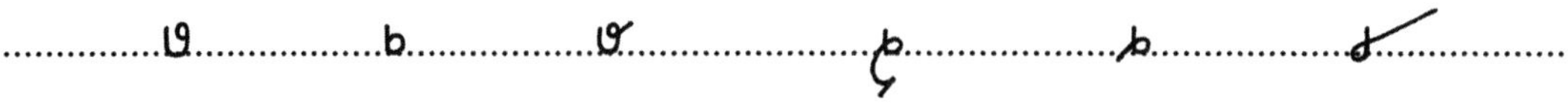

use   ease   usually   easily   easy   easier

Task 9.3

Read and write the following sentences

MP3

1
2
3
4
5

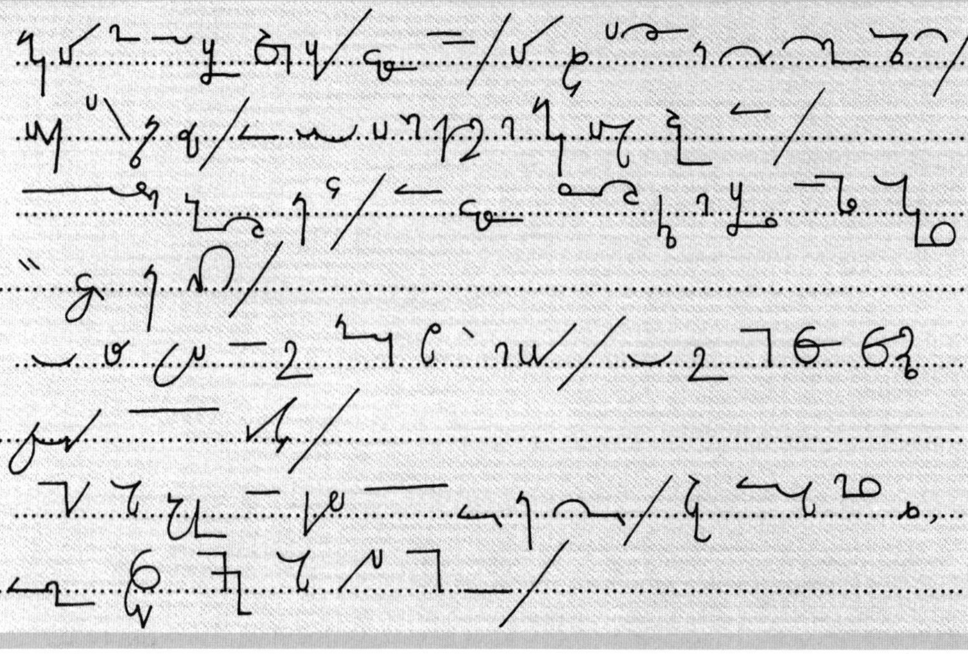

Words which begin with the prefix UN- may be shortened by writing the U indicator immediately before the remainder of the outline. In order to avoid confusing this with the E indictor, used for **ever/every,** take care to write the U indicator slightly above the writing line:

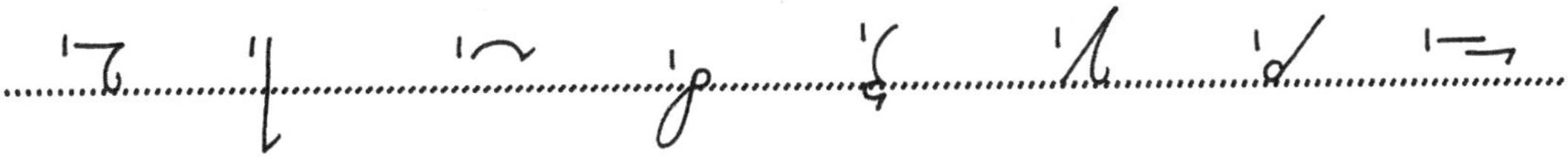

until unhappy untimely unsafe unlucky unroll unsure untidy

Task 9.4

Read and write the following sentences

MP3

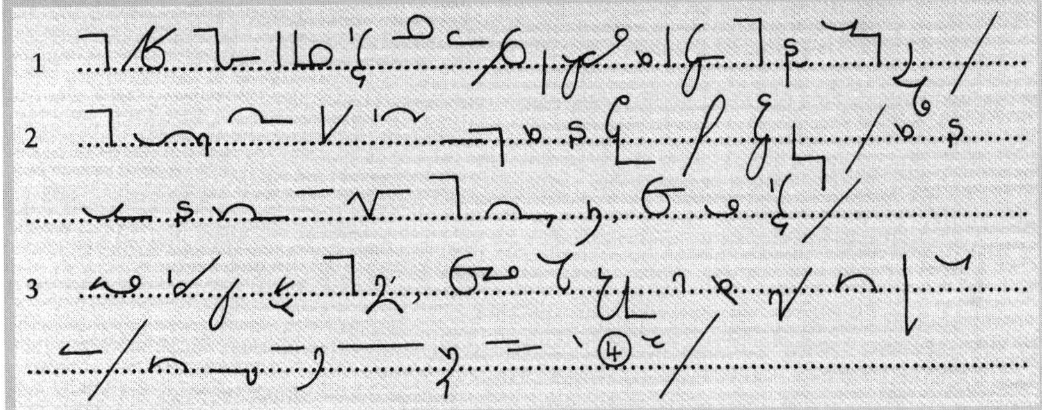

Letter O

Revision:

Full vowel **O** represents: **OR** ...... Indicator **O** represents: **OF** ....

Indicator O is turned on its side and blended with letter **M** to blend **OM** ..... and **MO** ....

(Take care not to close the two outlines or you may read this as letter **S**.)

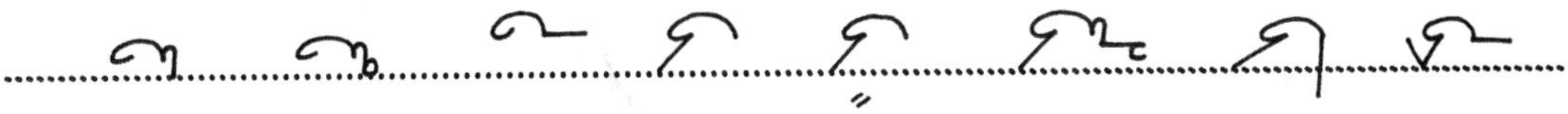

omen ominous omit room Rome romantic romp vomit

move remove memo ombudsman

Distinguishing outlines

The hook of the **N** is removed to give an outline which is easier to write:

on one

This theory is applied to other words:

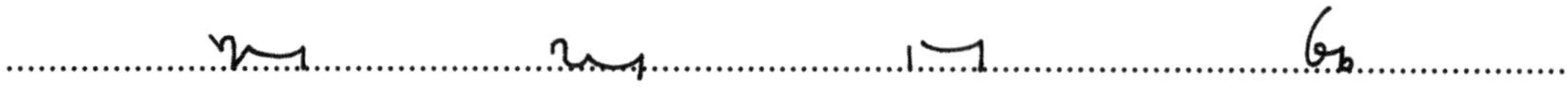

any**one** no-**one** every**one** lesson**s**

Special outlines – Unit 9

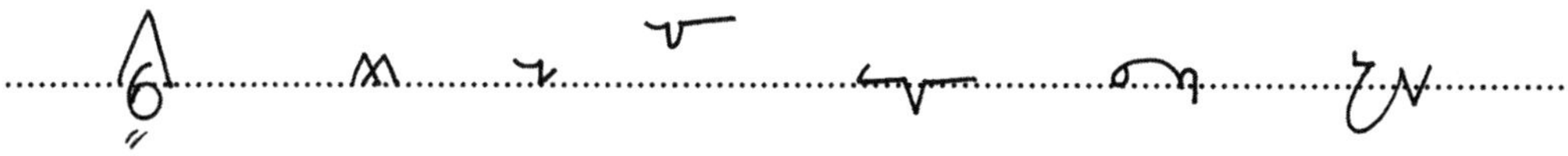

Archbishop area only ought individual someone equivalent

Word groupings

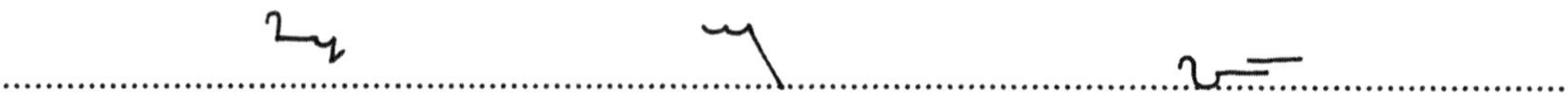

not only on the other hand no doubt

Task 9.5

Read and write 'Youth attacked in town centre bar'

MP3

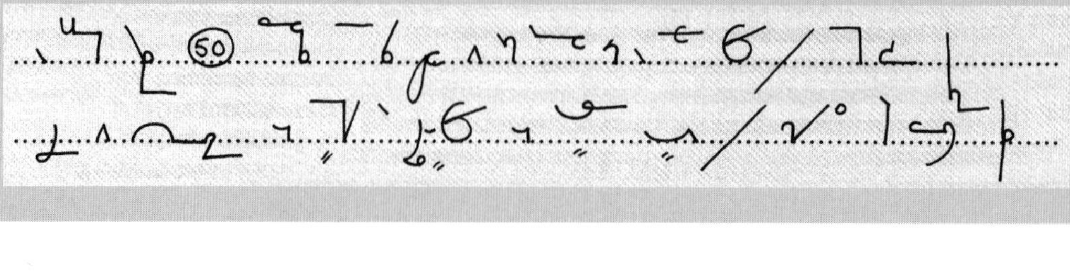

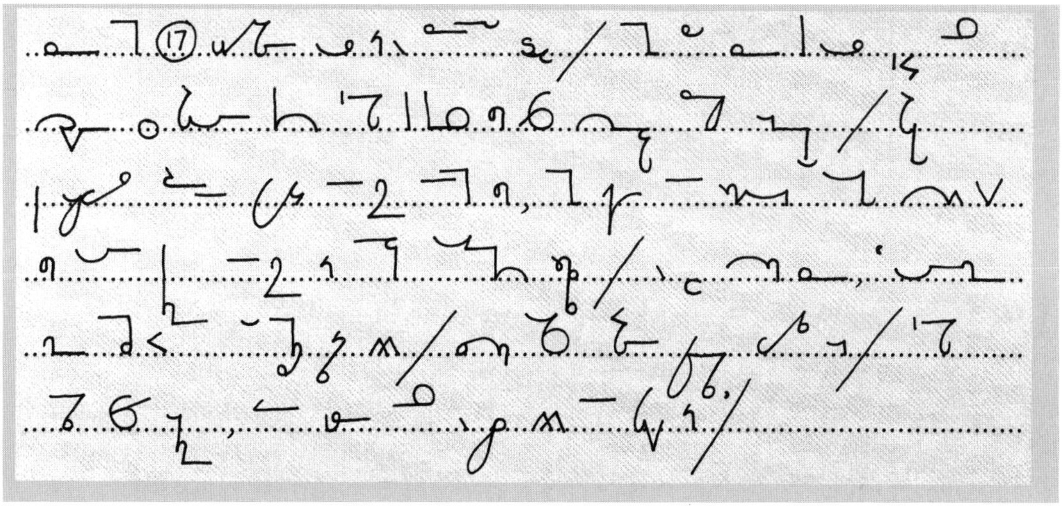

Task 9.6

Read and write 'Man arrested for attack on youth'

MP3

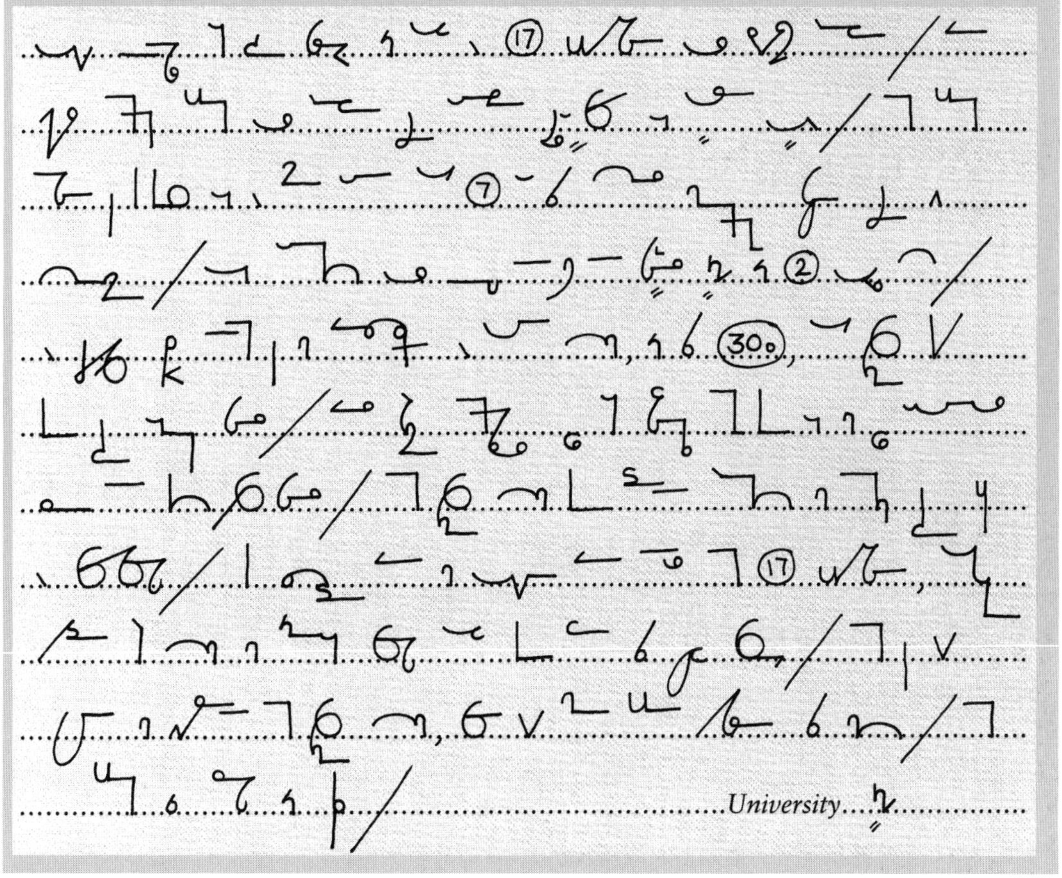

Unit 10
Vowel indicators used as word endings

Vowel indicators are used to represent word endings. The indicator is always written disjoined but close to the first part of the outline.

Indicator I for -ING

Indicator **I** must be written **downwards, disjoined** and **close** to the first part of the outline for **-ING**:

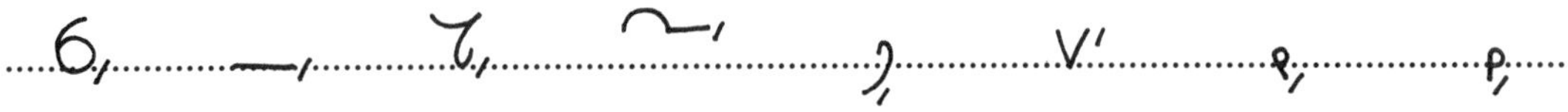

being doing willing meeting going having saying seeing

-ING may also be written as part of the word, not just as a word ending:

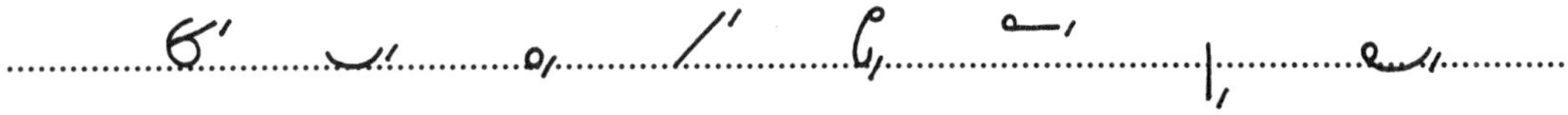

bring wing sing ring sling sting ping swing

If **-ING** is repeated the indicator is written twice – remember to write both downwards:

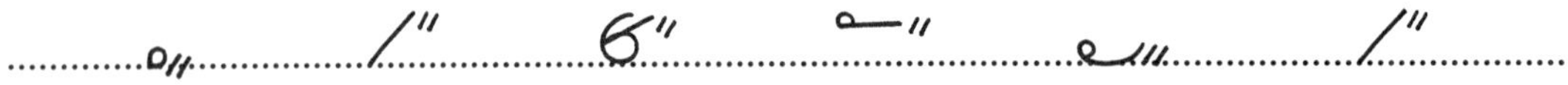

singing ringing bringing stinging swinging wringing

Other letters may be joined to the indicator in order to extend the word ending:

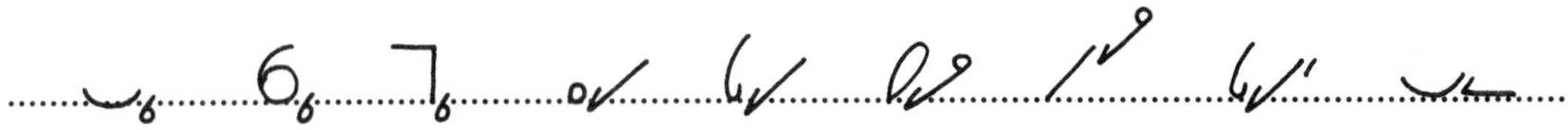

wings beings things singer linger fingers ringers lingering winged

In a grouping, the word **the** may be added to the indicator. In order to give a sharp angle and clearer outline TH is written:

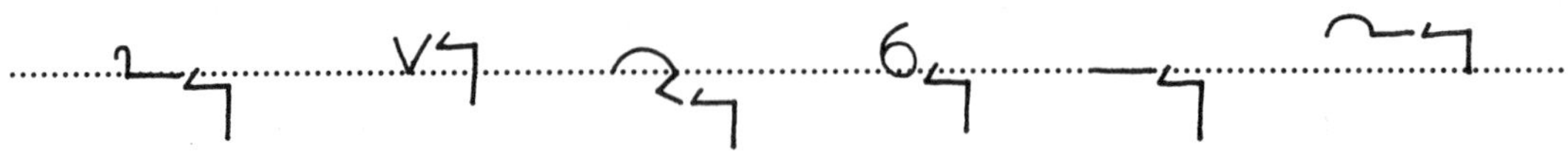

needing the having the making the being the doing the meeting the

Similarly, **this, these, those, them, they** may be added to **-ING**:

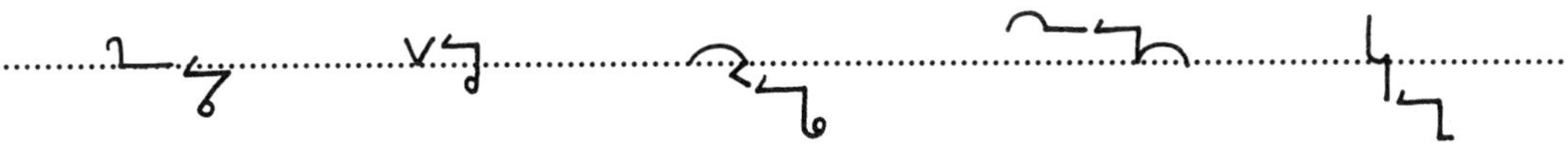

needing **this** | having **these** | making **those** | meeting **them** | hoping **they**

Words ending in **-INGE** may safely use the same word ending as **-ING**. Context helps transcription:

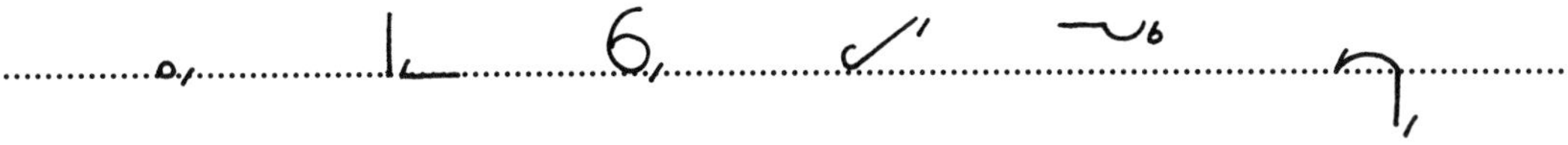

singe | hinged | binge | cringe | twinges | impinge

Words ending -INGLE

A disjoined letter **L** written downwards and in the position of **-ING** represents word ending **-INGLE**:

single | tingle | mingle | jingle

Other letters may be added to **-INGLE** to extend the word ending:

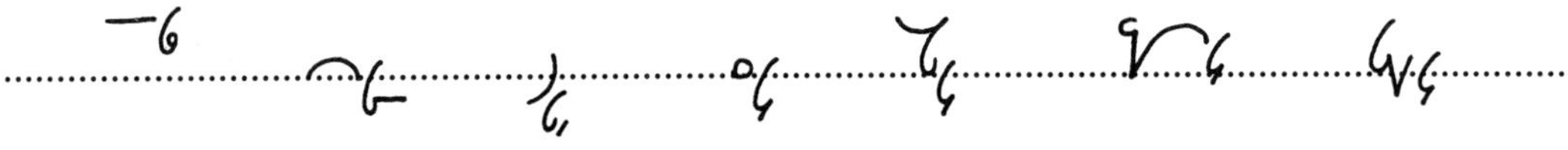

tingles | mingled | jingling | singly | willingly | charm**ingly** | lov**ingly**

In word groupings **-ING** or **-INGS** may be written to represent the word **thing** or **things**:

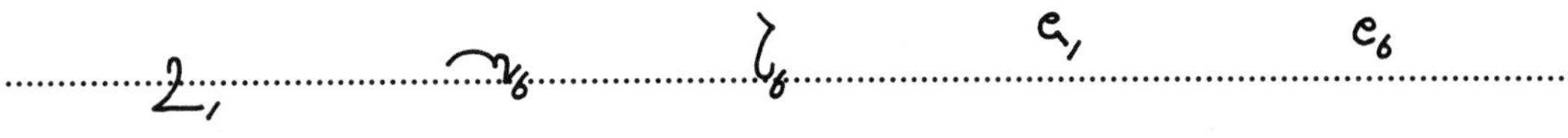

good **thing** | many **things** | all **things** | such a **thing** | such **things**

However, if a sentence starts with the word **things,** the outline **must be written in full** 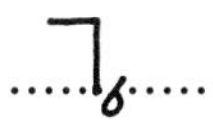

If you do not do this, you may try to read the word back as **is** and waste valuable transcription time.

Task 10.1

Read and write the following sentences

MP3

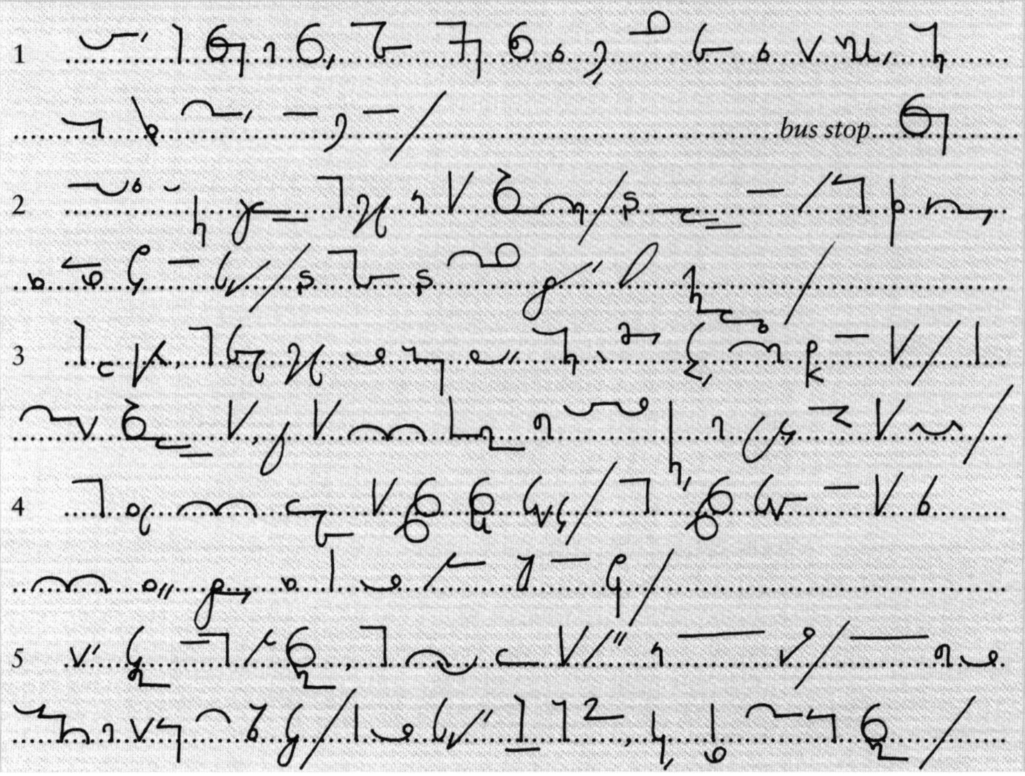

Indicator A for -ANG

Indicator **A** must be written **downwards, disjoined** and **close** to the first part of the outline for -ANG:

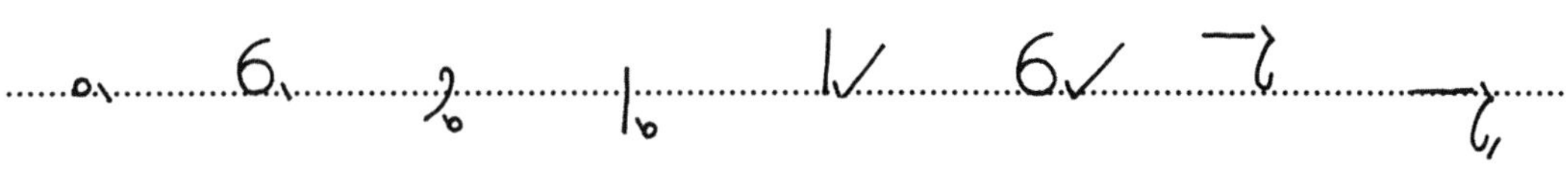

sang	bang	gangs	pangs	hanger	banger	tangle	dangling

Words ending in -ANGE may safely use the same word ending as -ANG. Context helps transcription:

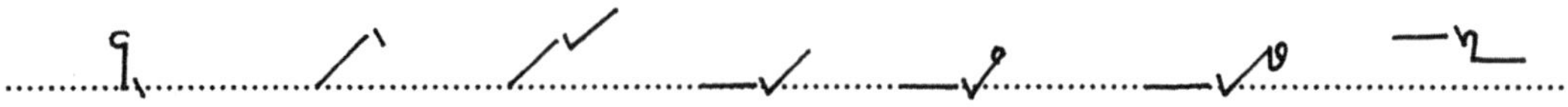

change	range	ranger	danger	dangers	dangerous	tangent

Indicator O for -ONG

Indicator O must be written **disjoined** and **close** to the first part of the outline for -ONG:

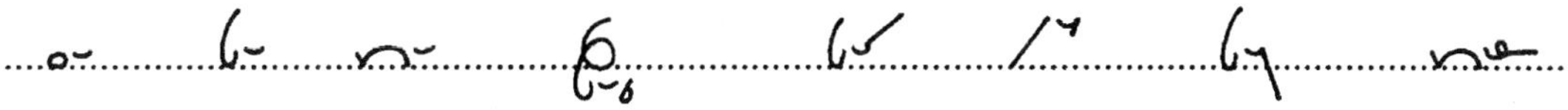

song long among bel**ongings** l**onger** wr**ongly** l**onghand** am**ongst**

Words ending in -**ONGE** may safely use the same word ending as -**ONG**. Context helps transcription:

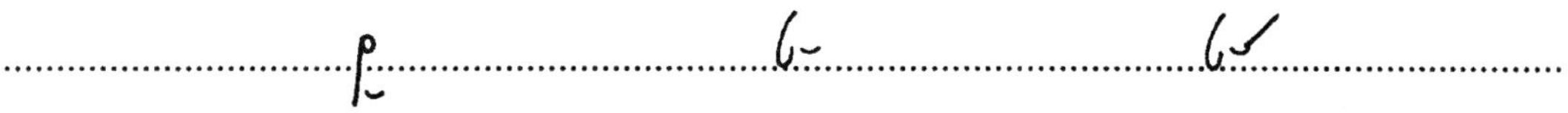

sp**onge** l**ounge** l**ounger**

Indicator U for -UNG

Indicator U must be written **downwards, disjoined** and **close** to the first part of the outline for -UNG:

l**ung** h**ung** sw**ung** yo**ung** yo**unger** r**ungs** j**ungle** h**ungry** b**ungle**

Words ending in -**UNGE** may safely use the same word ending as -**UNG**. Context helps transcription:

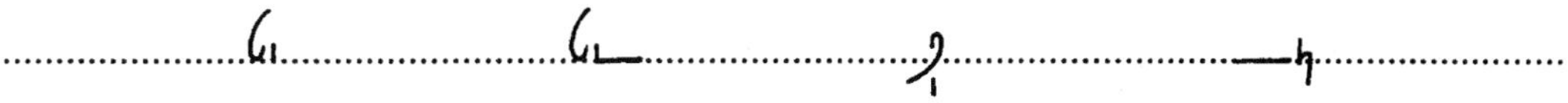

l**unge** l**unged** g**unge** d**ungeon**

Indicator E for -ENG

Indicator E must be written **downwards, disjoined** and **close** to the first part of the outline for -ENG:

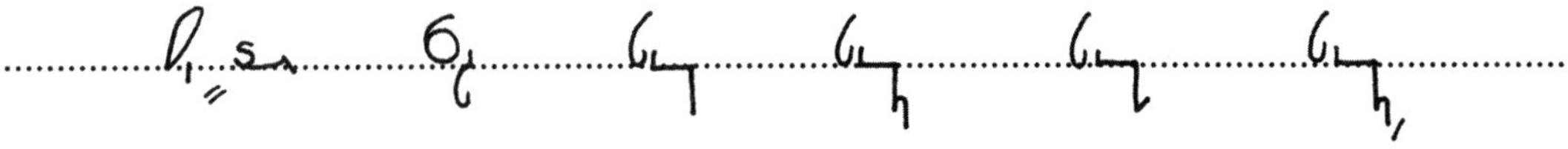

Feng Shui | Bengal | length | lengthen | lengthy | lengthening

Words ending in **-ENGE** may safely use the same word ending as **-ENG.** Context helps transcription:

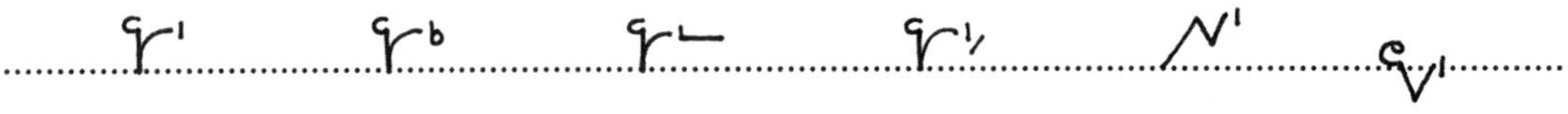

chall**enge** | chall**enges** | chall**enged** | chall**enging** | rev**enge** | scav**enge**

Task 10.2

Read and write the following sentences

MP3

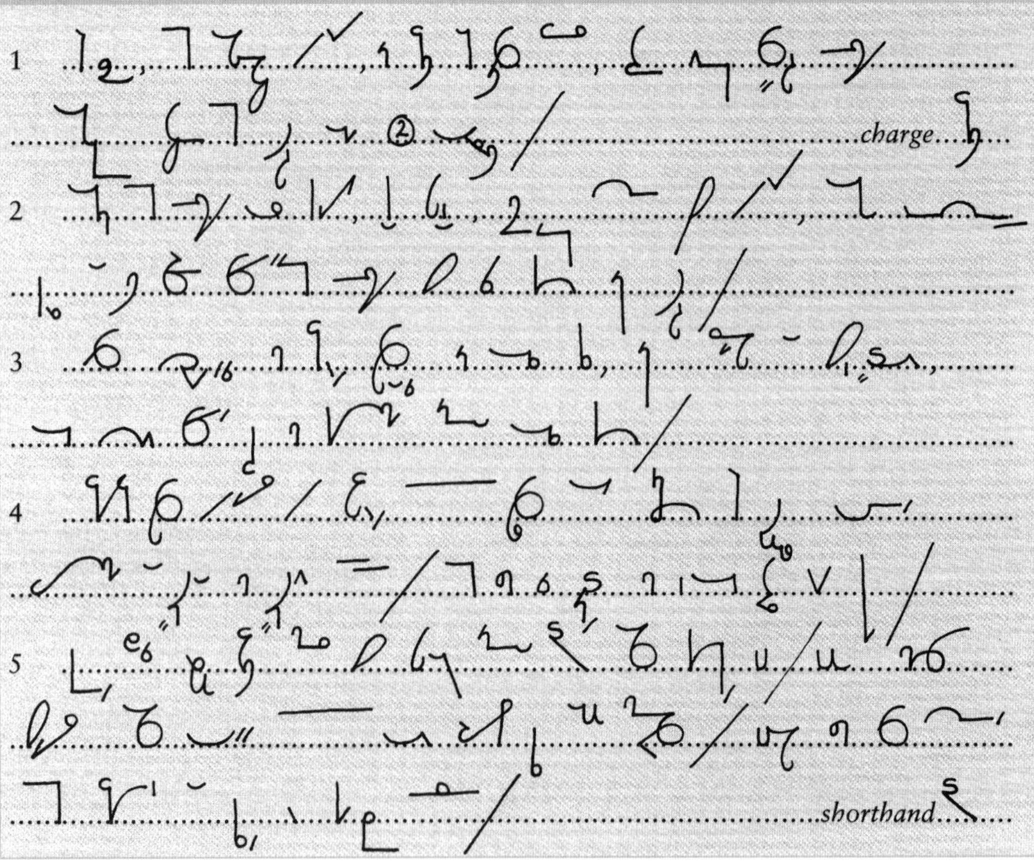

Special outlines – Unit 10

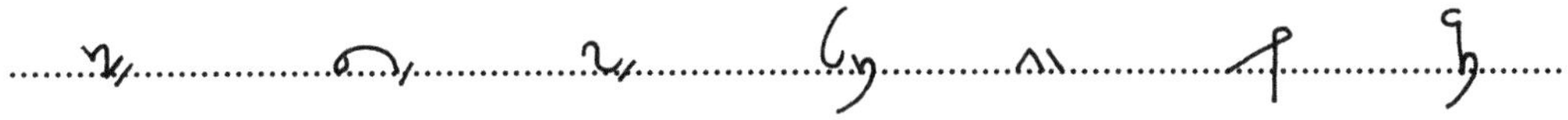

anything something nothing language arrange respect charge

Word groupings

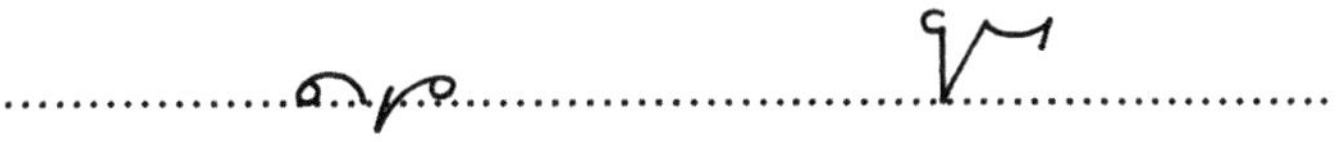

something else charged with

Task 10.3

Read and write 'Detached bungalow needed'

MP3

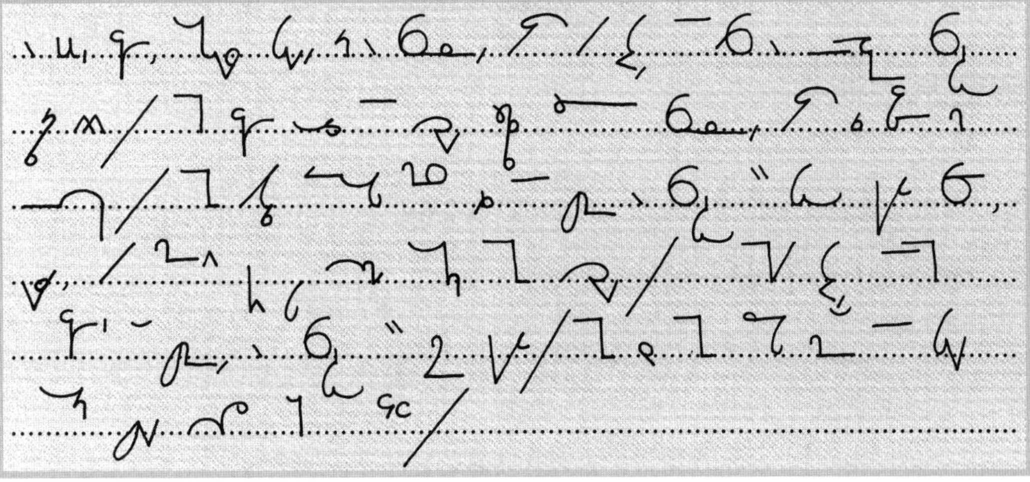

Task 10.4

Read and write 'When spring has sprung!'

MP3

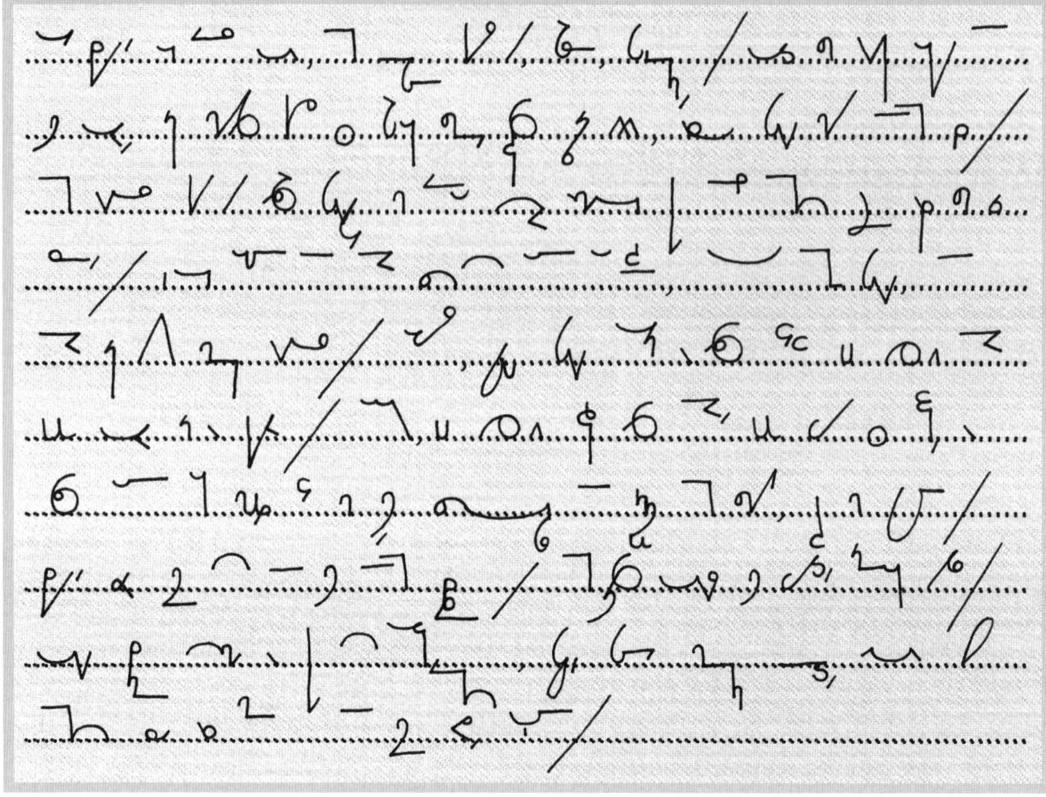

Unit 11
Extending vowel indicators as word endings and more new word beginnings

Adding letter **C** to vowel indicators gives more useful word endings. The **indicator + C** is always written disjoined but close to the first part of the outline.

Indicator A + C for -ANK

sank   rank   tank   crank   shrank   blank

Other letters may be joined in order to extend the word ending further:

ranked   tanker   cranking   blanket   spanking

When standing alone or at the start of a sentence, write **thank** .... and **bank** .... in full.

To save time, these words may be reduced in word groupings to the word ending -**ANK**:

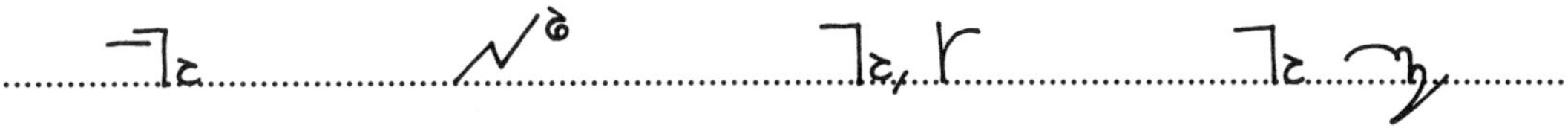

to the **bank**   river **banks**   the **banking** hall   the **bank** manager

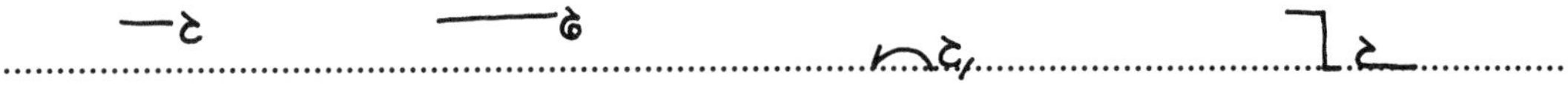

to **thank**   their **thanks**   I am **thanking**   they **thanked**

Indicator E + C for -ENK

There are no examples for words ending -**ENK**, but it may be used as part of certain proper nouns:

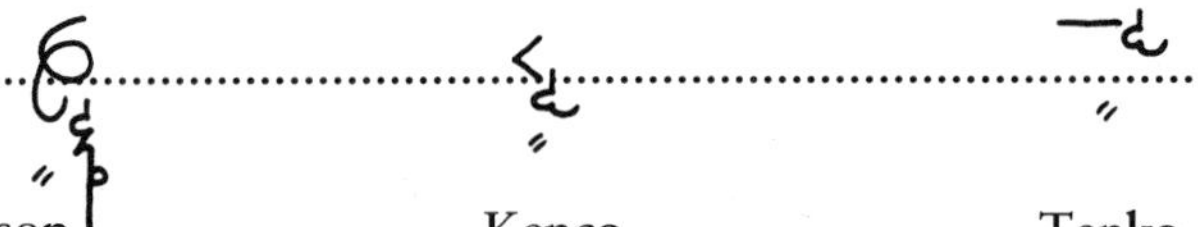

Blenkinsop Kenco Tenko

Indicator I + C for -INK

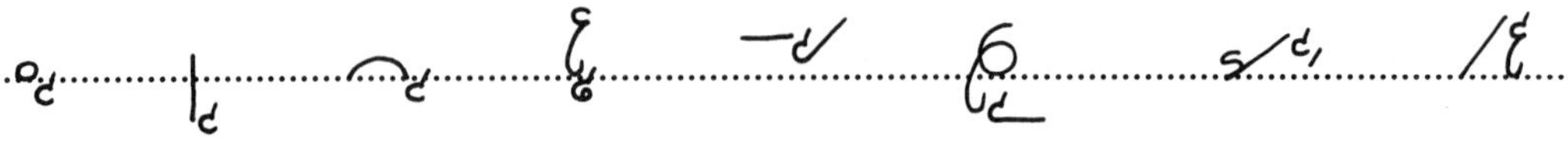

sink pink mink clinks tinker blinked shrinking wrinkle

When standing alone or at the start of a sentence, write the word **think**  in full.

To save time, this may be reduced in word groupings to the word ending -INK:

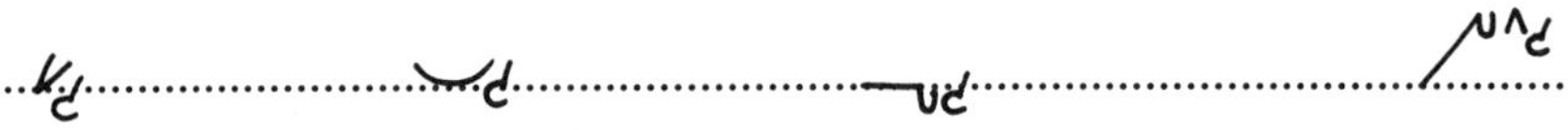

I think we think do you think are you able to think

Indicator O + C for -ONK

honk conk monk donkey bonkers conker honked honking

Indicator U + C for -UNK

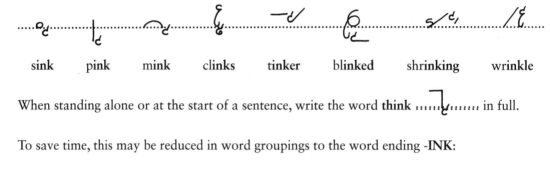

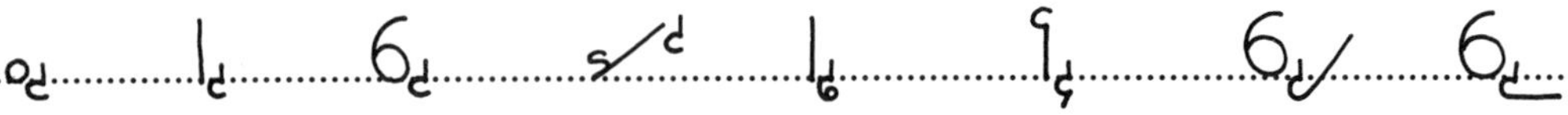

sunk hunk bunk shrunk hunks chunky bunker bunked

Task 11.1

Write the following sentences in neat Teeline outlines

MP3

1 I think the crank shaft on the old car collapsed.
2 The chunky pink jumper shrank in the wash.
3 I ate a chunky chocolate bar which the hunky man gave to me.
4 Sitting in the sun all day will give you wrinkled skin.
5 I would like to thank the person who moved the tanker.

ENC- and INC- as word beginnings

Omit the letter **N** and write the indicator **E** or **I** with letter **C** attached:

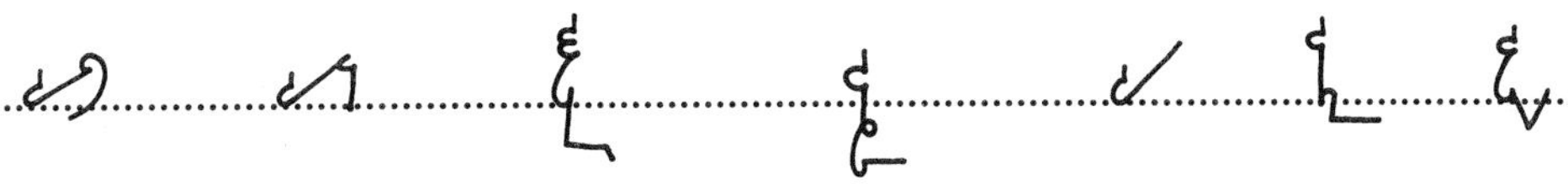

encourage encroach encyclopaedia encapsulate encore enchant enclave

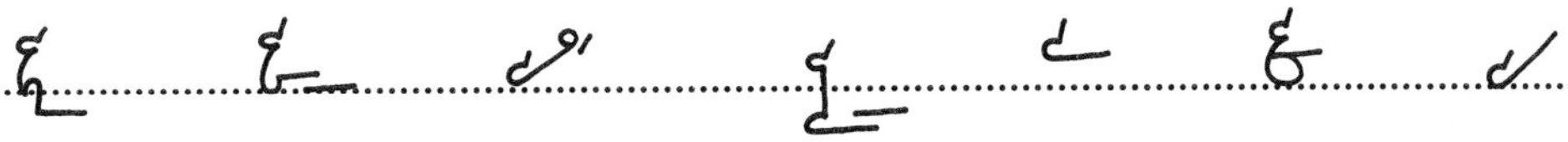

inclined included increasing incapacitate incite incubate incur

INS- as a word beginning

Omit the letter **N** and write the indicator **I** with letter **S** attached:

instead insure insulate insist insight insipid inspire instil

INT- as a word beginning

Omit the letter **N** and write the indicator **I** with letter **T** attached:

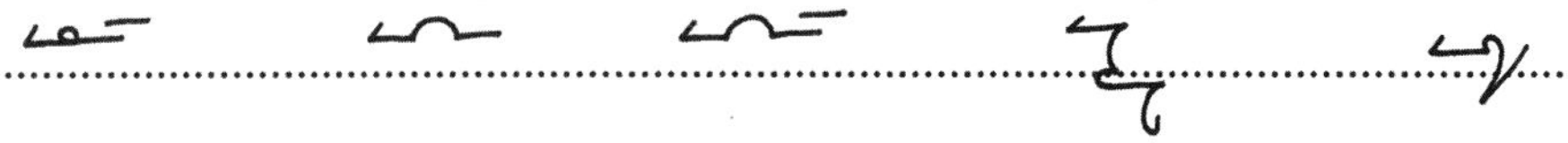

intestate **int**imate **int**imidate **int**ellectual **int**eger

Task 11.2

Read and write the following sentences

MP3

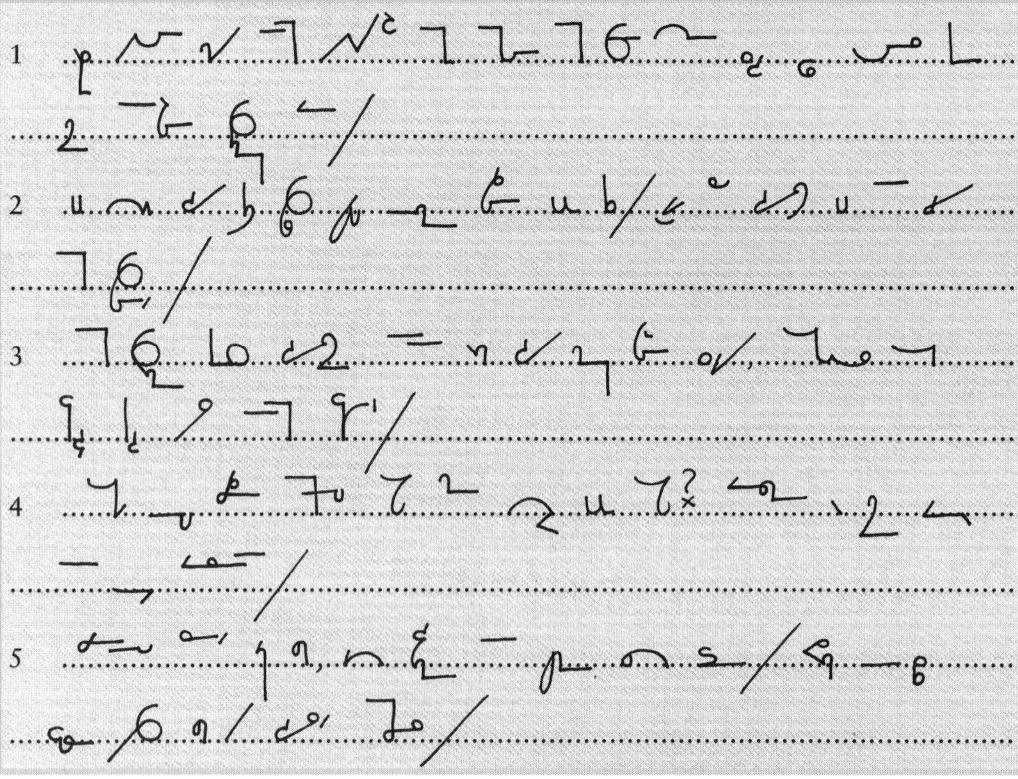

Special outlines – Unit 11

enclose enclosed enclosure inability

Word groupings

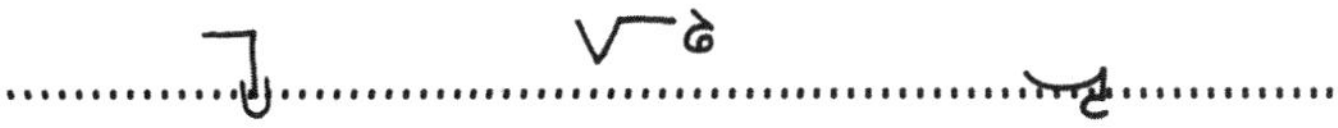

thank you vote of thanks we enclose

Task 11.3

Read and write 'Sheep'

MP3

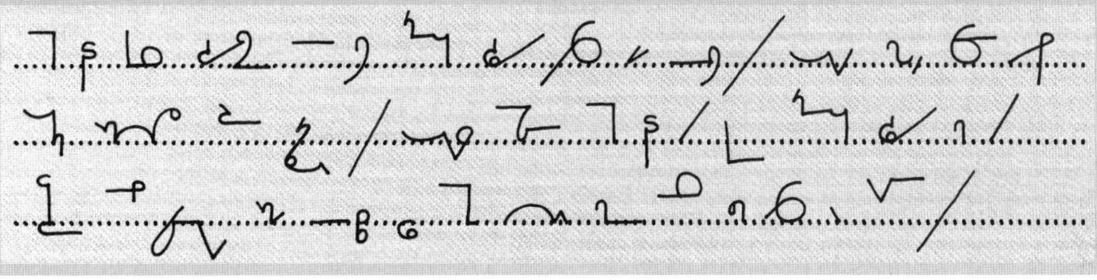

Task 11.4

Read and write 'Tanker sinks in channel'

MP3

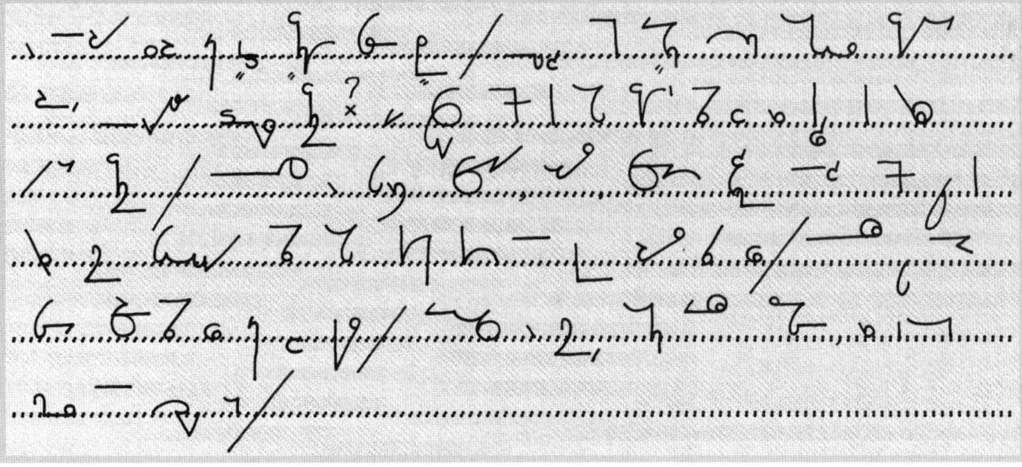

Task 11.5

Read and write 'Disappearing jobs'

MP3

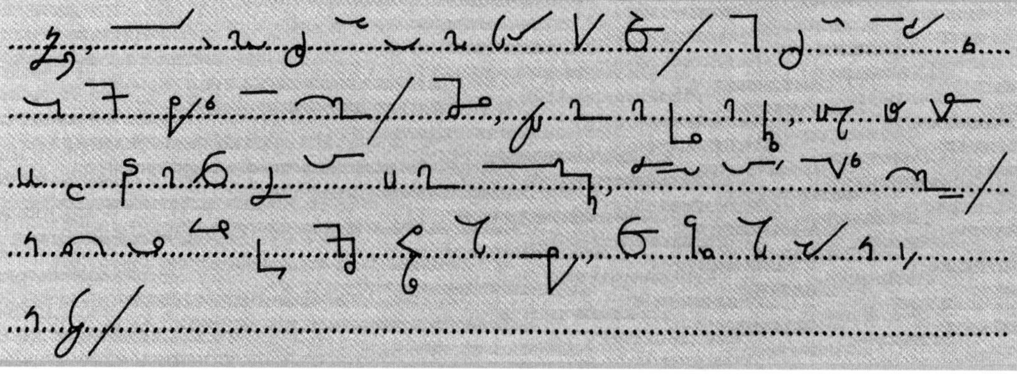

Task 11.6

Transcribe the following special outlines

MP3

1 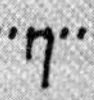

2 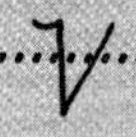

3 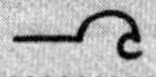

4 

5 

6 

7 

8 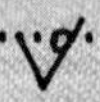

9 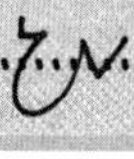

10 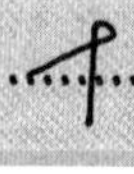

Unit 12
Words ending -NCE, -NCH and words beginning ANTI-, ANTE-, ANTA-

-NCE at the end of a word

Letter C must be **disjoined** and written **close** to the first part of the outline for words ending **-NCE**. Any vowel may precede this word ending:

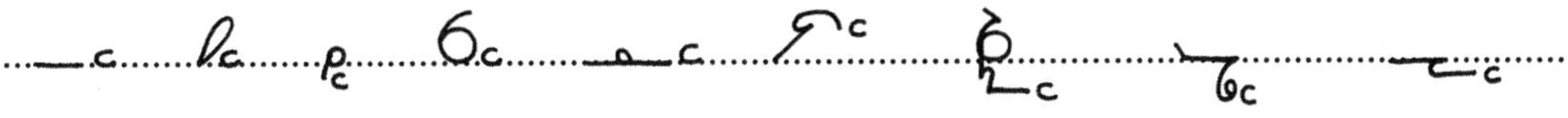

dance fence since bounce distance romance abundance adolescence decadence

Other letters may be joined to the C in order to extend the word ending:

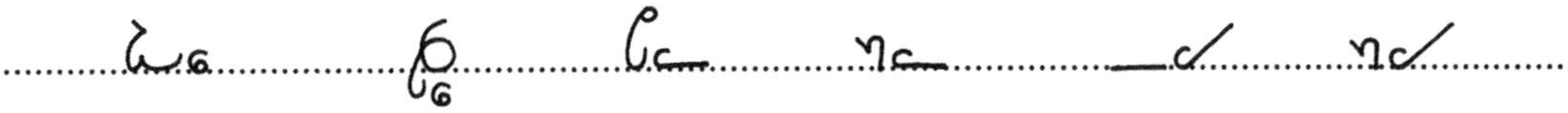

allowances balances silenced announced dancer announcer

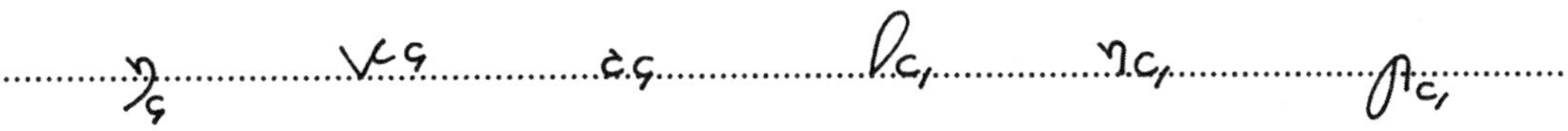

agency vacancy accountancy fencing announcing financing

Task 12.1

Read and write the following sentences

MP3

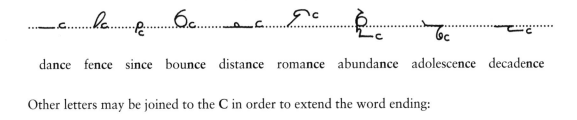

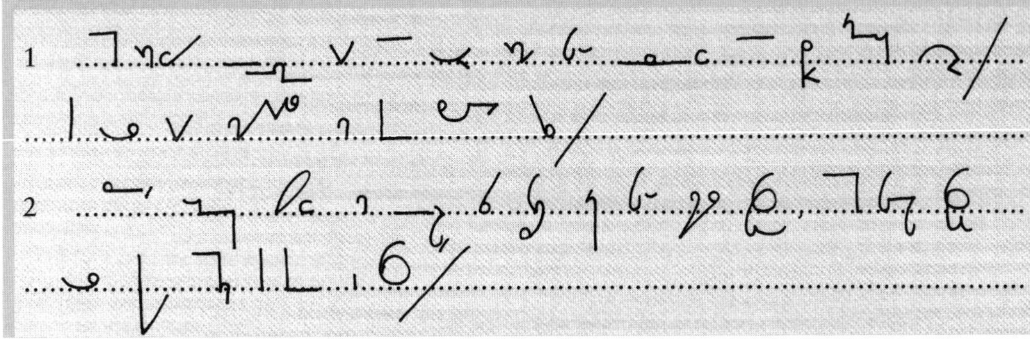

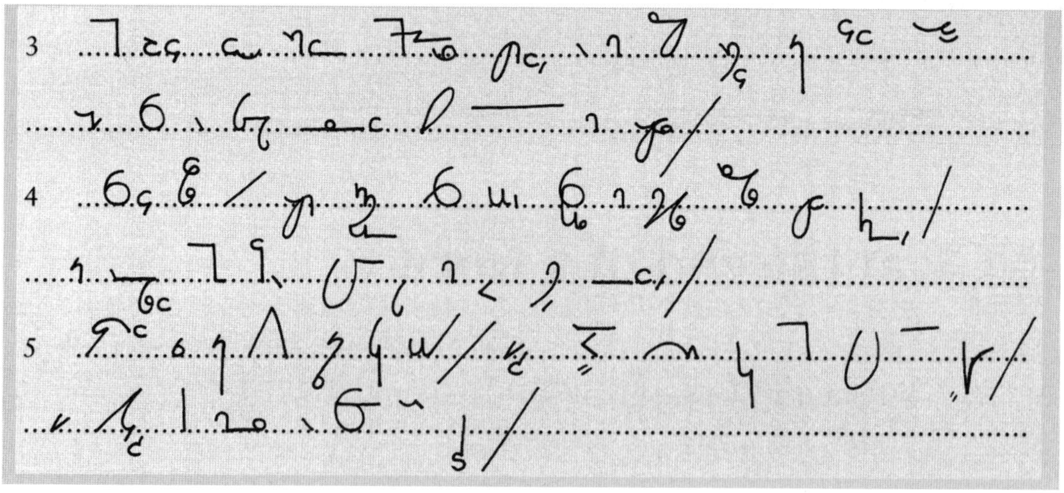

Revision:

Letter **C** …c.. represents common words **once** and **offence**

Letter **H** …|… represents common word **he**

Letters **CH** ……… represents special outline **chairman**

Special Outlines Unit 3 – the **H** is not written on common words ending in **CH**:

much ………. **each** ………. **such** ………. **which** ………. **too much** ……….

-NCH at the end of a word

CH must be **disjoined** and written **close** to the first part of the outline for words ending **-NCH**.

bra**nch** lau**nch** be**nch** pi**nch** wre**nch** mu**nch**

Other letters may be joined to **-NCH** in order to extend the word ending:

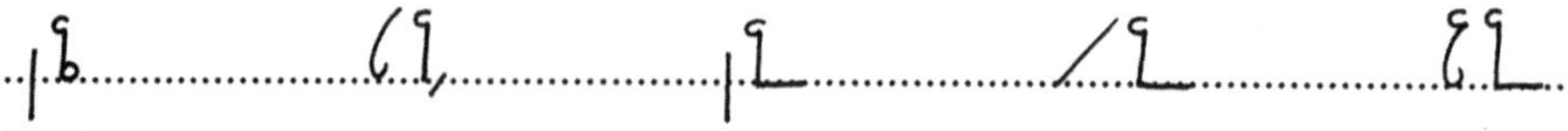

pi**nch**es lau**nch**ing pu**nch**ed wre**nch**ed cli**nch**ed

lunching munching puncher luncheon

Task 12.2

Read and write the following sentences

MP3

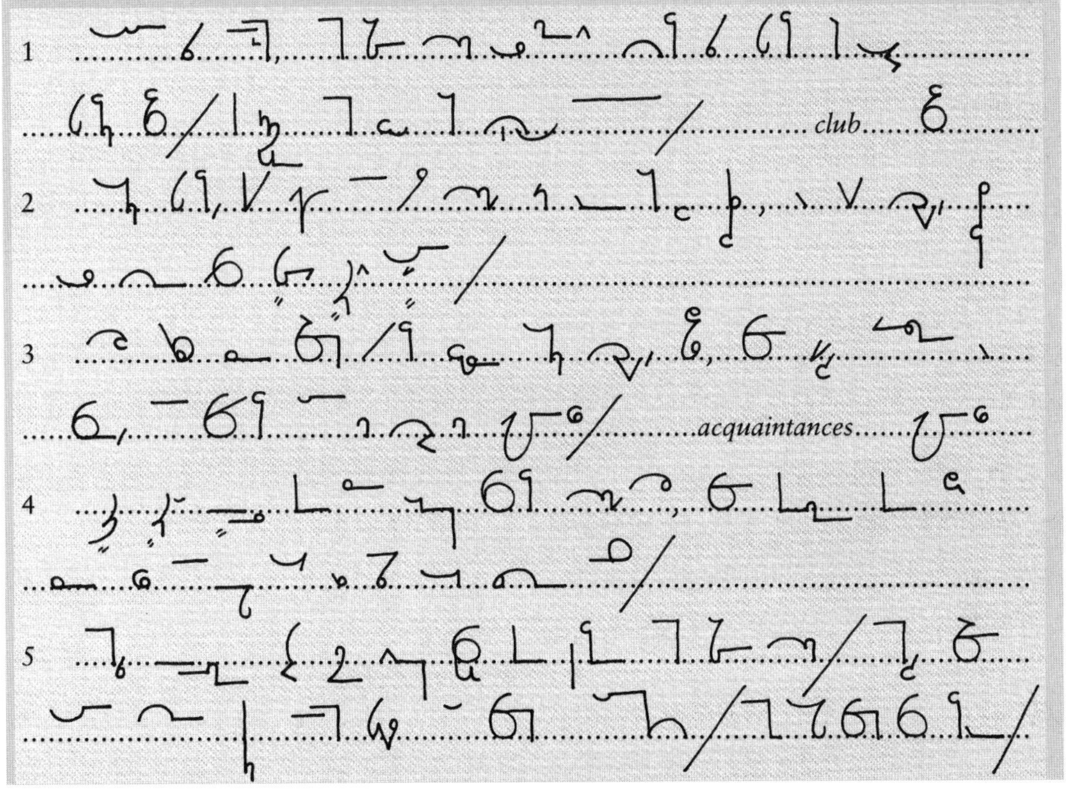

ANTI-, ANTE- and ANTA- at the beginning of words

Write letters **AN disjoined in the T position** and follow **closely** with the remainder of the outline:

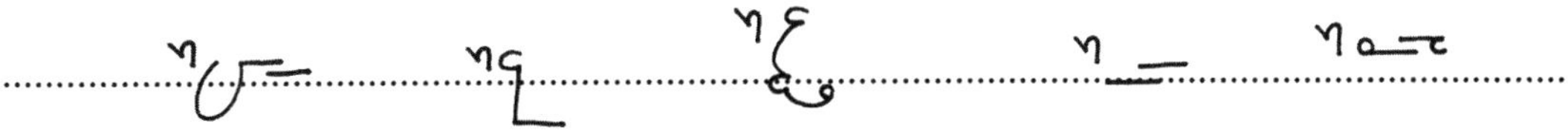

antiquated **anti**cipate **anti**-clockwise **anti**dote **anti**static

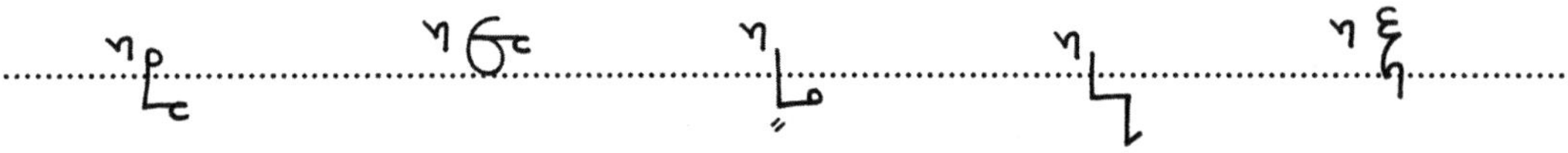

antiseptic | **anti**biotic | **Anti**podes | **anti**pathy | **anti**cyclone

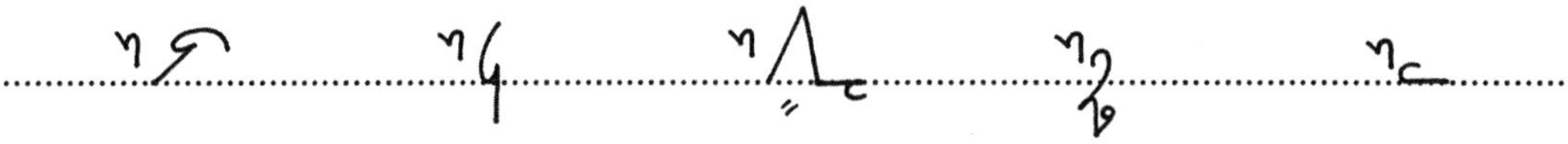

ante-room | **ante**lope | **Ant**arctic | **ant**agonise | **ant**acid

Task 12.3

Read and write the following sentences

MP3

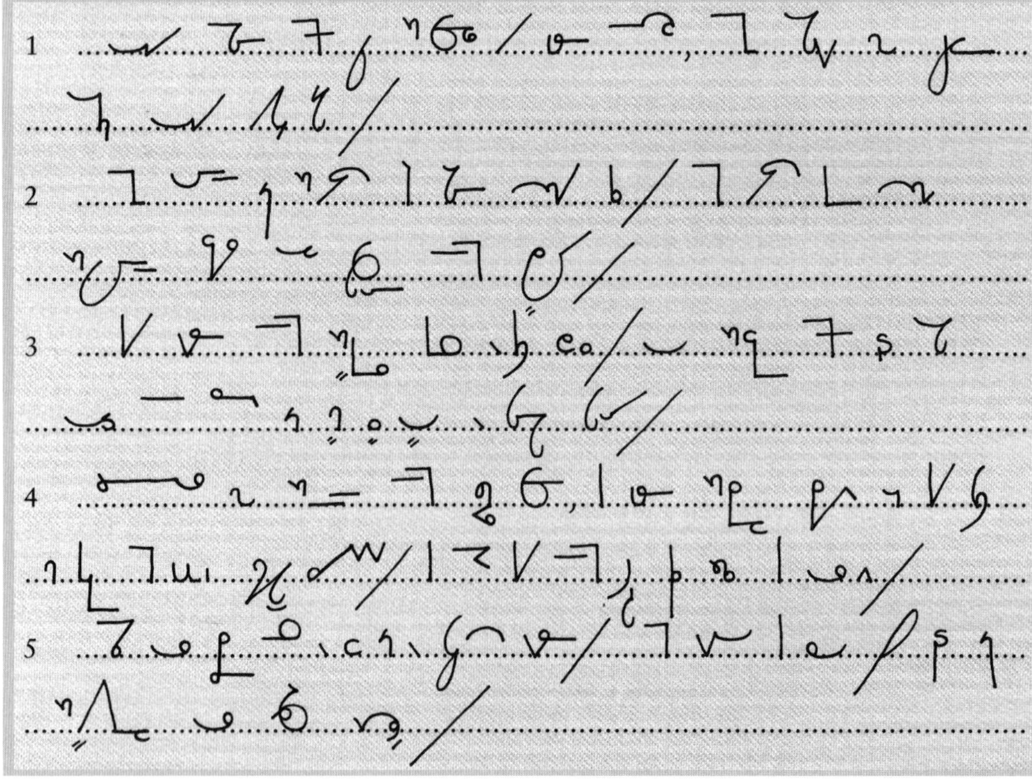

Special outlines – Unit 12

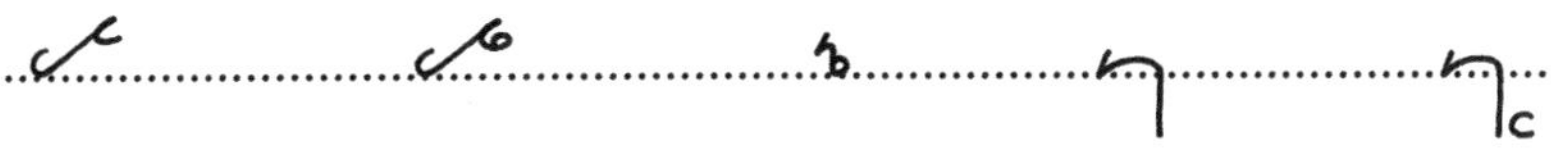

circumstance   circumstances   insurance   important   importance

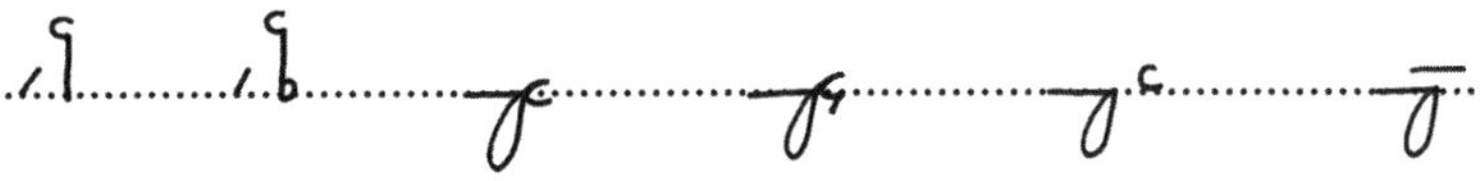

inch   inches   difficult   difficulty   difference   different

Word groupings

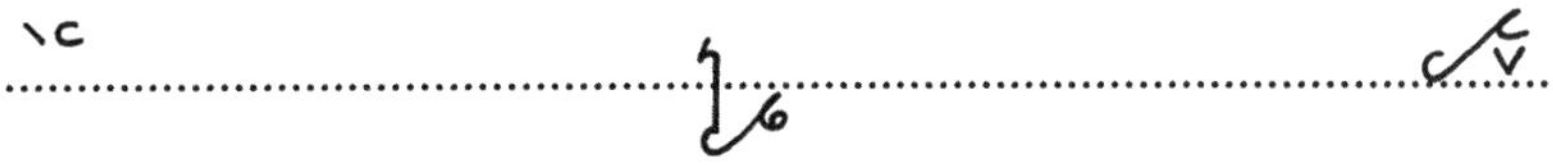

at once   in the circumstances   circumstantial evidence

it is important   most important   as much as   such as

Task 12.4

Read and write 'Kite-making takes off at museum'

MP3

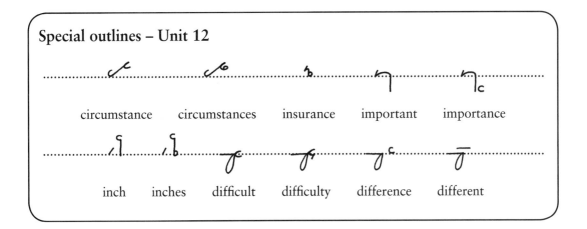

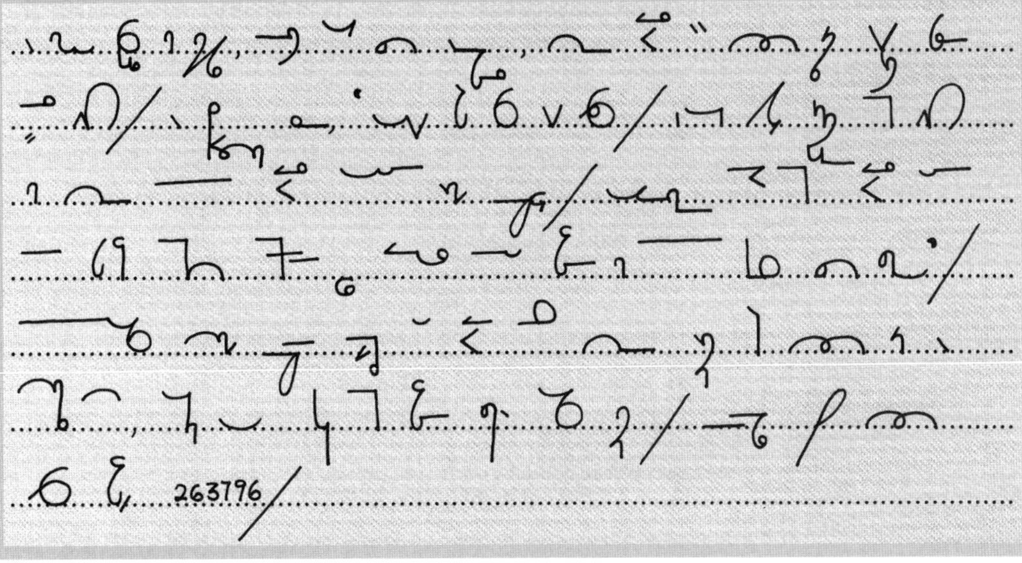

Task 12.5

Read and write '"Enough of this rubbish" say locals'

MP3

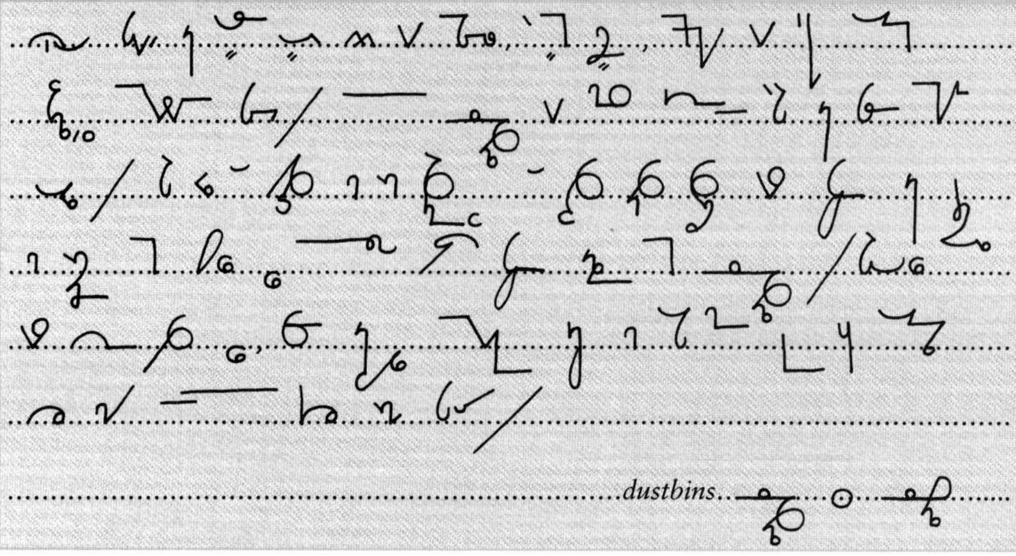

Letter L

L has three forms to make the joining of letters easier and clearer:

(1)  (2)  (3) 

(1) .... is most commonly used:

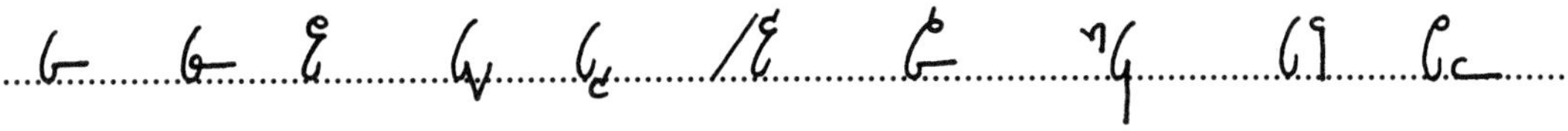

light last school live link wrinkle insulate antelope launch silenced

(2) .... do not write the curl at the end and it will be easier to join **L** to **C, G, M, N**:

lack leg lame land Teeline

(3) .... **never** used at the beginning of a word. Used for convenience, to make a clearer outline – if **L** follows a letter which has cut through the line, such as **G, P** or **J**, a downward **L** would interfere with the next line of Teeline, so upward **L** gives a neater note and takes the hand nearer to the writing line for the next outline:

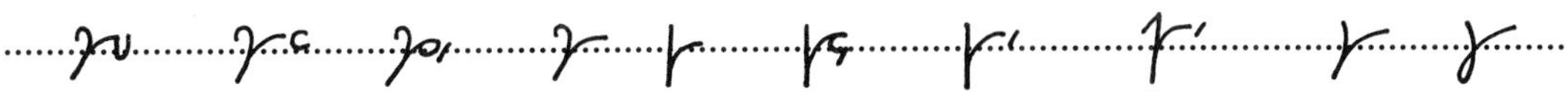

glue glance glazing goal pale policy pulling appalling jail jostle

Also use the upward **L** after **H, M** and **N**:

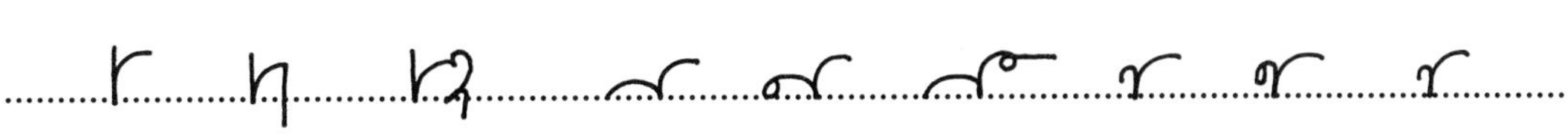

hill help hooligan male smell molest nail snail knoll

If indicator **I** follows upward **L**, the indicator is also written upwards:

hilly Molly smelly gully pulley jolly July

Task 13.1

Read and write the following sentences

MP3

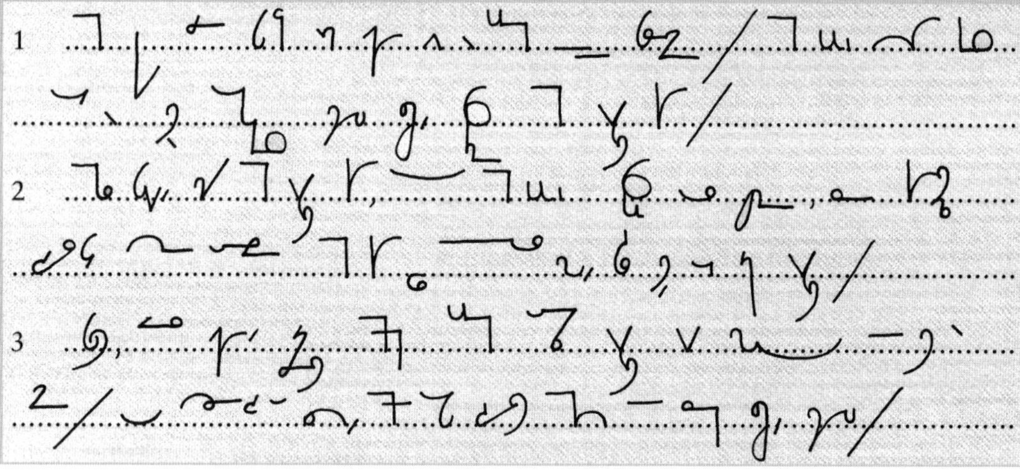

Words ending -ALITY, -ELITY, -ILITY, -OLITY, -ULITY

Revision:

words ending **-INGLE** are written by disjoining letter **L** and writing it downwards and close to the first part of the outline:

 **single**  **mingle** 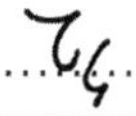 **willingly**

Write **upward L disjoined**, but **close** to the first part of the outline:

finality legality quality fidelity agility jollity utilities

The word **facility** when standing alone should be written  but in a word grouping, may safely be reduced to the word ending **-ILITY**:

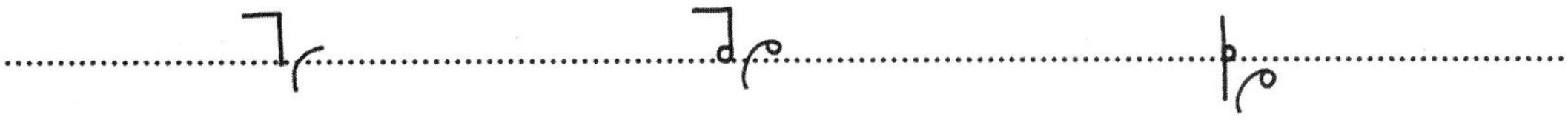

the facility | these facilities | hospital facilities

Task 13.2

Read and write the following sentences

MP3

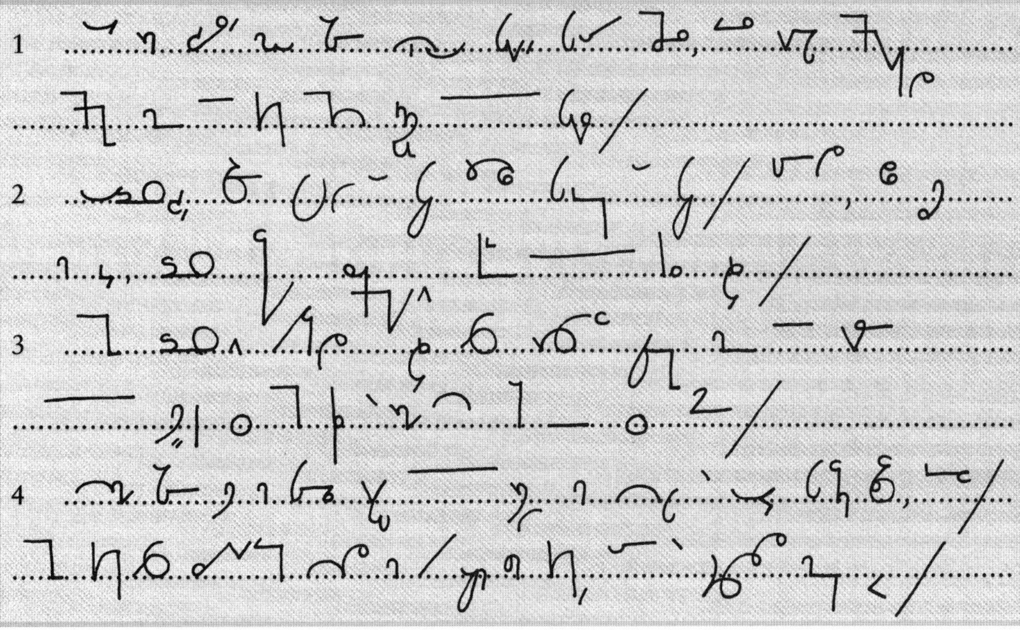

T and D after R and upward L

Always disjoin the letters T and D **after** an R or **upward** L:

route *but* road | court *but* cord | part *but* poured

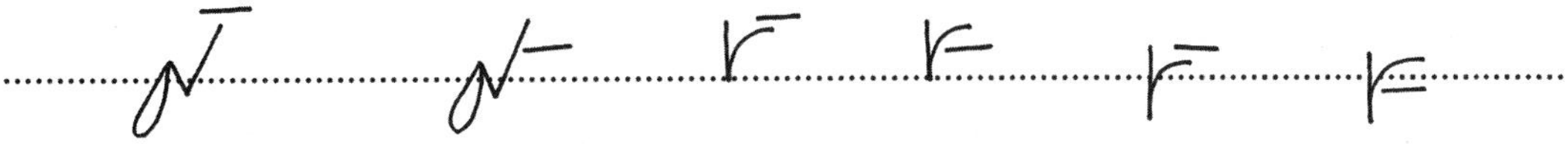

favourite *but* favoured | halt *but* held | pallet *but* pulled

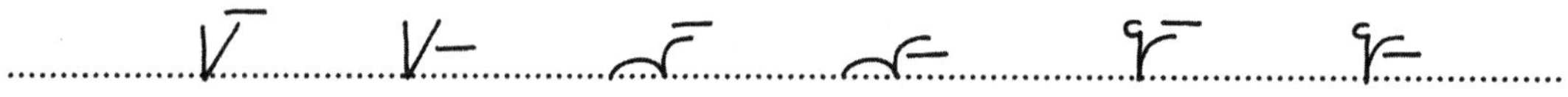

hurt *but* hard   moult *but* mailed   chalet *but* child

Task 13.3

Read and write the following sentences

MP3

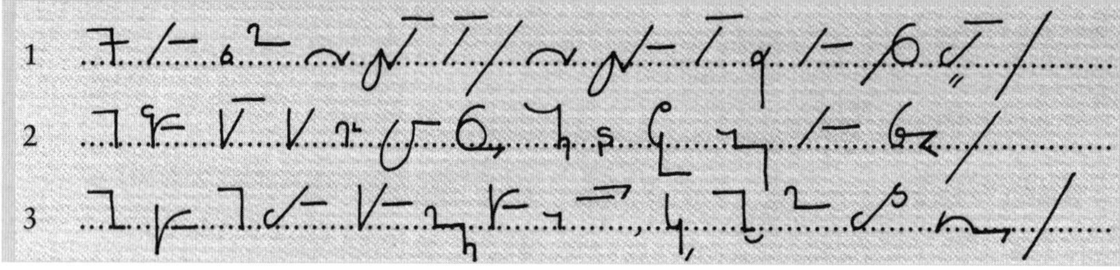

Words ending -ARITY, -ERITY, -ORITY, -URITY

Revision:

Letter **R** 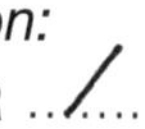 represents common words **are** and **auth<u>ority</u>**

Write R **disjoined** and upwards from the writing line. Do not cross through the line or you may think this is a full stop when transcribing:

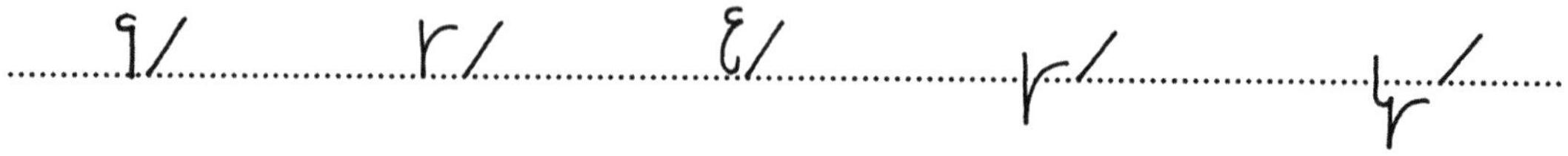

charity   hilarity   clarity   polarity   popul**arity**

sinc**erity**   tem**erity**   pri**orities**   min**ority**   seni**ority**   sec**urity**

Task 13.4

Read and write the following sentences

MP3

1 2 3

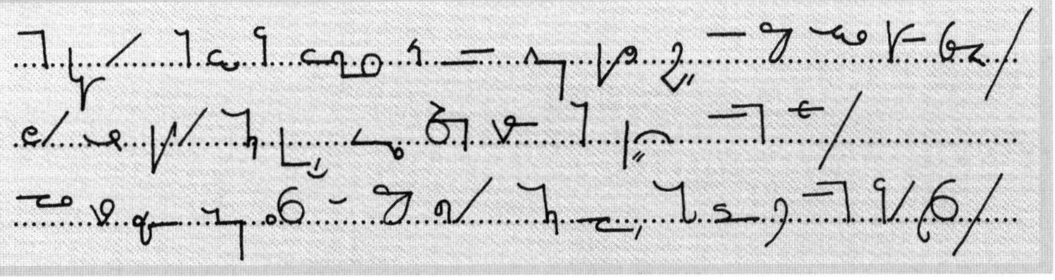

> **Special outlines – Unit 13**
>
> 
>
> resident establish satisfactory satisfied regularly
>
> 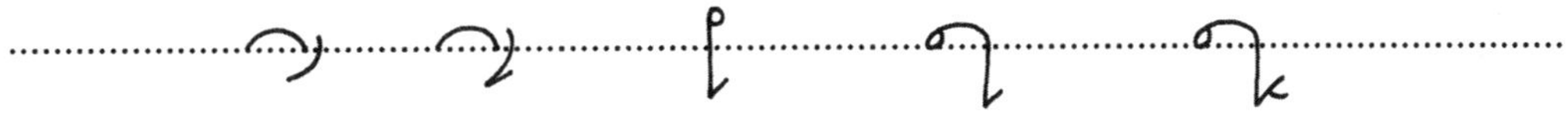
>
> major majority separately sympathy sympathetic

Word groupings

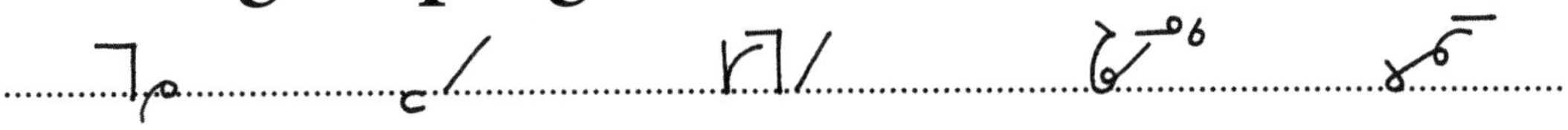

the facilities local authority health authority all sorts of things as a result

Task 13.5

Read and write 'M.P. supports local swimming pool'

MP3

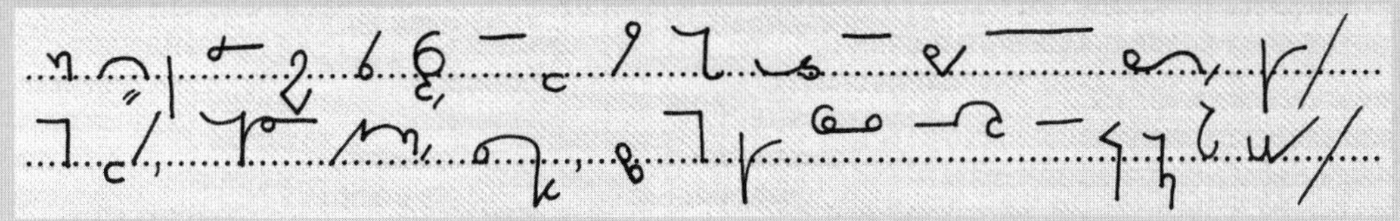

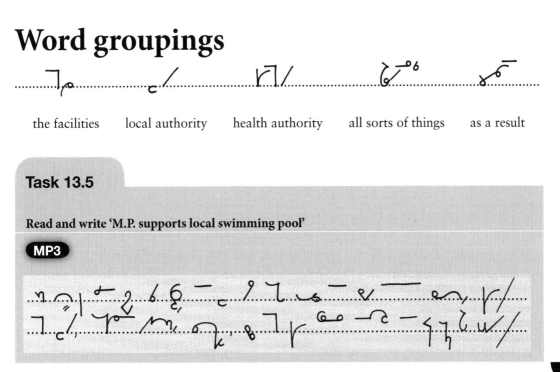

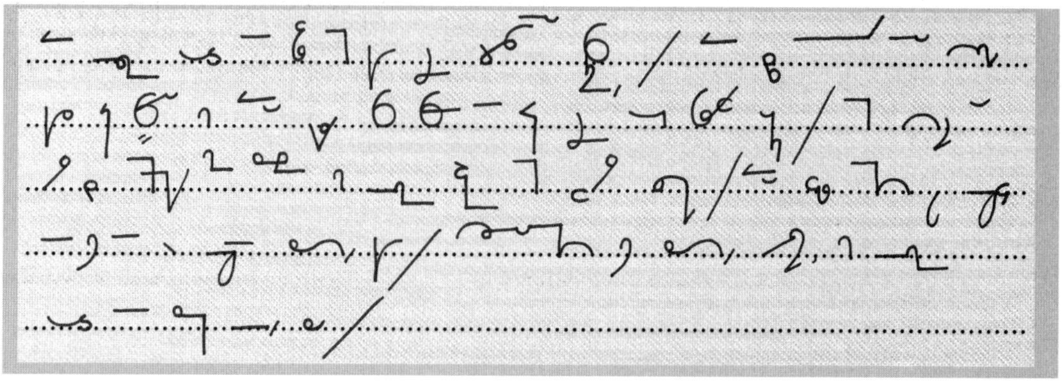

Task 13.6

Read and write 'Ideas needed for Charity Ball'

MP3

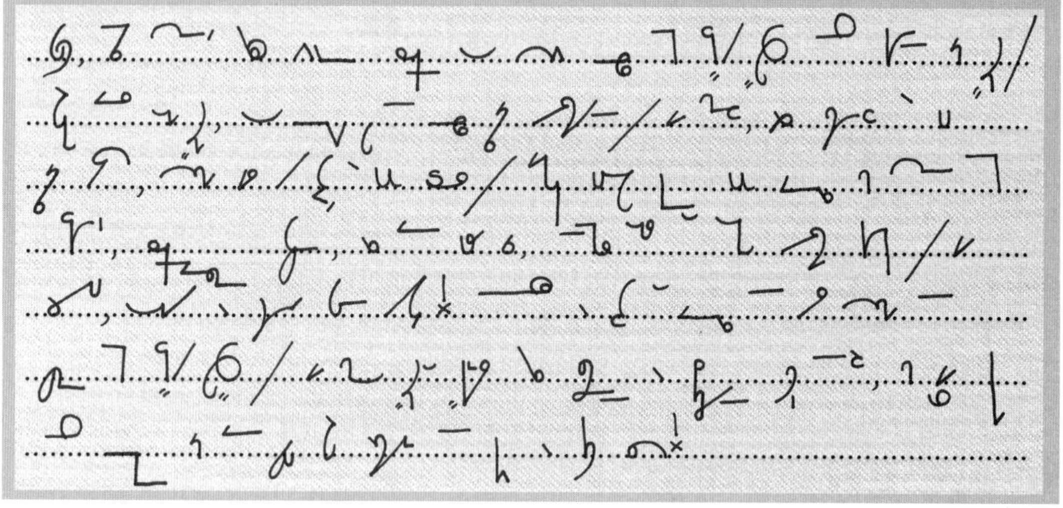

Letter F

Revision:

Letter **F** ..... written upwards represents common word **from**

F has two forms to make the joining of letters easier and clearer.

F can be written upwards .... or downwards ....

F is better written **downwards** before N, C, V and K:

fine face five fake

F is also written **downwards** before T, so that T can take its usual position – Top:

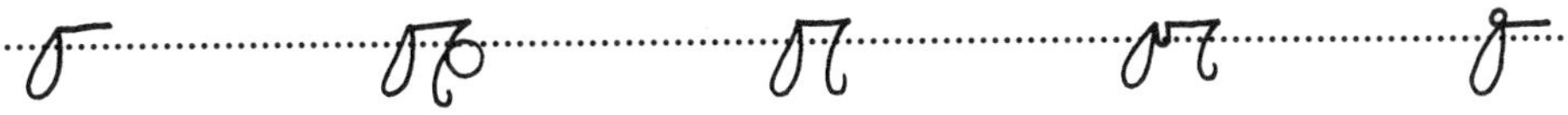

foot football fatal futile fist

F is written **upwards** before D, so that D can take its usual position – Down:

food fiddle fuddy-duddy

When T and D precede F, keep T and D in their usual position:

tough toffee tuft deaf defective defence defy

Task 14.1

Read and write the following sentences

MP3

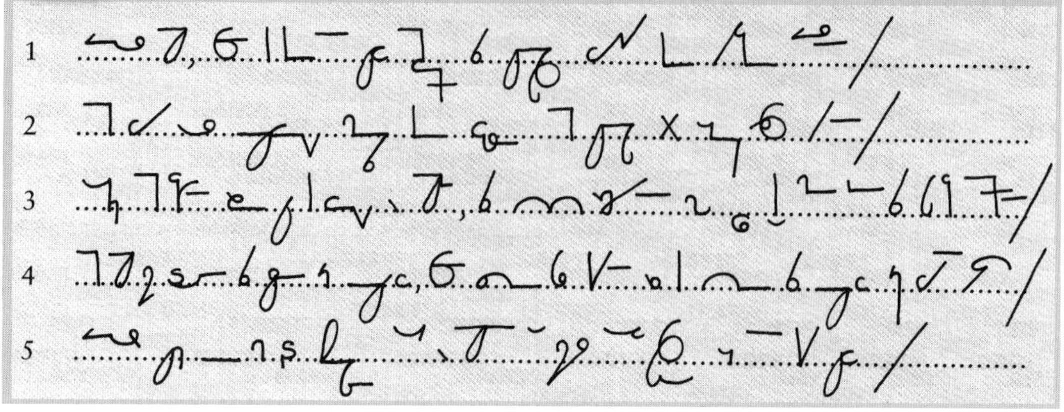

F blends

Blending Teeline letters saves writing time. Letter **F** blends well with other letters and there may or may not be a vowel between the blended letters.

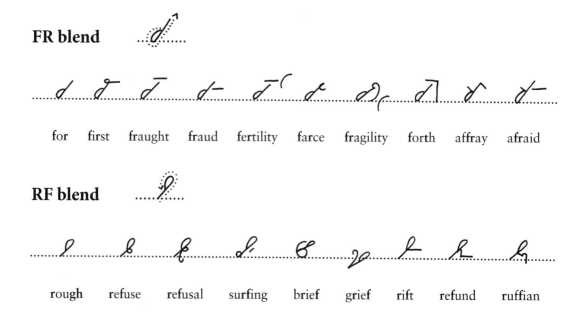

FR blend 

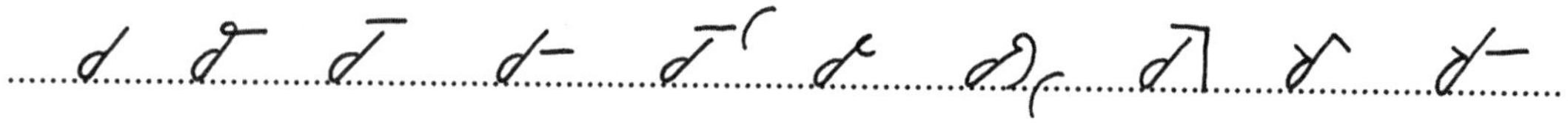

for first fraught fraud fertility farce fragility forth affray afraid

RF blend 

rough refuse refusal surfing brief grief rift refund ruffian

Words with RFR

When **R** is followed by **F** then **R** again, do not use the **RF** blend, but drop the **F**:

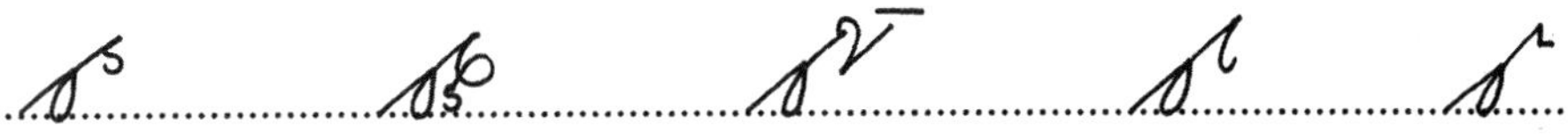

refresh refurbish refrigerate referral referee

FL blend 

flying flap flounce flinch follow faulty affluence afflicted baffle offal

rifle roughly reflected

The **FL** blend is useful for words ending -**FUL** and may be written using upward or downward **L**:

care**ful** use**ful** hope**ful** resent**ful** fear**ful** peace**ful** youth**ful** resource**ful** **ful**fil

cheer**fully** thank**fully** hate**fully** use**fully**

Task 14.2

Read and write the following sentences

MP3

1 

2 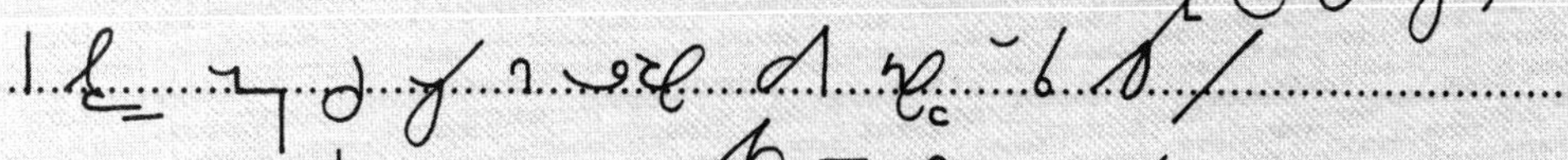

3 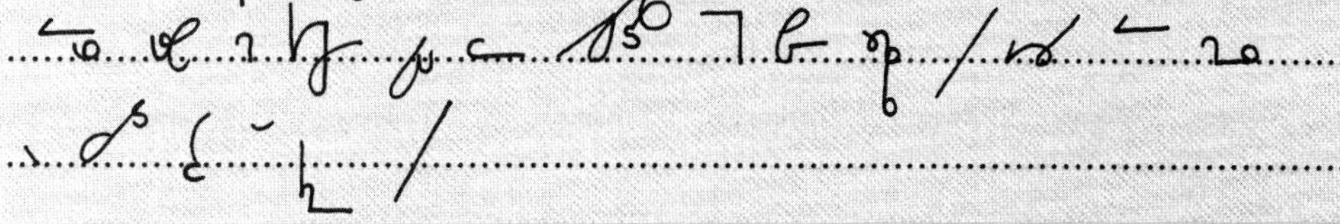

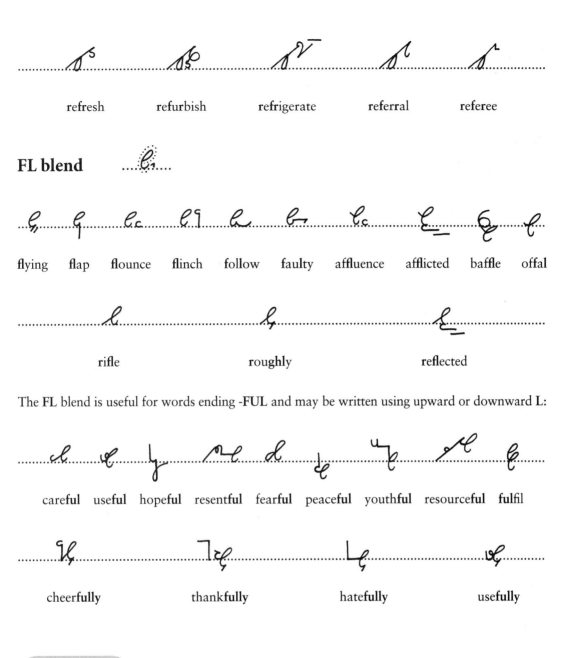

Words ending -FULNESS, -LESSNESS, -LOUSNESS

When -**FULNESS** ends a word, it is reduced to **FLS**, **disjoined**, and written **close** to the first part of the outline:

use**fulness**	forget**fulness**	hope**fulness**	joy**fulness**	thank**fulness**	cheer**fulness**

When -**LESSNESS** and -**LOUSNESS** end words, they are reduced to **LS**, **disjoined**, and written **close** to the first part of the outline:

use**lessness**	hope**lessness**	help**lessness**	fear**lessness**	thought**lessness**	rest**lessness**

cal**lousness**

Other letters that blend well with F

Take care when writing the **FM** blend; the **F** may look like **S** when written at speed!

fame	famous	family	fumble	feminine

fabric	fabulous	feeble	**half**	**chief**	**hefty**

Words with **FW/WF** may be blended, but it is not essential:

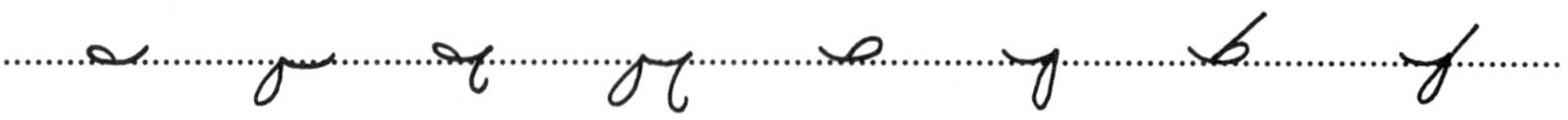

few *or* few fowl *or* fowl wife *or* wife wafer *or* wafer

When **N** is followed by **F,** a clearer outline is achieved by dropping **F** below the line:

enough	knife	infancy	infected	infested

Words which have **LF** do not blend: life .... bluff .... lift .... laughing ....

(the exception is special outline: .... **telephone**)

Words beginning or ending with self

Self when standing alone would be written .... although this is rarely needed.

Reduce **SELF** to **SL** when it is part of a word. It may be written either upwards or downwards:

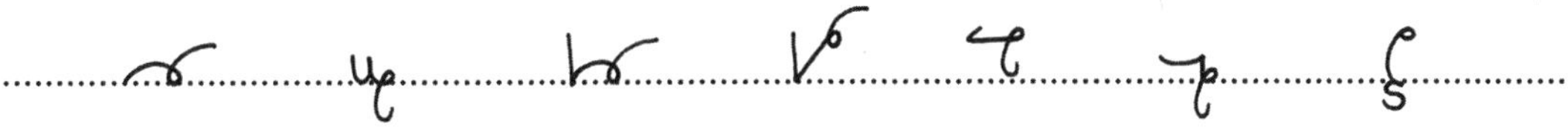

my**self**	your**self**	him**self**	her**self**	it**self**	one**self**	**self**ish

self-defence	**self**less	**self**-satisfied	**self**-supporting	**self**-esteem	**self**-taught

Add **S** to change the word ending to **-SELVES**:

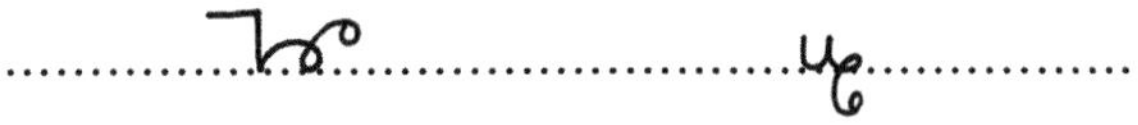

themselves	yourselves

Task 14.3

Read and write the following sentences

MP3

1 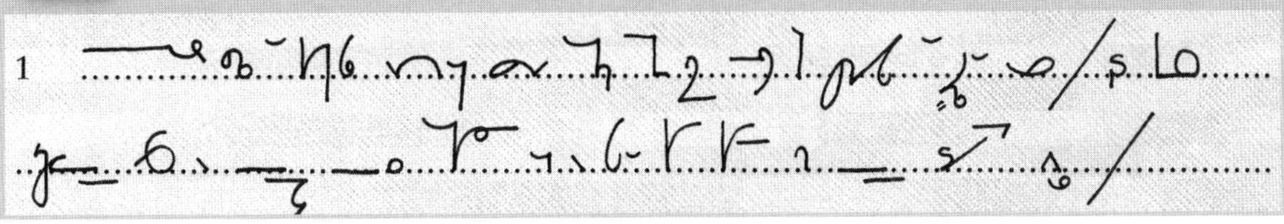

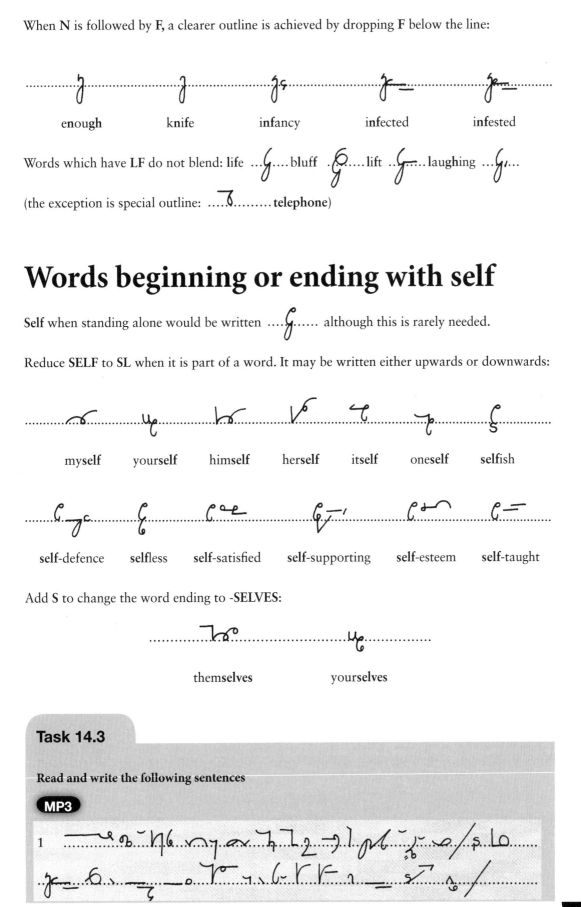

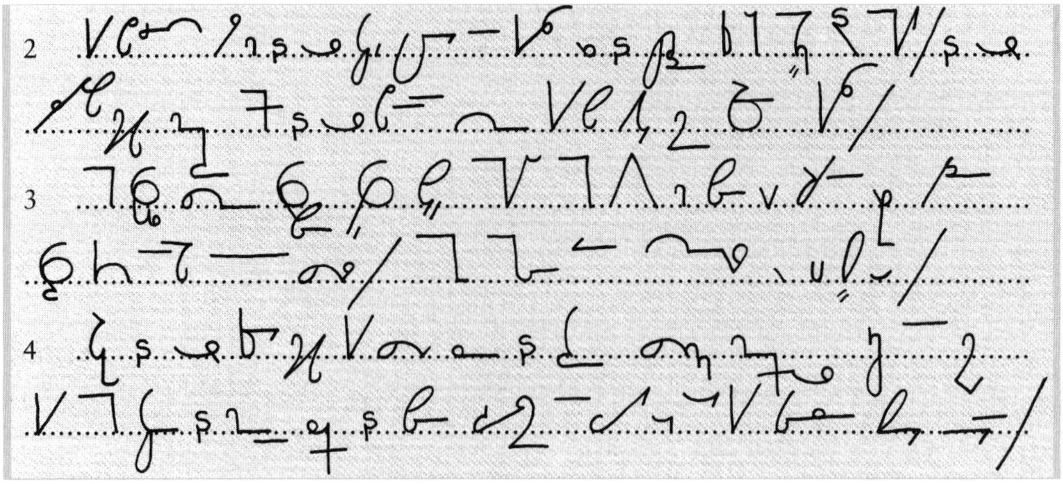

Special outlines – Unit 14

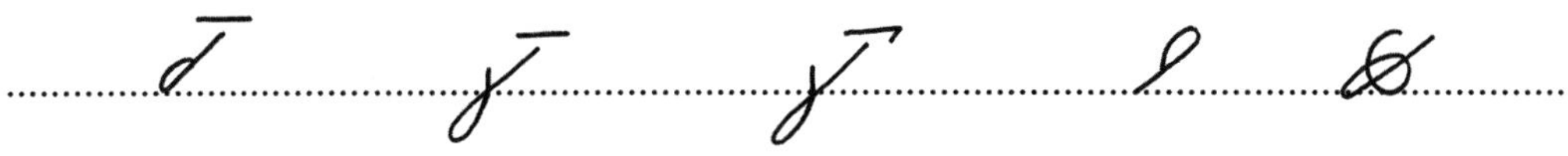

fortunate unfortunate unfortunately reference before

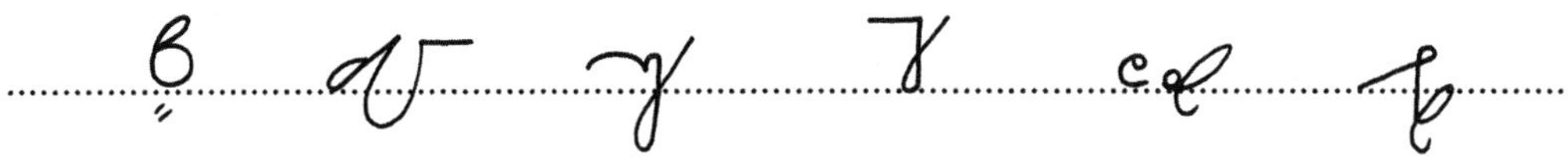

February frequent manufacture therefore successful respectful

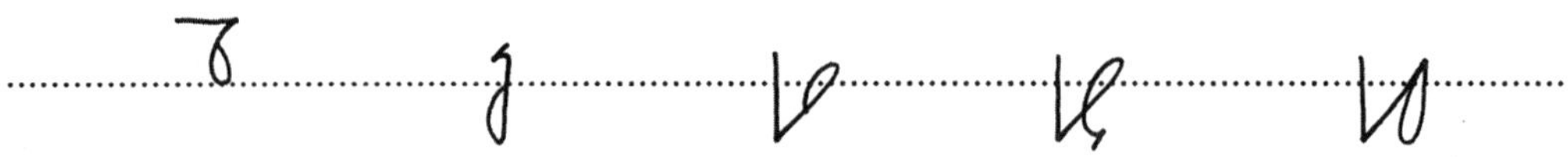

telephone inform perfect perfectly prefer

Word groupings

for the far from first of all for ever and ever as far as so far as

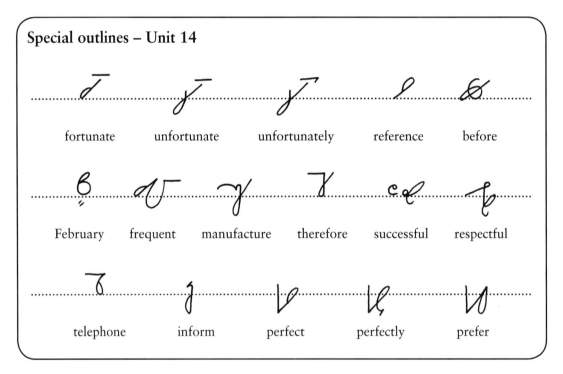

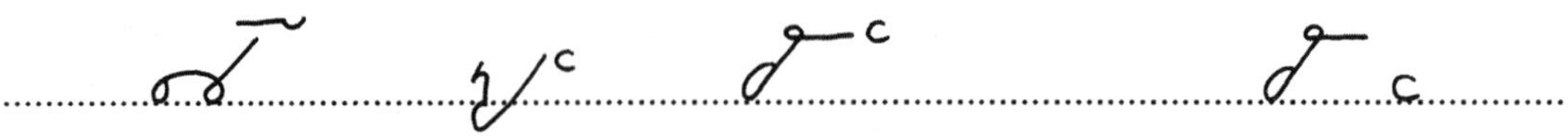

some sort of in accordance for instance (*do not confuse with* **first offence**)

Distinguishing Outlines

firm form farm

Task 14.4

Read and write 'New library books'

MP3

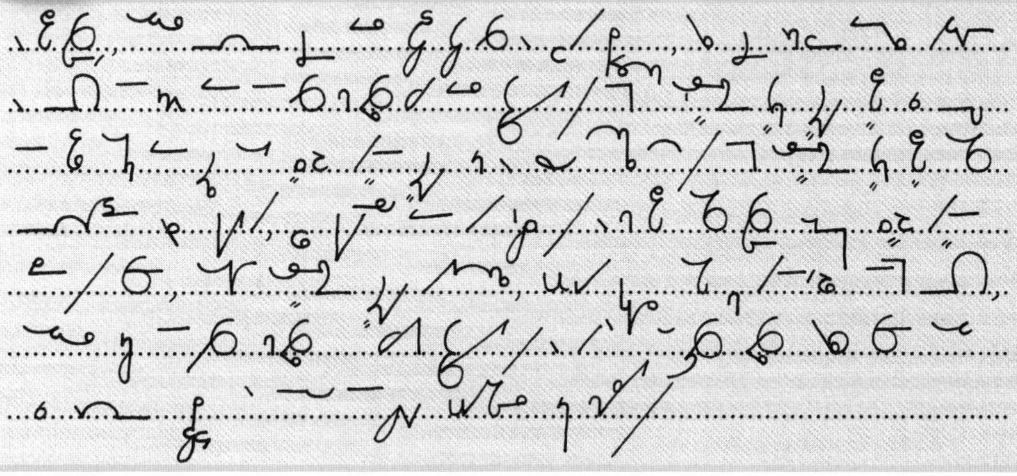

Task 14.5

Read and write 'Accident in the Alps'

MP3

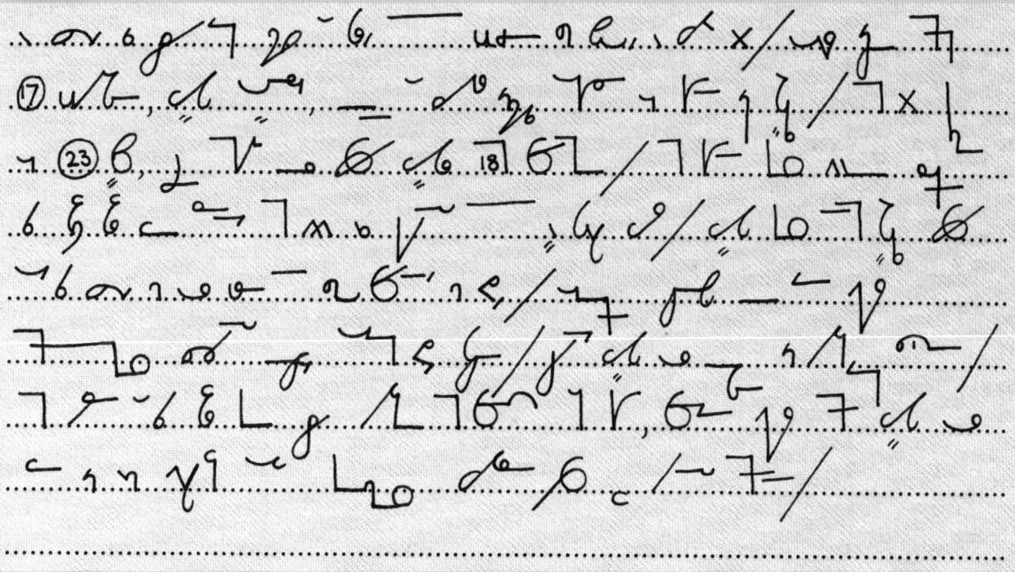

Unit 15
Words ending -MENT, -AVITY, -EVITY and -TIVITY

Revision:

Letter **M** represents common word **me** .... **time** .... **million** ....

Write the following words:

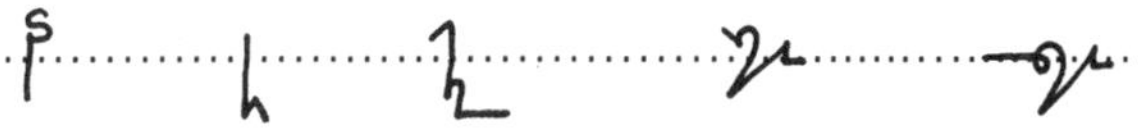

ship **pay** **appoint** **agree** **disagree**

Words ending -MENT

When standing alone write the word **meant** 

When used as a word ending, write a **smaller than normal sized** letter **M** in the **T** position, **disjoined** and **close** to the first part of the outline:

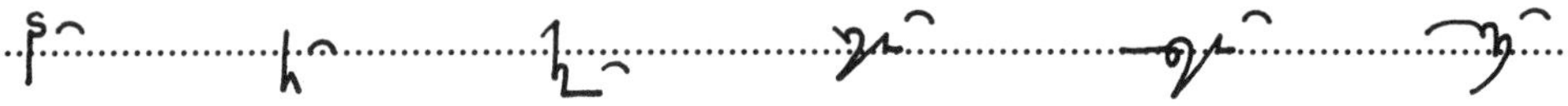

ship**ment** pay**ment** appoint**ment** agree**ment** disagree**ment** manage**ment**

Word ending -**MENT** can be extended by adding other letters:

-MENTAL

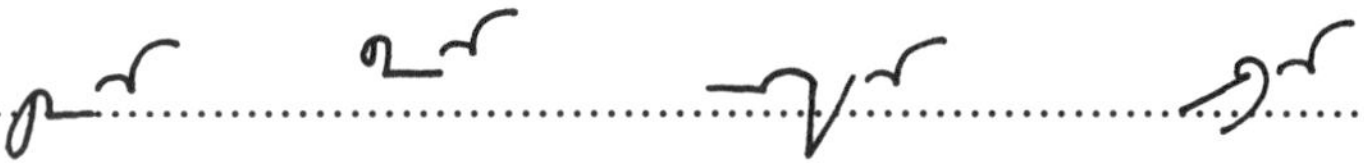

funda**mental** senti**mental** tempera**mental** regi**mental**

-MENTALLY

funda**mentally** senti**mentally** tempera**mentally** monu**mentally**

-MENTARY

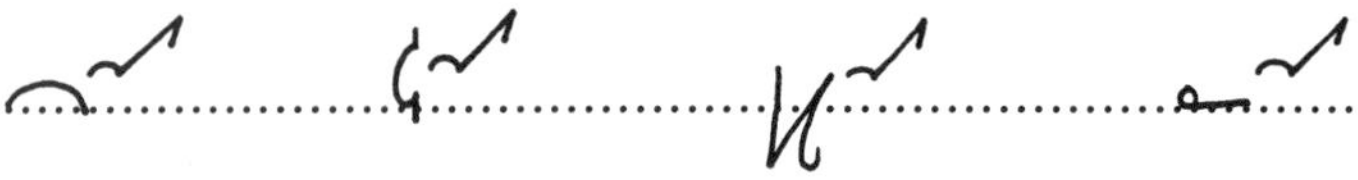

mo**mentary** ele**mentary** parlia**mentary** sedi**mentary**

-MENTALS

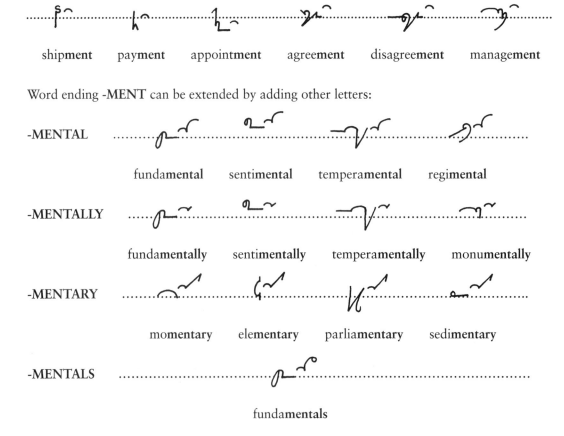

funda**mentals**

Task 15.1

Read and write the following sentences

MP3

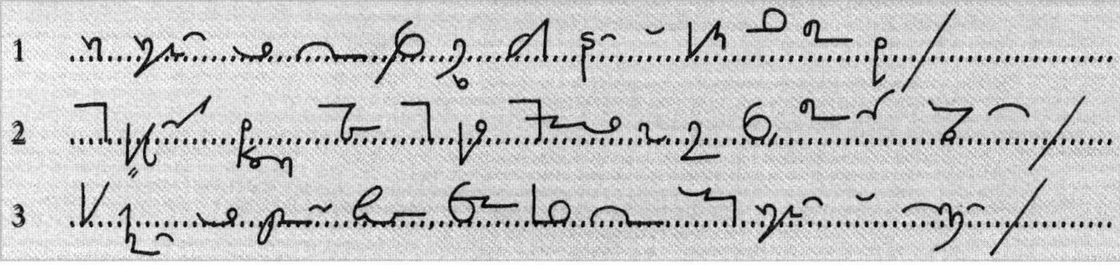

Revision:

Write the following words:

cave **grave** **deprave** **long**

Words ending -AVITY, -EVITY

Write letter V, **disjoined**, in the T position, **close** to the first part of the outline:

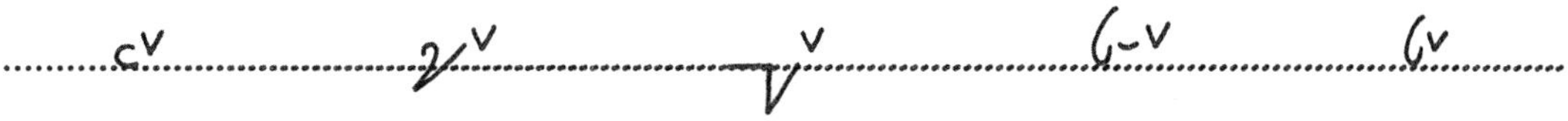

cavity gravity depravity longevity levity

Task 15.2

Read and write the following sentences

MP3

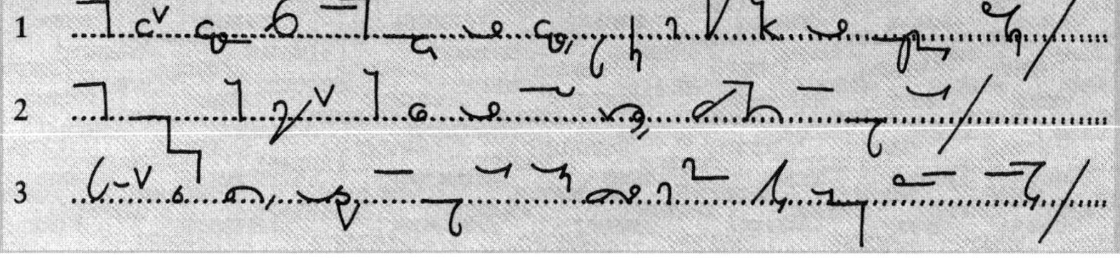

Revision:

Write the following words: 

active **relative** **sensitive** **native** **festive**

Words ending -TIVITY

Write TV, **disjoined** and in the T position, **close** to the first part of the outline:

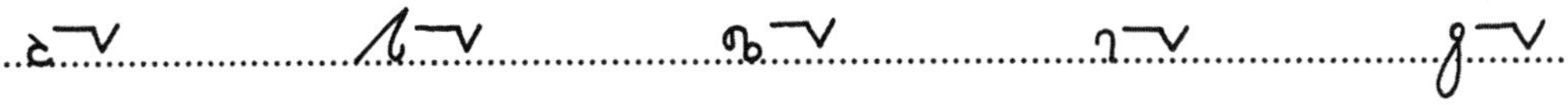

activity relativity sensitivity nativity festivity

Task 15.3

Read and write the following sentences

MP3

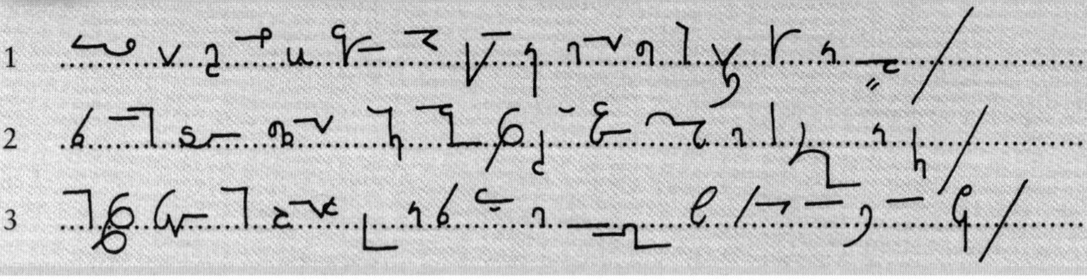

'REQUIRE' in word groupings

When standing alone **require** should be written in full 

However, in word groupings write **R through** the previous word to represent the word **require,** adding the appropriate word ending:

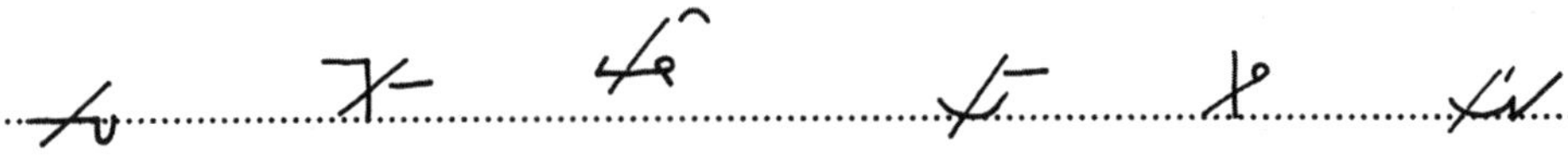

do you **require** the **required** it is a **requirement** we **required** he **requires** we are **requiring**

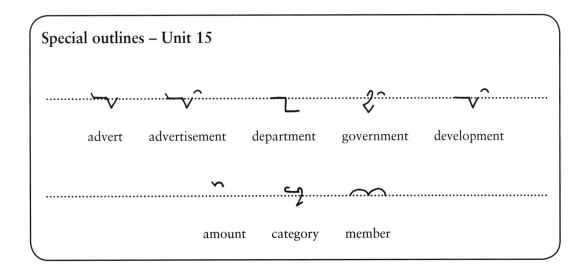

Special outlines – Unit 15

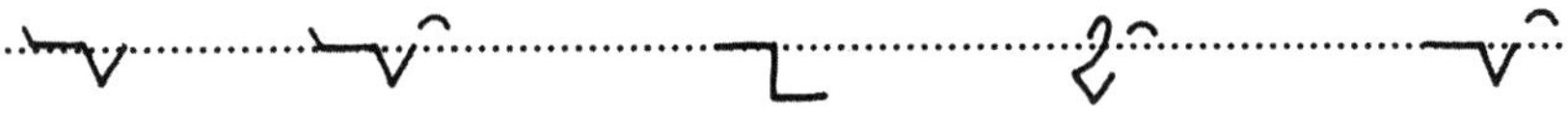

advert advertisement department government development

amount category member

Word groupings

not guilty in favour last minute

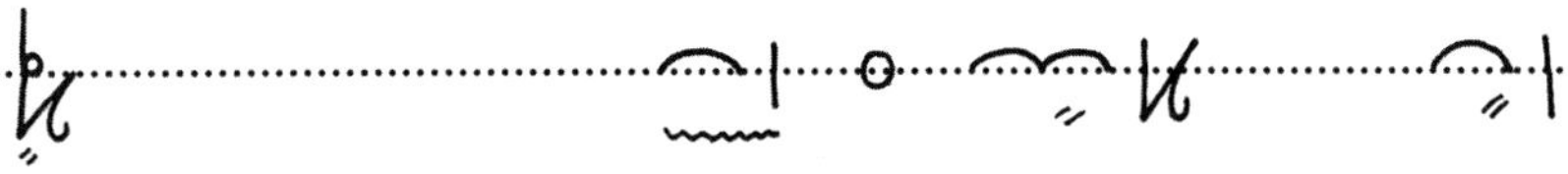

Houses of Parliament Member of Parliament M.P.

Task 15.4

Read and write 'Youths speak out at forum'

MP3

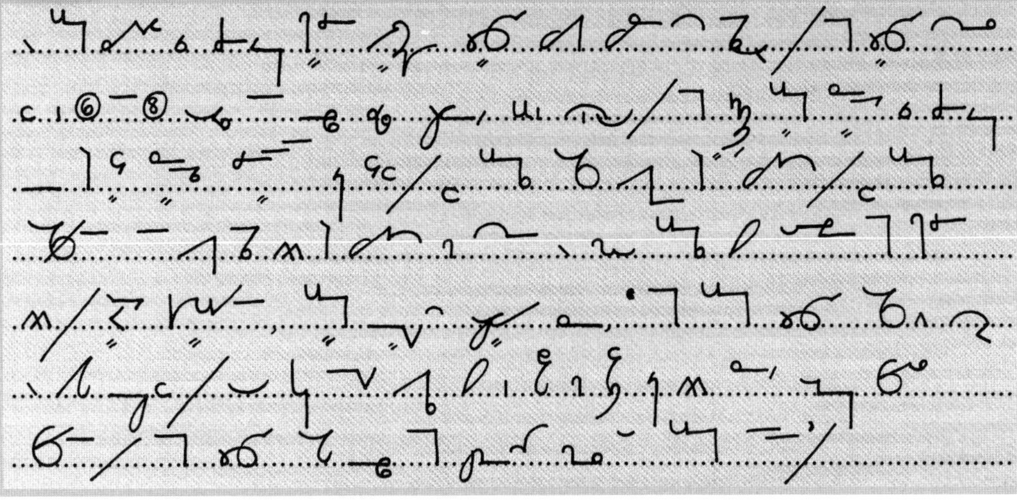

Task 15.5

Read and write 'Educating families about healthy eating'

MP3

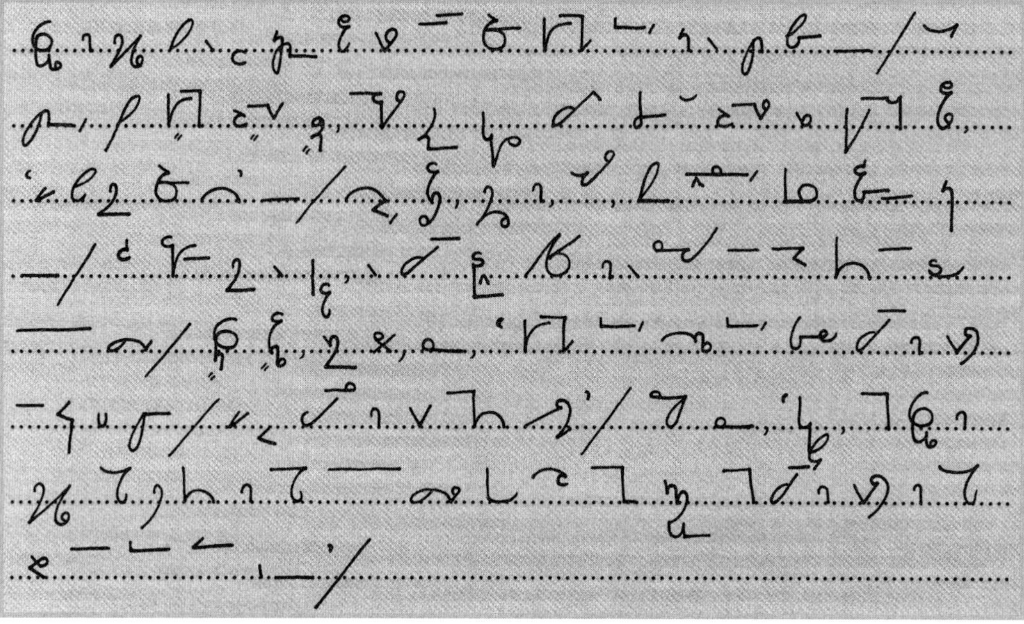

Unit 16
Words ending-SHUN, -SHL, -SHIP and -SHUS and words beginning SUPER-

Revision:

Letter **N** represents common words **and** .... **new** .... **knew** ....

and when hanging from the line **begin** .... **began** .... **begun** ....

Words ending -SHUN

Letter N written in the T position, **disjoined** and **close** to the first part of the outline represents words ending in the sound of **-SHUN**, however it is spelt:

mention occasion fashion ocean musician election passion

Other letters may be added to -SHUN:

occasions motions suggestions emotional sensational educational

efficient patience impatience deficiency sufficiency efficiency

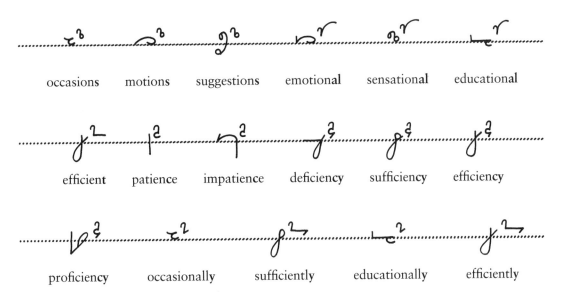

proficiency occasionally sufficiently educationally efficiently

When T or D are followed by -SHUN it is quicker to join -SHUN:

reputation | hesitation | addition | situation | additional

Similarly, after word ending **-MENT** join **-SHUN** for words ending **-MENTATION**:

documentation | regimentation | sedimentation

Although very rarely necessary, vowels may be added to make transcription easier:

possession | position | solution | diminution

Task 16.1

Read and write the following sentences

MP3

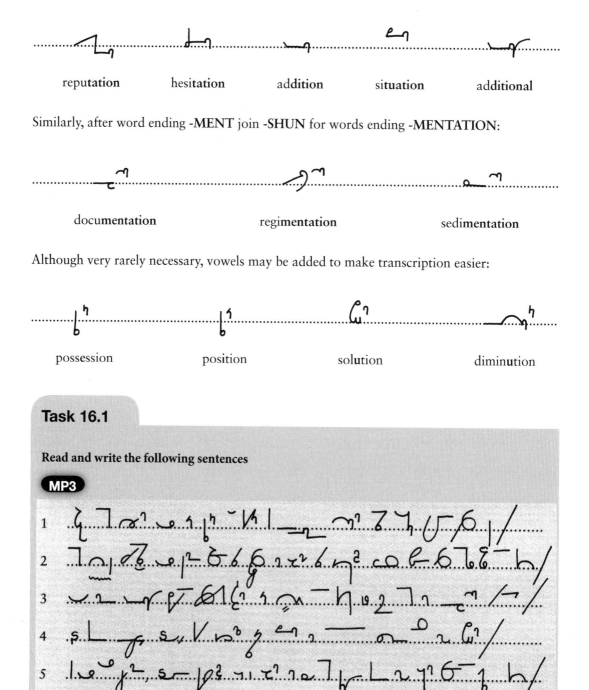

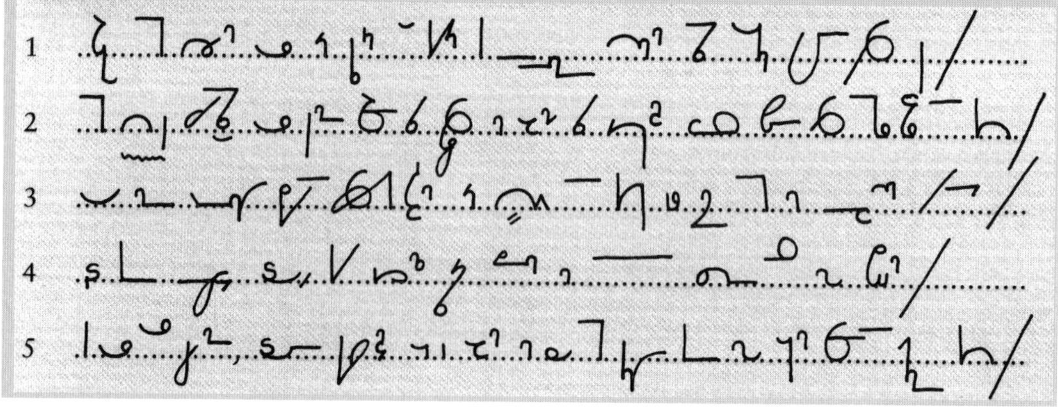

Revision:

SH represents special outline **shall** ...S.....

Words ending -SHL

SH is written **disjoined** and **close** to where the first part of the outline ends. This represents words ending in the sound of **-SHL,** however they are spelt.

*It might help you to remember to disjoin -SHL by thinking '**shells float**'*

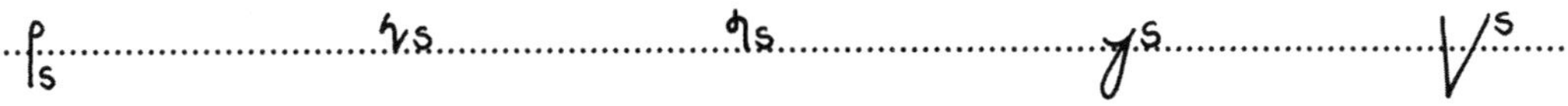

spe**cial** | ini**tial** | essen**tial** | offi**cial** | par**tial**

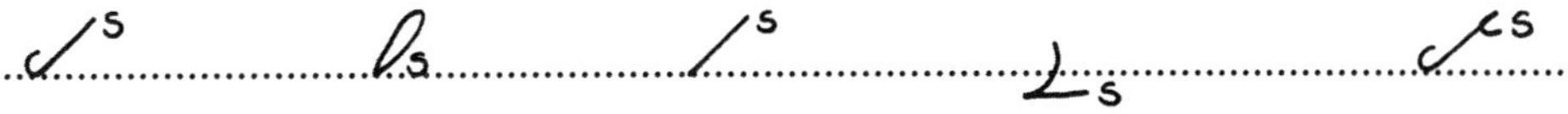

cru**cial** | fa**cial** | ra**cial** | judi**cial** | circumstan**tial**

High speed outline: **social**  and **social services** 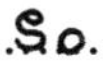

Other letters may be added to -SHL:

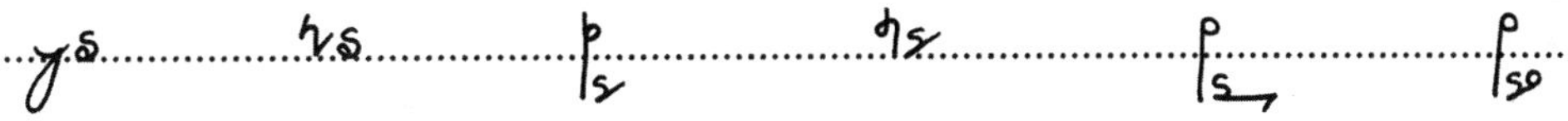

official**s** | initial**s** | especial**ly** | essential**ly** | special**ity** | special**ise**

official**dom** | social**ism** | social**istic**

Task 16.2

Read and write the following sentences

MP3

1
2
3

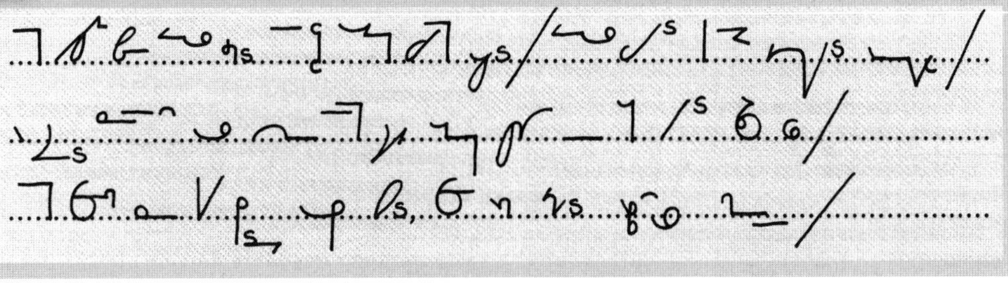

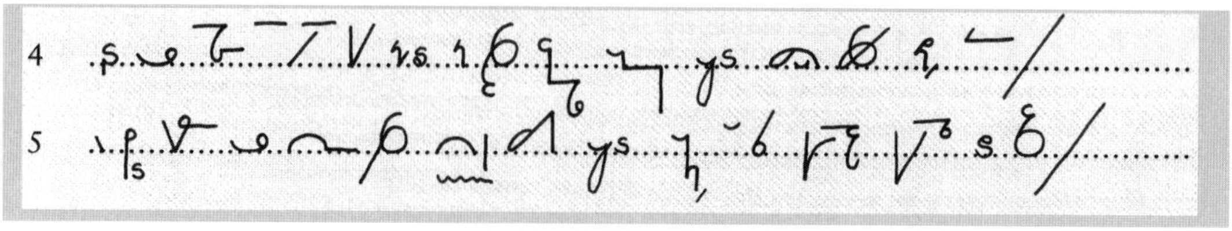

Words ending -SHIP

SH is **joined** to the outline for words ending in **-SHIP.**

It might help you to remember to join -SHIP by thinking ***'ships are docked'***

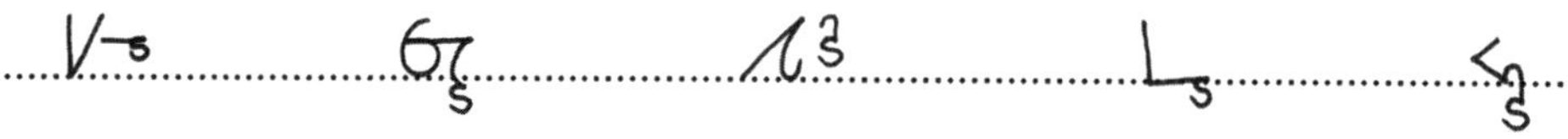

hard**ship** battle**ship** relation**ship** head**ship** kin**ship**

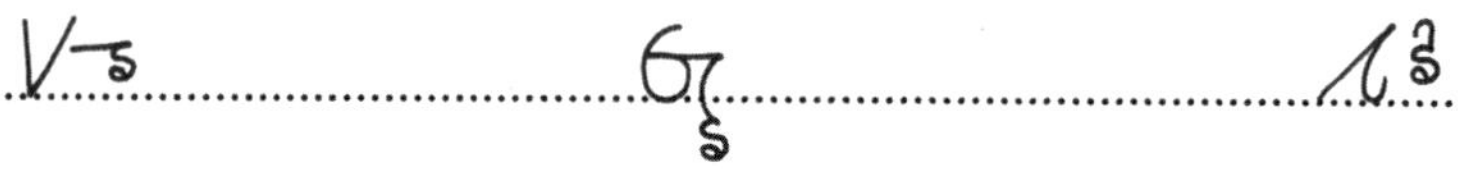

hard**ships** battle**ships** relation**ships**

Task 16.3

Read and write the following sentences

MP3

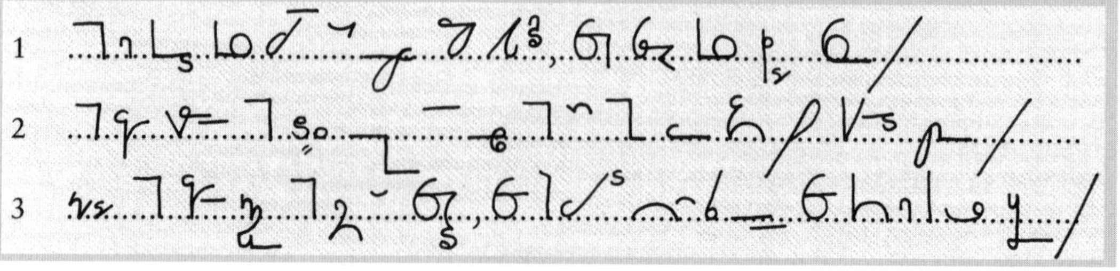

Words beginning SUPER-

Letter S **with U indicator** is **disjoined** and written **above** the rest of the outline:

superfine **super**stition **super**fluous **super**ficial **super**sede **super**annuation

supervision supervisor supersonic superhuman superior superiority

Task 16.4

Read and write the following sentences

MP3

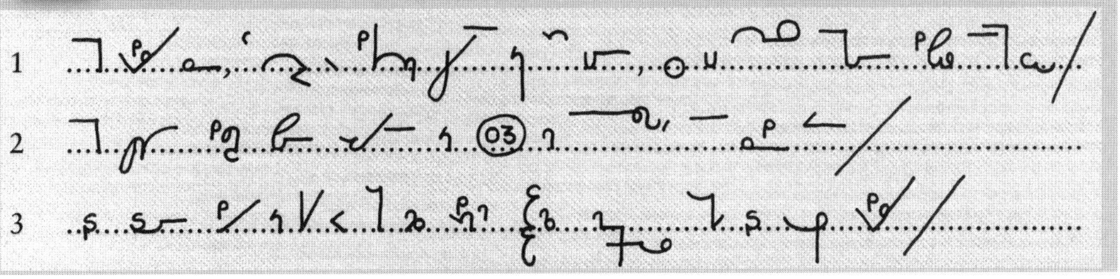

Words ending -SHUS

When words end in the sound of **-SHUS**, however it is spelt, outlines are easier to write if you **join SHS** to the first part of the outline:

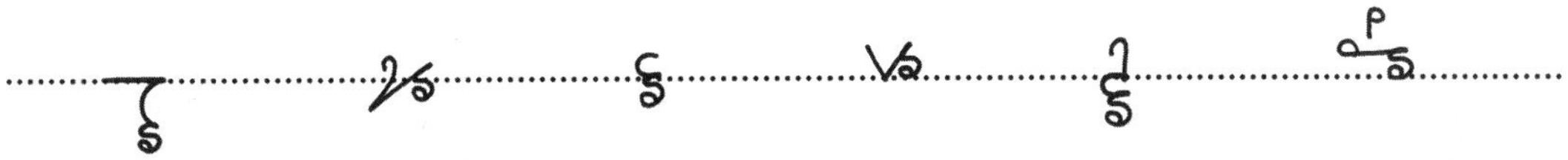

delicious gracious cautious vicious noxious superstitious

Task 16.5

Read and write the following sentences

MP3

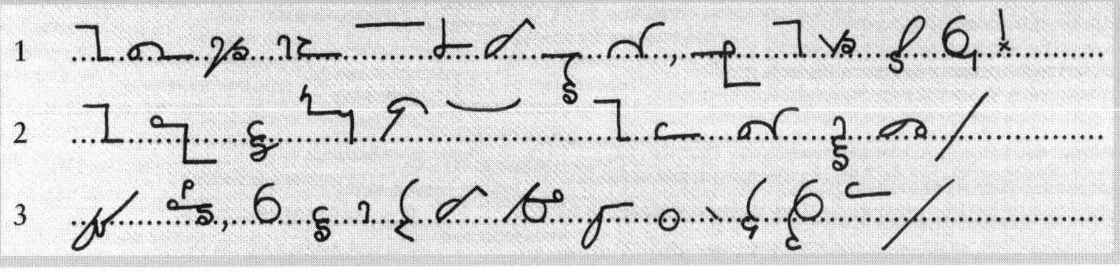

Special outlines – Unit 16

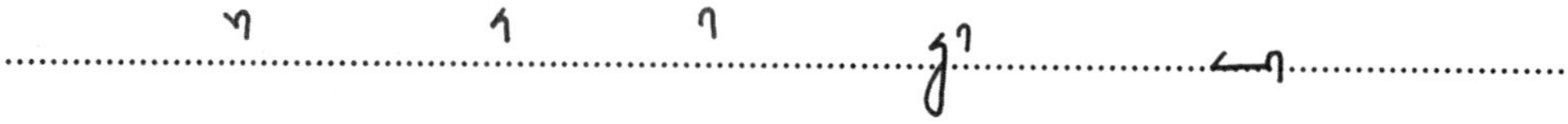

attention intention station information identification

application electrician qualification financial substantial

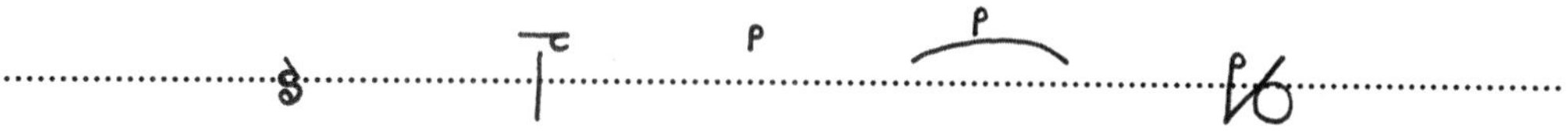

anxious particular super supermarket superb

Distinguishing outlines

specialist specialised

Task 16.6

Read and write 'Police station to open longer hours'

MP3

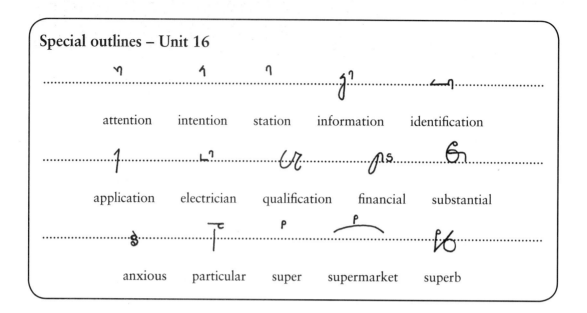

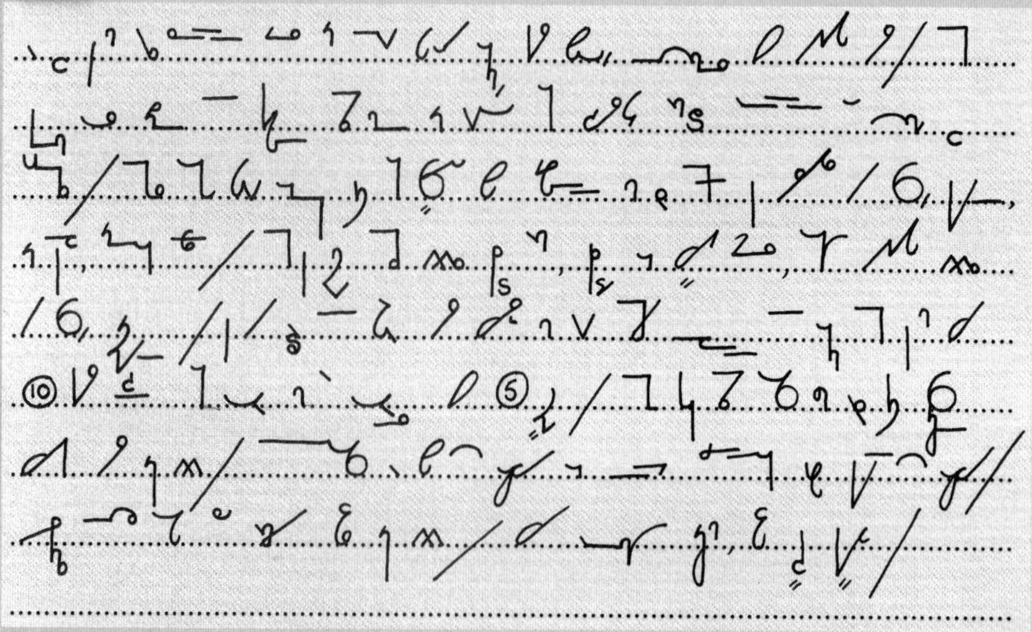

Revision:

Letter **T** represents common word **to** ....

A double length letter **T** represents common words **their** or **there** ....

Letter **D** represents common words **do** or **day** ....

TR blend

When T and R occur **next to each other, or if there is a vowel between** the T and R, the letters are blended and written as a slightly more than double length T. The blend may be used anywhere in an outline but, as usual, if the word begins with T, a vowel, or an S, start the outline in the T position:

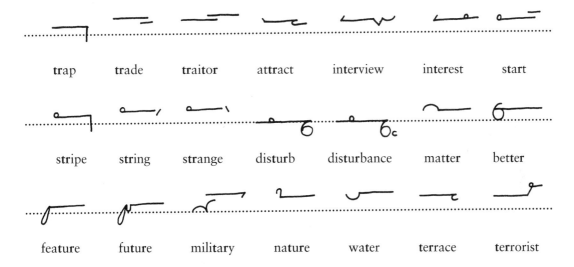

trap trade traitor attract interview interest start

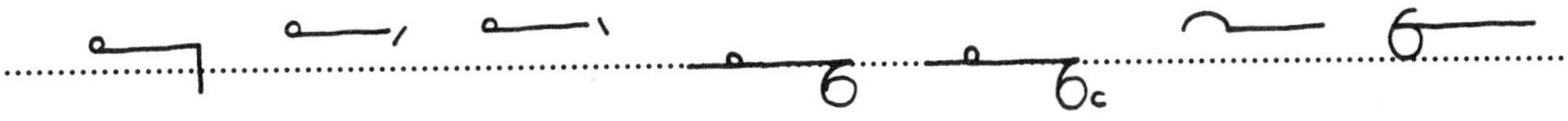

stripe string strange disturb disturbance matter better

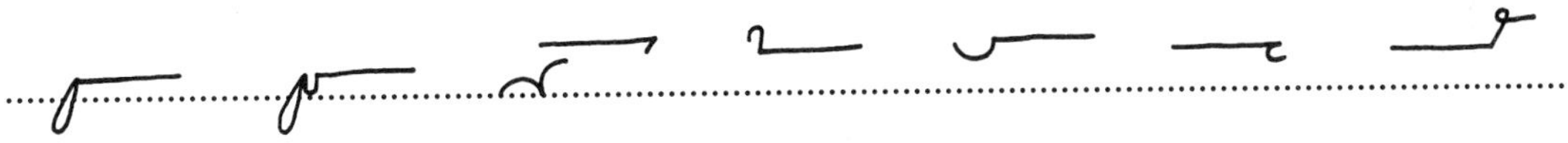

feature future military nature water terrace terrorist

DR blend

Similarly, when D and R occur **next to each other, or if there is a vowel between** the D and R, the letters are blended and written as a slightly more than double length D. The blend may be used anywhere in an outline but, as usual, if the word begins with D, a vowel, or an S, start the outline in the D position:

drive drink drugs address during dirty dark sadder

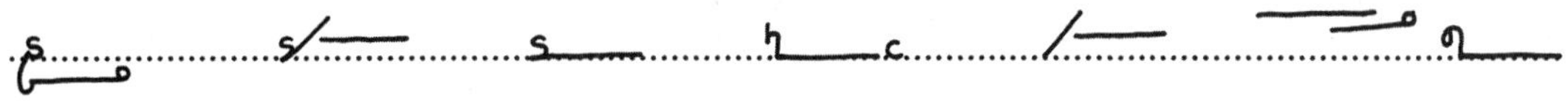

shoulders shredder shudder endurance reader traders sender

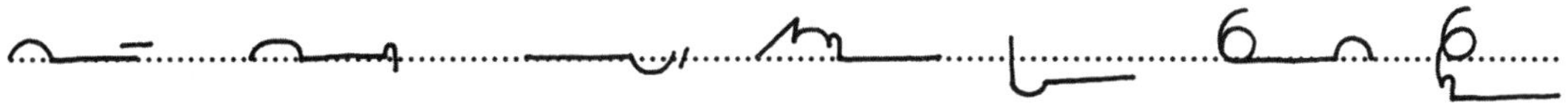

moderate moderation drawing remainder powder bedroom blunder

Task 17.1

Write the following words in Teeline

MP3

travel .... terminal .... history .... later .... enter ....

Madrid .... drooping .... withdraw .... slander .... corridor ....

Task 17.2

Read and write the following sentences

MP3

1 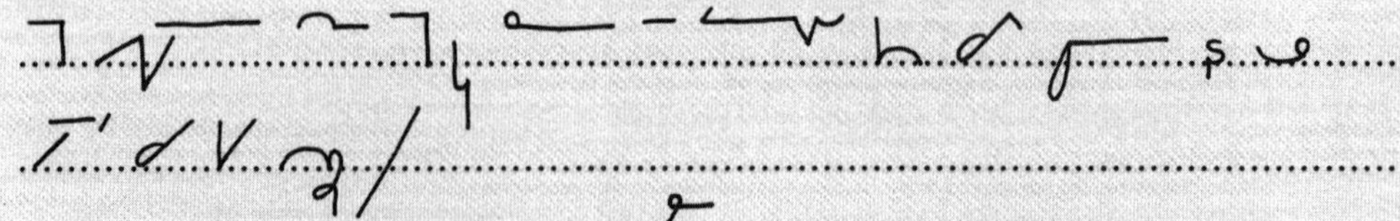

2 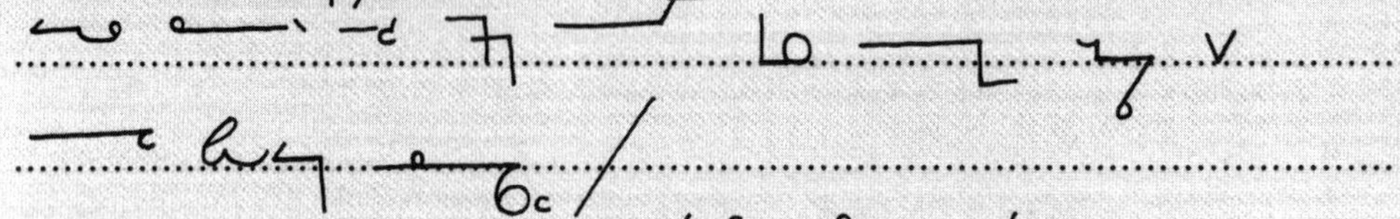

3 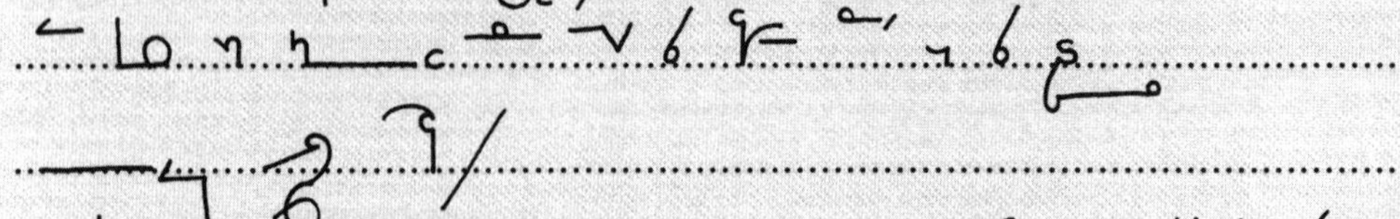

4 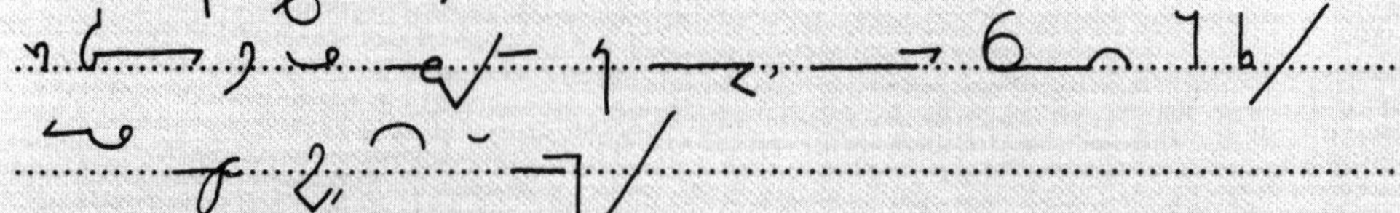

5 

TN, DN and TRN, DRN

Letters T and D can both be blended with N, by smoothing out the hook on N.

TN

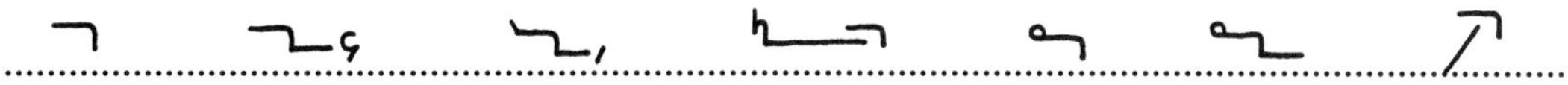

tan tendency attending entertain stain stand retain

DN

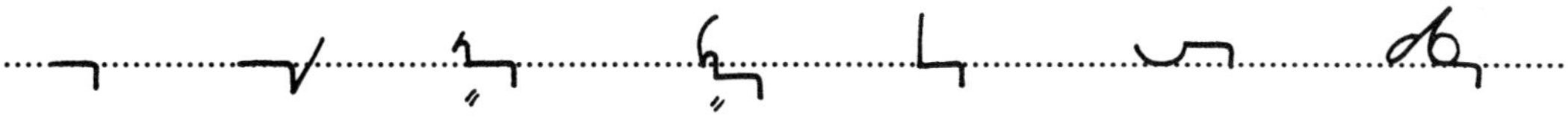

dine dinner Indian London hidden wooden forbidden

TRN

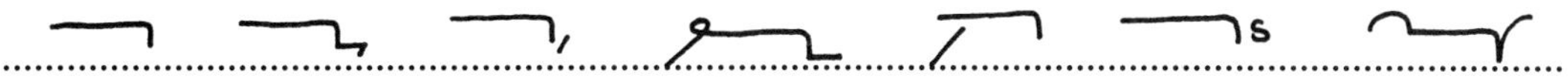

train trendy turning restaurant return torrential maternal

DRN

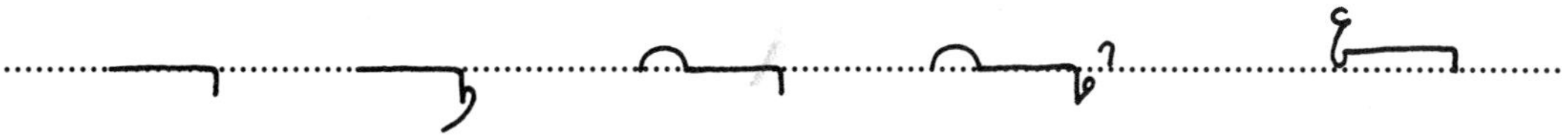

drain drainage modern modernisation cauldron

Task 17.3

Read and write the following sentences

MP3

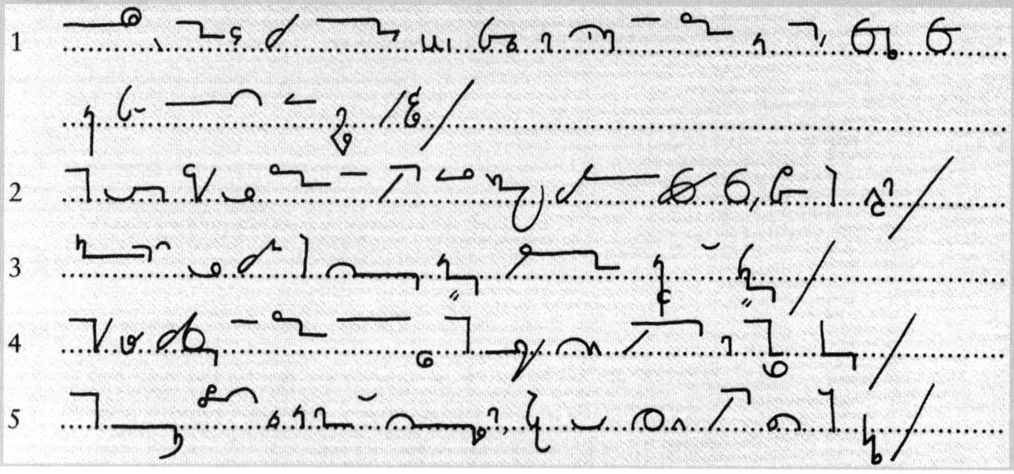

Special outlines – Unit 17

yesterday identify general generally

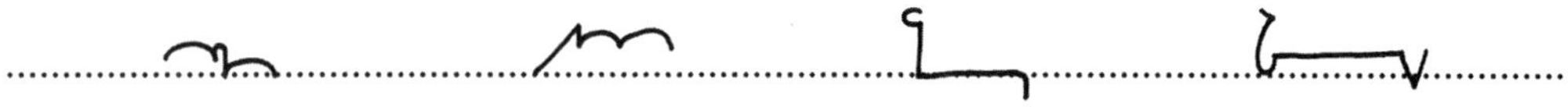

minimum remember children alternative

Distinguishing outlines

industries industrious

Word groupings

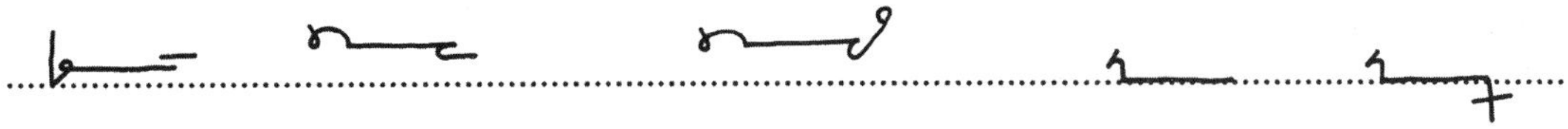

high street | as a matter of fact | as a matter of course | in order to | in order that

name and address | names and addresses

Task 17.4

Read and write 'A rewarding future in entertainment'

MP3

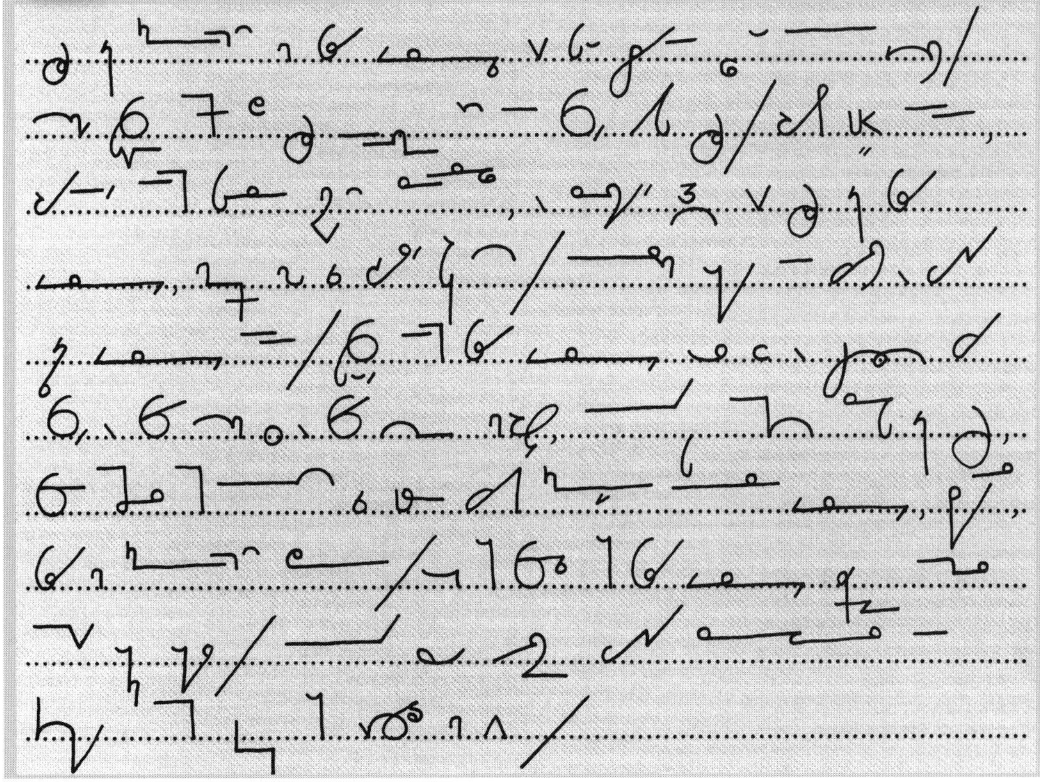

Unit 18
THR, CTR and RN blends and words ending -NESS

Revision:

A double length letter **T** represents common words **their** or **there**

there is **is their** **has there been** **there has been** **there is no**

THR blend

The **TR** blend may also be used to show the sound of **THR** when it comes in the **middle or at the end** of a word:

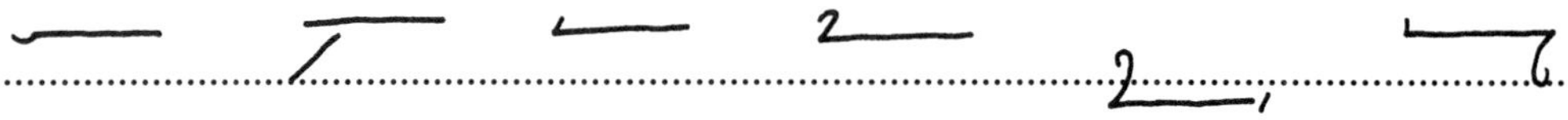

other rather either neither gathering ethereal

smothered bother mother father author authoritarian

But never use the **THR** blend **at the beginning** of a word:

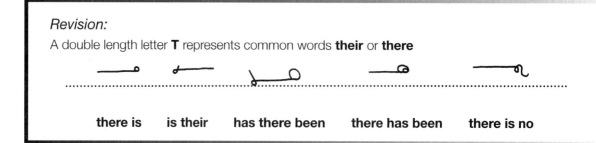

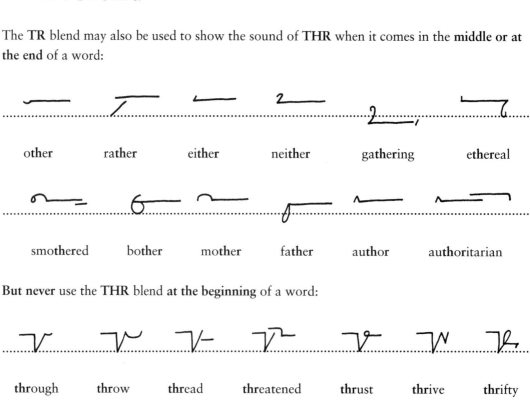

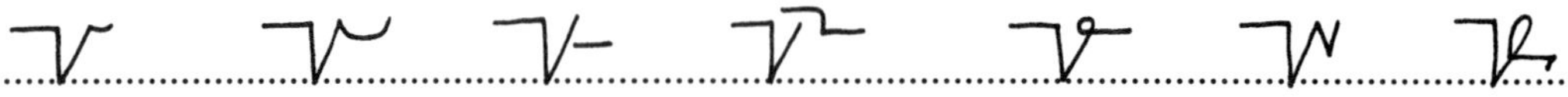

through throw thread threatened thrust thrive thrifty

Task 18.1

Read and write the following sentences

MP3

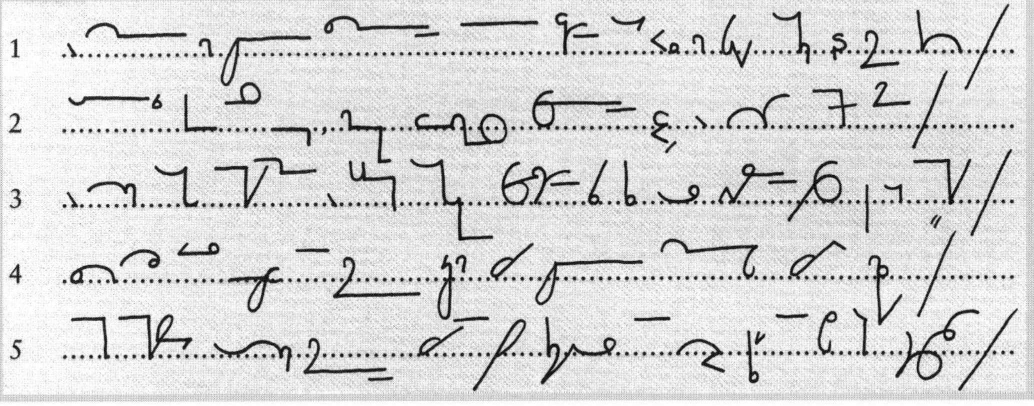

CTR blends

Revision:

C was blended with **T** and **D** (see Unit 7) in such words as:

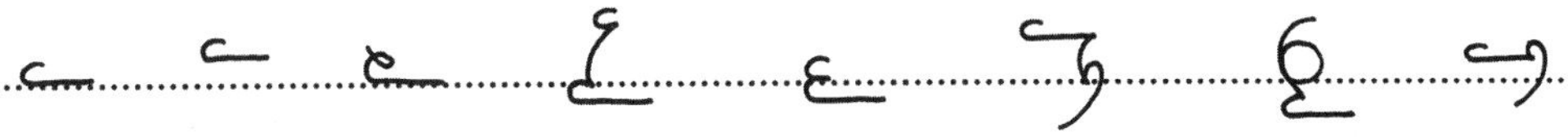

coul**d** **c**u**t** as**ked** colle**ct** coo**ked** **c**a**t**alogue ba**ked** **c**o**tt**age

This principle of blending is used in the **CTR** blend:

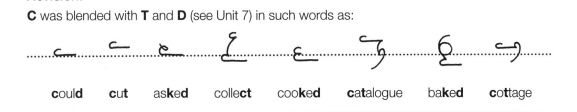

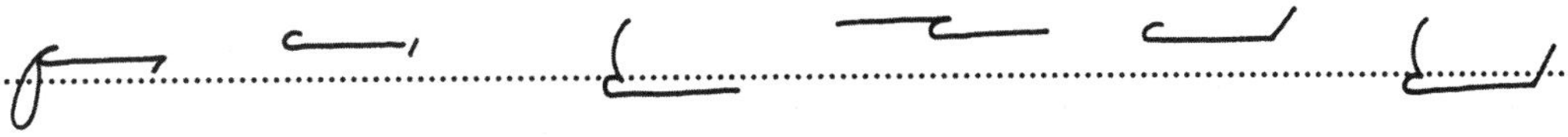

factory catering lecture tractor cater<u>er</u> lectur<u>er</u>

Task 18.2

Read and write the following sentences

MP3

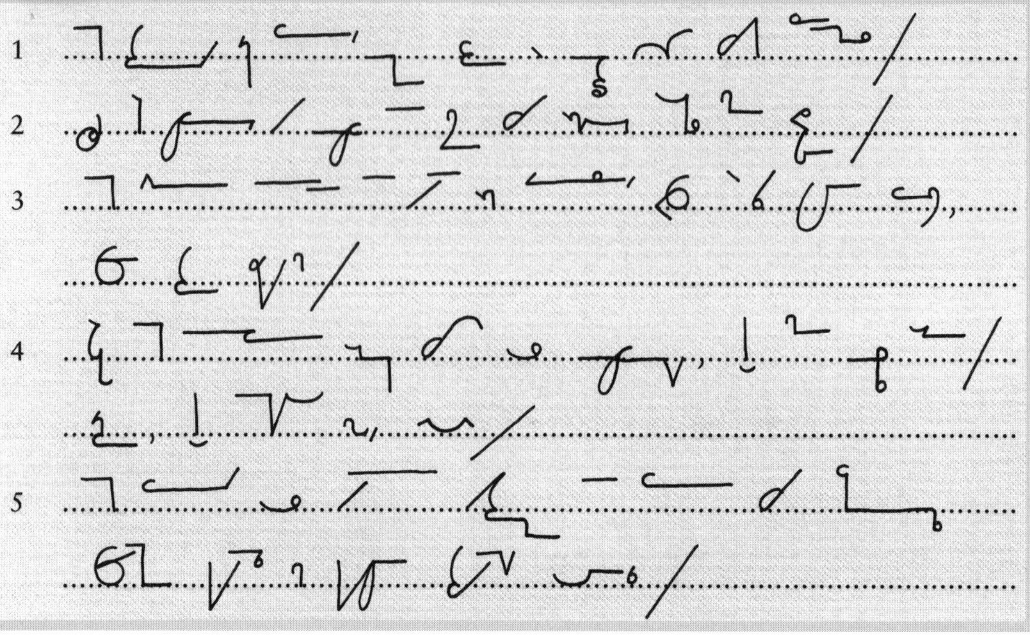

RN blend

Blend letters **R** and **N** so that they make a smooth, continuous line, with the straight stem of **N** pointing down towards the writing line:

run raining burn foreign parent coroner journalist

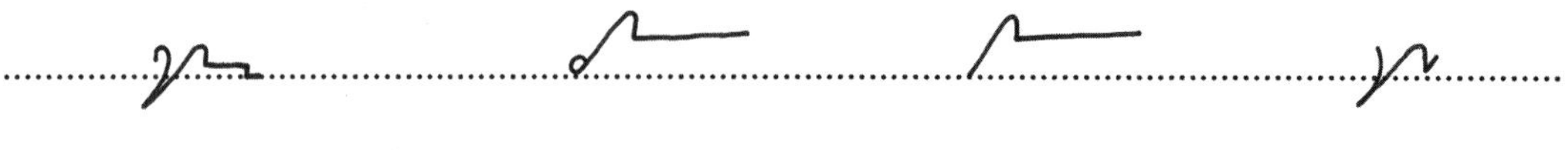

guarantee surrender render journey

Task 18.3

Read and write the following sentences

MP3

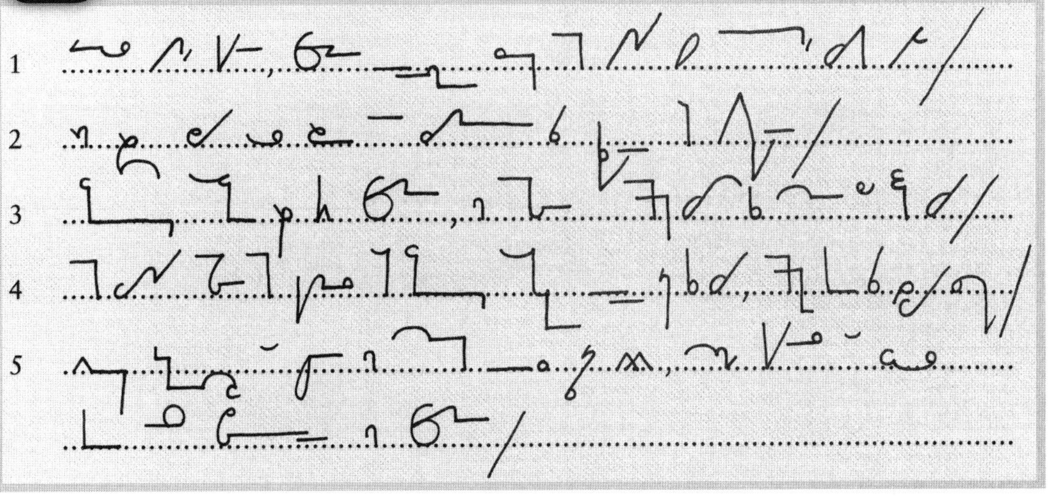

Words ending -NESS

When words end in **-NESS** use full letters **NS** to distinguish between similar outlines: 

neat | neaten | neat**ness**

sweet | sweeten | sweet**ness**

light | lighten | light**ness**

Special outlines – Unit 18

significant | insignificant | society | association | residents' association

Distinguishing outlines

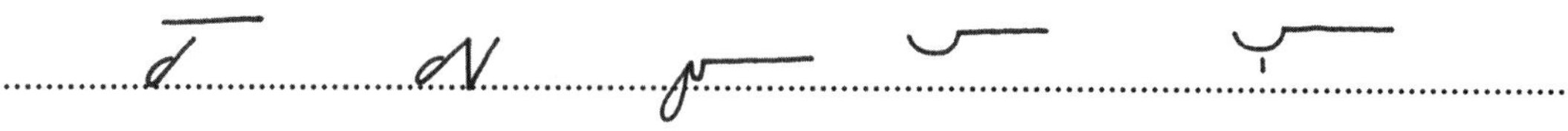

farther further future water weather/whether

Word groupings

during their whether or not some other car park

Task 18.4

Read and write 'Boost for tourism'

MP3

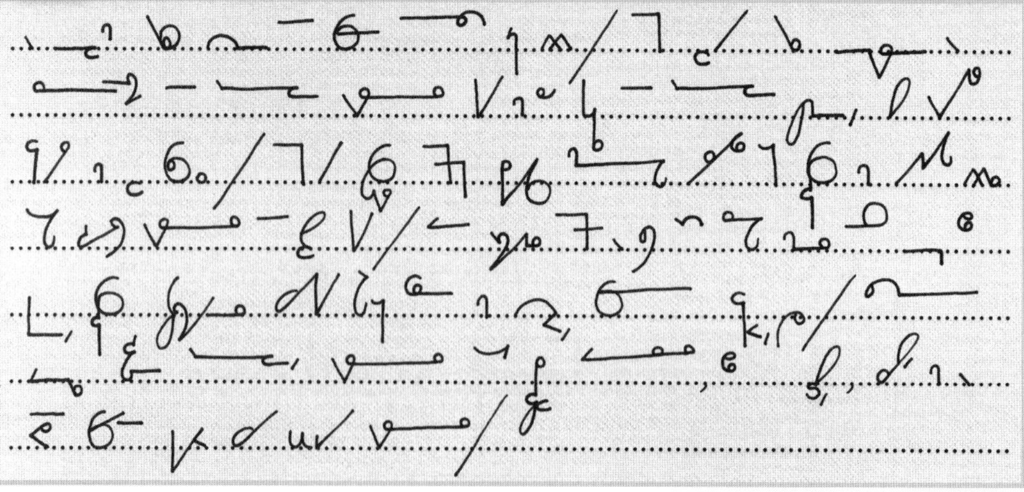

Task 18.5

Read and write 'Surfer thanks lifeguards'

MP3

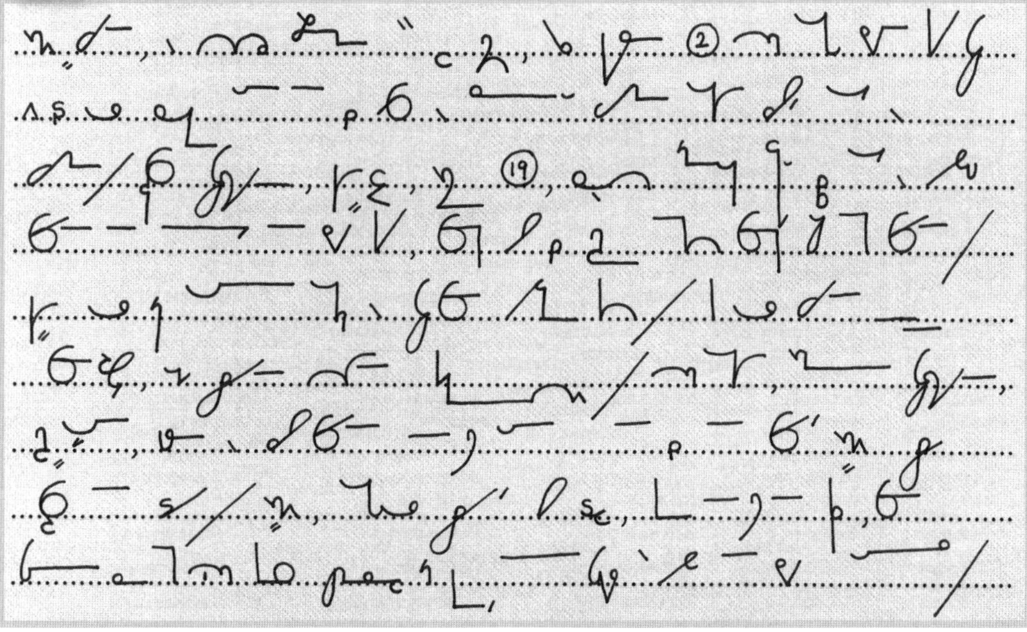

Unit 19
LR, MR and WR blends

Revision

Letter **L** represents common words **letter** .... or **a lot/a lot of** ....

LR blend

Letter **L** is written slightly more than **double** in **length** to show that letter **R** is in the word. There may or may not be a vowel between the **L** and **R**. The same rules apply to **LR** as applied to the different forms of **L**.

(Revise theory at Unit 13 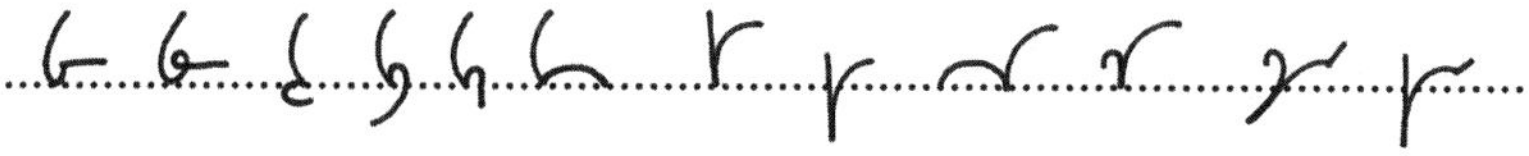)

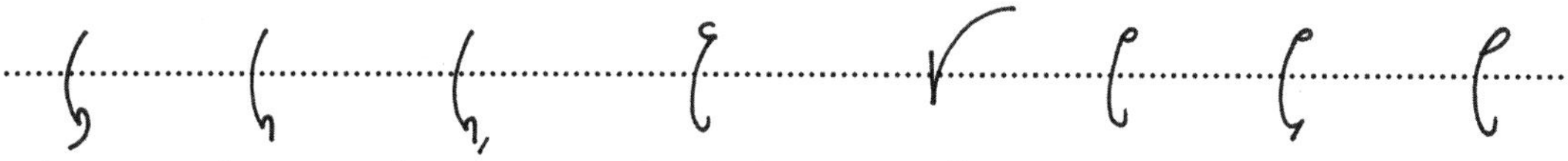

large learn learning clear/colour pillar slur salary fuller

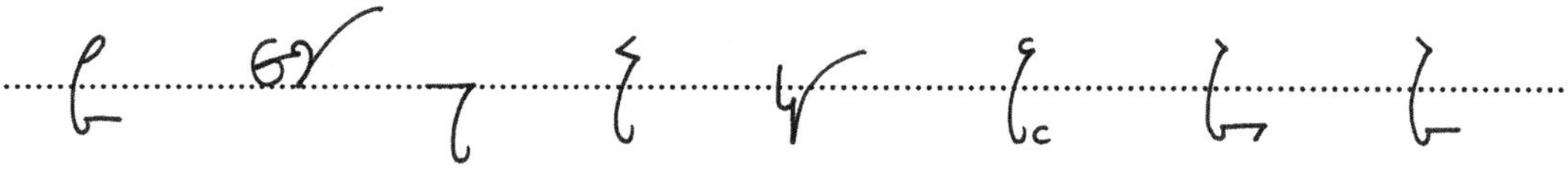

flirt burglar dealer killer popular clearance already alright

Task 19.1

Read and write the following sentences

MP3

1
2
3

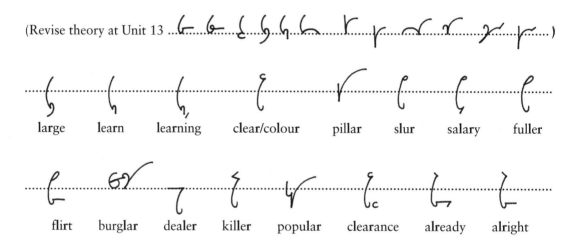

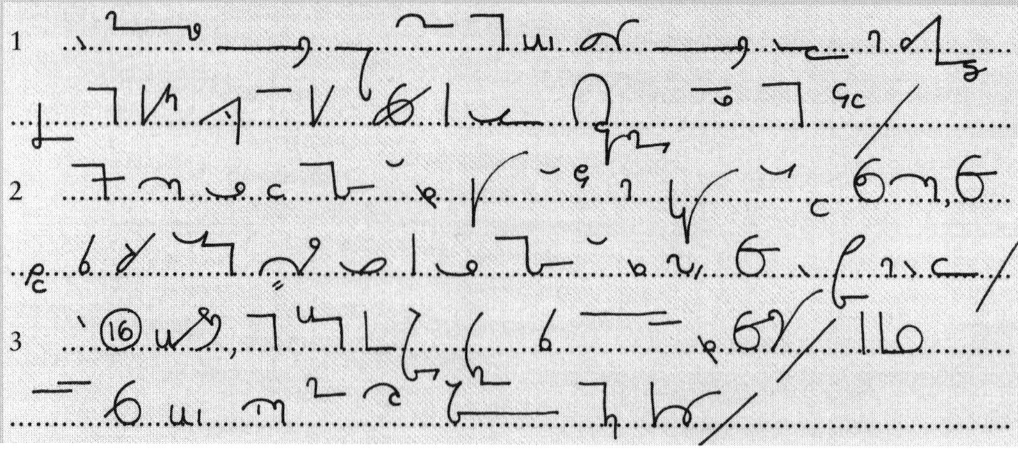

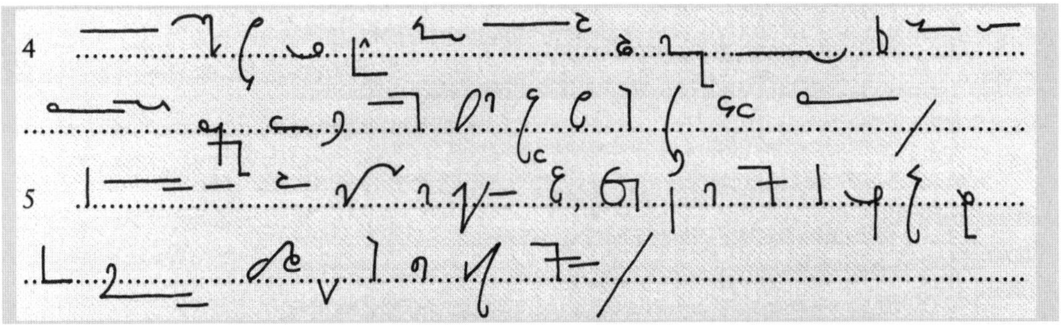

Revision:

Letter **M** represents common words **me** … **time** … **million** ......

Smaller than normal size **M** written in the **T** position represents words ending -**MENT,** as in special outline **government** …

MR blends

more Mr Mrs morning merely summer mortgage mortality

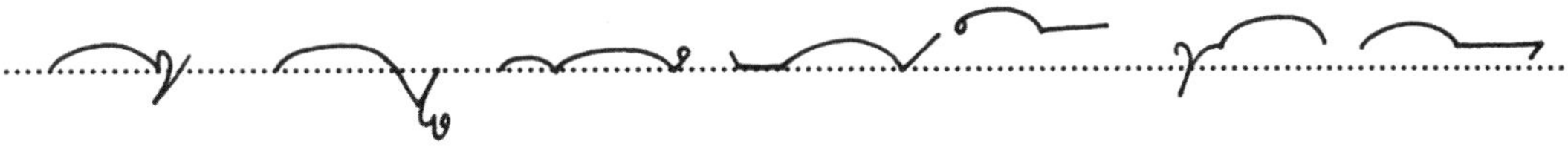

merger marvellous memories admirer smarter glamour mortuary

Task 19.2

Read and write the following sentences

MP3

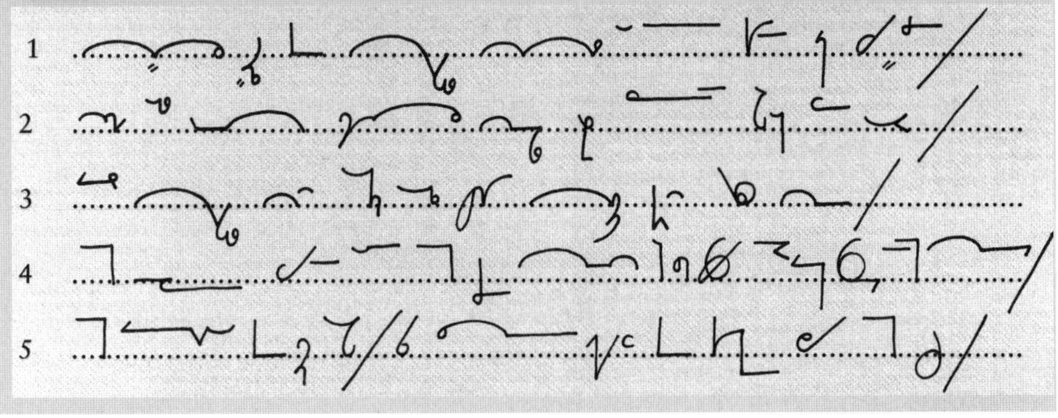

Revision:

Letter **W** represents common words **we** ...... **Wales** ......

Smaller than normal size **W** written in the **D** position represents:

the word **would** when it follows other words in a grouping ......, ..., ... etc

word endings -**WARD, -WORD, -WOOD, -WIDE** as in: **towards** ...... **crossword** ......
oakwood ...... **nationwide** ......

and the word **forward** in groupings, as in **look forward** ......

WR blends

were worse worst worry worried lower flower worthless

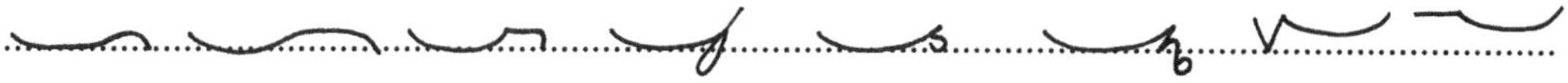

warm warmer warden warfare worship weariness viewer tower

Task 19.3

Read and write the following sentences

MP3

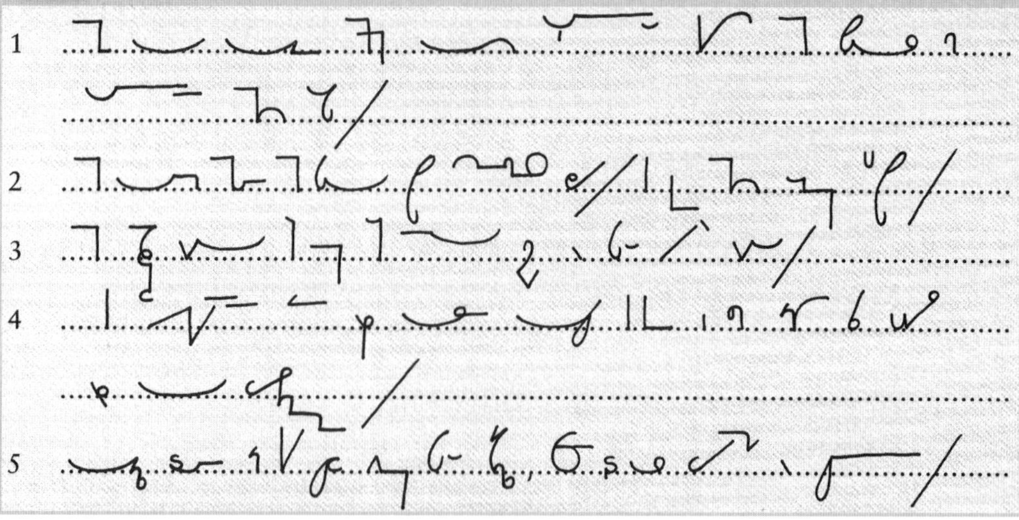

WK and WRK blends

When joining **W** or **WR** to **K**, slide the pen/pencil back down the **W** or **WR** to write the **K**:

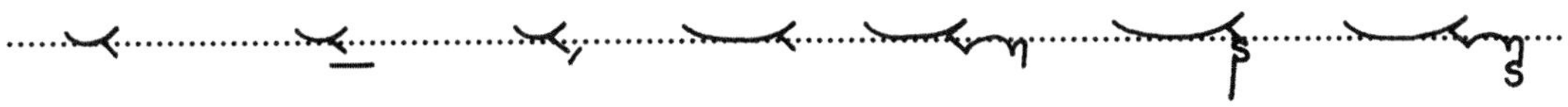

week/weak weekend walking work workman workshop workmanship

Change **K** to **C** when joining **R** or **D**:

weaker worker worked

Task 19.4

Read and write the following sentences

MP3

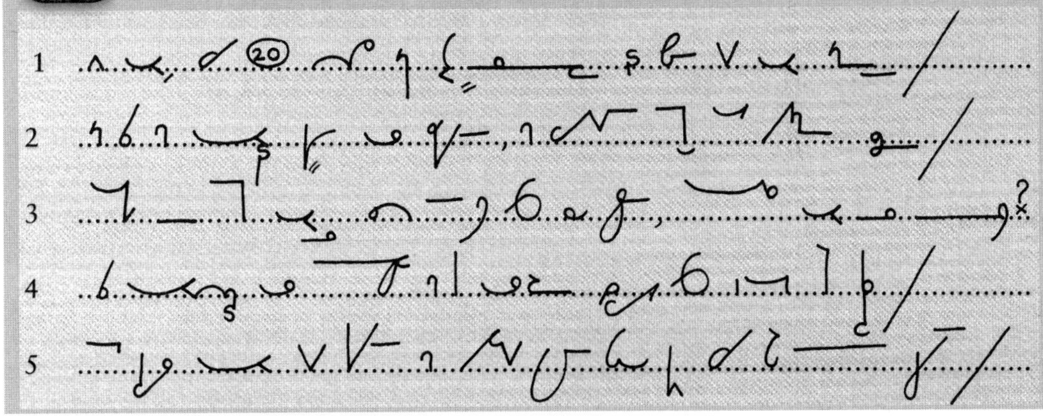

Revision:

Remember to take care with the size of your outlines, especially:

-MENT  **would, -WARD, -WORD, -WOOD, -WIDE** 

M  **W** 

MR  **WR** 

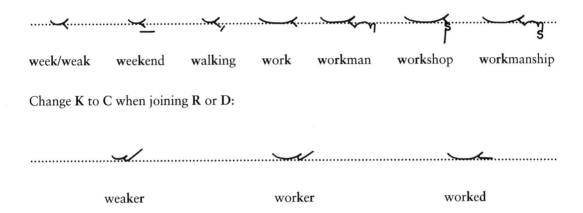

Special outlines – Unit 19

landlord our tomorrow emergency motorway remarks world

Distinguishing outlines

were where small smaller similar

Word groupings

The word **than** may be reduced to full letter **N** when it follows other words in a word grouping:

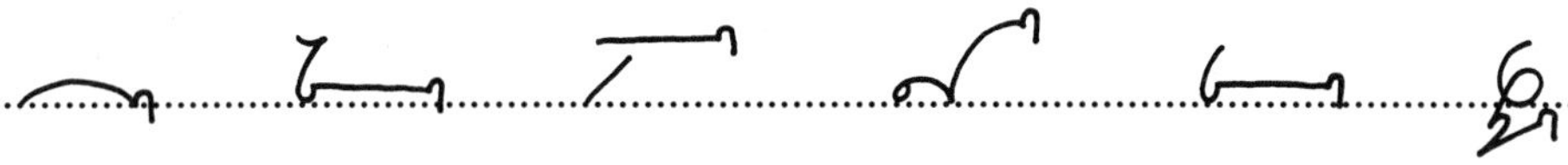

more than older than rather than smaller than later than bigger than

worthwhile this morning smaller and smaller larger and larger

more and more more or less more and more important much more important

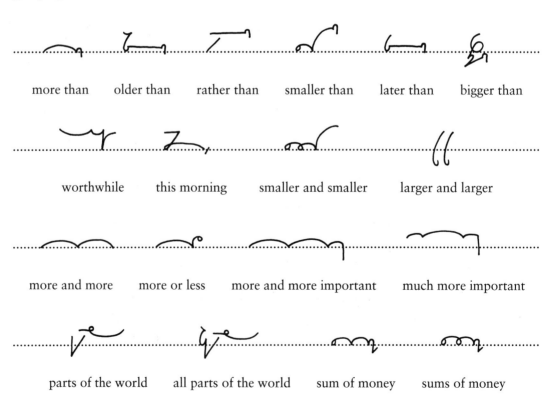

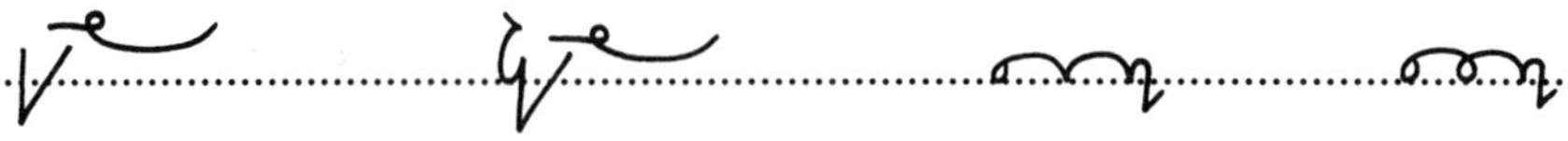

parts of the world all parts of the world sum of money sums of money

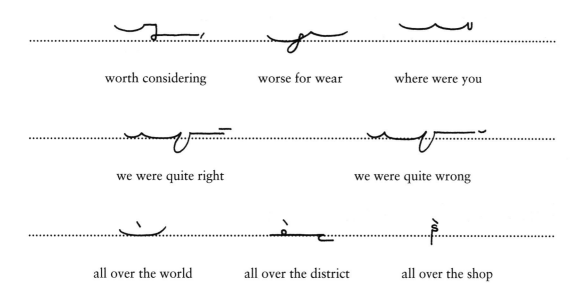

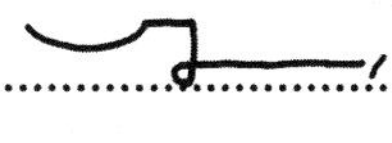
worth considering

worse for wear

where were you

we were quite right

we were quite wrong

all over the world

all over the district

all over the shop

Task 19.5

Read and write 'Award for foster carer'

MP3

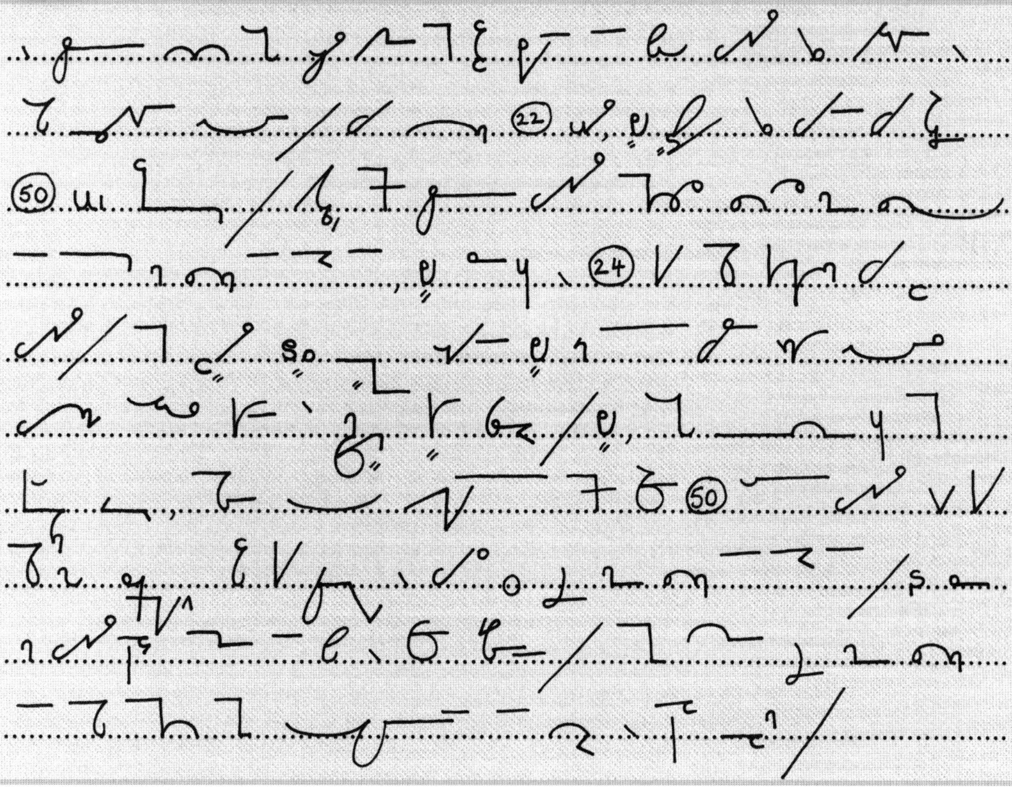

Unit 20
Colloquialisms, numbers, currencies and measurements

Colloquialisms

If colloquial forms of speech are used, then it is necessary to write an apostrophe above the outline:

Compare

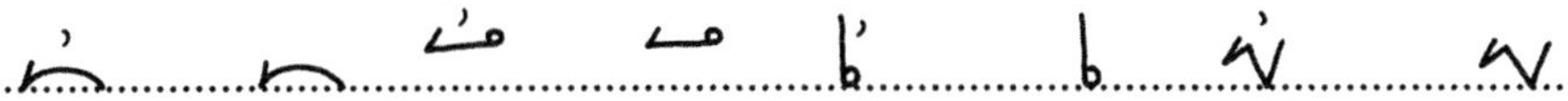

I'm *but* I am it's *but* it is he's *but* he is I've *but* I have

Numbers

As explained in Unit 2, numbers between 1 and 99 may be written as figures and then circled in your Teeline notes to avoid the possibility of them being read as Teeline outlines.

Larger numbers should be written as follows:

Hundred

Write the **DR** blend under the number:

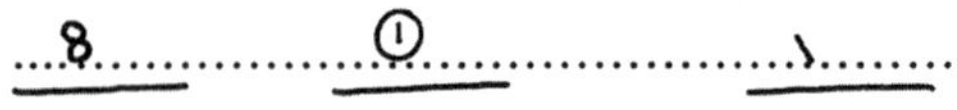

800 100 a hundred

The **DR** blend may be used in phrases:

There were hundreds of

Thousand

Write letter **T** above the number:

8,000

The letter **T** may be used in phrases:

There were thousands of

Hundred thousand

DR blend with letter **T** above it:

800,000

This may be used in phrases:

There were hundreds of thousands of

Compare

There were hundreds and thousands of

Million

Letter **M** under the figure:

8,000,000

Hundred million

DR and **M** under the figure:

8 hundred million

Thousand million

T and **M** above the figure:

8 thousand million

Billion

B written next to the figure: 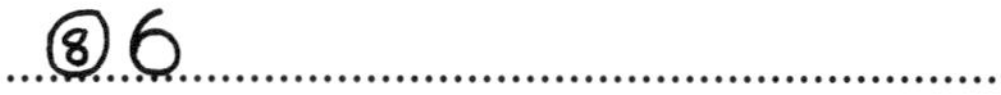

8 billion

but, take care with: 

6 billion *and* 5 billion

If you do not circle the figures you may transcribe these as **66** and **56**!

If the words cannot be written with a figure or incorporated into a word grouping, then write the full outline:

hundred thousand billion

Fractions are written in the usual way, but without the line dividing the figures:

2/3 9/16

but, don't forget:

half

Per cent is written as **PR** next to the figure:

100% 50% 10% 1%

Currencies

When writing **Pounds Sterling,** write a **dot after** the figure:

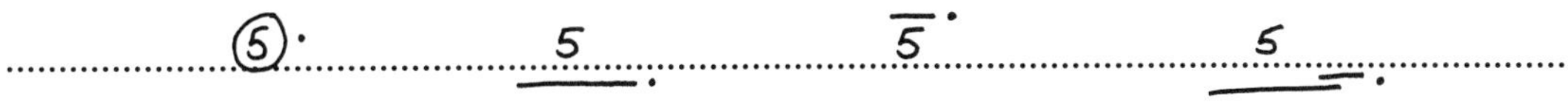

£5 £500 £5,000 £500,000

The dot may also be used for the words **point, spot, dot:**

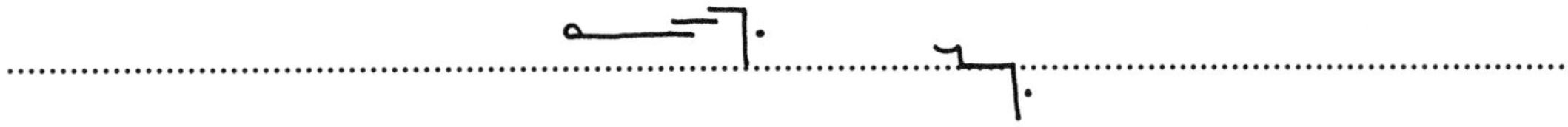

Straight to the point On the spot

Full **U** vowel with **O** indicator written **through** the U = **Euro:** 

21 Euro

DS written below the figure for the word **Dollars:**

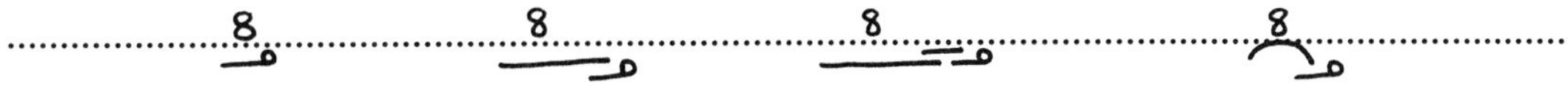

\$8 \$800 \$800,000 \$8 million

Dates beginning with the year two thousand, should be written by omitting the **2** and **0,** and simply writing the final two digits:

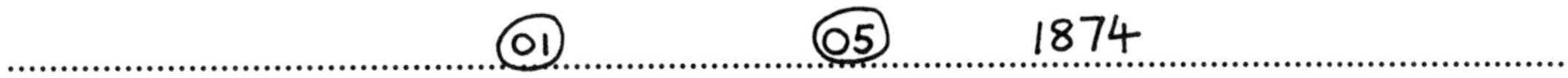

2001 2005 *but* 1874

Century may be written by enclosing the figure with a large letter C: 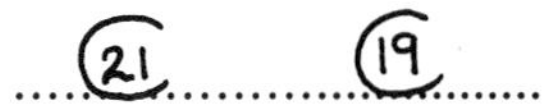

21st century 19th century

Measurements

gram	80 grams
kilogram	12 ¼ kilograms
metre	6 ½ metres
*centimetre	7 centimetres
kilometre	2,000 kilometres
litre	8.5 litres
*centilitre	25 centilitres
millilitre	3 millilitres

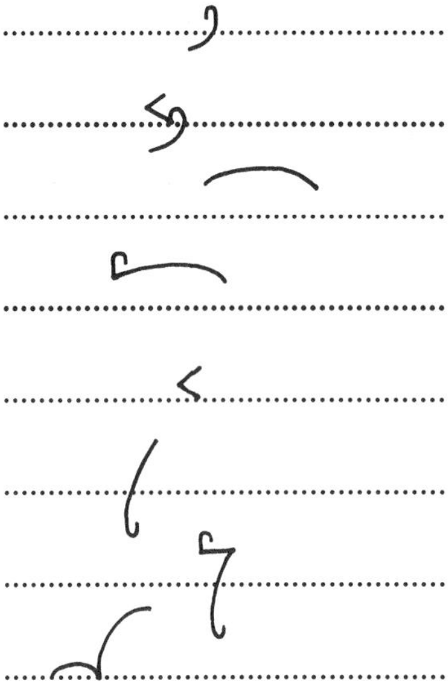

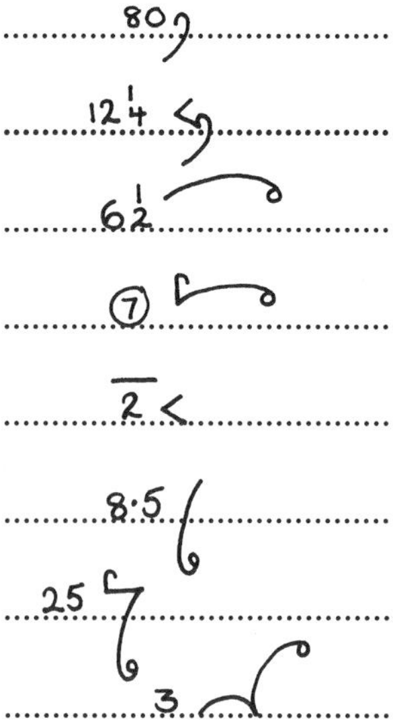

* Note the use of the CN blend to be covered in a later Unit. Start as if writing a C, but continue with the straight down stroke of N.

Task 20.1

Read and write the following sentences

MP3

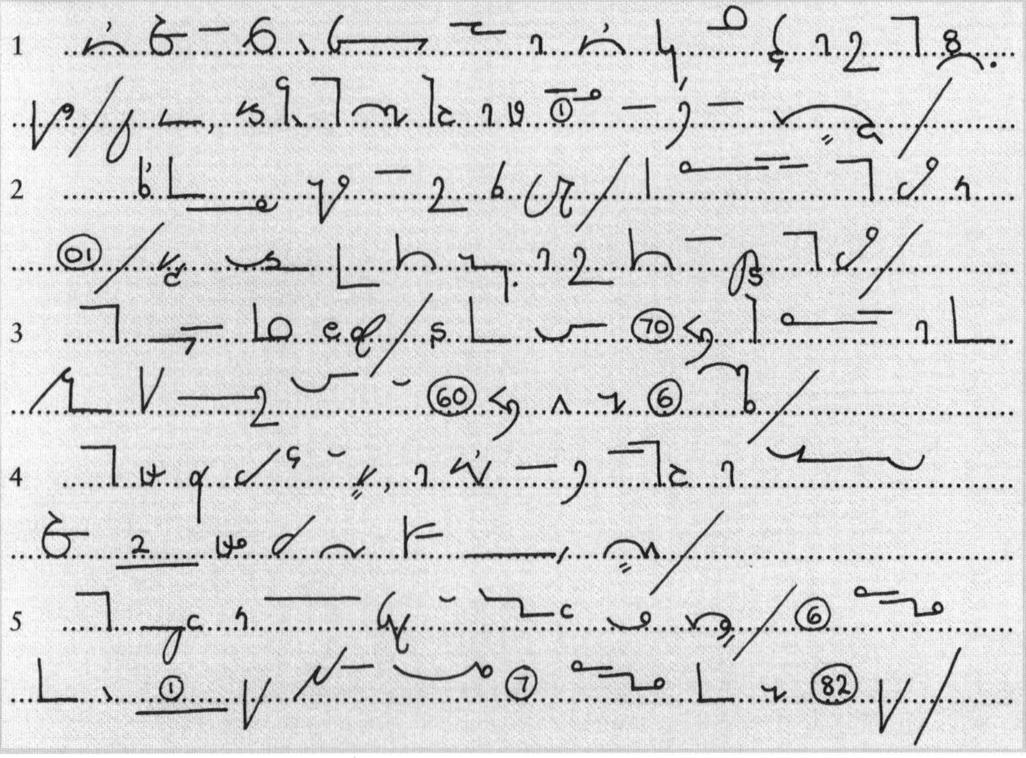

Unit 21
X blends

Revision:
Letter **X** represents common words **accident** ..X.. or **cross** ..X.

Blend letter X with other letters by writing one of the strokes of X through another letter. It is most often the first stroke of X which is used ......\......

If words begin with **EX** there is no need to write vowel **E** because **E** can be heard in the sound of **EX**:

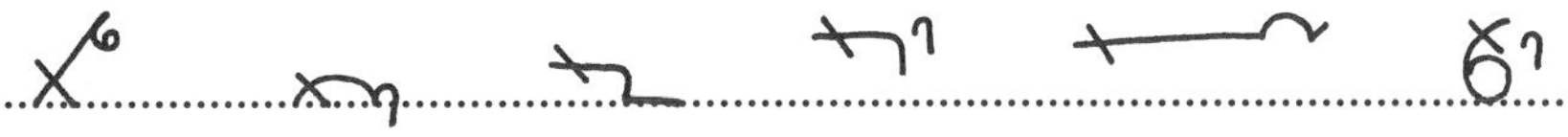

exercise examine extend extension extremely exhibition

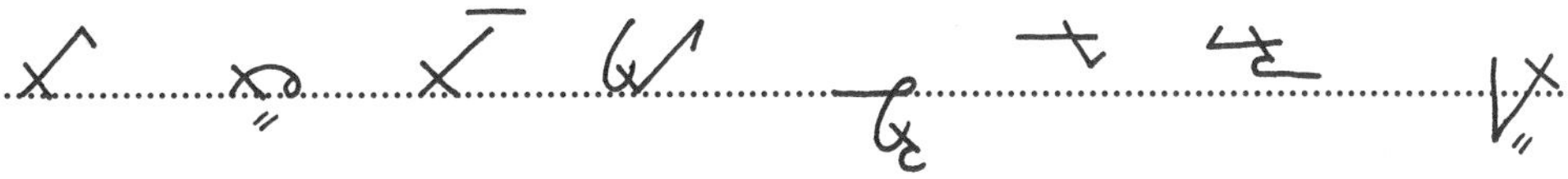

X-ray Xmas exert luxury dyslexic taxi intoxicate Pyrex

In words which blend **HX**, **PX** and **NX** a better outline results if the **H**, **P** or **N** is sloped slightly. This helps an **X** to be seen in the outline and makes transcription easier:

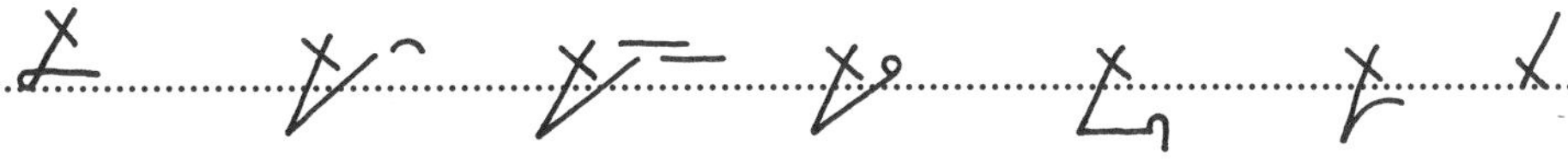

exhaust experiment exported express expedition expel hoax

next annexe

X is written in full in the words:

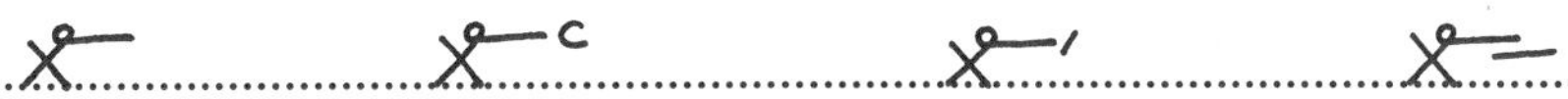

exist existence existing existed

Task 21.1

Read and write the following sentences

MP3

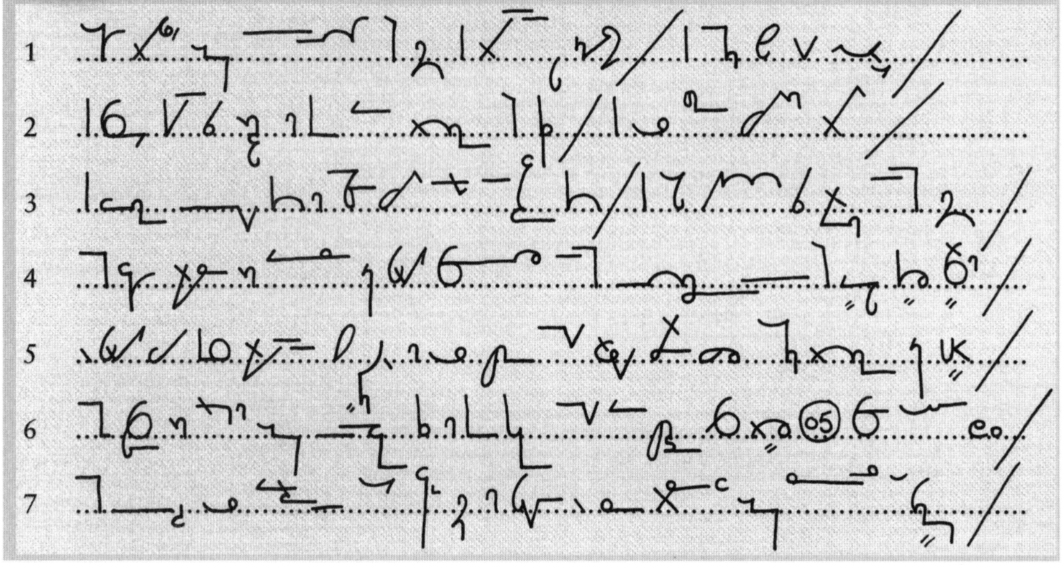

If words begin with **EXC** there is no need to write **E** or **C** if they can be heard in the sound of **EX**:

excel   excellent   excellence   excerpt

If words begin with **EXC** and the **C** has a **definite sound**, the **C** must be written:

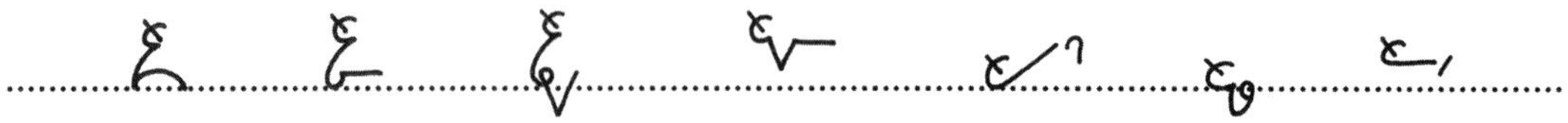

exclaim   exclude   exclusive   excavate   excursion   excuse   exciting

It is possible to have more than one blend in an outline:

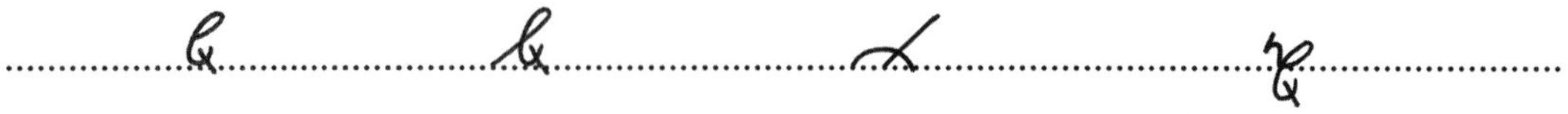

flex (**fl** + **lx**)   reflex (**rf** + **fl** + **lx**)   mixer (**mx** + **xr**)   influx (**fl** + **lx**)

Task 21.2

Read and write the following sentences

MP3

1 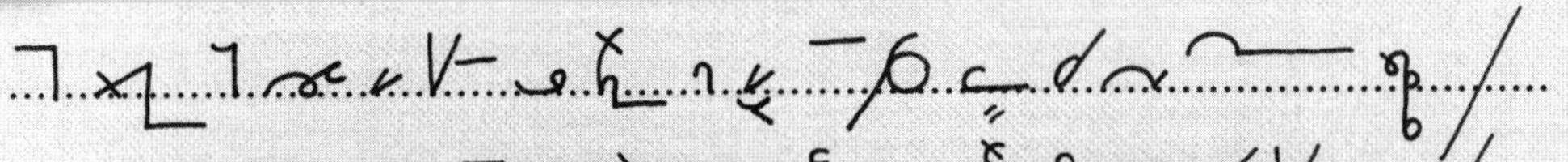

2 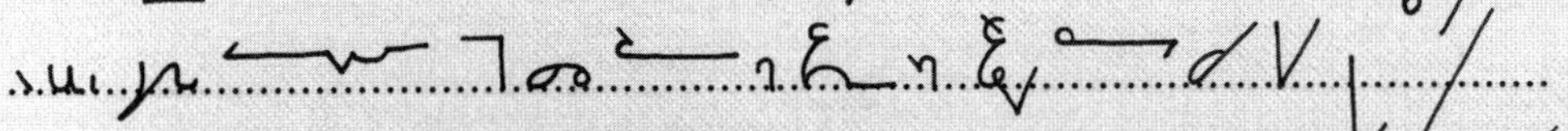

3 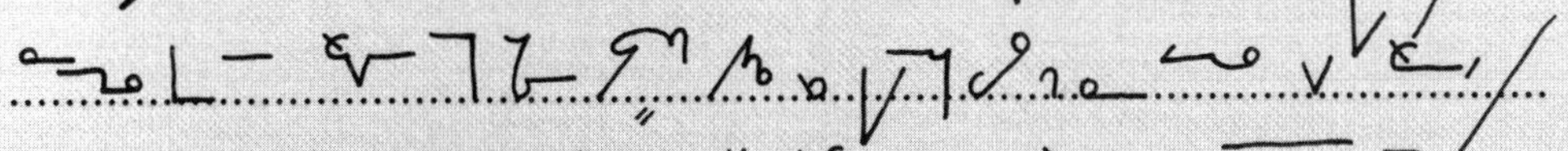

4 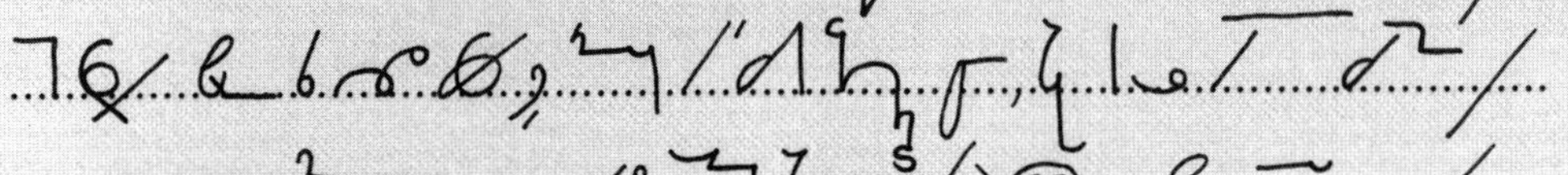

5 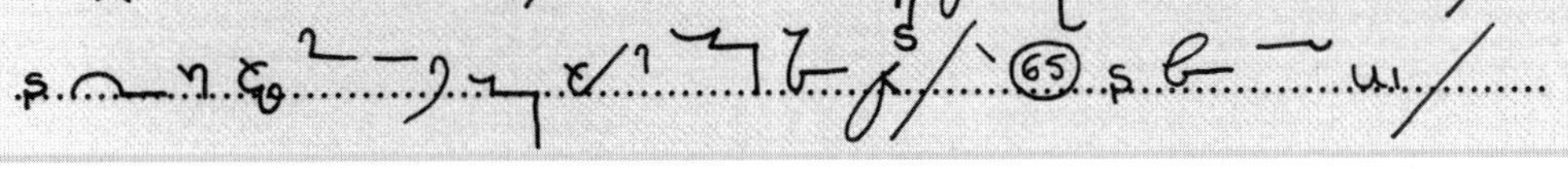

Special outlines – Unit 21

examination | experience | inexperience | maximum | approximately

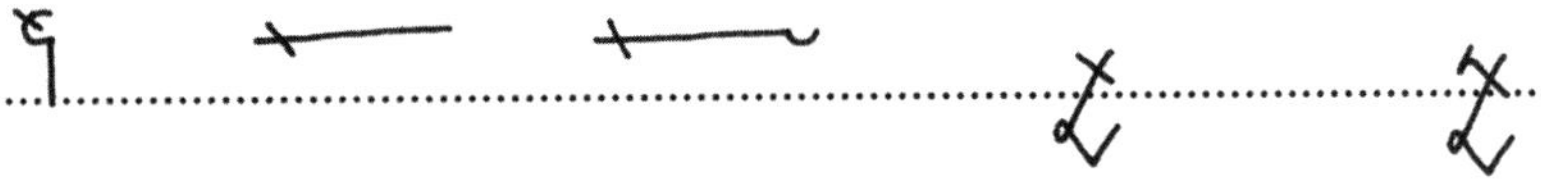

exchange | extra | extraordinary | expensive | inexpensive

Distinguishing outlines

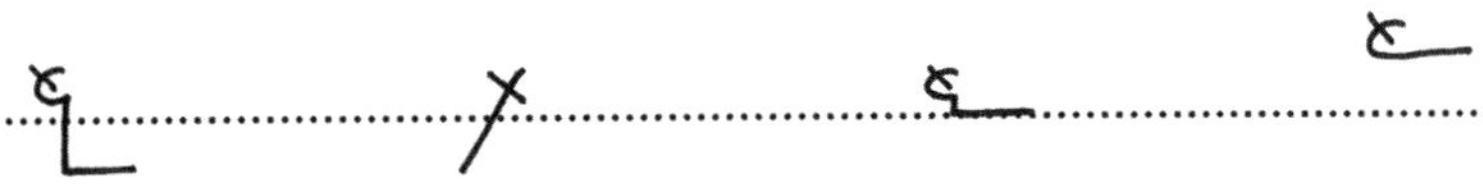

except | expect | exceed | exact

Word groupings

for example

chief executive

Task 21.3

Read and write 'Help your local hospice'

MP3

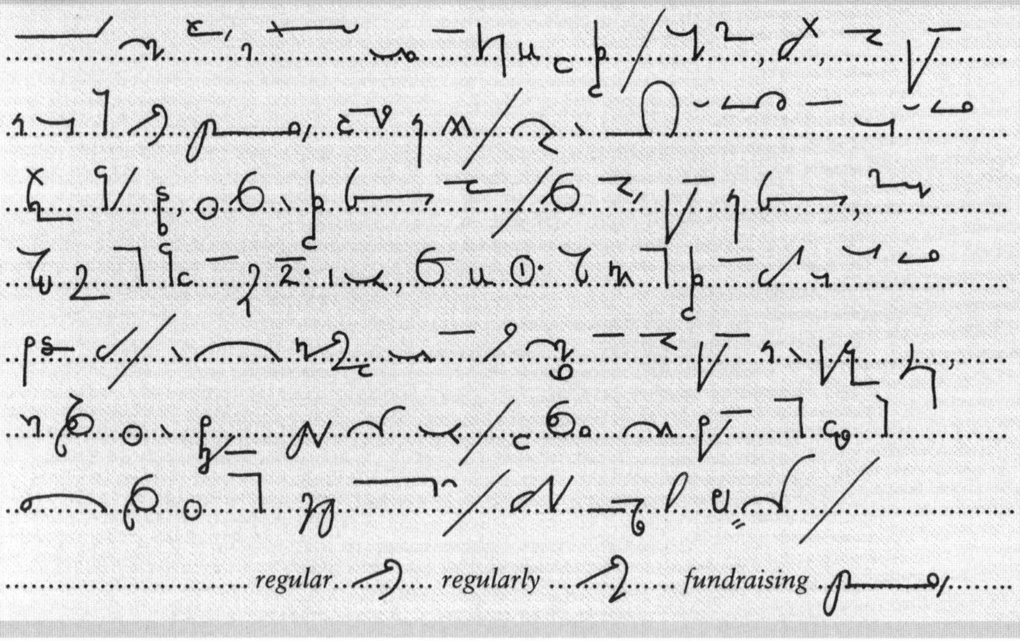

Task 21.4

Read and write 'Mistake with nail glue'

MP3

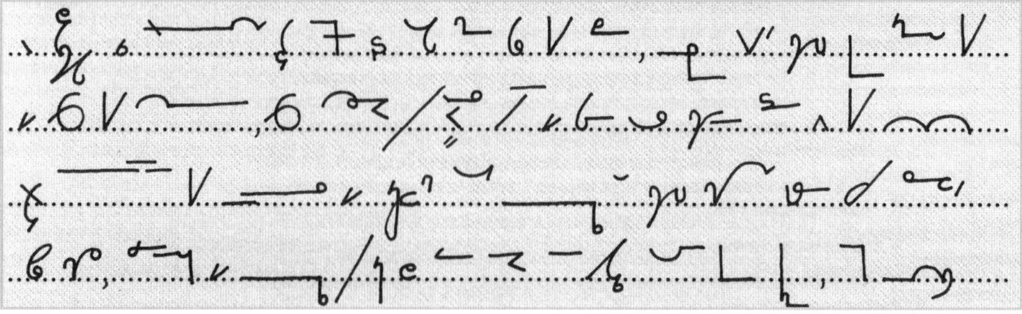

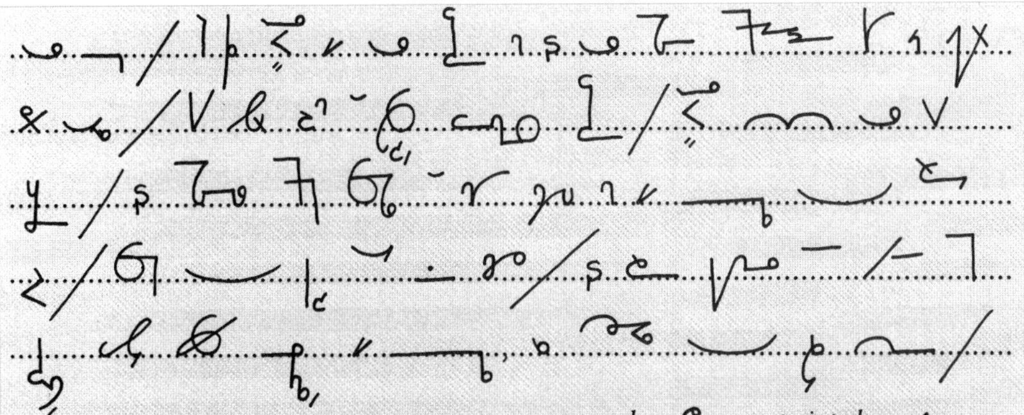

second  pointed 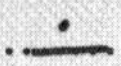

Task 21.5

Transcribe the following special outlines

MP3

1 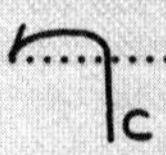 ....

2 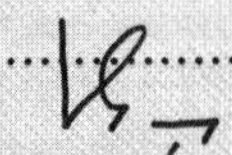 ....

3 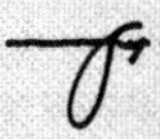 ....

4 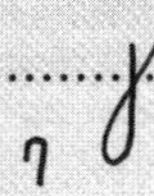 ....

5 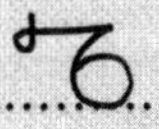 ....

6 ....

7  ....

8 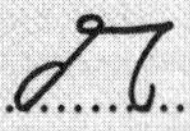 ....

9  ....

10  ....

11  ....

12  ....

Unit 22
CM blends and words beginning RECOM-

Revision:

Letter **C** represents common words **once** ...... or **offence** ......

and when hanging from the writing line **local** ......

Letter **C** represents the word ending -**NCE**:

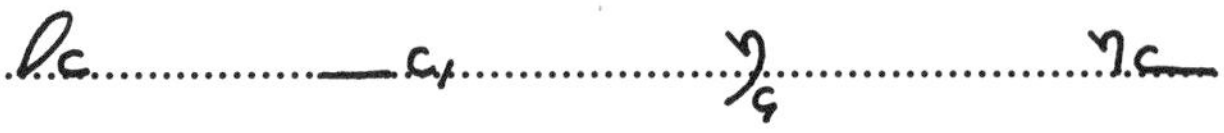

fence dancing agency announced

The letters C and M should be blended so that letter C is as wide as letter M and flattened slightly:

CM blend

The **CM** blend may occur anywhere in an outline. A vowel always occurs between the letters C and M. The sound of C may be hard or soft (as in S).

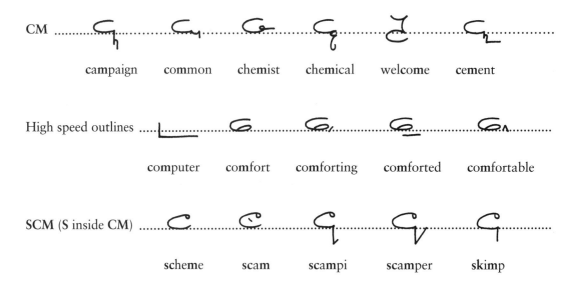

CM

campaign common chemist chemical welcome cement

High speed outlines

computer comfort comforting comforted comfortable

SCM (S inside CM)

scheme scam scampi scamper skimp

ACCOM (attach A indicator)

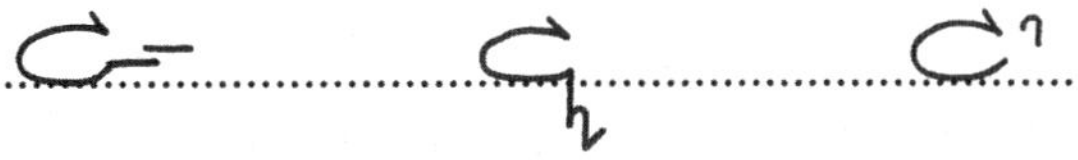

accommodate   accompany   accommodation

UNACCOM/UNCOM (disjoin U indicator)

unaccompanied   uncommon   uncommonly

ENCOM/INCOM (omit N)

encompass   income   incoming

Words beginning RECOM-

Write **RC** for words beginning **RECOM-**  Do not use the **CM** blend. *Note high speed forms.*

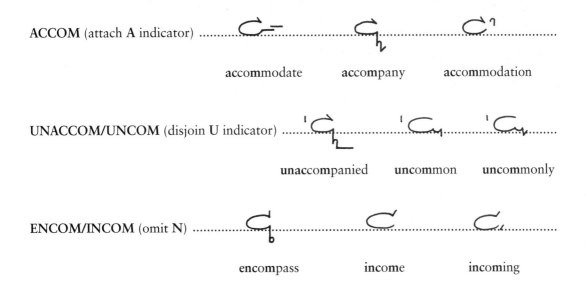

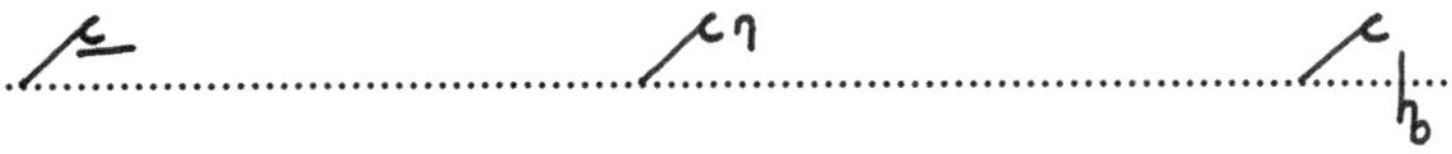

recommend   recommendation   recompense

Task 22.1

Write the following words in Teeline

MP3

camper	competence	competition	comments ....
camber	chameleon	comparison	camouflage ....
composed	commuter	accompaniment	ecumenical ....

Task 22.2

Read and write the following sentences

MP3

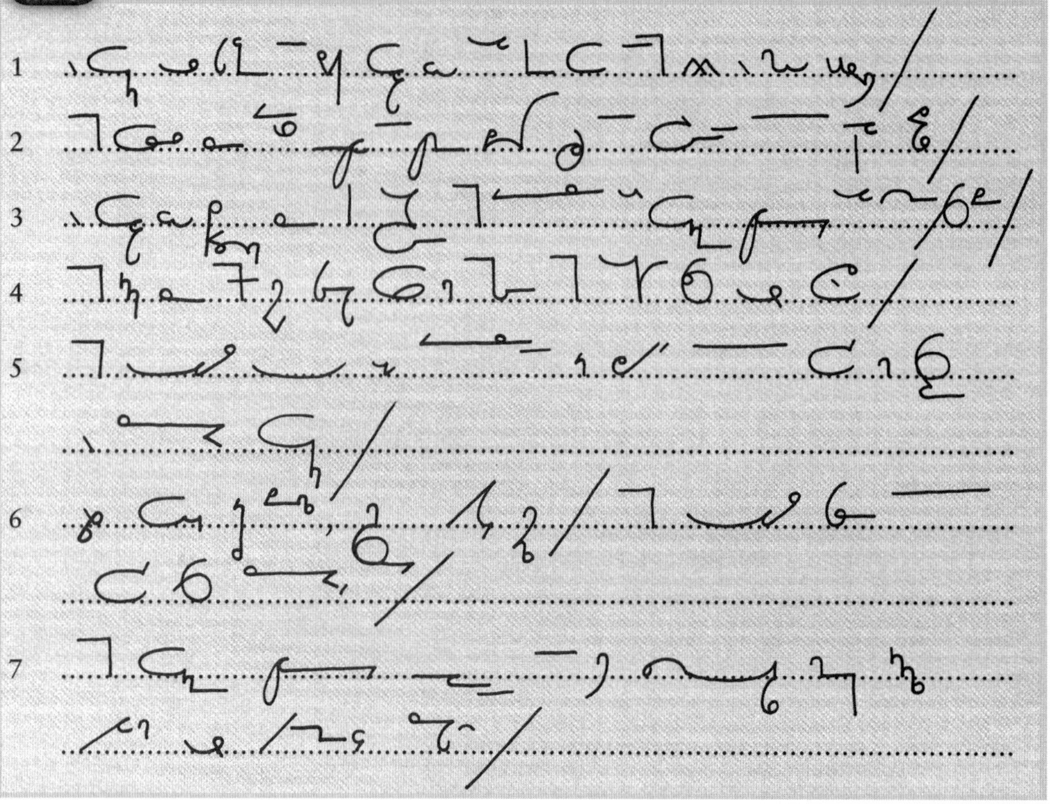

Special outlines – Unit 22

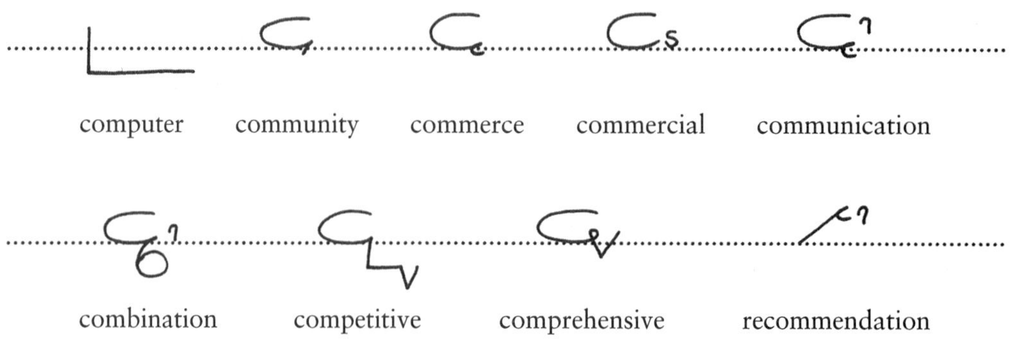

Distinguishing outlines

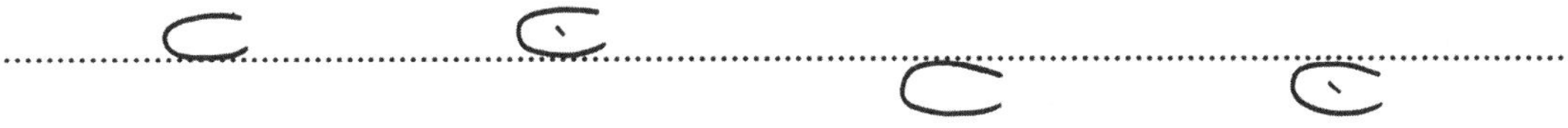

come came become became

Word groupings

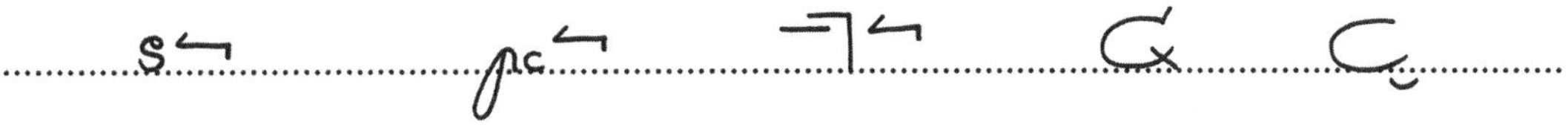

social committee* finance committee to the committee income tax come forward

*Note the use of ITE for the word COMMITTEE in word groupings

come to the conclusion come straight to the point House of Commons Community Association

Task 22.3

Read and write the following sentences

MP3

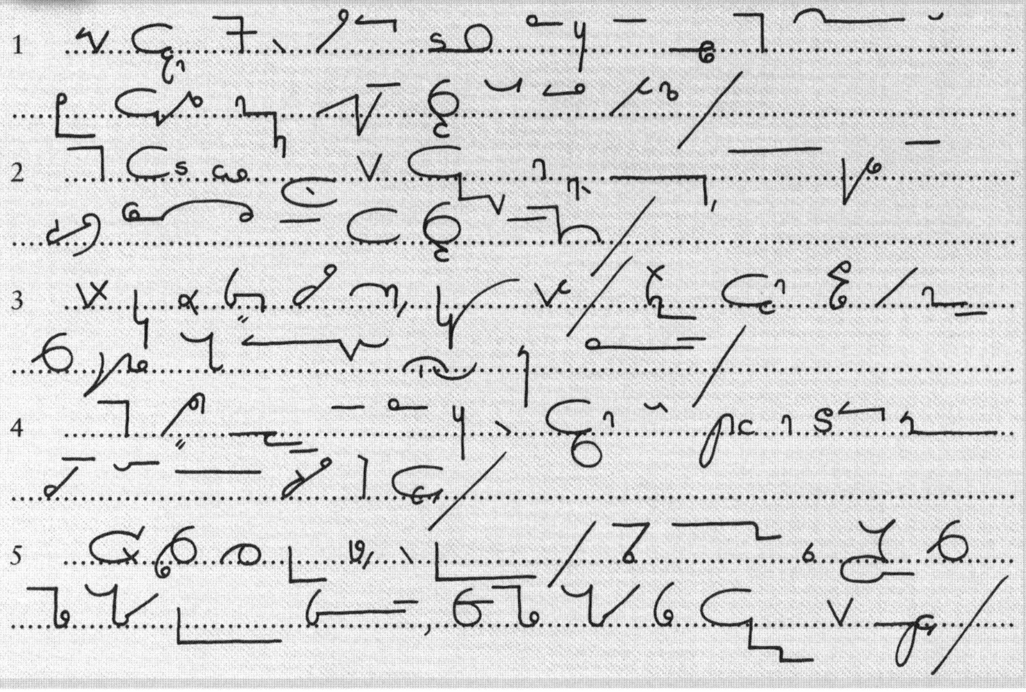

Task 22.4

Read and write 'Speed cameras'

MP3

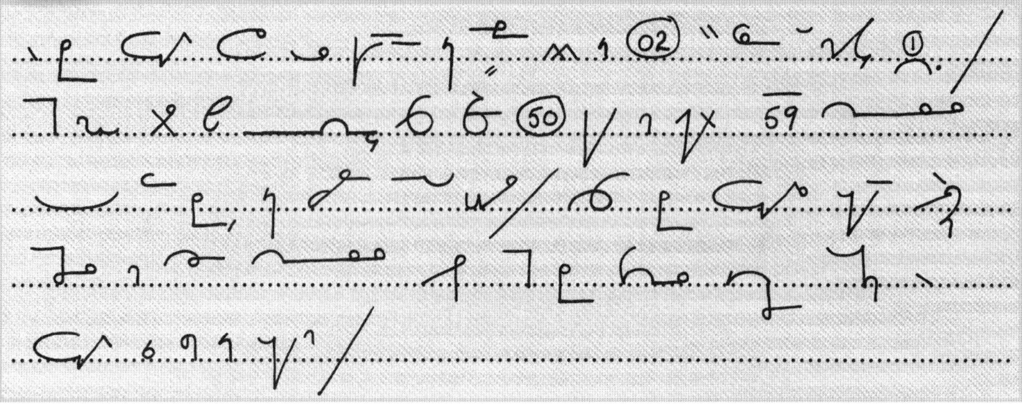

Task 22.5

Read and write 'Hi-tech police force'

MP3

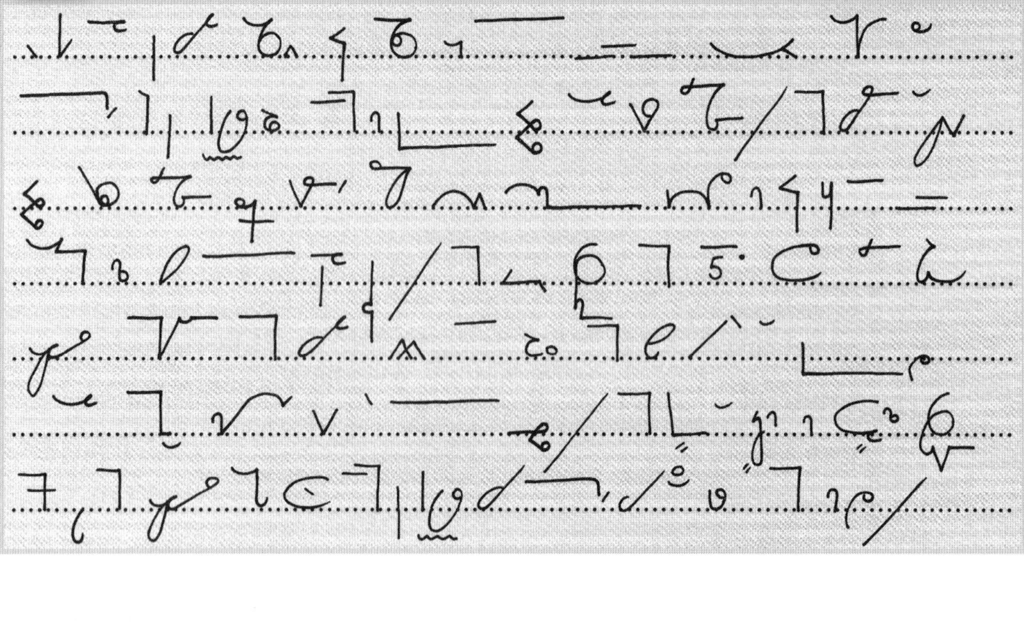

N and V blends

Revision:

Letter **N** represents common words **and** .... or **new/knew** ....

and when hanging from the writing line **begin**, **began**, **begun** ....

and is used as word ending -**SHUN ocean**........, **addition** ...., **station**........

Letter **V** represents common words **have**, **very**, **versus** ....

and when hanging from the writing line **evidence** ....

and when above the writing line **above** ....

NV blend ....

The letters N and V may be blended by sloping N so that it forms the first part of V. Other letters may also be blended with NV. Any vowel sound may occur between the two blended letters:

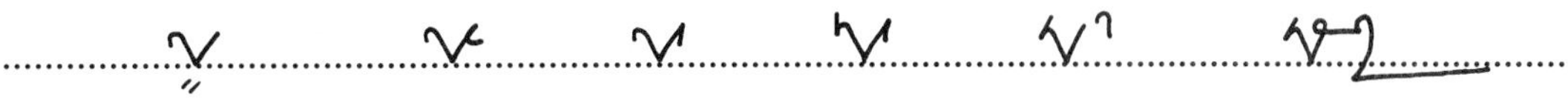

November novice navy envy invasion investigator

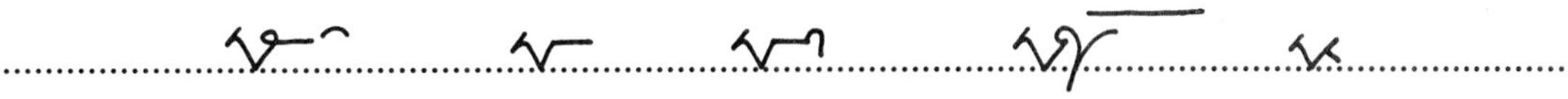

investment invite invitation invigilator invoke

VN blend ....

Write letter V and blend the hook and downstroke of N. Ensure the downstroke of N remains pointing downwards:

van venue avenue vinyl veneer vendor

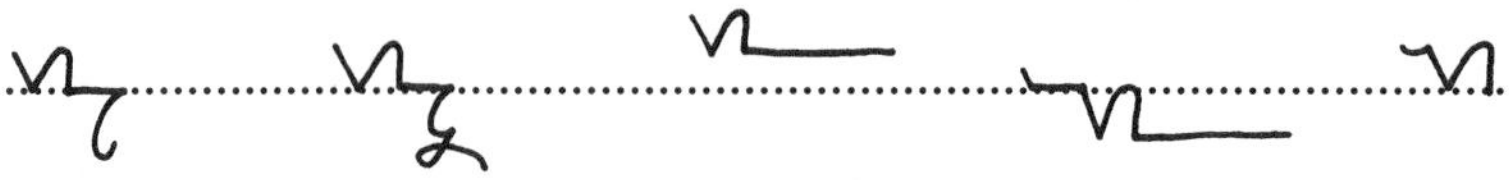

vandal vandalism venture adventure oven

NVN blend 

invent invention inventory

VL blend 

Write V and slide the pen/pencil back down the **V** with **L**:

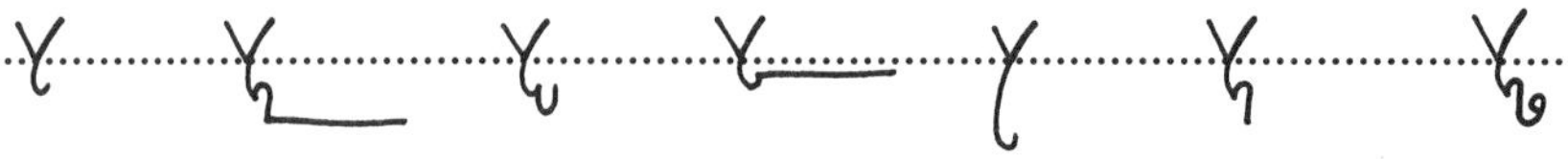

vile volunteer value vulture valour villain villainous

vulgarity villa valid volume voluptuous volition volatile

envelope involve involuntary

VR blend 

Write letter V but lengthen the second stroke of **V** to show **R**:

vary river reverse savour severely vertical verdict

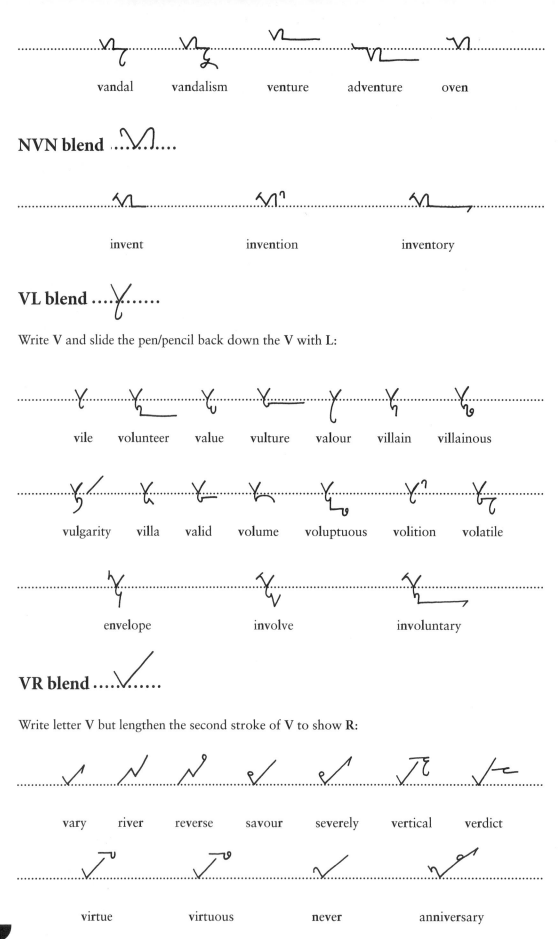

virtue virtuous never anniversary

Task 23.1

Read and write the following sentences

MP3

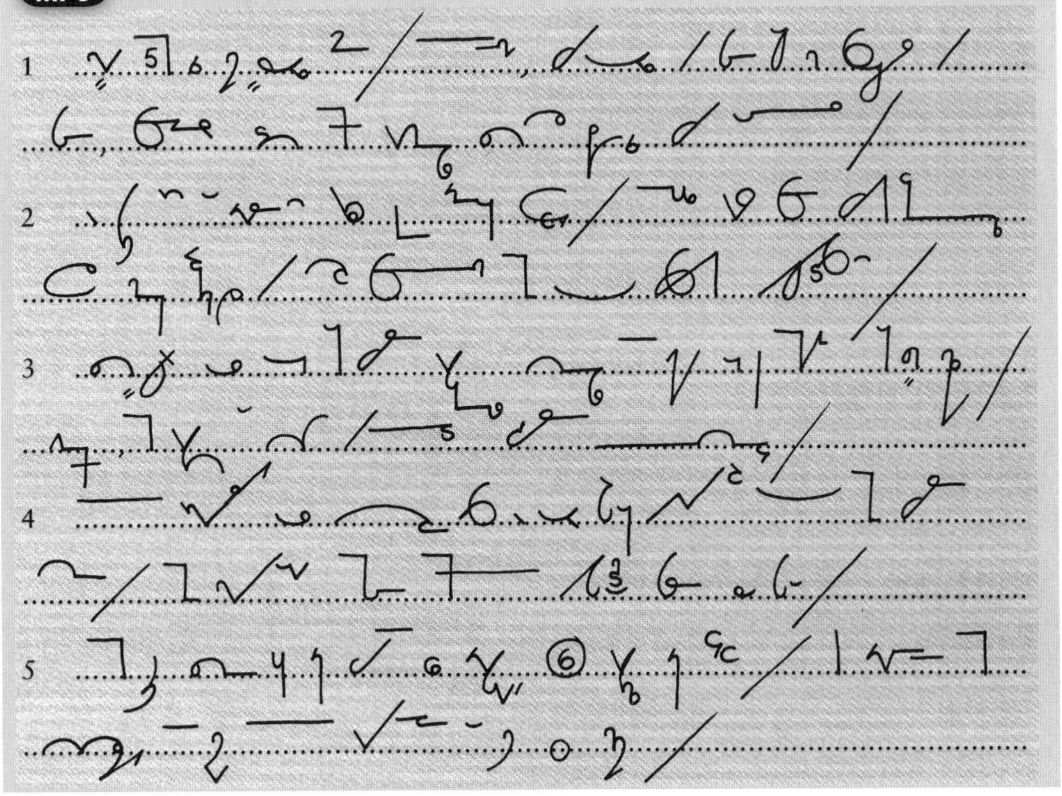

Words beginning EV and EVER/EVERY

EV 

When words begin with the letters EV write the E indicator first, disjoined between the letter V:

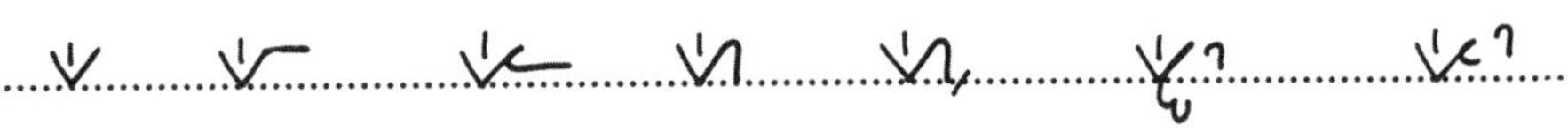

eve evade evacuate even evening evaluation eviction

evolve event eventful eventually evasive evaporate

EVER/EVERY ……

Revision:

E indicator represents common words **EVER** and **EVERY** ……

everything everyone everywhere everybody **ever** since **ever** more

Words ending **-EVER** are written with a disjoined letter **V** beneath the previous part of the outline:

how**ever** what**ever** which**ever** whatso**ever** **never**theless

WN and NW

WN ……

Write **W** and turn the hook of **N** on its side, inside the curve of **W**:

win/won want/went wind own owner ownership found bound

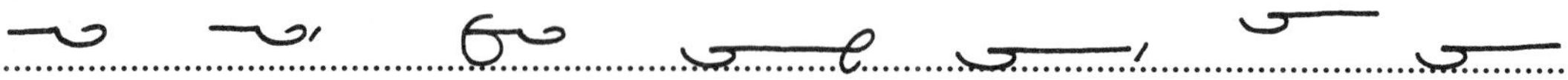

town twinning between wonderful wondering winter wander

NW ……

Turn the hook of **N** on its side and write this inside the curve of **W**:

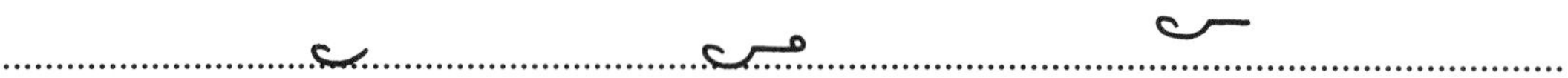

now nowadays newt

Task 23.2

Read and write the following sentences

MP3

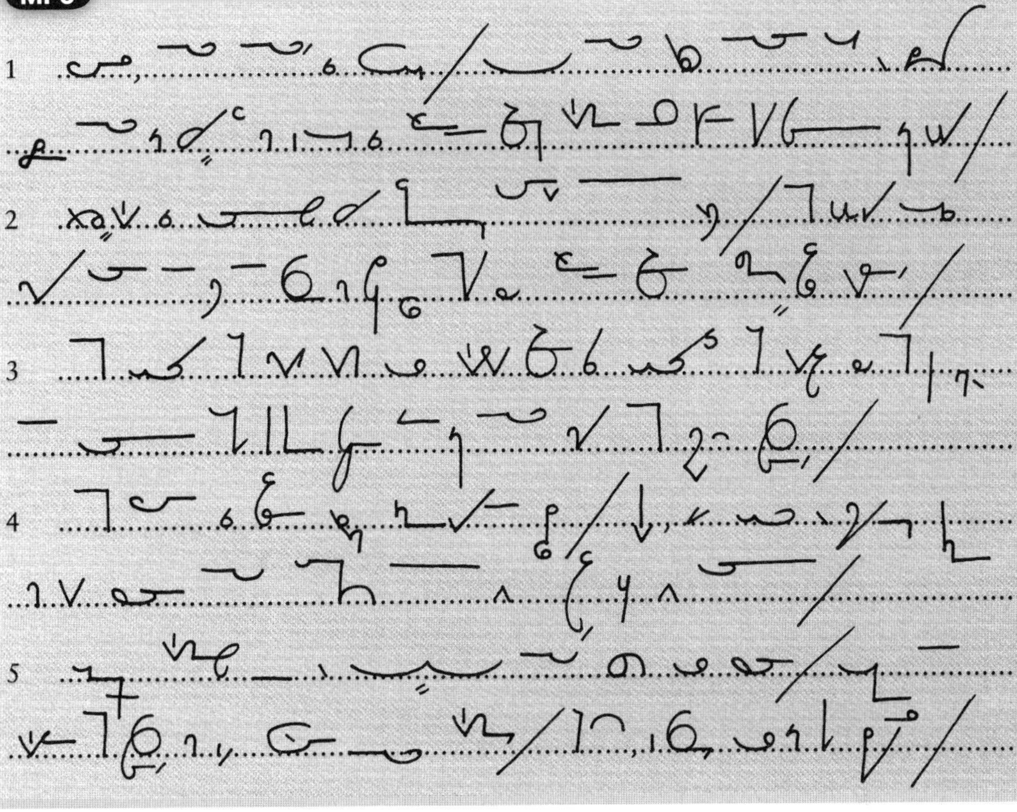

Special outlines – Unit 23

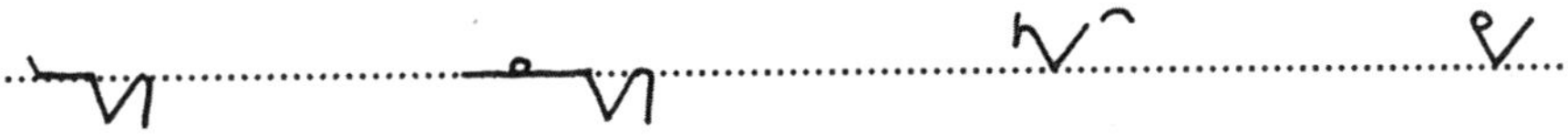

advantage disadvantage environment several

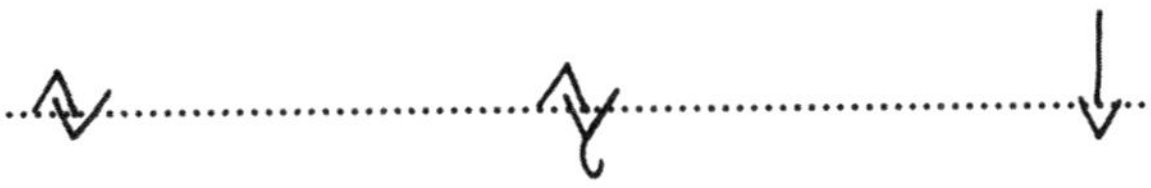

arrive arrival however

Distinguishing outlines

lovely | lively | new/knew | now | no | know

Word groupings

in our | in our view | in our opinion | well known | in which

no doubt | upside down

Task 23.3

Read and write the following sentences

MP3

1
2
3
4
5

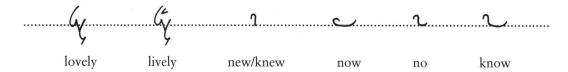

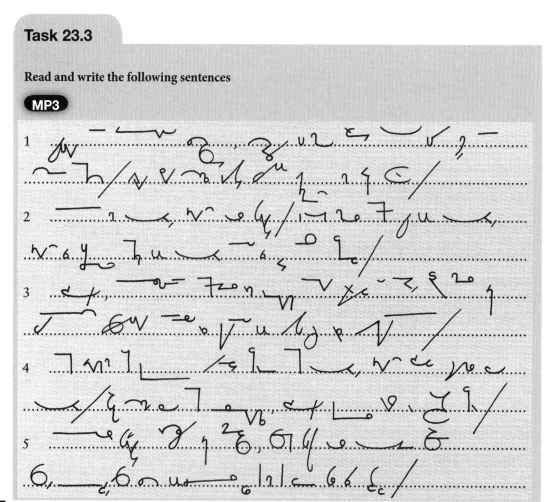

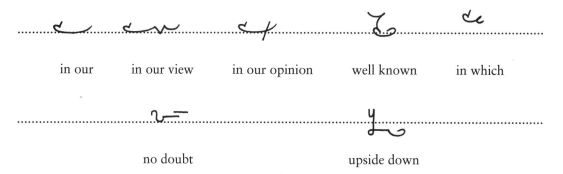

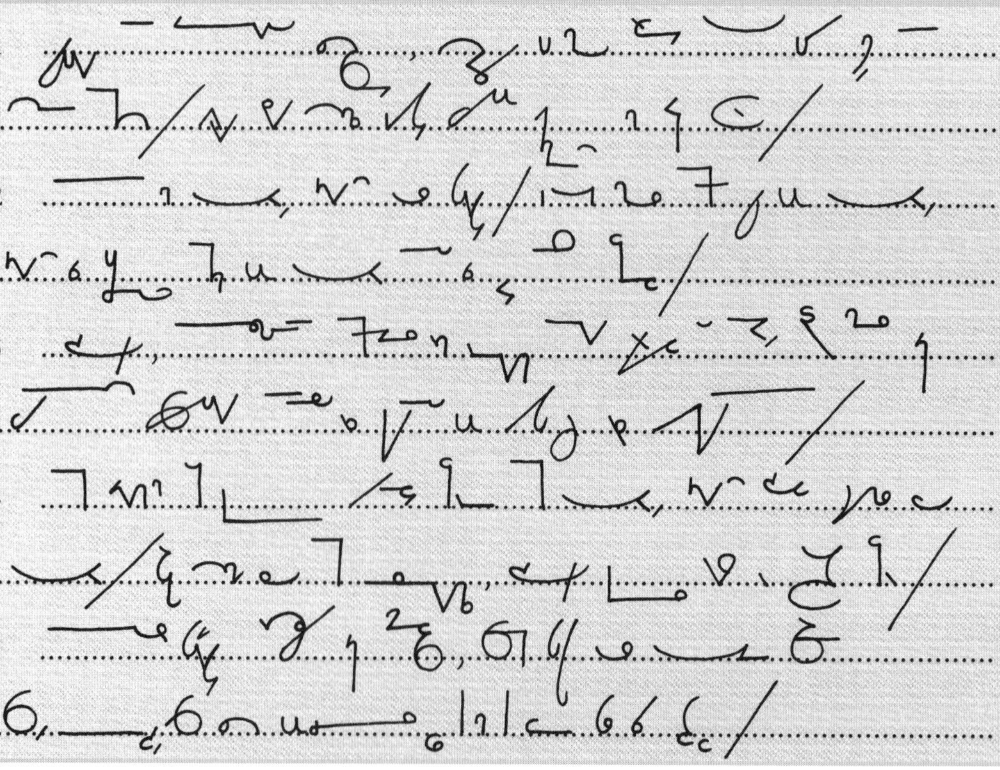

Task 23.4

Read and write 'Police to stop rising tide of violence'

MP3

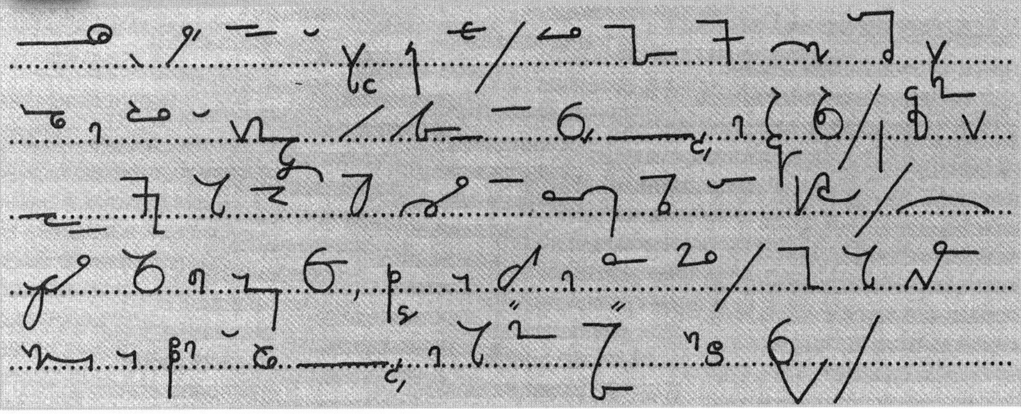

Task 23.5

Read and write 'Successful airline business'

MP3

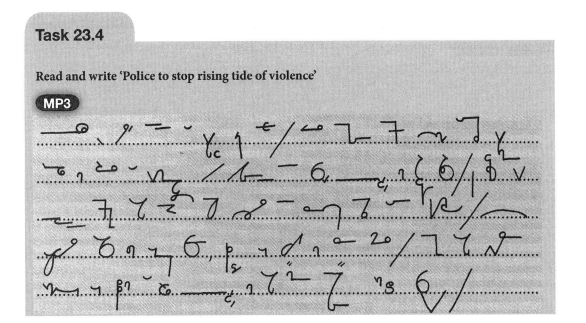

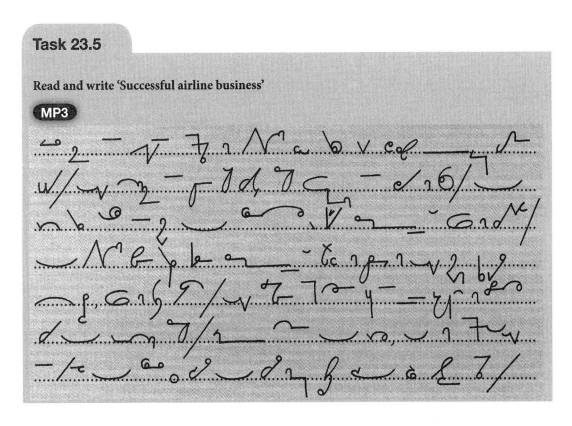

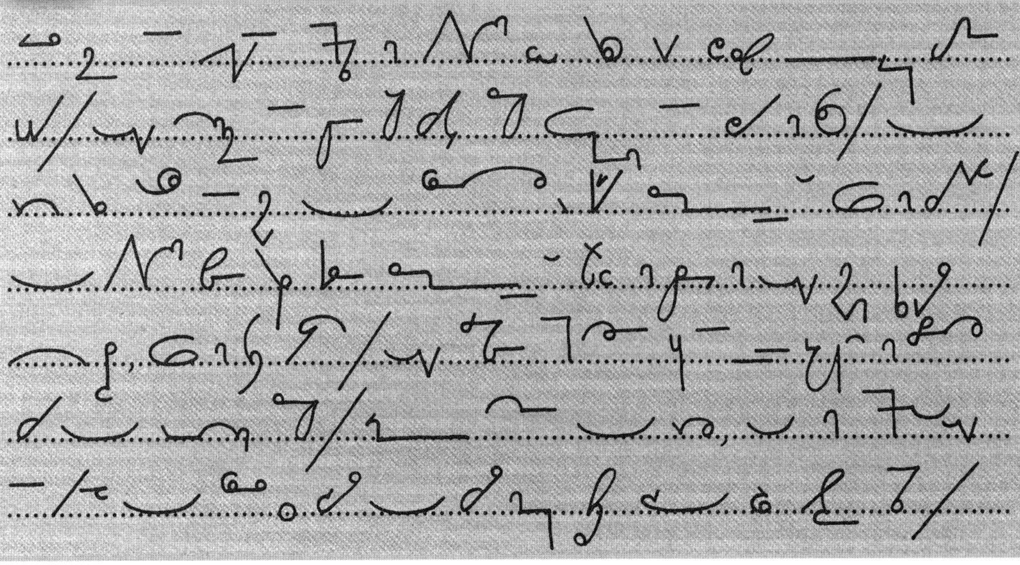

Unit 24
CN blends

Revision:

Letter **C** represents common words **once** .... or **offence** ....

or when hanging from the writing line **local** ....

and when used as a word ending -**NCE** ....

Letter N represents common words **and** or **new/knew** ....

or when hanging from the writing line **begin/began/begun** ....

and when used as a word ending -**SHUN** ....

CN blend ....

The CN blend looks like a letter **N** written in reverse. Start as if to write letter C, but straighten the stroke into N. A vowel always occurs between the **C** and **N**. The **C** may have a hard or soft sound:

can cancel candidate contain concern continue continually

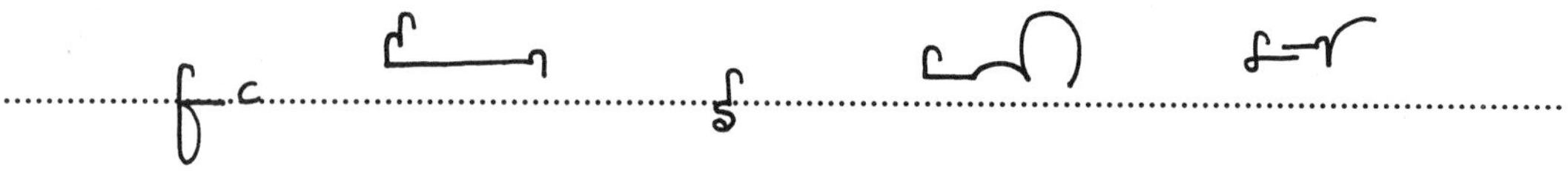

confidence concentration conscious contamination constitutional

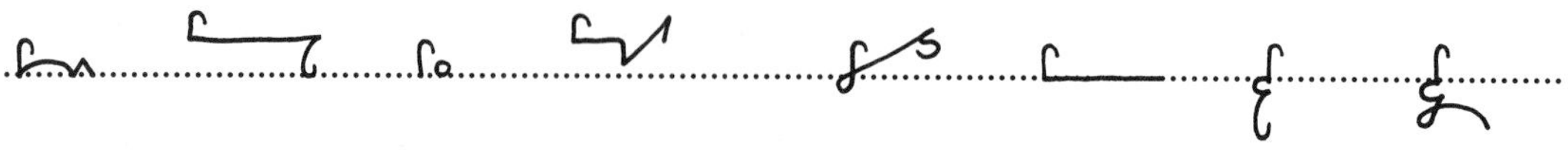

cinema central census centenary censorship cinder cynical cynicism

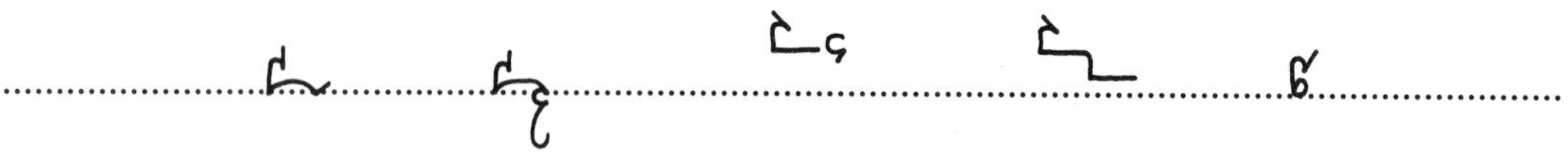

economy economical accountancy accountant icons

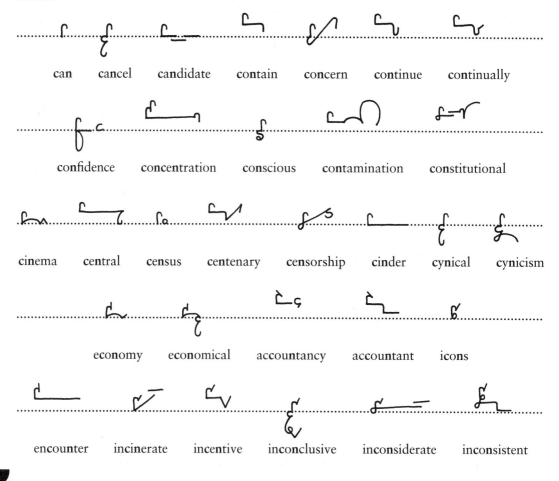

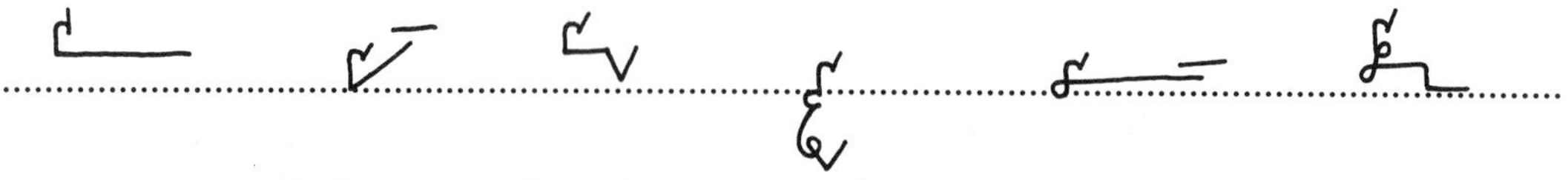

encounter incinerate incentive inconclusive inconsiderate inconsistent

SCN blend ……

Write the **S** circle inside the **CN** blend:

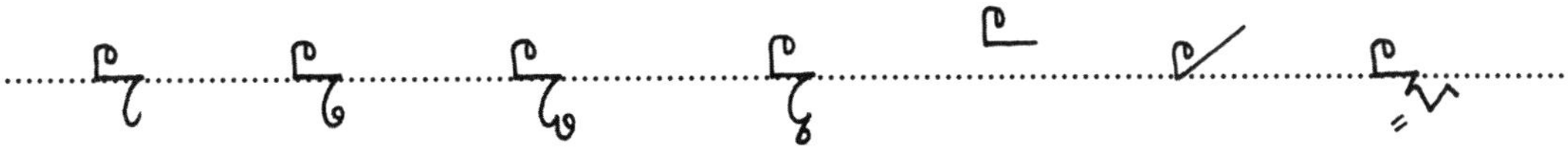

scandal scandals scandalous scandalize scant scanner Scandinavia

Task 24.1

Read and write the following sentences

MP3

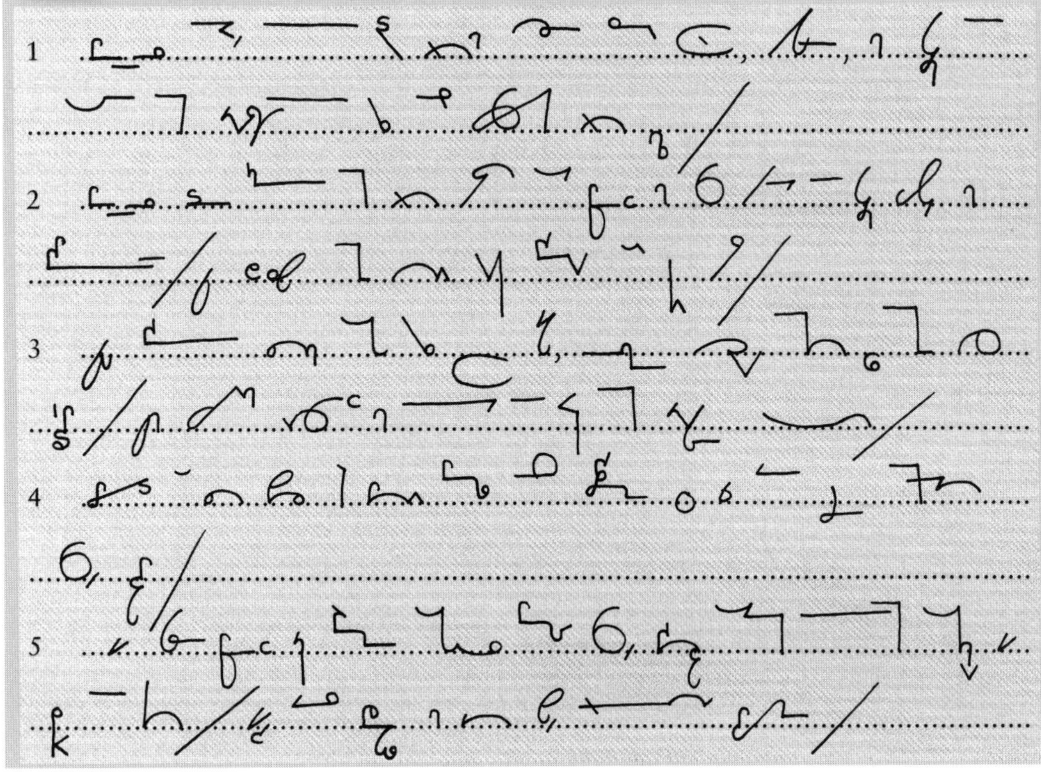

CNV blend ……

Slope the **CN** blend to form the first part of letter **V**:

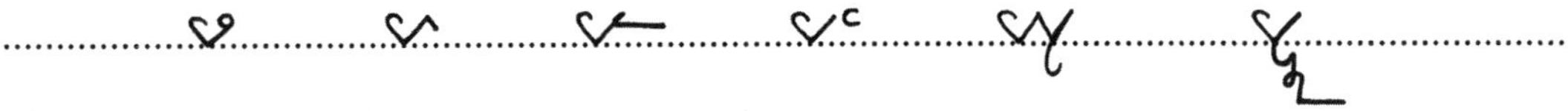

canvas convey convict convince convivial convalescent

CNVR blend ...  ......

converse conversation converge convert conversant

CNVN blend ...  ....

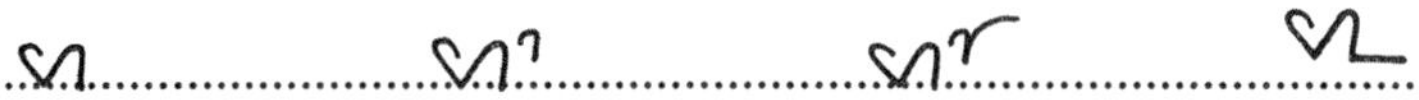

convene convention conventional convent

Task 24.2

Read and write the following sentences

MP3

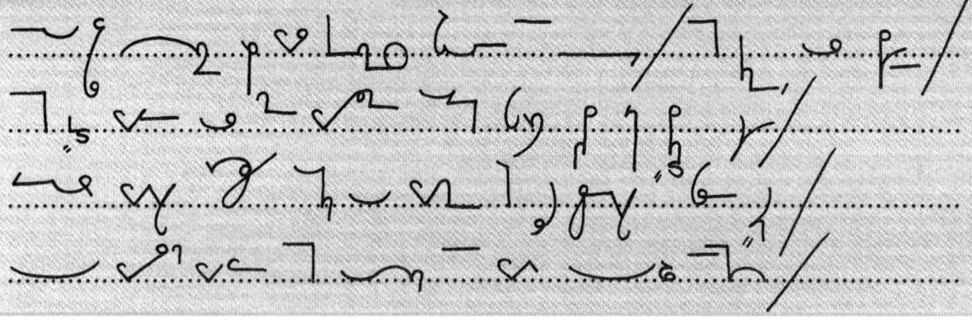

1

2

3

4

Special outlines – Unit 24

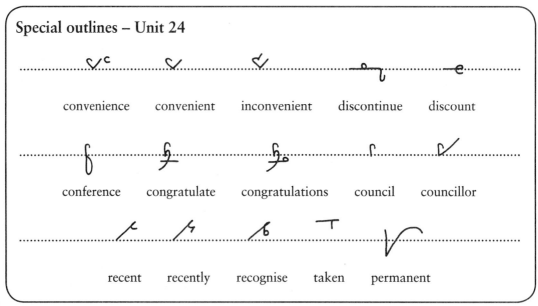

convenience convenient inconvenient discontinue discount

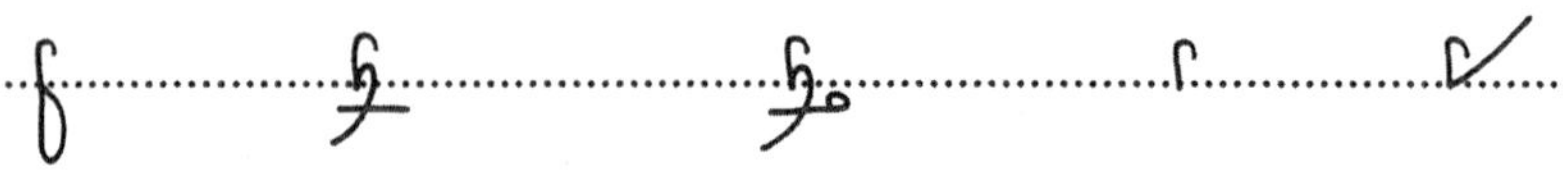

conference congratulate congratulations council councillor

recent recently recognise taken permanent

Distinguishing outlines

county country century cannot can't

Word groupings

county council borough council town council council tax

I can we can you can can you

Task 24.3

Read and write the following sentences

MP3

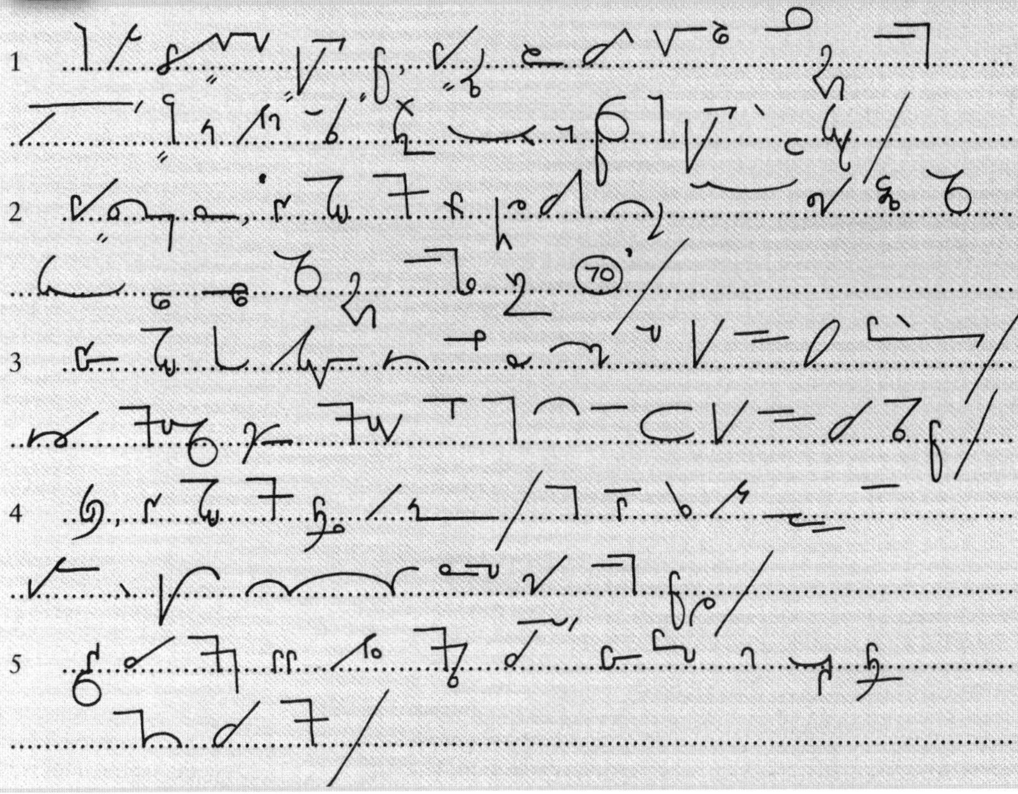

Task 24.4

Read and write 'Fines for dropping litter'

MP3

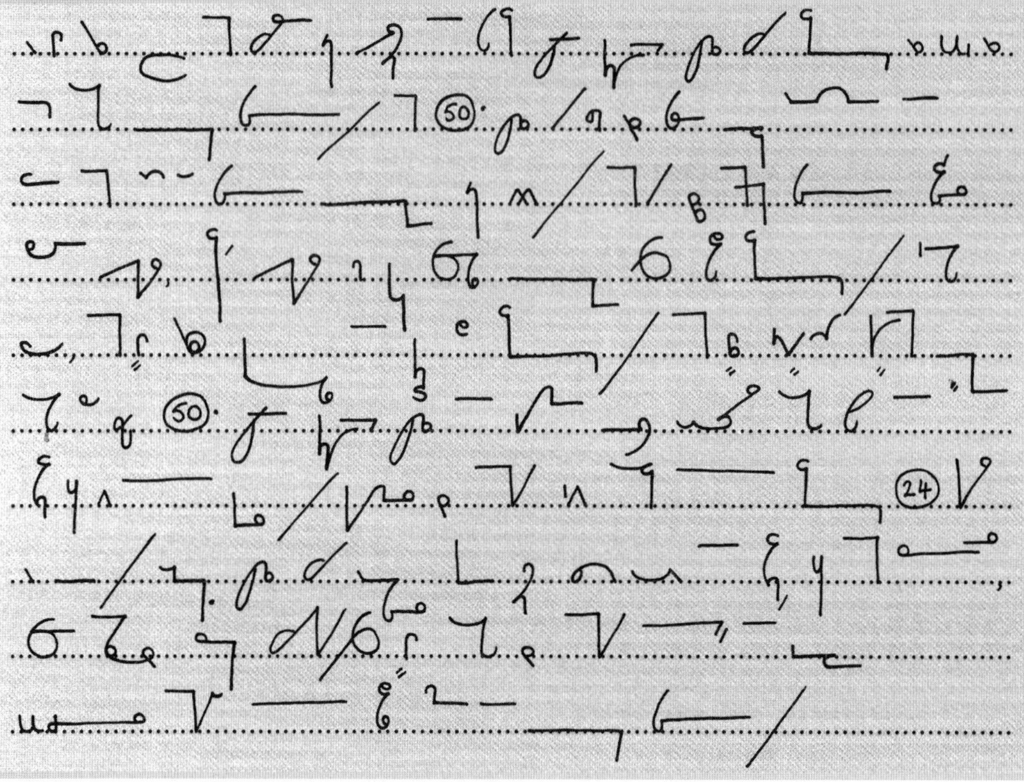

Task 24.5

Read and write 'Fake cash machines'

MP3

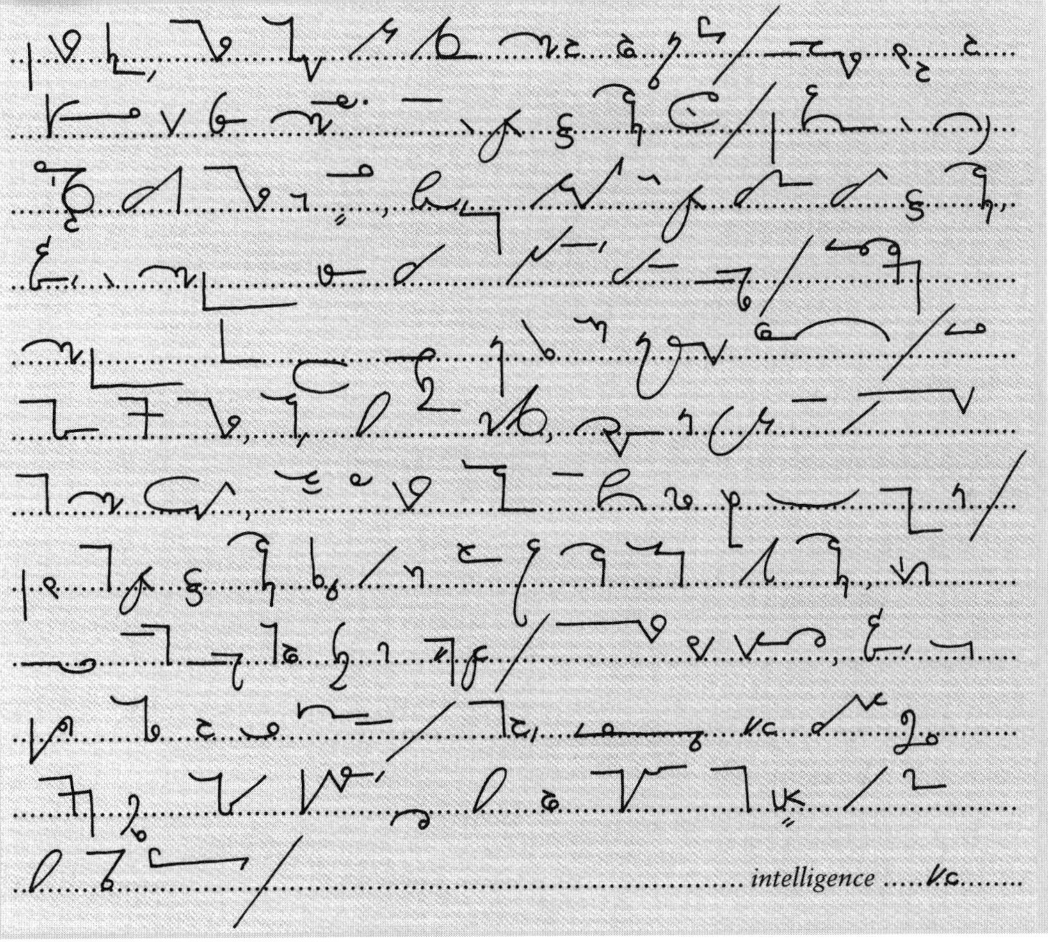

Unit 25
P blends

Revision:
Letter **P** represents common words **police**, **pence** or **page** ....

Letter **V** represents common words **very**, **have** or **versus** ....

when hanging from the writing line **evidence** ....

and when above the line **above** ....

and when used as word ending -**EVER whatever** .... **however** ....

PV blend ....

Slope letter P to form the first stroke of letter V:

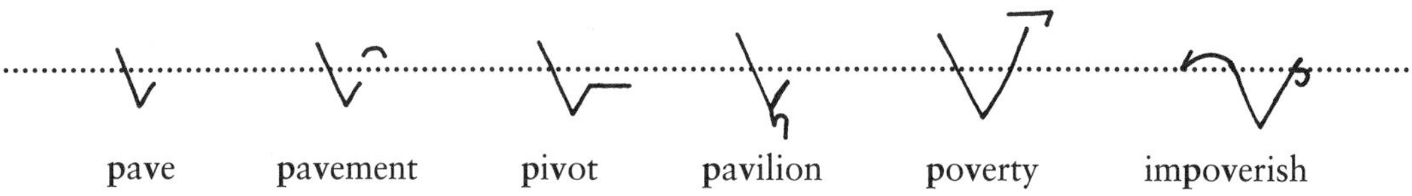

Revision:
Letter **L** represents common word **letter** ....,

when hanging from the writing line **a lot/a lot of** ....,

when disjoined and written downwards, words ending -**INGLE** ....

and when disjoined and written upwards, words ending -**ALITY**, etc ....

PL blend ....

Written as letter L in the P position at the beginning of words. Only ever used when PL occur together – **never** a vowel between PL.

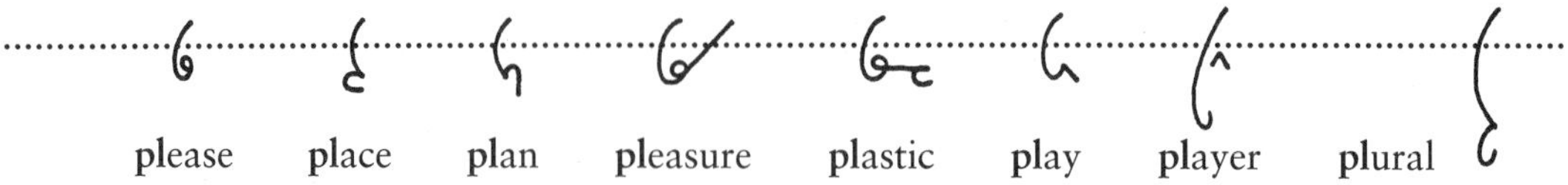

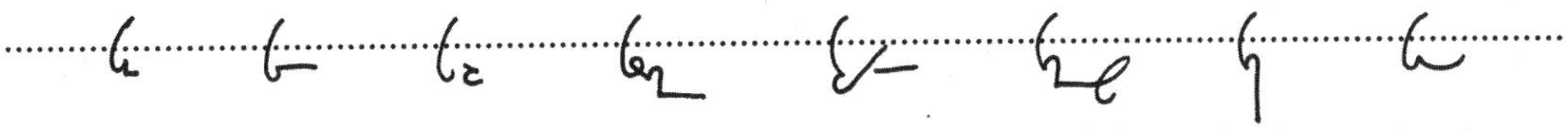

plea plead plank pleasant placard plentiful plinth plough

An initial vowel or an **S** may be added:

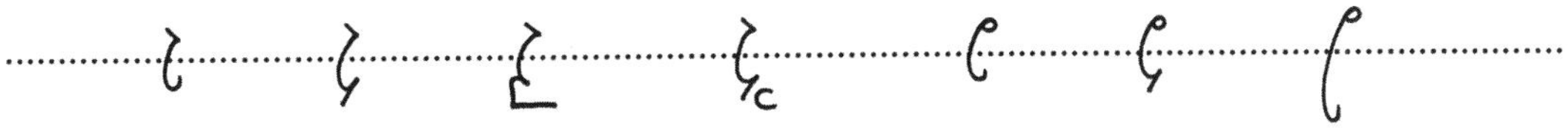

apple apply applicant appliance supple supply supplier

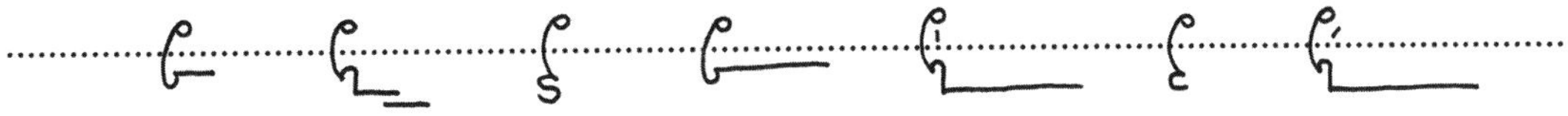

split splendid splash splatter splendour splice splinter

In the **middle** or at the **end** of a word, **PL** is written through the preceding consonant:

reply replica replay duplicate display deploy sample amplify

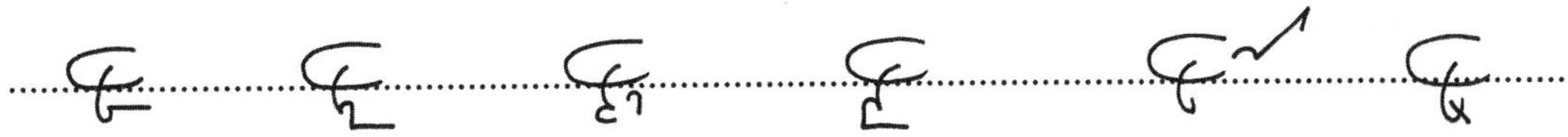

complete complaint complication complacent complimentary complex

Task 25.1

Read and write the following sentences

MP3

1
2

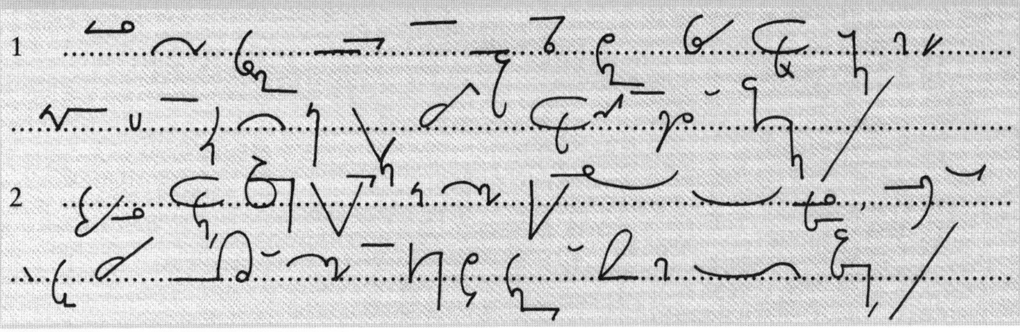

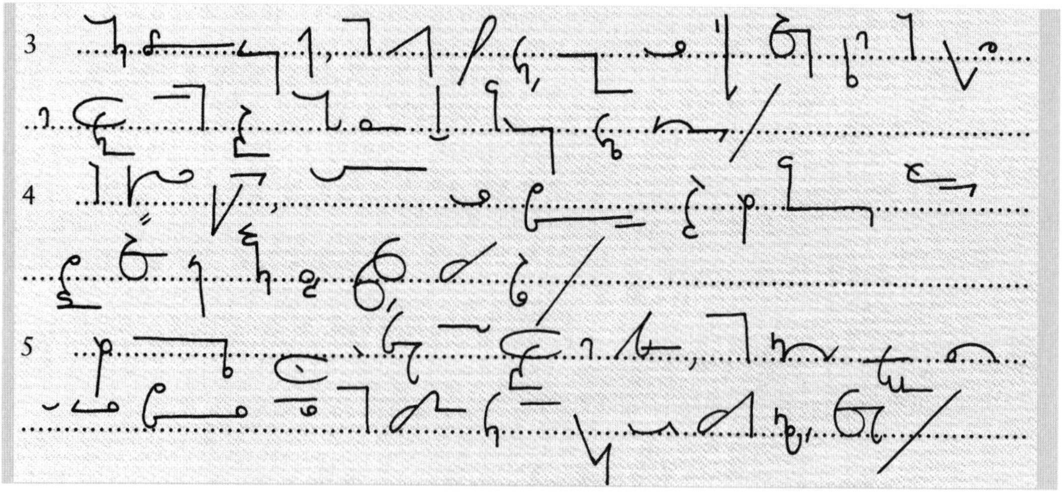

XPL blends ....

Write the first stroke of **X** and then blend **PL** with it:

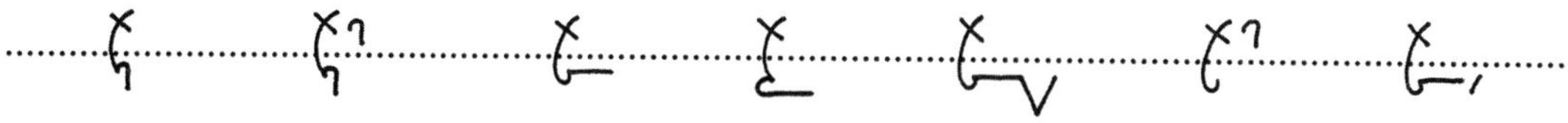

explain	**expl**anation	**expl**oit	**expl**icit	**expl**etive	**expl**osion	**expl**oding

XPLR blends ....

Write the first stroke of **X** and then blend with **PL** lengthened to include **R**:

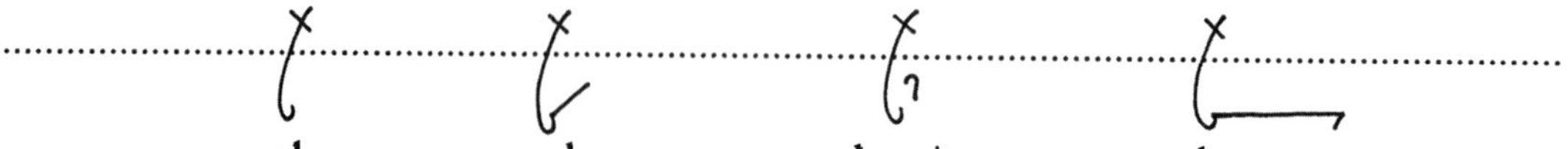

explore	**explorer**	**exploration**	**exploratory**

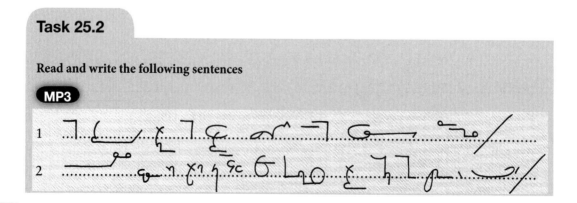

Task 25.2

Read and write the following sentences

MP3

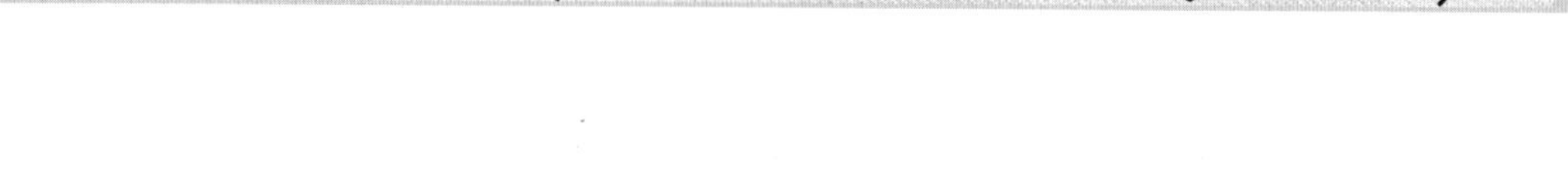

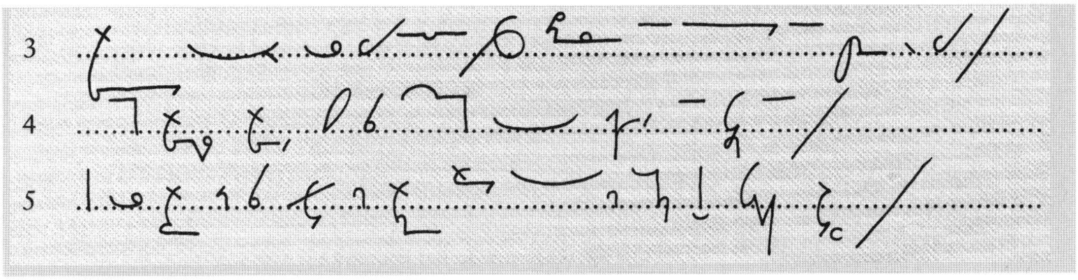

PB blends 

The circle of **B** is written on the side of **P**:

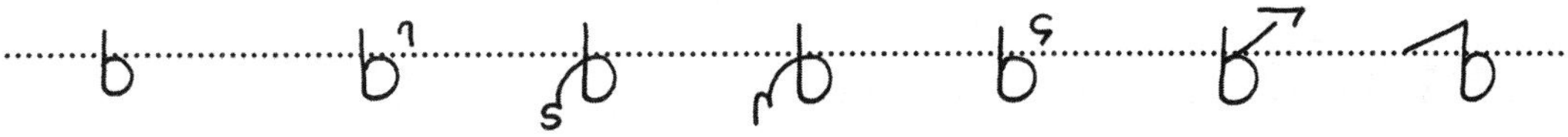

public* publication publish publican publicity puberty republic

Special outlines – Unit 25

people employ employment employer public*

Distinguishing outlines

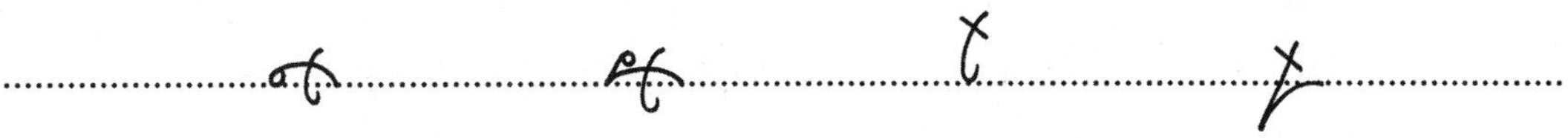

sample simple excel expel

Word groupings

members of the public we should be pleased we are pleased to know

it is my pleasure | I am pleased | your reply

Task 25.3

Read and write the following sentences

MP3

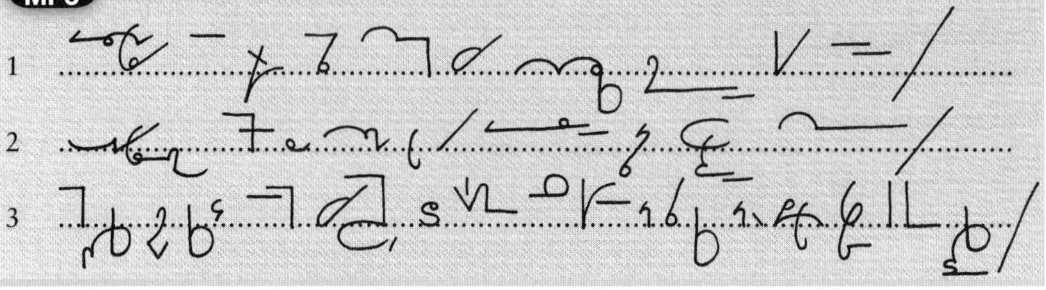

Task 25.4

Read and write 'Riverside Festival success'

MP3

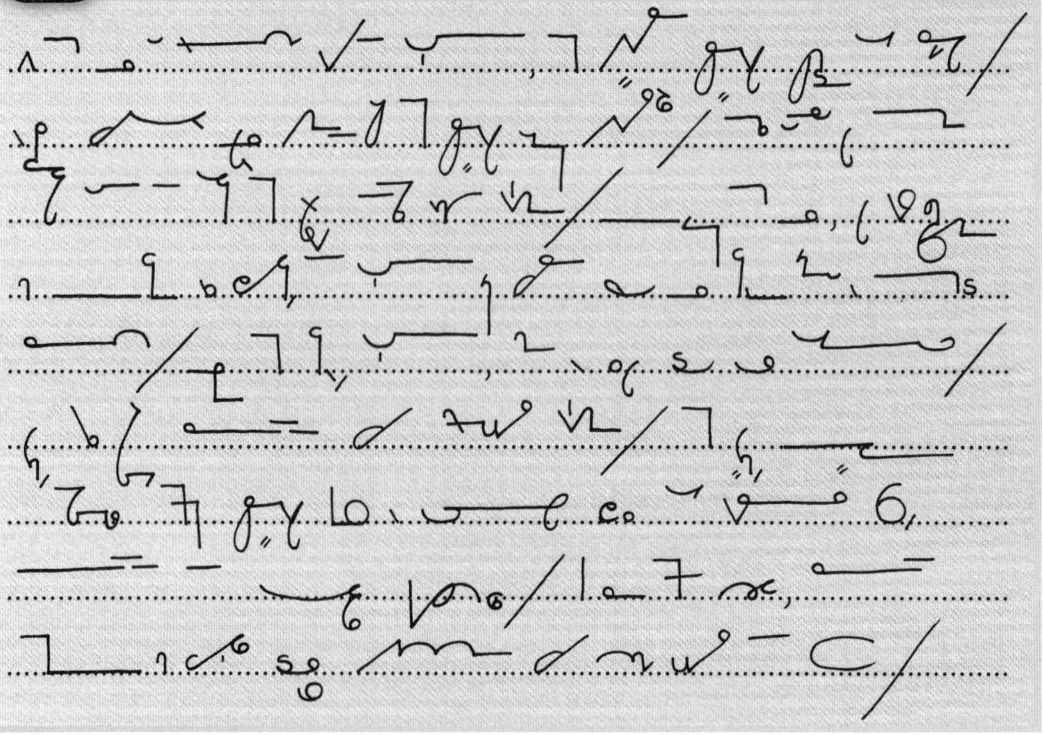

Task 25.5

Read and write 'Waste collection'

MP3

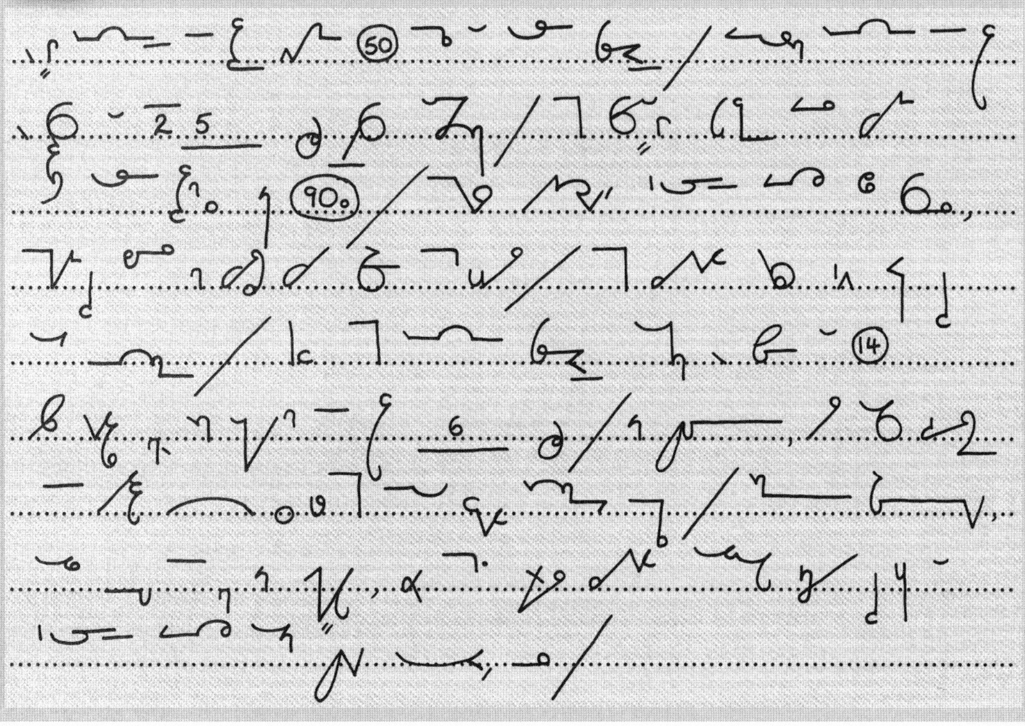

Unit 26

Full vowels used as word endings

Full vowel A

Revision:

Full vowel **A** represents common words **able**/**able to**, **ability** or **after** .........,

is used for words beginning **AU** .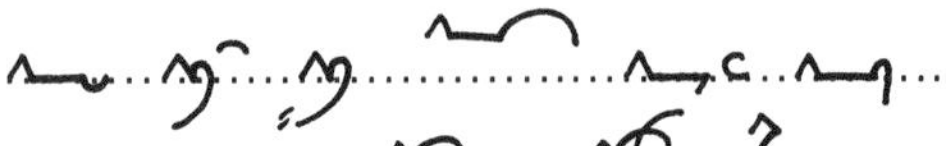...,

when above the line for words beginning **AUTO**- 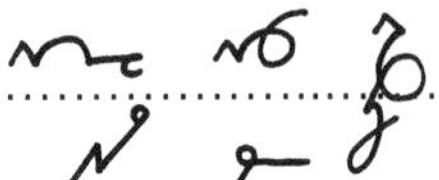..........

and is used before letter **R** .....

(Revise theory at Unit 9)

Full vowel A, which represents the words **able** and **ability**, may be disjoined from the first part of an outline to represent words ending -ABLE and -ABILITY:

li**able**/li**ability** cap**able**/cap**ability** reli**able**/reli**ability** vi**able**/vi**ability**

Other letters may be added to extend the word ending:

valu**ables** l**abelling** c**abled** dis**abled** reason**ably** honour**ably** favour**ably**

Full vowel I

Revision:

Full vowel **I** represents common words **I**, **eye** or **intelligent** ..............

A better outline results if **I** is written in full before letter **L** ......

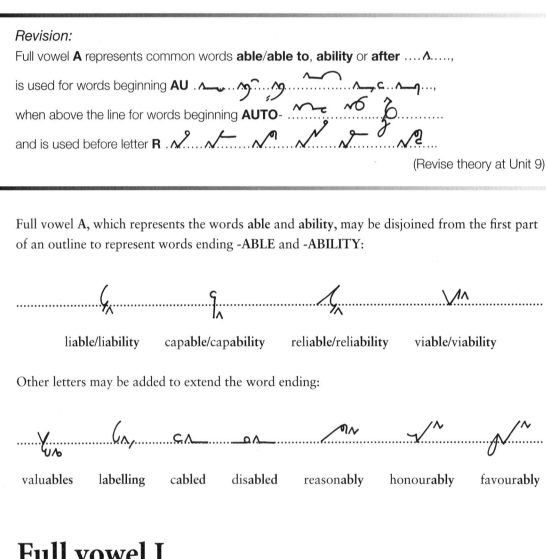

Full vowel I may be disjoined from the first part of an outline to represent words ending -IBLE and -IBILITY:

visible/visibility sensible/sensibility accessible/accessibility plausible/plausibility

Full vowel **I,** with the **I** indicator added, represents -**IBLY**:

compat**ibly** terr**ibly** leg**ibly** poss**ibly**

Task 26.1

Write the following words in neat Teeline outlines

MP3

available/availability ...... durable/durability ...... gables ...... lovable ...... nibbles ......

adaptable/adaptability ...... gullible/gullibility ...... horribly ...... flexible/flexibility ......

Full vowel E

Revision:

Full vowel **E** represents common words **electric** .... or **England** ....

E is written in full before letters **P** and **Q**

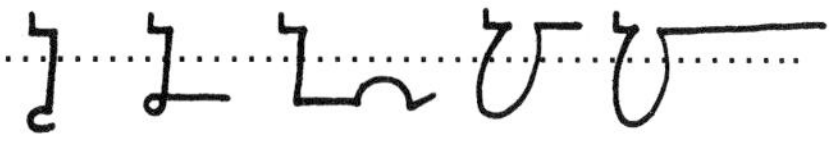

Full vowel E may be disjoined from the first part of an outline to represent words ending -EB(B)LE and -EBEL. Other letters may be added to extend the word ending:

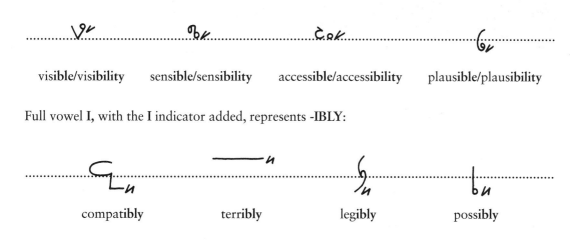

rebel pebbles trebling pebbly

Full vowel O

Revision:
Full vowel **O** represents common word **or** ....

Full vowel O may be disjoined from the first part of an outline to represent words ending -OB(B)LE, -OUBLE and -OBILITY. Other letters may be added to extend the word ending:

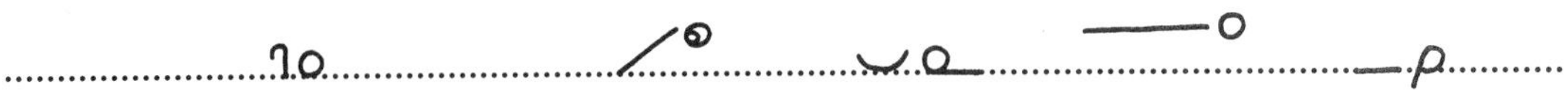

noble/nobility/knobble roubles wobbled trouble doubly

Full vowel U

Revision:
Full vowel **U** represents common word **you** ....
Above the line full **U** represents words beginning **UPPER-** ....
Written on the line **U** represents words beginning **ULTRA-** ....

Full vowel U may be disjoined from the first part of an outline to represent words ending -UB(B)LE and -UBILITY. Other letters may be added to extend the word ending:

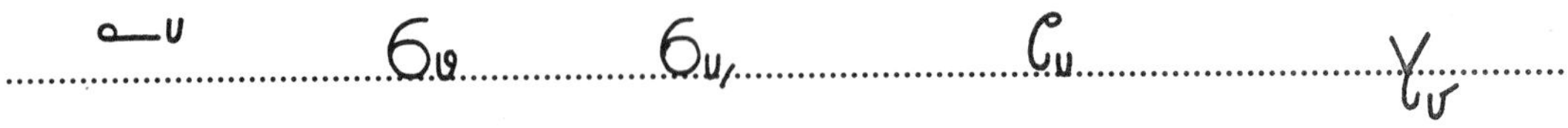

stubble bubbles bubbling soluble/solubility volubly

Task 26.2

Read and write the following sentences

MP3

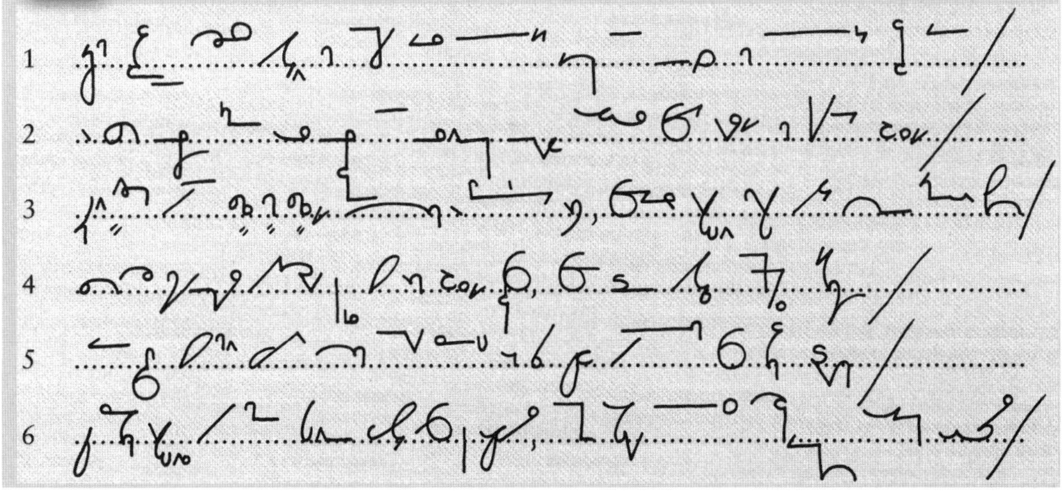

Special Outlines – Unit 26

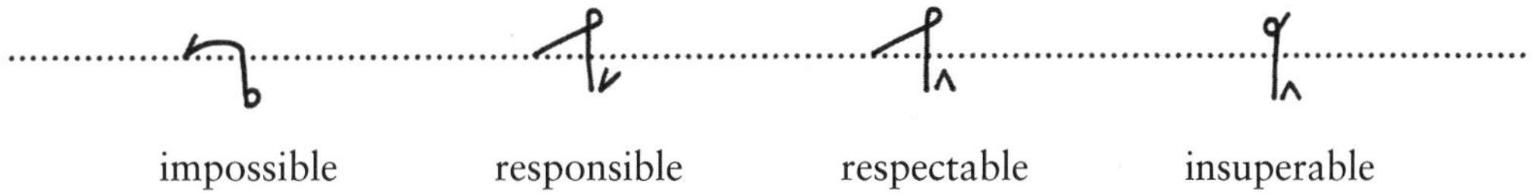

Task 26.3

Read and write the following sentences

MP3

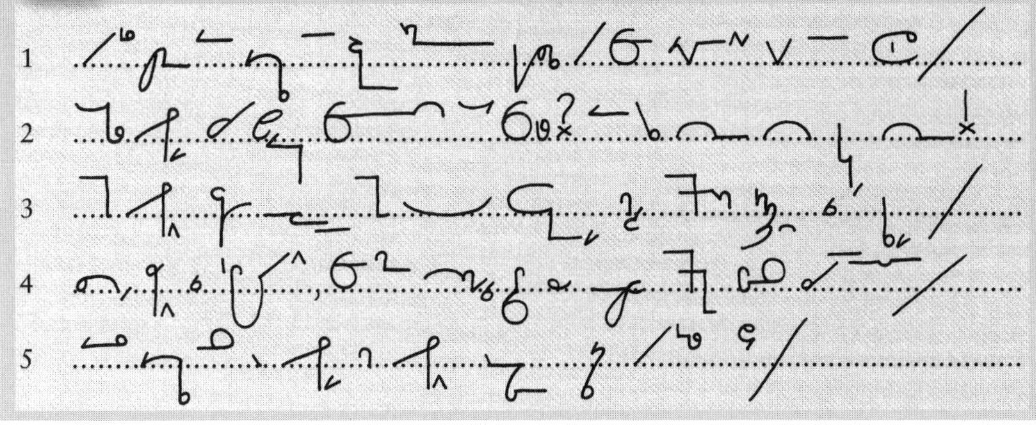

Task 26.4

Read and write 'Disabled charity busker's parking ticket'

MP3

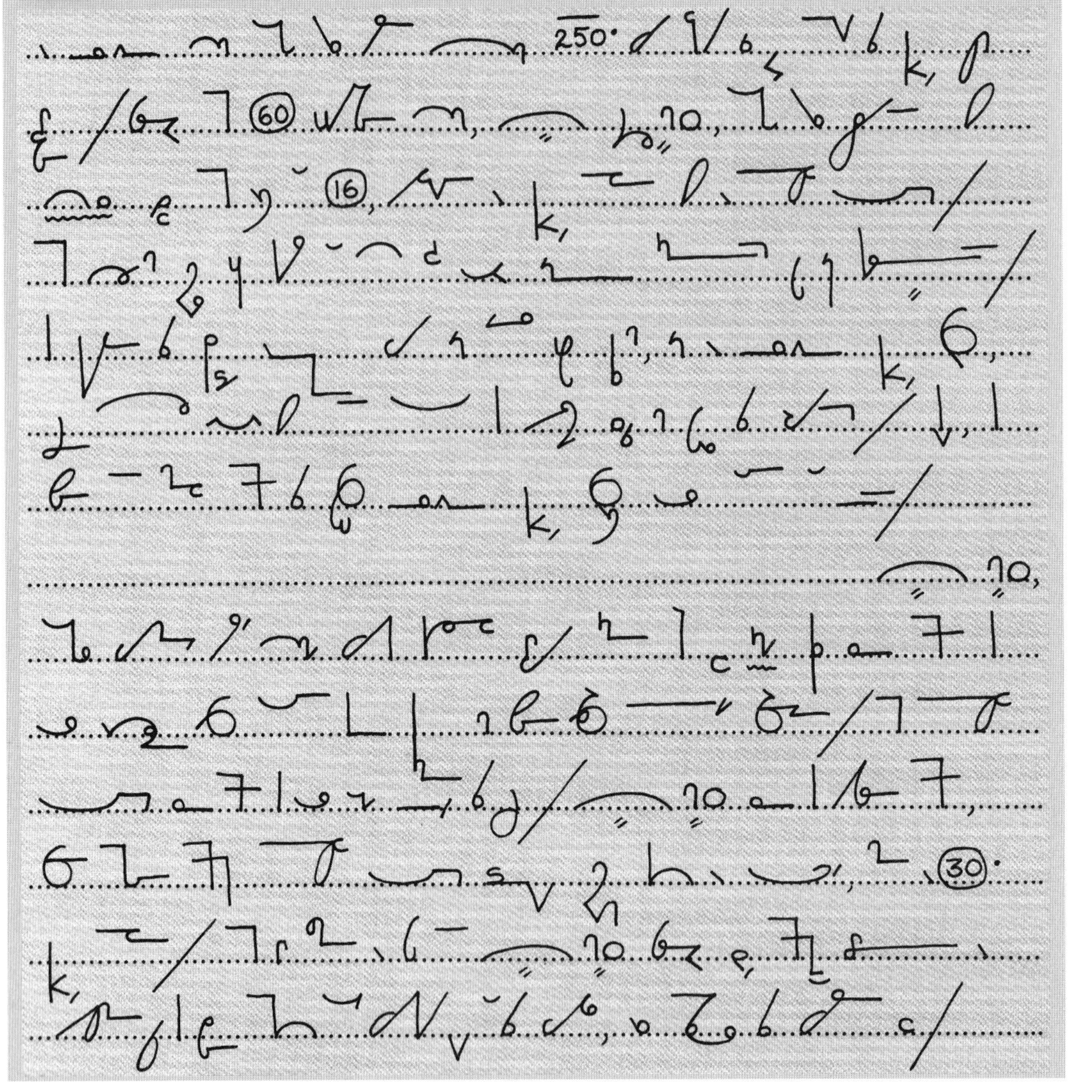

Unit 27
More word beginnings and endings

Words beginning UNDER-

Full vowel **U**, with the **DR** blend attached represents words ending **UNDER-**. This may be joined or disjoined from the part of the outline which follows. It is also used for the word **under**:

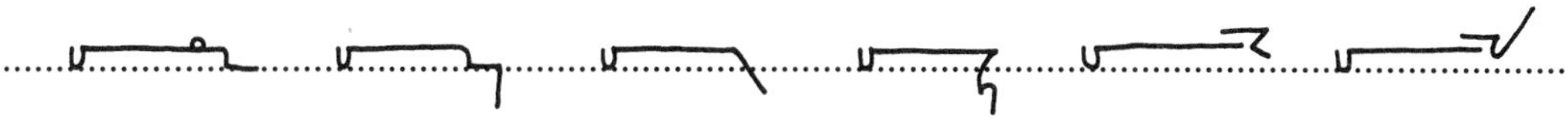

understand underneath underhand underline undertake undertaker

Words beginning TRANS-

Omit letter **N** and write **TRS**:

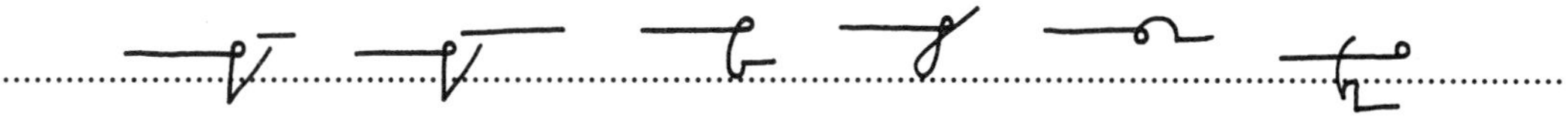

transport transporter translate transfer transmit transplant

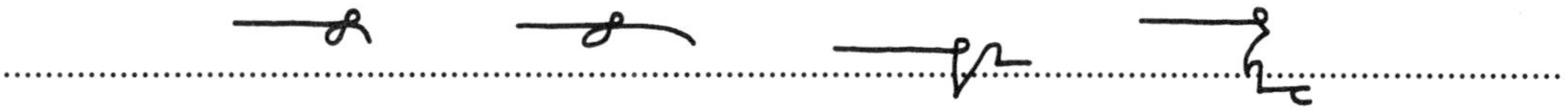

transform transformer transparent transatlantic

Words beginning OVER-

Write the **O** indicator **over** the rest of the outline:

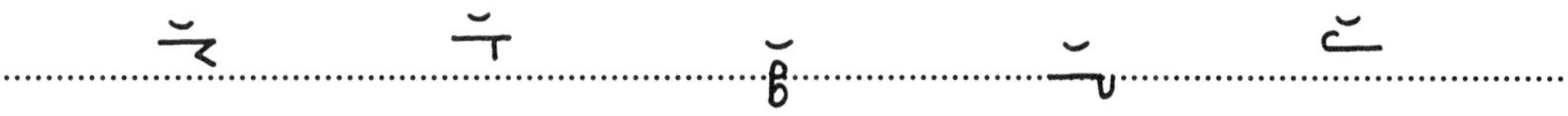

overtake overtaken overseas overdue overcoat

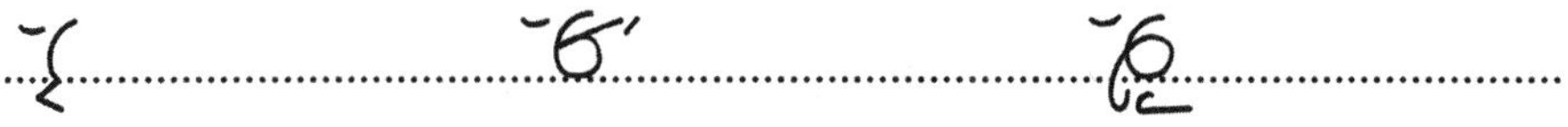

overlook **over**bearing **over**balanced

Words ending -OVER

Write **VR under** the first part of the outline. Very useful at the end of a sentence:

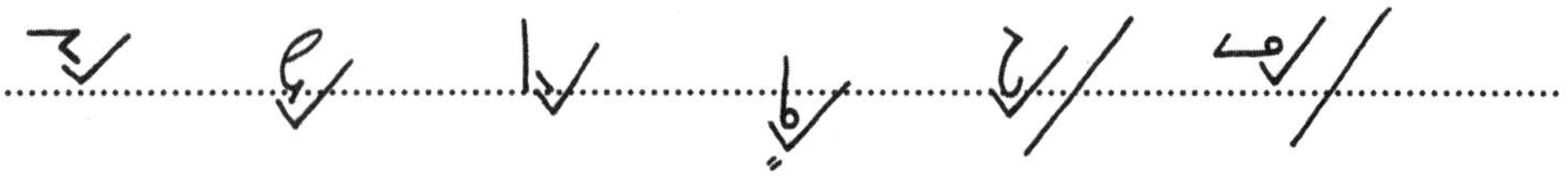

takeover flyover hangover Passover all over. it is over.

Task 27.1

Read and write the following sentences

MP3

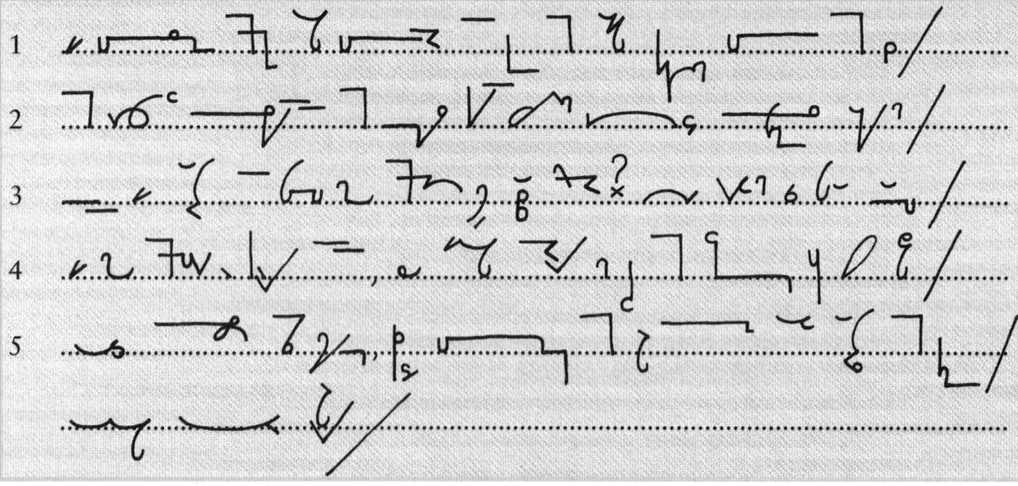

Words beginning MULTI-

Write a normal sized **M over** the remainder of the outline for words beginning **MULTI-**:

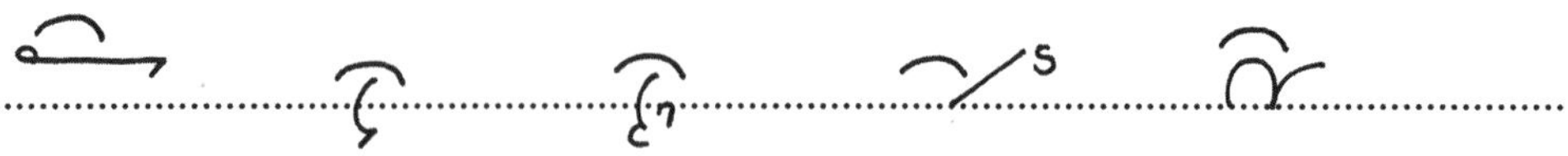

multi-storey **multi**ply **multi**plication **multi**-racial **multi**-national

Words beginning SEMI-

Write letter **S** on the line, **disjoined** but **immediately before** the rest of the word:

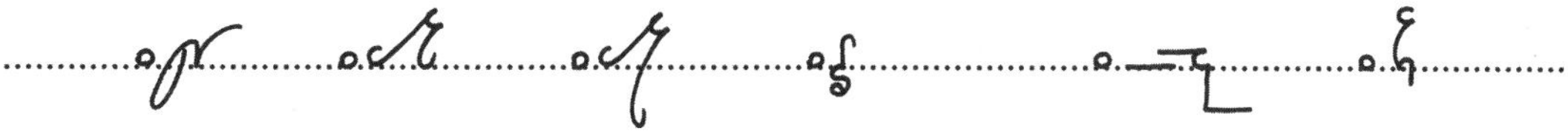

semi-final **semi**-circle **semi**-circular **semi**-conscious **semi**-detached **semi**-colon

Words ending -JECT and -JECTION

In order to avoid a difficult outline, reduce words ending **-JECT** and **-JECTION** by omitting **CT**:

inject injection object objection objectives objected

subject subjective subjected reject rejection rejected

Task 27.2

Read and write the following sentences

MP3

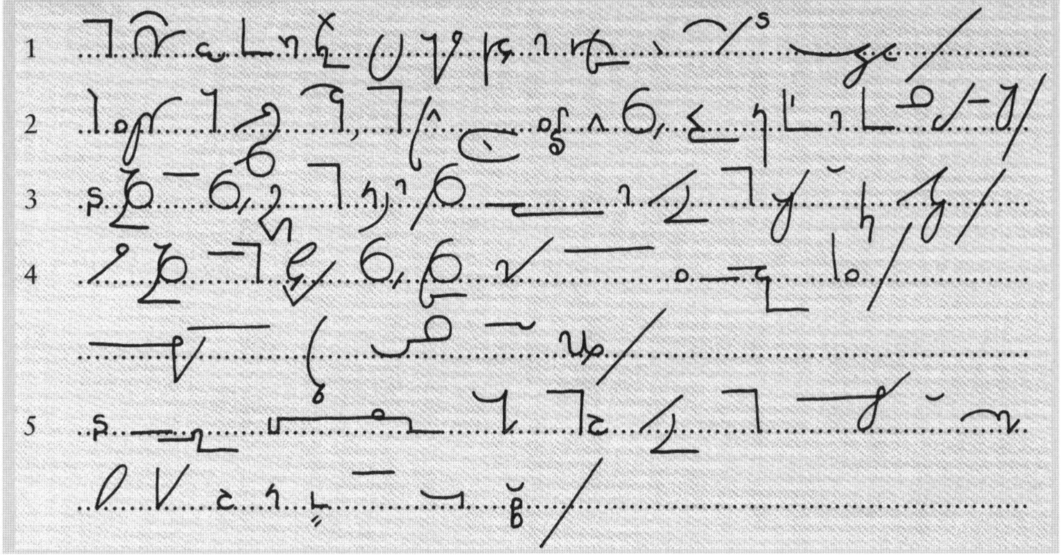

Word groupings

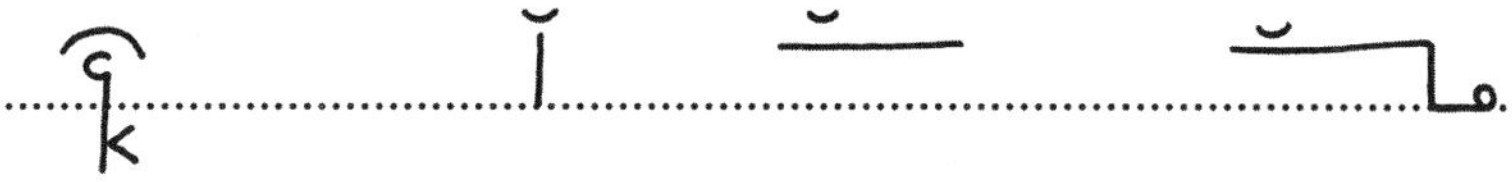

multi-storey car park | over the | over there/their | over their heads

over and over | over and over again | over and done with

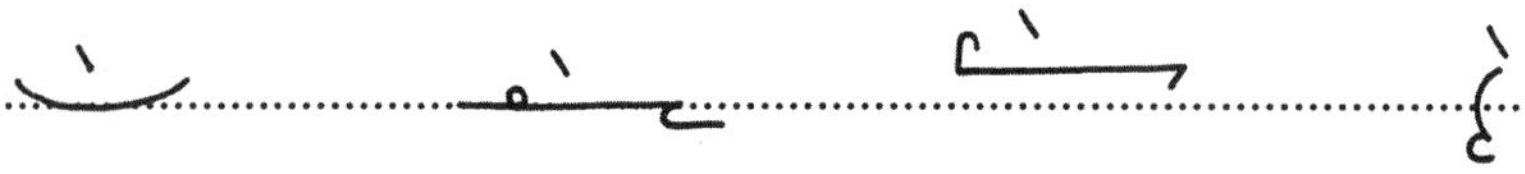

but also: all over the world | all over the district | all over the country | all over the place

Task 27.3

Read and write the following sentences

MP3

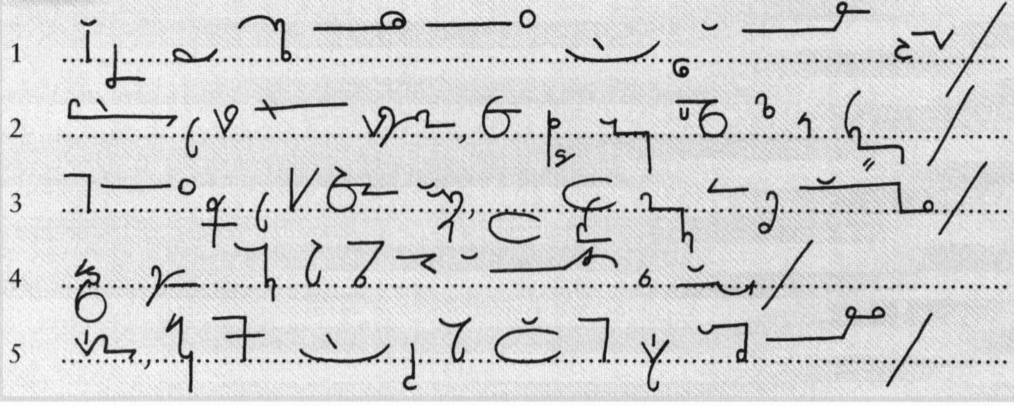

Task 27.4

Read and write 'Headteachers help police'

MP3

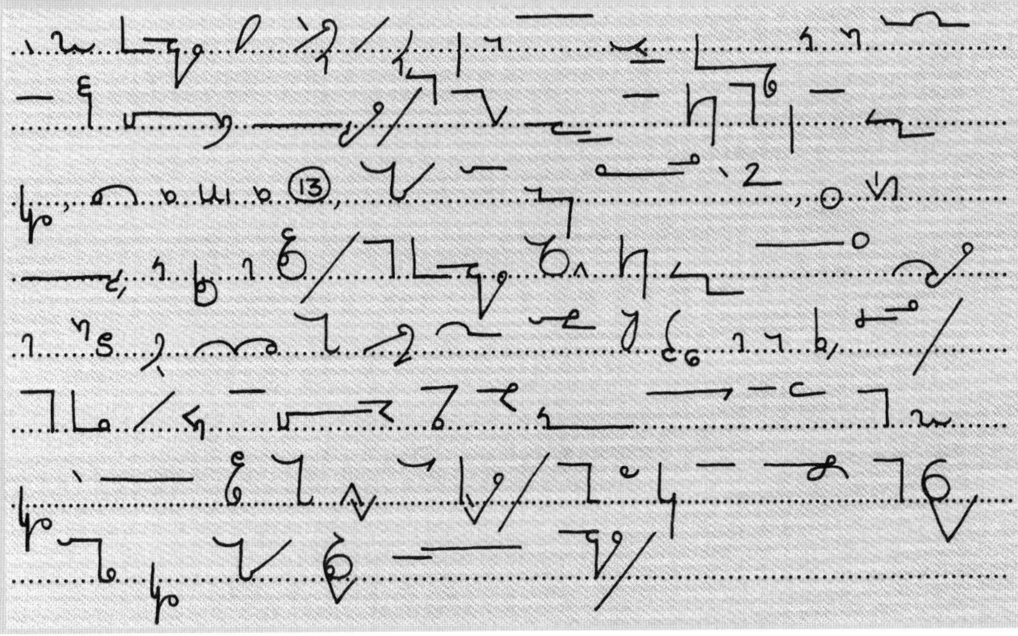

Words beginning ELECTRO- and ELECTRI-

Revision:

Full vowel **E** represents common words **electric** .... and E**ngland** ....

and words ending -**EBEL/EB(B)LE** ...

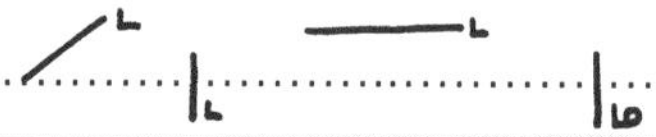

Write full vowel E disjoined and immediately in front of the rest of the word for words beginning ELECTRO- and ELECTRI-:

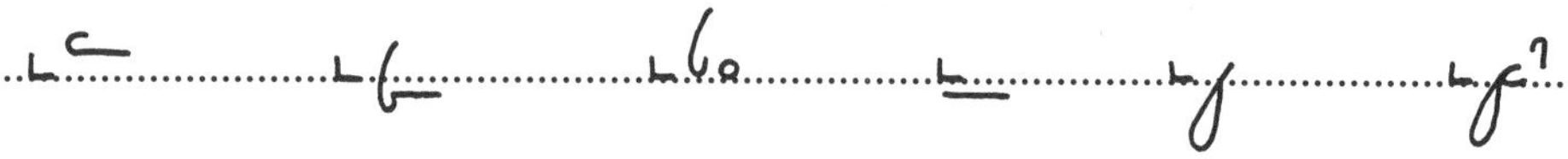

electrocute **electro**plate **electro**lysis **electro**de **electri**fy **electri**fication

Words beginning MAGNA-, MAGNE-, MAGNI- and MAGNO-

Write letters MG disjoined and on the writing line:

magnanimous **magne**tic **magni**fy **magni**ficent **magno**lia

Words beginning MICRO-

Write MC disjoined and on the writing line:

microphone **micro**wave **micro**chip **micro**scope **micro**-climate **micro**film

Task 28.1

Read and write the following sentences

MP3

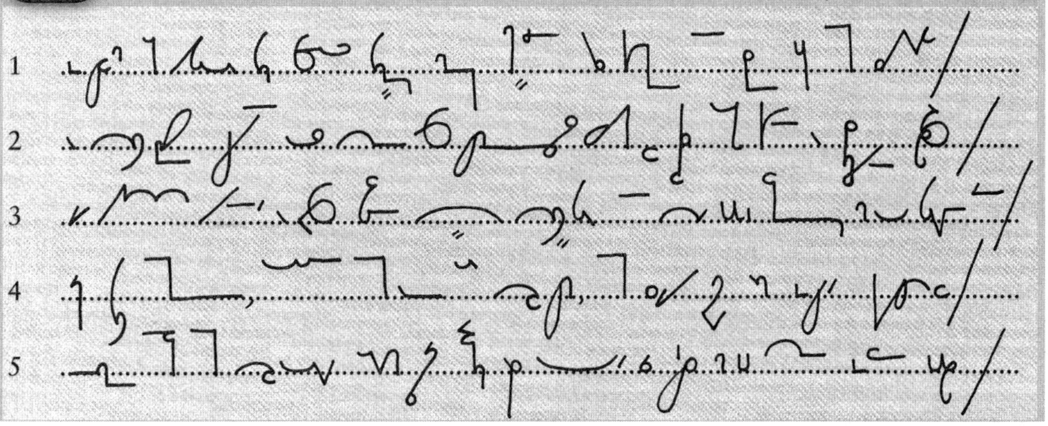

Words beginning ATOMIC-

Write **AMC** in the **T** position:

atomic energy

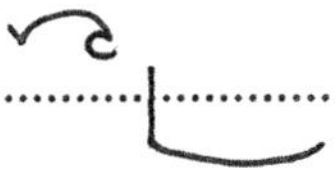

atomic power

atomic fuel

Words beginning TECH-

Write TC for the word **technical:**

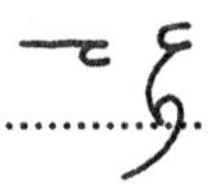

technical college

technical training

technical terms

Write TCN for the word **technological:**

technological age

technological skills

Words ending -OLOGY and -ALOGY

Write an O indicator, **disjoined** and in the T position for words ending **-OLOGY** and **-ALOGY:**

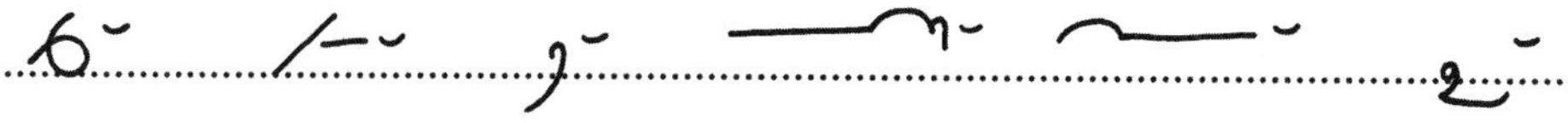

bio**logy** radio**logy** geo**logy** termin**ology** meteor**ology** zoo**logy**

gynaeco**logy** psycho**logy** physio**logy** phren**ology** gene**alogy**

Other letters may be added to the word ending:

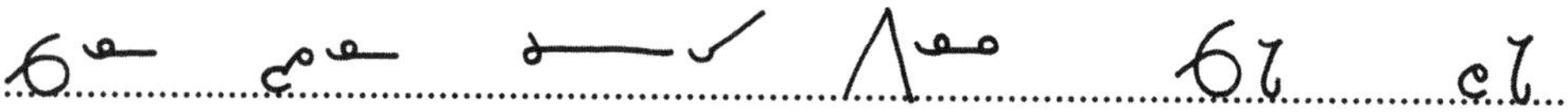

bio**logist** psycho**logist** astro**loger** archae**ologists** bio**logical** socio**logical**

Task 28.2

Read and write the following sentences

MP3

1
2
3
4
5

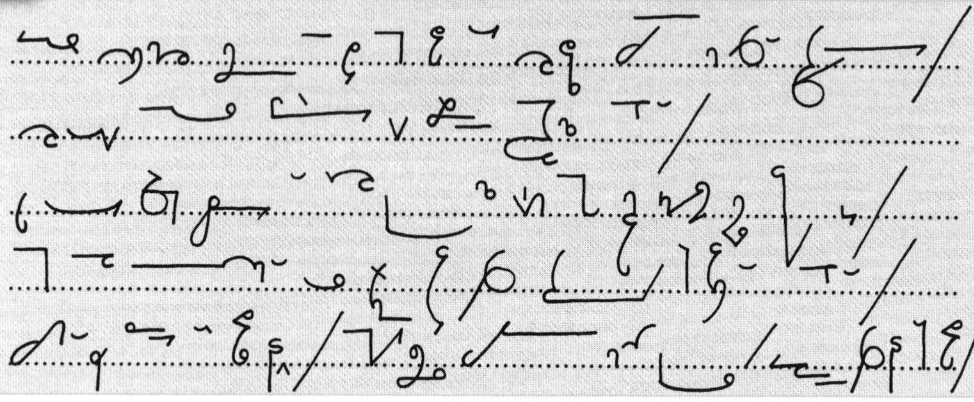

Special outlines – Unit 28

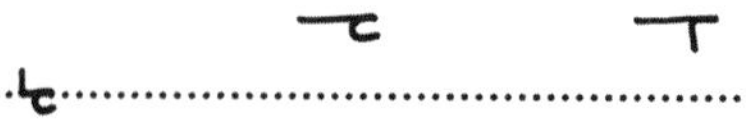

electronic technical technological

Distinguishing outlines

psychology

sociology

Word groupings

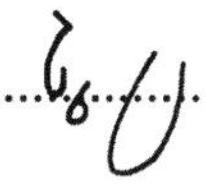

all things being equal

Task 28.3

Read and write 'Rightful owners asked to come forward'

MP3

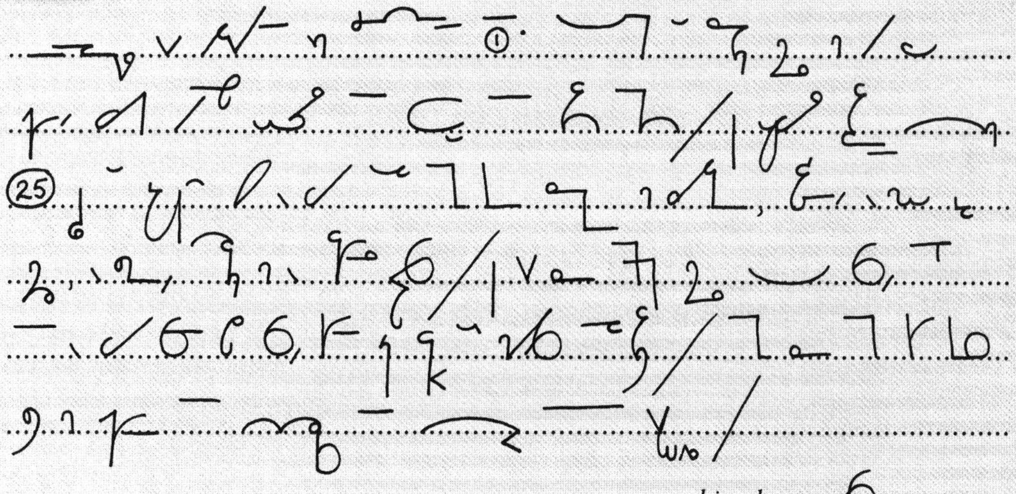

bicycle

Task 28.4

Read and write 'Appeal for new blood donors'

MP3

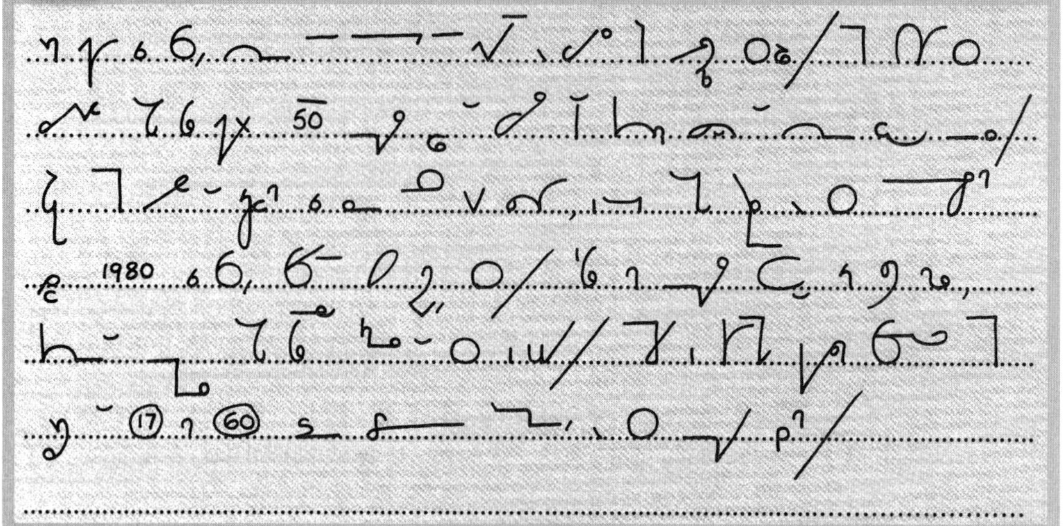

The R principle – BR, CR, GR and PR and words ending -GRAPH and -GRAM

When letter **R** follows immediately after **B, C** or **G** it is not necessary to write **R.** Simply write the letter which follows through the **B, C** or **G.**

BR

break **br**oken **br**illiant **br**own **br**andish **br**ibery **br**idge

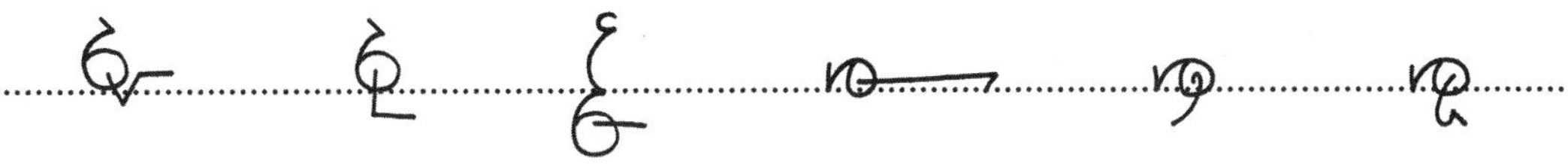

ab**br**eviate a**br**upt cele**br**ate em**br**oidery um**br**age um**br**ella

BUT when a vowel occurs between **BR** write letter **R** as part of the outline:

broad *but* board **br**ow *but* borrow **br**ain *but* barn

Task 29.1

Read and write the following sentences

MP3

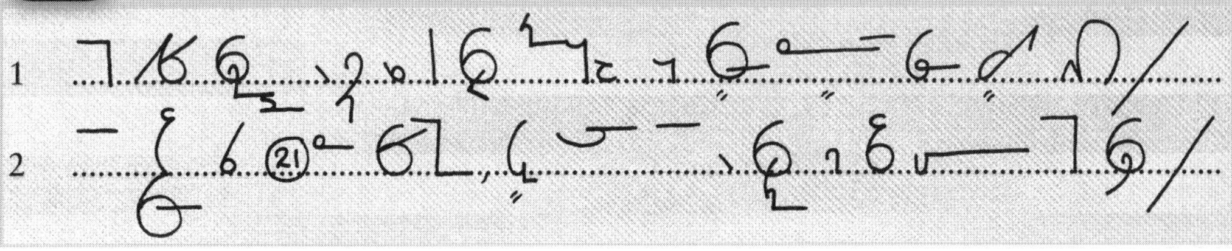

CR

crime crop crave craft cracked cramp credit

concrete secret consecrate acrobatics decrepit incredible incriminate

BUT when a vowel occurs between **CR** write letter **R** as part of the outline:

cruel *but* curl crib *but* curb crate *but* cart

Task 29.2

Read and write the following sentences

MP3

1
2

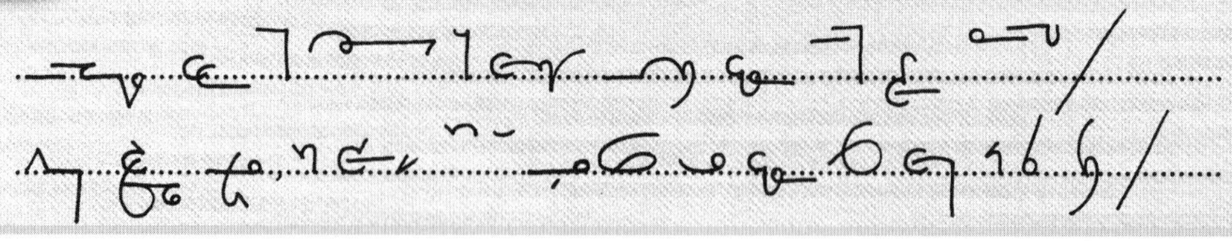

GR

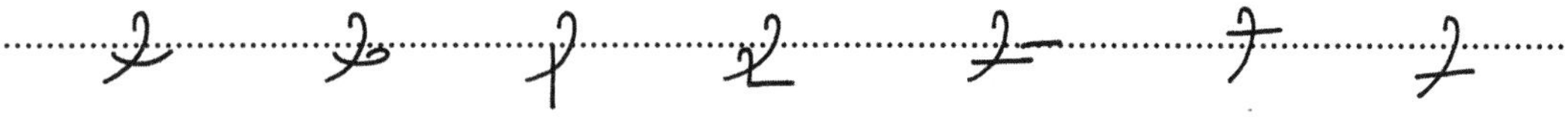

grow grown grip ground graduate great greed

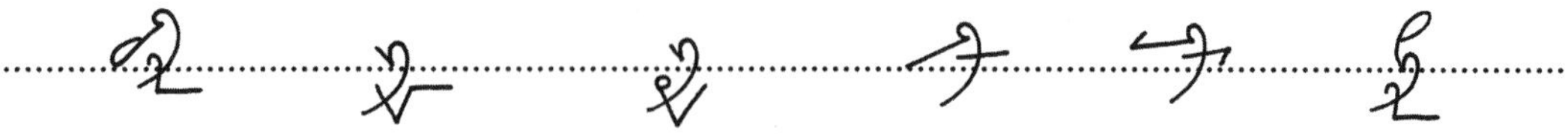

fragrant aggravate aggressive regret integrity flagrant

But when a vowel occurs between **GR** write letter **R** as part of the outline:

grim *but* germ grade *but* guard grill *but* girl

Task 29.3

Read and write the following sentences

MP3

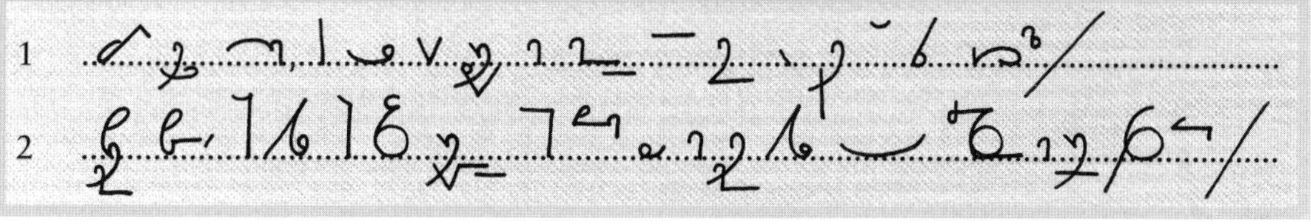

A better outline is achieved by writing **T** to the **top** of an outline and **D down** at the bottom of an outline:

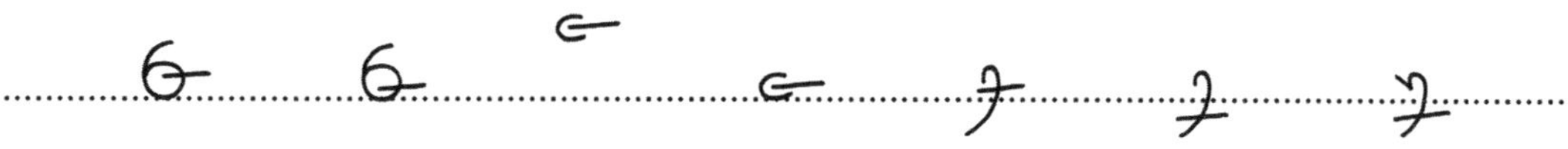

bright broad crate crude great grade agreed

If it is easier to write an outline without applying the **R** principle, then you should do so:

across cry bruise fabric agree crust grace

Task 29.4

Read and write the following sentences

MP3

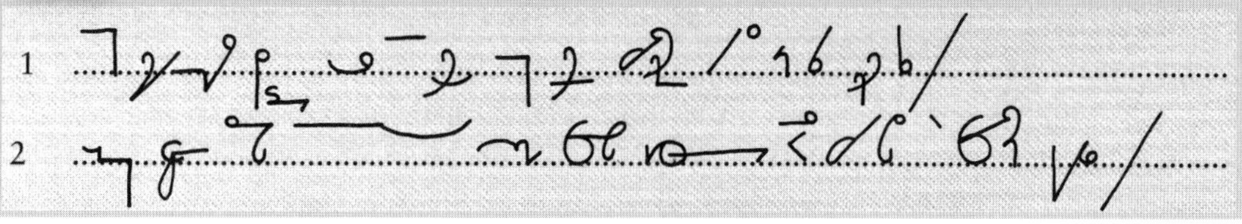

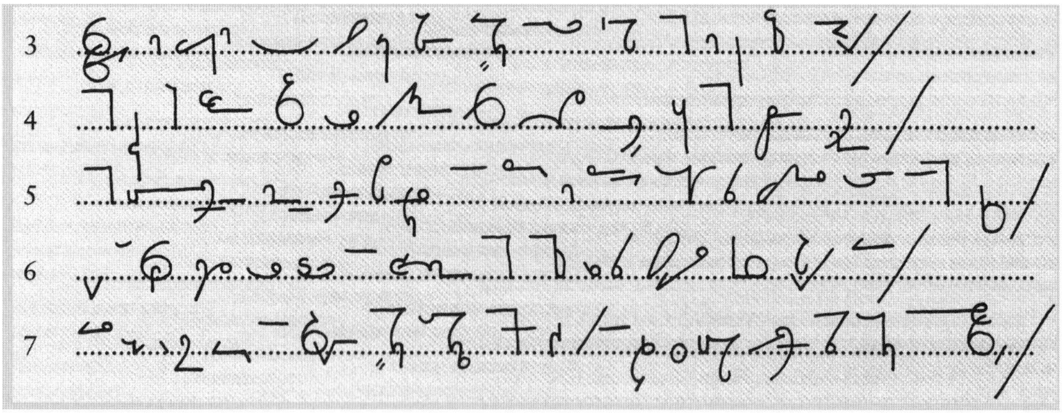

PR

The **R** principle may be applied to words which have **PR** in them when no vowel occurs between the letters **P** and **R**. Horizontal strokes **D, M, T,** and **W** are written through **PR,** with **D** down and **T** top to help reading back. Vertical strokes are written next to **PR** so that they can be seen, for example **PR** followed by **P**:

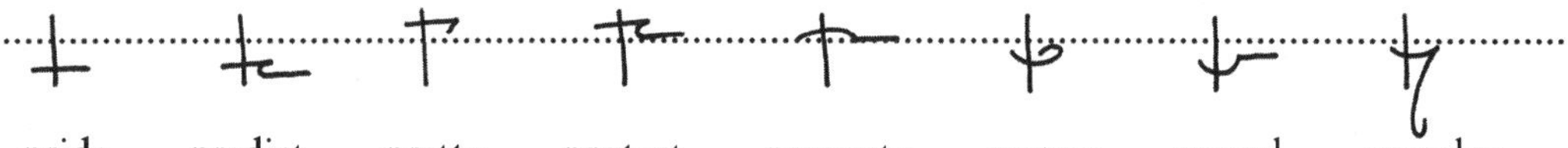

pride predict pretty protect promote prawn proud prowler

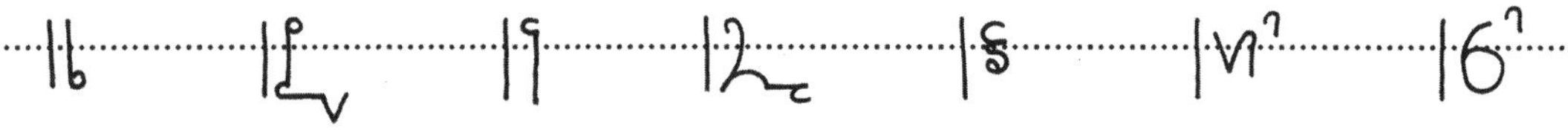

propose prospective preach pragmatic precocious prevention probation

BUT when a vowel occurs between **P** and **R** write letter **R** as part of the outline:

prompt *but* permit prosecute *but* persecute prison *but* parson

If it is easier to write an outline without applying the **R** principle, then you should do so:

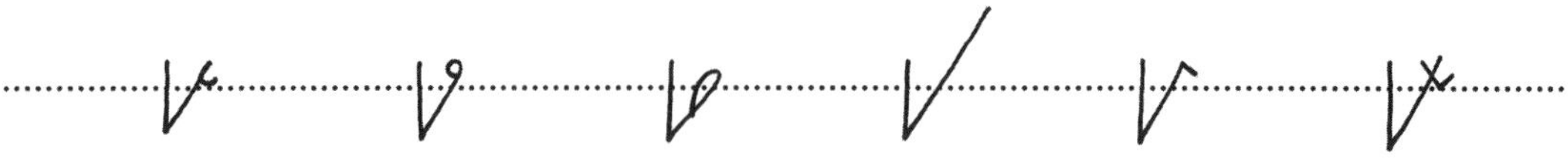

price press proof prior pray proxy

Exception – the **R** principle is not used when words already have disjoined endings:

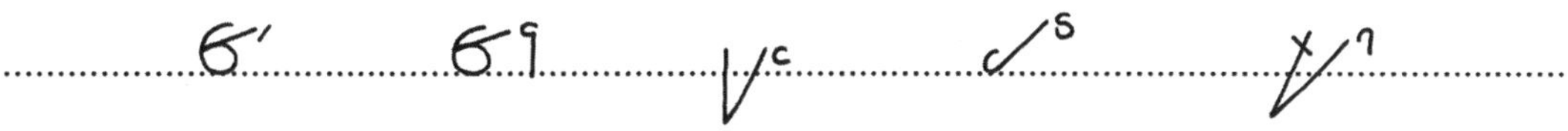

bri**ng** bran**ch** prin**ce** cru**cial** expre**ssion**

Task 29.5

Read and write the following sentences

MP3

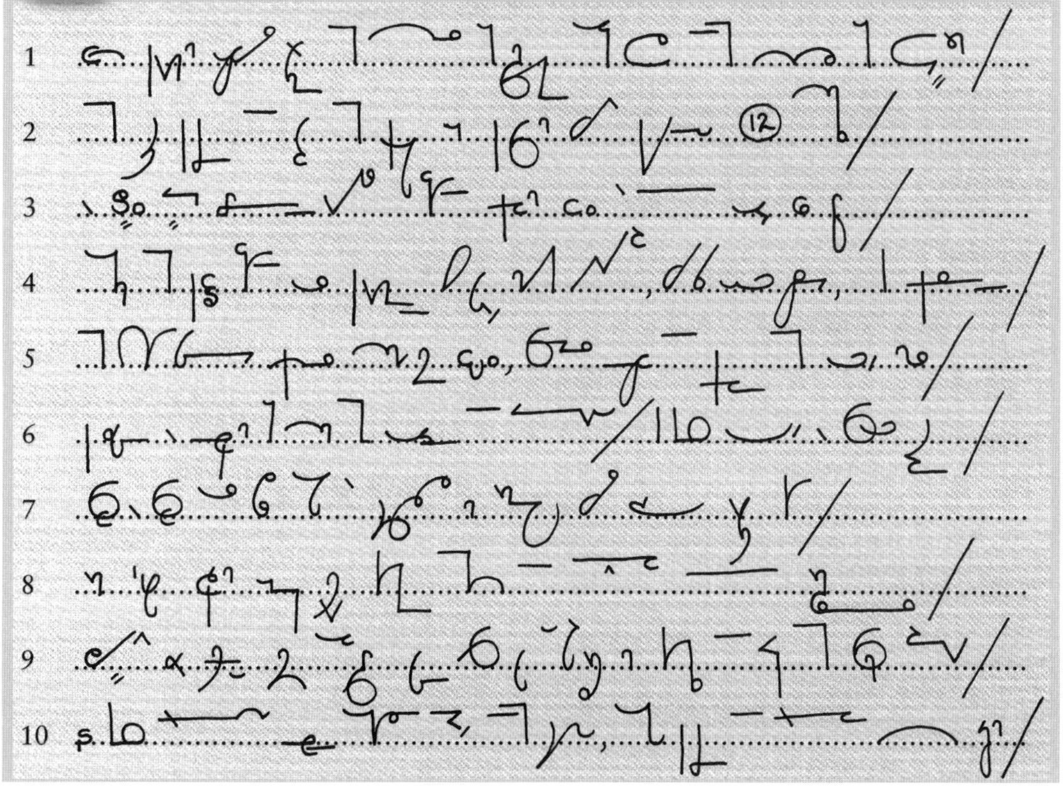

Words ending -GRAPH

The word **graph** is written in full 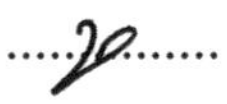

When **-GRAPH** is written as a word ending, omit **R** and blend **G** and **F**:

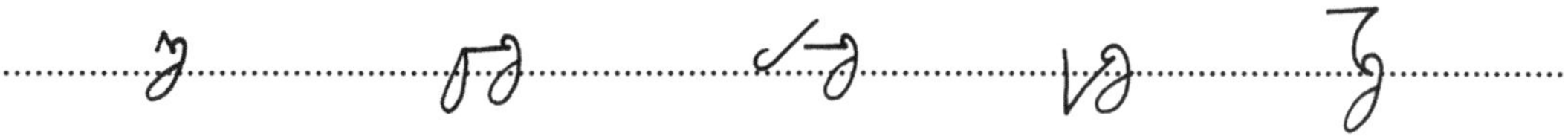

auto**graph** photo**graph** cardio**graph** para**graph** tele**graph**

Other letters may be added to extend the word ending:

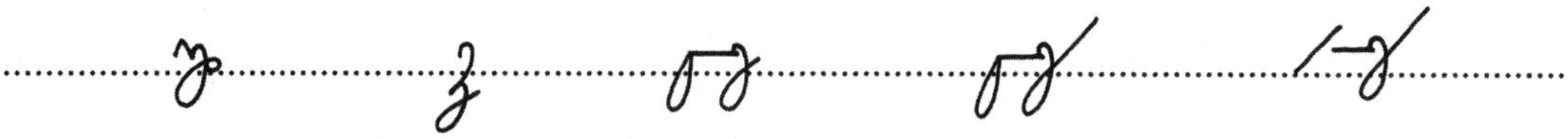

autographs geography photography photographer radiographer

Words ending -GRAM

The word **gram** is written in full 

When **-GRAM** is written as a word ending, omit **R** and write **G** and **M**:

anagram diagram monogram mammogram pictogram program(me)

Other letters may be added to extend the word ending:

anagrams diagrams diagrammatic programmer

Task 29.6

Read and write the following sentences

MP3

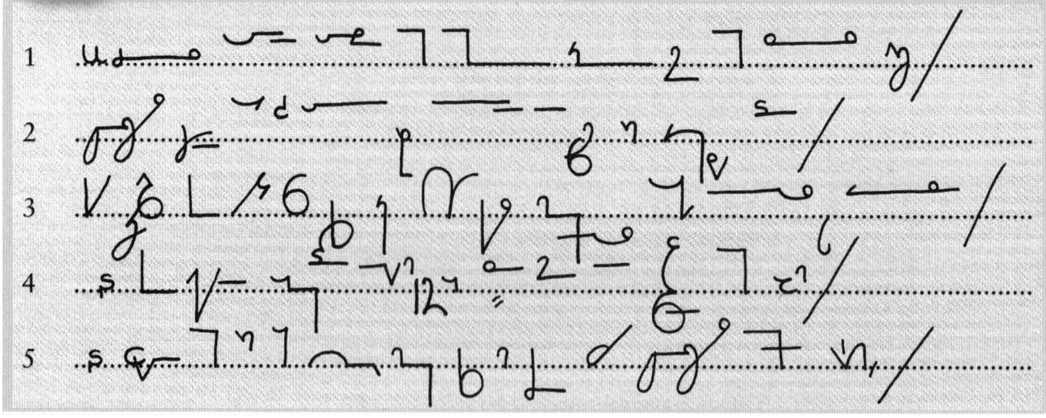

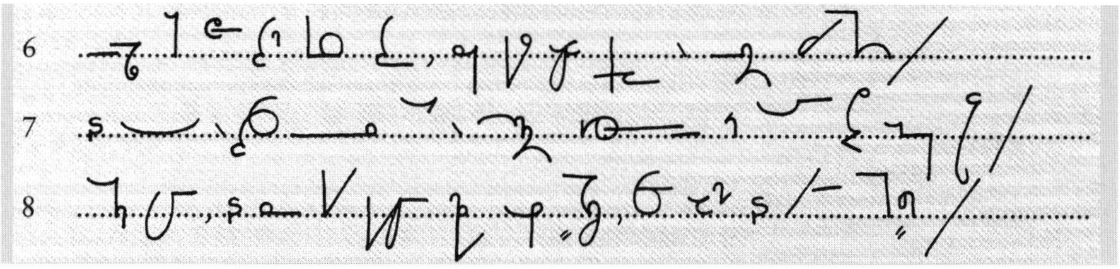

Special outlines – Unit 29

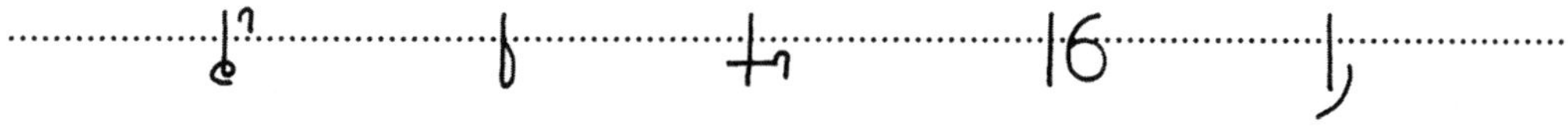

prosecution profit production problem prejudice

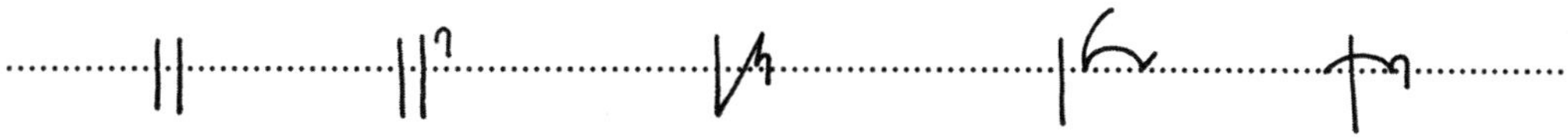

prepare preparation principle/principal preliminary prominent

proportion probable probably improve improvement

subscription subscriber agriculture appropriate

Word groupings

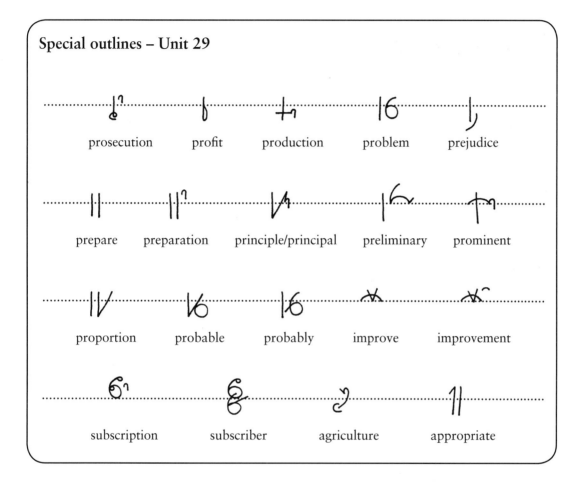

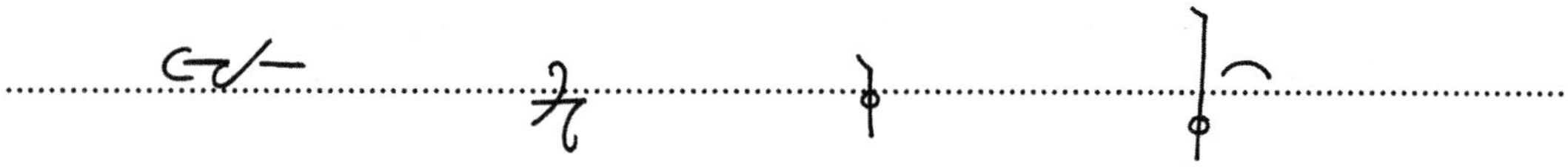

credit card great deal at present at the present time

Task 29.7

Read and write 'Firefighter caught speeding'

MP3

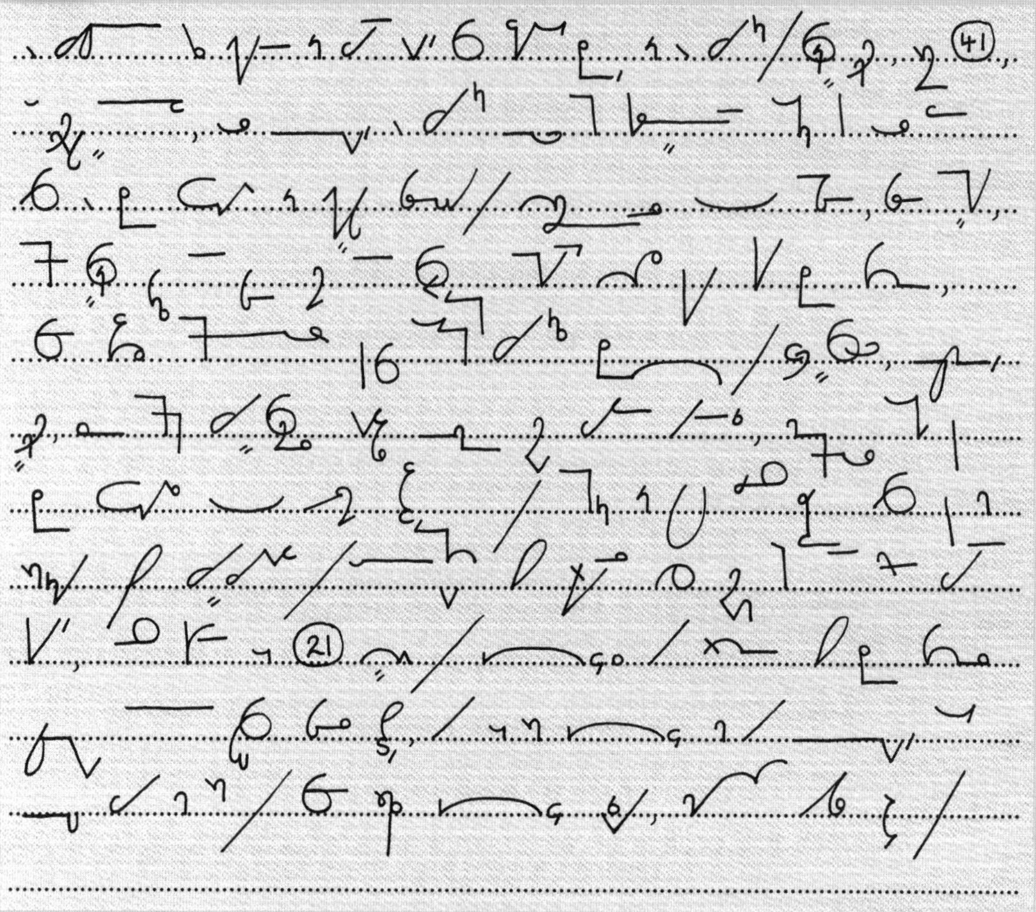

Unit 30
The R principle – AR, OR, UR

When words **begin with the vowels A, O** or **U** and are followed by letter **R**, the **R Principle** may be applied. Simply write the consonant which follows **R** through the **full vowel.**

AR

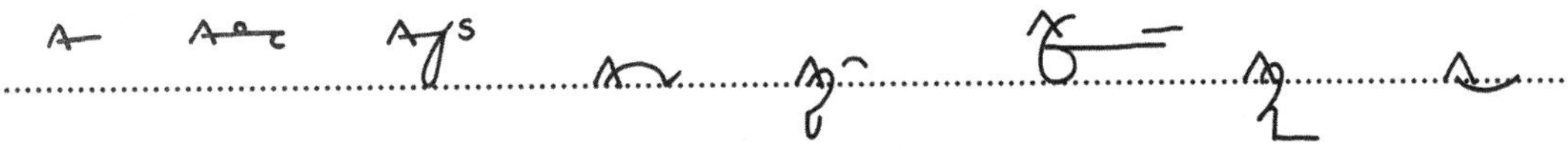

art artistic artificial army argument arbitrate arrogant arrow

OR

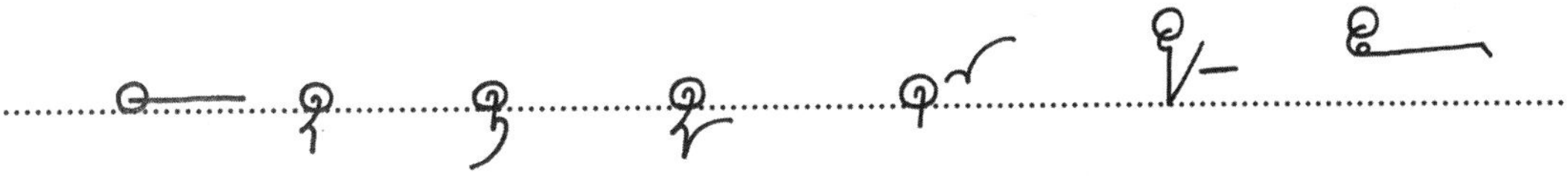

order organ orange original ornamental orchard orchestra

UR

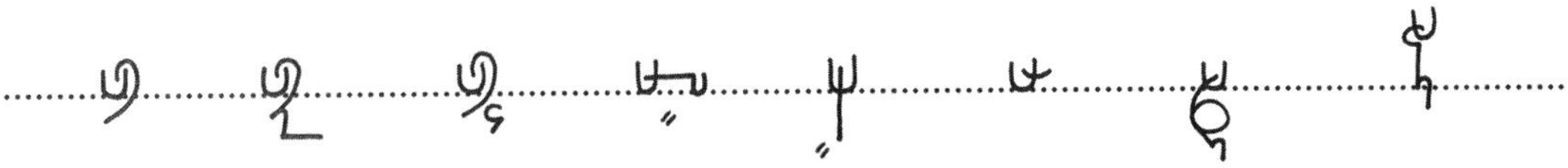

urge urgent urgency Urdu Europe euro urban urchin

Task 30.1

Read and write the following sentences

MP3

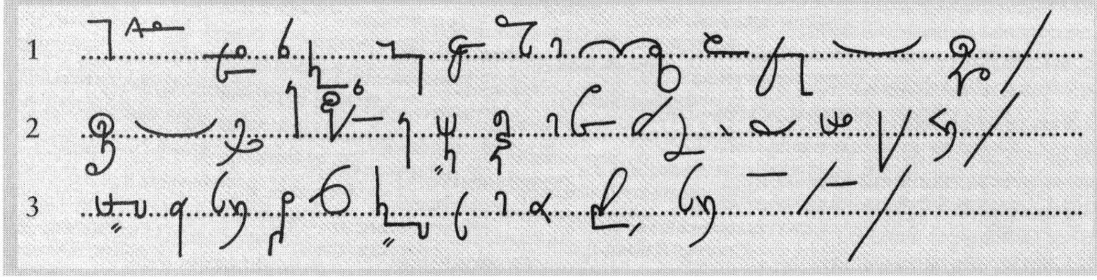

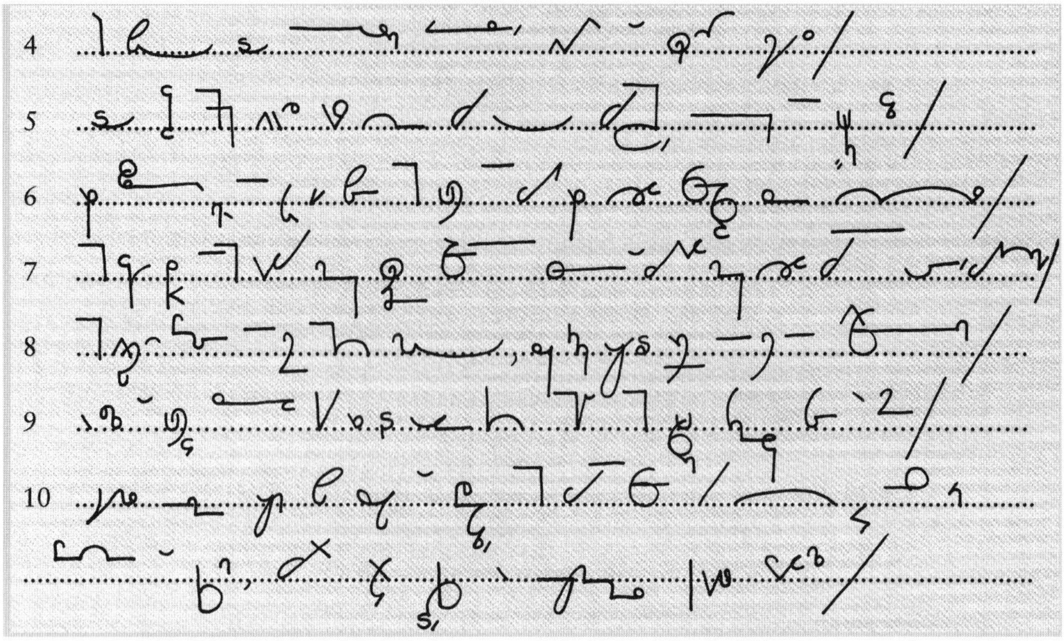

Special outlines – Unit 30

ordinary

ordinarily

organisation

Word groupings

at home and abroad

Task 30.2

Read and write 'Revised plan for new homes'

MP3

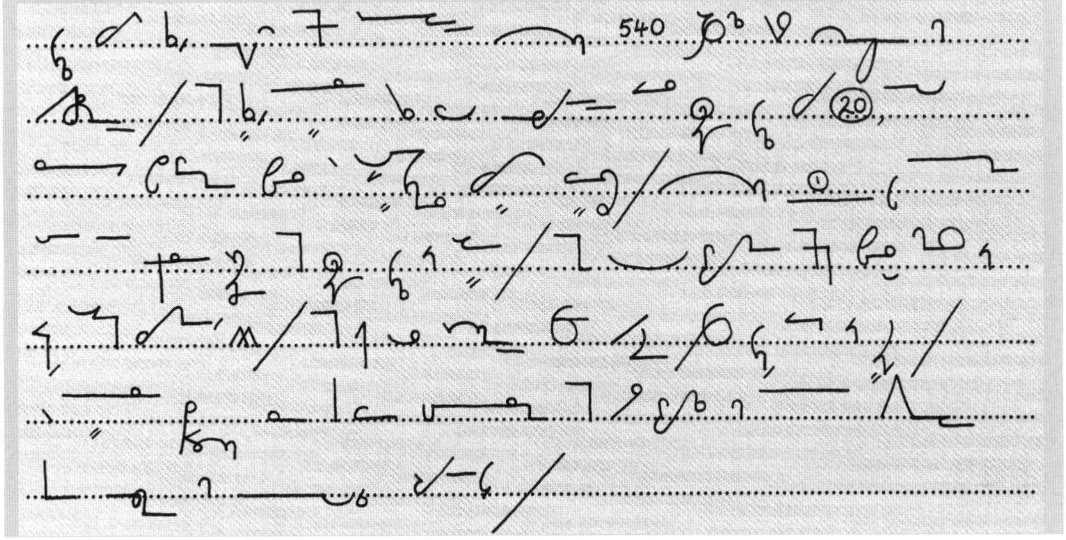

Task 30.3

Read and write 'Church hit by vandalism'

MP3

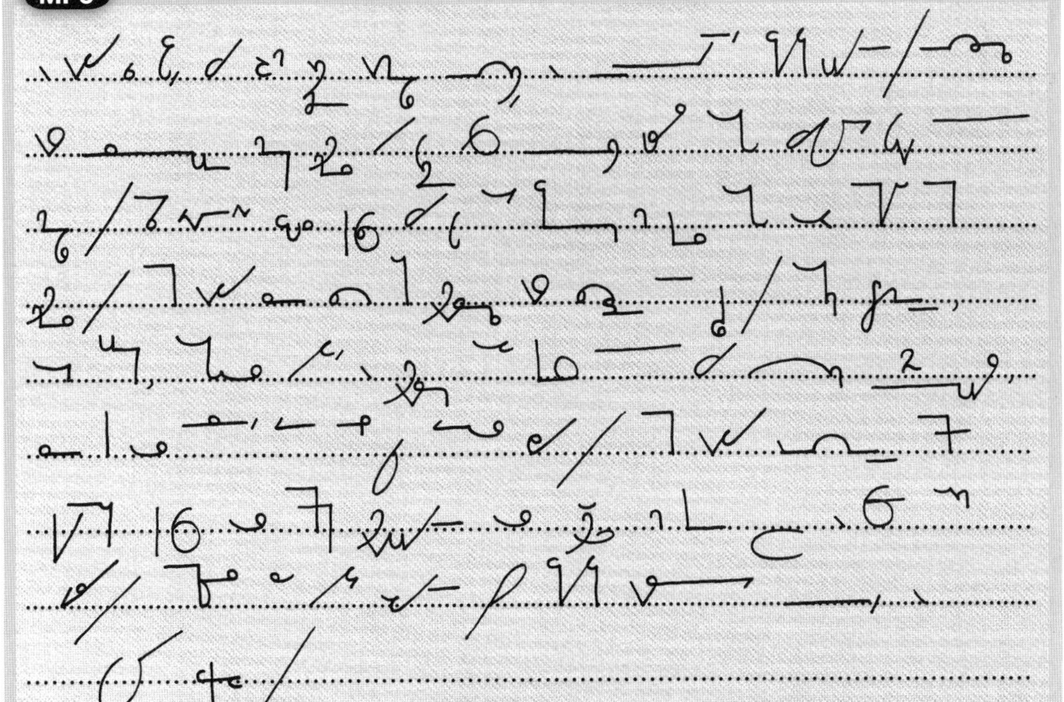

Unit 1 – The Teeline alphabet

Task 1.1

Memorise letters A– M of the alphabet by using a 'drill sheet'.

Task 1.2

Memorise letters N–Z of the alphabet by using a 'drill sheet'.

Task 1.3

Memorise common words represented by the letters A–M.

Task 1.4

Transcribe the following words represented by the letters A–M.

local	from	guilty	time	be	at	ever	like
				been		every	
me	a lot	he	kind	do	once	able	a
	a lot of		knowledge	day	offence	able to	
						ability	
						after	
go	letter	Ireland	million	electric			
gentleman							
guilt							

Task 1.5

Memorise common words represented by the letters N–Z.

Task 1.6

Transcribe the following words represented by the letters N–Z.

begin	your	police	or	very	you	we	of
		pence		have			
		page		versus			
evidence	accident	Wales	Scotland	to	accident black spot	south	and
	cross						new
							knew
began	above	question	are				
		equal	authority				

Task 1.7

Write the Teeline outlines for the following sentences.

1
2
3
4
5
6
7
8
9
10

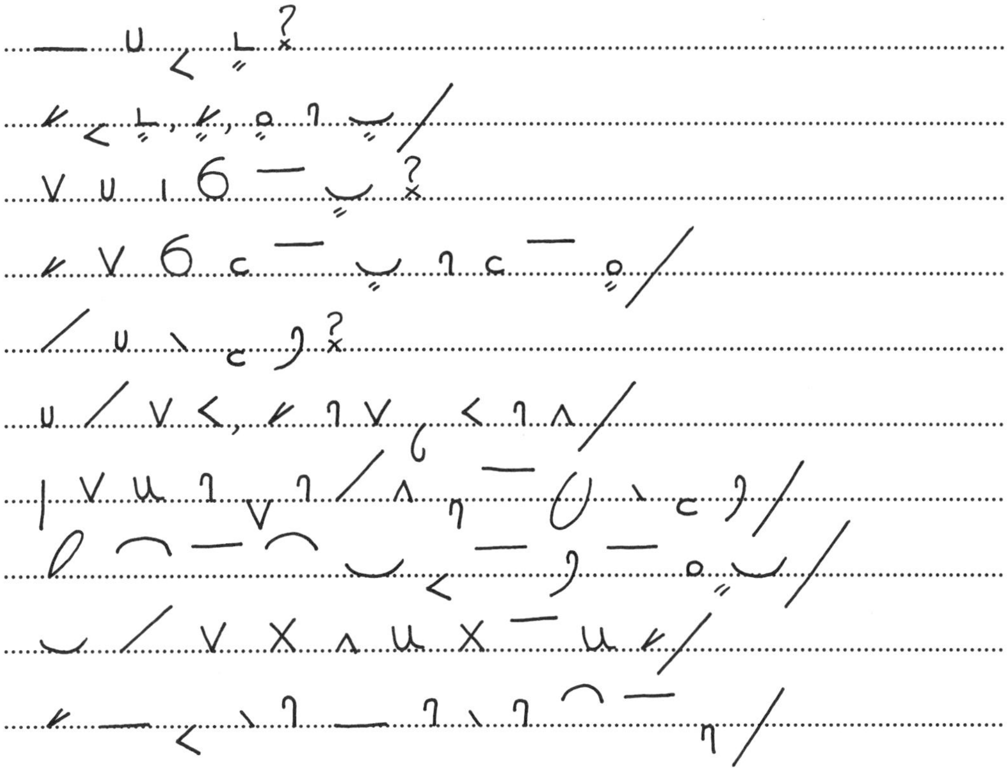

Task 1.8

Join letters of the alphabet as shown.

Task 1.9

Copy the outlines below.

no so us up pr ox hk jk pk

Unit 2 – The basic principles of writing Teeline

Task 2.1

Read the following paragraph.

As a journalist you will need to write fast and accurate Teeline notes so that you are able to write that memorable quote for your newspaper. Spend part of each day learning the common words and other outlines which will help to increase your writing speed. Teeline is a skill subject and that skill will become automatic with daily practice. Good luck and enjoy your learning.

Task 2.2

Remove the unnecessary letters in the following words to reveal the Teeline skeleton.

bld	pr	lv	mn	yr
lvl	ps	dm	vc	acpt
rl	rs	tf	gv	mng

Task 2.3

Read the following Teeline outlines.

prc	fnd/t	grl	pnd/t	nd
nt	cl	hnd/t	mn	wmn
bhnd	rpd/t	prs	ns	ppr

Task 2.4

Read and then neatly copy the following sentences.

1 If you have an opportunity, make good use of your[10] time[11].

2 I believe it will take up a lot of your[10] time. It will be time well spent if you do[20] a little every day[24].

3 He told me he will go with you. Will Monday[10] be a good day to go? You might be able[20] to have a cup of tea as you talk with[30] him. You will get all you need from him[39].

4 He gave her a vivid account of a car accident[10].

5 It happened at 9 o'clock last Wednesday[7].

Task 2.5

Write the following sentences in neat Teeline outlines.

1
2
3
4
5

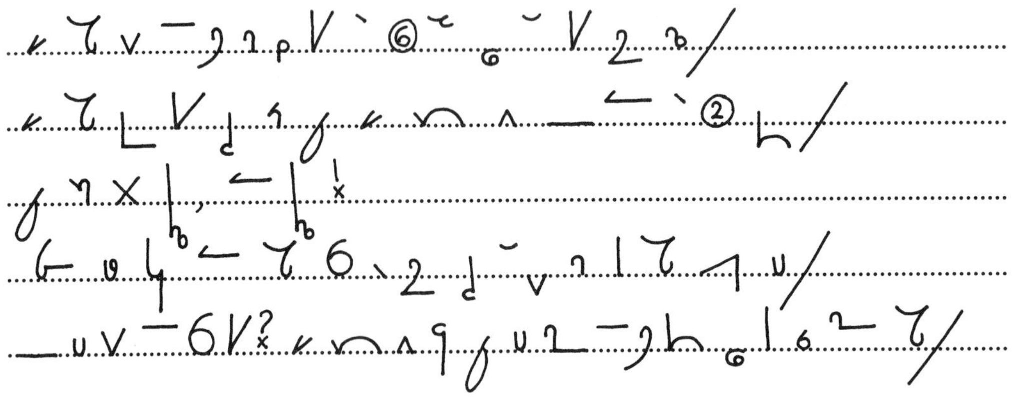

Unit 3 – Additional Teeline characters

Task 3.1

Read and copy the following words.

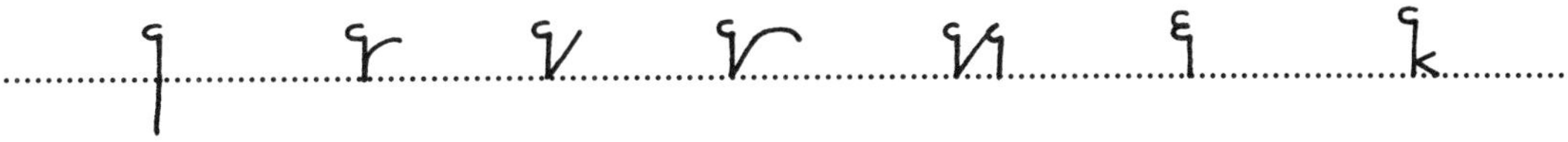

chap chill chair charm church coach choke

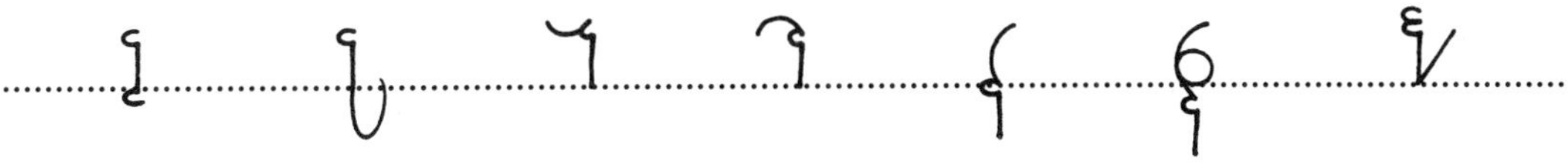

check cheque watch match latch batch catcher

Task 3.2

Read and copy the following words.

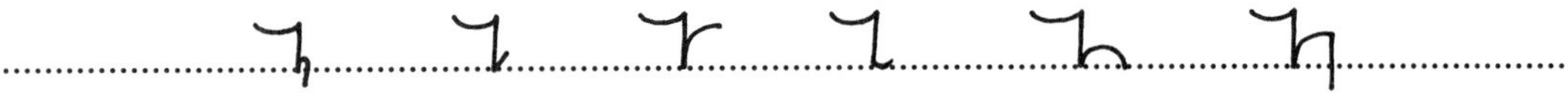

when why while who whom whelp

wheelchair wheeze whimper whip

Task 3.3

Read and copy the following words.

shop should sharp shook she shoot

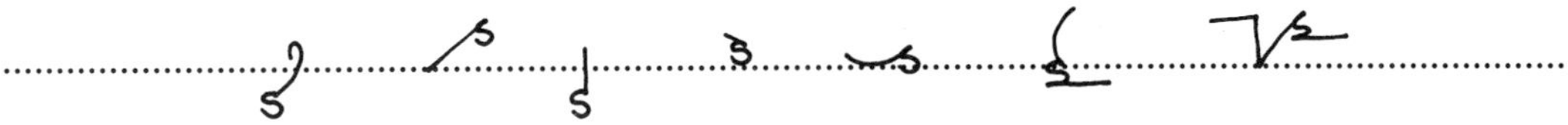

gash rush push ash wish lashed thrashed

Task 3.4

Read and copy the following words.

them thin both clothes thrilled Thursday thumped

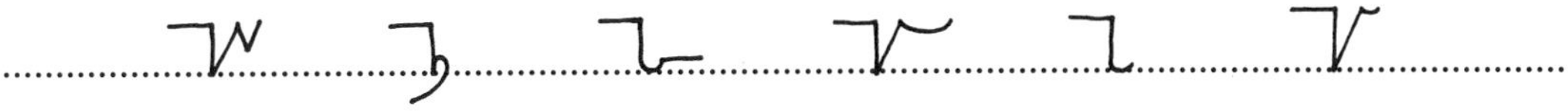

thrive thug thought throw though through

Task 3.5

Read and copy the following words.

await avail avoid axe aquatic appeal appear

Task 3.6

Read and copy the following words.

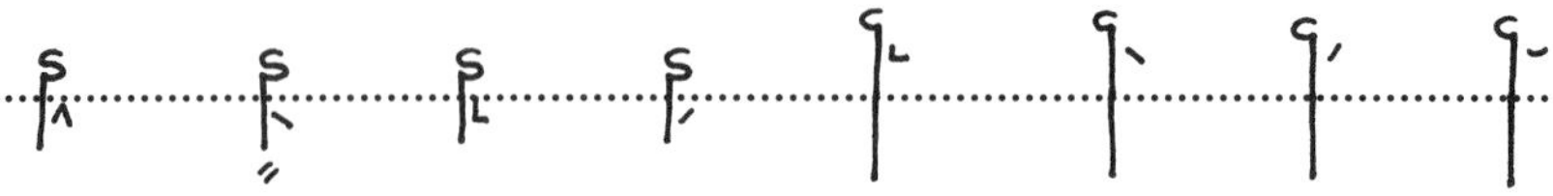

shape Shap sheep ship cheap chap chip chop

man main mean mine women woman

Task 3.7

Write the following words in Teeline.

Asia die toe shoe oak clue tie

Task 3.8

Read the following sentences and write from dictation.

1 Let us look at the damage to the shop. There[10] are a lot of clues[15].
2 There was evidence to show the police when they got[10] there at 7 o'clock[14].
3 They said they will go through it to show the[10] judge when they need it[15].

Unit 4 – S and plurals

Task 4.1

Read and then practise the outlines written in the following passage

Where shall we go today? We could meet you at[10] about 2 o'clock. We will be able to go to[20] the zoo by bus. When we see all the animals[30] there we will have a really good time. We will[40] see you near the bus stop just outside the church[50].

Unit 5 – Word groupings and G or J

Task 5.1

Read and write the following sentences.

1 When **will you have** finished the blue book? I loaned[10] it **to you last year**[15].

2 **I shall be** finished **as soon as possible. It is**[10] **a** good book, but **I have** not had time to[20] look at it[23].

3 **I am sure you wish to see** me soon, and[10] **we should** meet up **as soon as you have** time[20].

4 **I am sure that this is** a good idea. When[10] **do you** suggest[13]?

5 **We could say** Saturday at 2pm. How **about it**[10]? Give me a call when **you are able to do**[20] **so**[21].

Task 5.2

Read and write the following paragraph.

John, **I will** go **to the** local shop to buy[10] your Sunday newspaper. **I will** go there **as soon as**[20] **possible**. If **I do not** get there early, **I might**[30] **not be able to** get the paper **that you** like[40].

Task 5.3

Read and write 'Accident at the bus stop'.

There was chaos **in the town centre** when a car[10] hit a bus as **it was** about to **leave the**[20] bus stop. The car and bus have both been damaged[30]. The bus **had been** outside the cake shop, and **there**[40] **are** thought **to have been** many girls **from the** local[50] school there **at the** time. **At least** two **of the**[60] girls had to go **to the** hospital **after the** accident[70]. We believe **they have been** in shock and **have had**[80] minor injuries to their heads and legs. **They have had**[90] a check up **and the** girls **have been** told they[100] **will be able to** go home today. **I am sure**[110] we all wish them well **and that they will be**[120] well again soon[123].

Task 5.4

Read and write 'New shop to open in June'.

I am happy **to be able to tell you** today[10] **that this** company **is to** open a new shop **at**[20] **the** Oak Lane **Leisure Centre. We shall** need **a lot**[30] **of** new staff and **we have received** many requests from[40] local **men and women** about these jobs. We hope **to**[50] **have** some Saturday jobs **so that the** youths here **will**[60] **be able to** make some money and also perhaps spend[70] it **in the** shop **and the leisure centre! We shall**[80] sell newspapers, magazines and sweets to name just some **of**[90] **the** goods **we shall be able to** offer. **There has**[100] **been** no business **of this** kind anywhere nearby, so **it**[110] **will be** good **to have** it open very soon. **We**[120] **are sure that the** new shop **will be** a huge[130] success when it opens in June[136].

Unit 6 – Word groupings, word endings and more new Teeline characters

Task 6.1

Read and write the following sentences.

1 **I would like** **to see** you rewarded. **I am sure**[10] you deserve it because **of your** success **in your** new[20] job which **you have** just begun[26].

2 **What would you** like **to see** **as a** reward? **I**[10] **will** **give you** the choice. Tell me **what you would**[20] really like and **I will** buy it[27].

3 I believe a new pair of blue shoes **would be**[10] very nice, **if that is** not **too much** to spend[20]. **I would like** them to go with the new bag[30] which I bought[33].

4 **That is a** good idea. **Shall we** meet **in the**[10] **town centre**? **I do** need to go into the **town**[20] **centre** soon **and that will be** a good opportunity **to**[30] **do so**[32].

5 Yes, **that is a** very good idea. **I shall be**[10] **able to** see you at 2 o'clock. **Where would you**[20] like to meet me? **I would** suggest the café where[30] **I met you** last time, **so that I will be**[40] **able to** **at least** buy you a cup of coffee[50].

Task 6.2

Read and write the following sentences.

1 The salesman will accept the nomination of his peers **as**[10] **the** Chairman **of the** national company. He said **he would**[20] **look forward** and do his best[26].

2 He seemed a little nonchalant to me and I thought[10] he **should not** get the job because he **does not**[20] seem **to have the ability** **to do it**[28]!

Task 6.3

Read and write the following sentences.

1 Girl Guides and Cubs have to know **the words of**[10] **the** National Anthem used in England. 'God **Save the** Queen'[20].

2 They also need to know the names of **all the**[10] saints of England, Ireland, Scotland and Wales **as well**[19].

3 **Most of us** have a mobile phone **these days**, so[10] **we are able to** make a call at almost any[20] time **of the** day or night from just about anywhere[30].

4 A massive bomb blast happened at 6 o'clock today **at**[10] **the** Embassy in China. A **number of men and women**[20] from England have injuries **from the** blast[27].

5 The designer was very enthusiastic. He said the new clothes[10] he had designed **would be** made with synthetic wool **which**[20] **would be** as soft **as that** from a real sheep[30].

Task 6.4

Read and write 'Magazines with puzzles'.

The **number of** magazines which are sold **in the** newsagents'[10] shops **these days** quite amazes me. **There are** a **number**[20] **of** them which appeal to all ages nationwide. Sometimes it[30] appears **that there is** **too much** choice. I like to[40] buy a magazine with puzzles in it **at least** once[50] every month. **This month** the magazine **will be** a bumper[60] issue. **I am** very enthusiastic **about it**. **I**

might stumble[70] across a crossword **that I am able to do**! I[80] often jumble up the letters in a wordsearch which does[90] make it very awkward to solve. My husband looks bemused[100] at my attempts **to do** the puzzles, but I amble[110] through the magazine with much enthusiasm[116].

Unit 7 – Letters T (top) and D (down)

Task 7.1

Write the following words in Teeline.

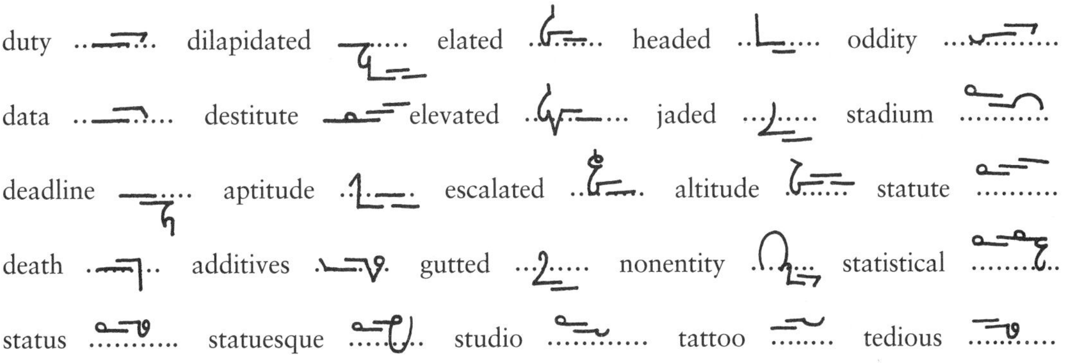
duty
dilapidated
elated
headed
oddity
data
destitute
elevated
jaded
stadium
deadline
aptitude
escalated
altitude
statute
death
additives
gutted
nonentity
statistical
status
statuesque
studio
tattoo
tedious

Task 7.2

Read and write the following sentences.

1 The topic **had been** debated **in the** House many times[10]. Nobody there could decide what **to do about it**[19].

2 The bedsit at the bottom of the house was robbed[10]. The robbers took an old video and a new DVD[20].

3 The tidal wave hit the coast **in the** south and[10] devastated the houses near the beach[16].

4 The headline title **in the** daily newspaper was designed to[10] titillate **so that** sales **would be** higher **that day**. The[20] couple **in the** news said they **had been** devastated, but[30] remained devoted[32].

5 The little girl told her daddy that her toothache was[10] really bad **and that** she was in **a lot of**[20] pain. He told her **he would** get a bottle of[30] pills **and they would** help the nasty pain to go[40].

Task 7.3

Read and write 'The robot'.

A robot **has been** bought by a couple who live[10] **in the** huge detached house **at the** bottom of **Oak[20] Wood** Lane. They hope **that their** new robot will keep[30] their house clean and tidy while **they are** not there[40].

Task 7.4

Read and write 'Jobs for food lovers'.

There are many kinds of careers **if you are** keen[10] **to have** a job where **you are** close to food[20]. You might like a job in a bakery or a[30] takeaway. It might seem a little quirky, but **at least**[40] **you will be** close to food **each day** or night[50]. **You will be able to** eat **a lot of** curry[60], pizza, jacket potatoes or kebabs which **have been** cooked by[70] you or your colleagues. **It is a** bit **of a**[80] risk, **but it could be** just the ticket **if you**[90] **do not** care **about the** size and shape **of your**[100] body[101]!

Task 7.5

Read and write 'Attack on eighty-three year-old woman'.

There was a savage attack upon an eighty-three **year**[10] **old** woman as she slept in her bed at her[20] home in Coach Lane. The incident happened last Monday **in**[30] **the** early hours. Jane Hill was robbed of her antique[40] jewels. She is believed **to have** injuries to her head[50] **as well as** to her left hip and leg. Her[60] eyes are black and she has bruises to **most of**[70] her body. A neighbour, who has asked not **to be**[80] named **at this** stage, said he saw the attacker **leave**[90] **the** house of Jane Hill at about 2am. The[100] neighbour **could not** sleep and had, **in fact**, got up[110] to make a cup of tea **at that** time together[120] with his wife. The **police would like** to hear from[130] anybody **who is able to** help them[137].

Unit 8 – Letter Y

Task 8.1

Read and write the following sentences.

1 **I am sorry there has been** cause to delay. The[10] reason **I am** late is because **I could not** find[20] my house key[23].

2 **We shall have** a pie and pea supper as **I**[10] **shall be** too busy to cook a big meal when[20] I get home. **Could you buy the** pies **as you**[30] pass the shop[33]?

3 Guy **is a** very good teacher **at this** college. Although[10] **he is** busy he still finds time to make his[20] class laugh **a lot**[24].

4 The lady **in the** dock apologised **to the** judge. She[10] had had **too much** sherry **that day** and **did not**[20] realise where she was when the incident happened[28].

5 Ray said **he would** repay May some day, but **did**[10] **not** know when **that would be** because he had no[20] job and no money. Poor Ray and poor May[29]!

Task 8.2

Read and write the following sentences.

1 Although the little girl was noisy and nosey she was[10] chosen **to be** the Queen **of the** May Day pageant[20].

2 The girl's mum was very happy when she spoke of[10] her little royal relative, but annoyed **most of the** mums[20] and dads **at the** local school because **she would** not[30] shut up **about it**[34].

3 **At the** school **in the town centre**, some **of the**[10] boys **have been** rewarded with toys, and **I hope** they[20] will really enjoy them[24].

4 The baby boys, called Roy and Ray, **could not** take[10] cow's milk and had **to have** soya milk. They seemed[20] to like it and soon began to thrive[28].

5 The vicar said that he was happy **to see** so[10] many **at the** church at **such a** joyous time and[20] wished all **of them** well[25].

Task 8.3

Read and write the following sentences.

1 Sadly, **we are not able to** swim **in the** sea[10] today. The waves are really too big to make it[20] safe. **It will do us** no good **to be** annoyed[30].

2 **I shall** watch closely **to see if the** boy pays[10] the girl **at the** shop. He **did not** pay last[20] time and left very quickly[25].

3 The lawyer spoke effectively **about the** new system. **It would**[10] **be** effective after 1 January, sadly. **It had been** hoped[20] **to have the** system by December[26].

Task 8.4

Read and write 'Destitute old lady'.

The man **from the** local **estate office** spoke **to the**[10] old woman. She told him **about the** bad **state of**[20] her house and how she had got behind with her[30] bills. She **had not been able to** pay any **of**[40] **them**. She had no oil, coal, gas or electricity and[50] her house was very cold and damp. '**I am sorry**[60]' the man said. He also said that he was annoyed[70] that she **had been** left in **such a** poor state[80] and thought **that it would be** necessary to find **somewhere**[90] **else** to live immediately. He said **he would** speak to[100] somebody about this when he got back to his office[110]. The old lady said that **she would** speak **to the**[120] local press if **it was** beyond his ability to help[130]. No old person **should be** allowed **to be** destitute **in**[140] **this day and age**[144].

Task 8.5

Read and write 'Help for destitute old lady'.

A spokesman **at the estate office** said **he would** look[10] immediately **at the** case **of an** old lady who **had**[20] **not been able to** pay the bills to allow her[30] to heat her home. The house was in a **state**[40] **of** decay, and despite **the fact that** he was very[50] busy, he said **he would** deal **with the** case without[60] delay. He thought he **might be able to** put her[70] into a bedsit, while repairs are made to her house[80]. He knew **that it would be** disruptive, but thought **that**[90] **it would be** best **at the end of the day**[100].

Task 8.6

Read and write 'A happy ending!'

I told you about the destitute old lady **who had**[10] lived in a house **which was** in a dilapidated state[20]. She **has been able to** go back to her home[30] after just eight weeks. It took that much time **to**[40] **do all the** jobs to get the house into a[50] good **state of** repair **so that she would be able**[60] **to** live there again. June White said she was delighted[70] to get the key to her home **from the estate**[80] **office** manager, Paul Goode, **who had been** so kind to[90] her. She said that she was amazed and **could not**[100] believe how good the house looked. Just eight **weeks ago**[110] it had looked beyond repair. The walls **had been** painted[120] and new carpets **had been** laid. She had talked to[130] a very kind woman about her bills and **had been**[140] **able to** get **some money** to help **with the** arrears[150]. **She would** still have to pay the money which she[160] owed but, because **of the** help she **had received**, she[170] knew that **she would** not get into **such a** bad[180] state of debt again[184].

Unit 9 – Use of vowels

Task 9.1

Read and write the following sentences.

1 He bought the blue automatic car in August. The car[10] had an audio system and an aerial[17].

2 The police had the authority and arrested the **men and**[10] **women** who stood **at the** picket line last Monday with[20] their Union[22].

3 We agree **that the** girl showed some aptitude and she[10] took up archery **so that** she could represent her school[20].

4 The noisy arcade was immediately behind the **leisure centre** and[10] near **to the** shops **in the town centre**[18].

5 The woman was stabbed **in the** abdomen. She was seen[10] soon **after the** incident, **at the** local hospital, by a[20] nurse[21].

Task 9.2

Write these words in Teeline and use a dictionary if you are not familiar with their meaning.

airgun  aerated  aeronautic  airless 

aerospace  airbed  airtight  archaic 

autobiography  autobahn  autopsy  arched 

autumnal  aural  archipelago  archer 

auk  audacity  archivist  archway 

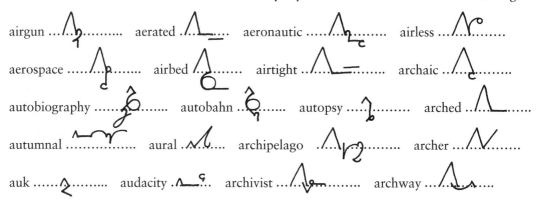

Task 9.3

Read and write the following sentences.

1 **I hope you are** not too upset **about the** uproar[10] caused today. **You are** easily uppermost in my mind **at**[20] **this** time[22].

2 **You have the** upper hand **in this** issue. **I do**[10] owe you an apology and **I hope you will** accept[20] it[21].

3 **There was an** epidemic **in the** city. It caused stomach[10] pains and upsets to those **who had been at a**[20] café **in the** afternoon[24].

4 We usually queue to get **into the** sale at new[10] year. We get the best bargains **if we are** there[20] early[21].

5 **They are** well equipped to pursue their idea **in the**[10] media. Although **it will not be** easy, **I do not**[20] believe **that they** will rue the day[27].

Task 9.4

Read and write the following sentences.

1 The robber thought he **had been** unlucky **to be** caught[10] **by the** police officers as he left the shop **with**[20] **the** jewels[22].

2 The woman met her untimely death as she slipped **from**[10] **the** cliff path. As she walked she aimed to avoid[20] the muddy edge, but was unlucky[26].

3 **I was** unsure if **I would like** the gym, **but**[10] **it is** well equipped and **as a** beginner **I am**[20] happy with it. **I am** due to go there again[30] today at 4 o'clock[34].

Task 9.5

Read and write 'Youth attacked in town-centre bar'.

A youth **has had** fifty stitches to his face after[10] an attack in a **town-centre** bar. The incident happened[20] just after midnight on Thursday at Joe's Bar on West[30] Way. Nurses **at the** Cottage Hospital said the seventeen year[40] old was in a **state of** shock. They also said[50] he was unlikely **to be** moved or allowed home until[60] he **had been** seen by medical staff **on the ward**[70]. Although police officers acted quickly to get **to the** scene,[80] they appeal to anyone who may have seen what happened[90] to get in touch **with them as soon as possible**[100]. A local man said, '**We do not** need these kind[110] of thugs **in this** area. Someone **will be** killed **if**[120] **this** carries on. Until this bar opened, it used **to**[130] **be** a safe area to live in[137]'.

Task 9.6

Read and write 'Man arrested for attack on youth'.

We have details **of the** incident **last week** in which[10] a seventeen year old was savagely attacked. It appears **that**[20] **the** youth was attacked just outside Joe's Bar on West[30] Way. The youth told police he **had been** on a[40] night out with seven of his mates **and that they**[50] left just after midnight. One **of them** was due to[60] go to Leeds University in two weeks' time. A **passer-by**[70] spoke **to the** police and **it seems that** a white[80] man, in his thirties, with blond hair had picked **on**[90] **the** lads. **It is** alleged **that this was** because **of**[100] **the** clothes they had on and because **of what was**[110] said to him **by the** lads. The blond man had[120] shouted **at them** and then picked up a **beer bottle**[130]. He smashed it and waved it towards the seventeen year[140] old, **who had** rushed **at the** man and **into the**[150] bottle which had cut his face badly. The police have[160] questioned and arrested the blond man, but have not yet[170] released his name. The youth is still in hospital[179].

Unit 10 – Vowel indicators used as word endings

Task 10.1

Read and write the following sentences.

1 Waiting **at the** bus stop and being told **that the**[10] bus is going **to be** late is very annoying when[20] one **has a** meeting to go to[27].

2 Twinges of pain affected the girl in her abdomen. She[10] decided to **ring the** hospital immediately as **it would be**[20] silly to linger. She thought she **might be** suffering from[30] appendicitis[31].

3 **At the** local park, the little girl was **on the**[10] swing when a nasty looking man spoke to her. He[20] **might have** abducted her, if her mum **had not** seen[30] **what was** happening and quickly took her away[38].

4 The single mum cuddled her baby boy lovingly. The baby[10] loved to hear his mum singing softly as he was[20] rocked off to sleep[24].

5 Having listened **to the** rock band, the **man and woman**[10] could hear ringing in their ears. Their son was **with**[20] **them** and **having the** time **of his** life. He was[30] lingering **at the end of the** night, hoping **he would**[40] **be meeting the** band[44].

Task 10.2

Read and write the following sentences.

1 **At the** zoo, the wildlife ranger, in charge **of the**[10] big cats, looked **after the** Bengal tiger **who had** left[20] the jungle only two **weeks ago**[26].

2 When the tiger was hungry, **he would lunge forward, getting**[10] **the** meat **from the** ranger, who admitted pangs of guilt[20] about **bringing the** tiger from his home **in the** jungle[30].

3 By **moving things** and changing belongings in one's house, **in**[10] **the** style of feng shui, one may bring peace and[20] harmony into one's home[24].

4 Church bell ringers are clanging their bells with enthusiasm **at**[10] **the** joyous wedding ceremony of John and Jane today. The[20] sun is shining and everyone looks very happy[28].

5 Putting **such things as your** college notes from longhand into[10] shorthand **will be** helping you. Your nimble fingers **will be**[20] winging their way **across the** pages **of your** notebook. **You**[30] **will** soon be **meeting the** challenge of passing a high[40]-speed test[42].

Task 10.3

Read and write 'Detached bungalow needed'.

A young couple, **who have been** living in a bedsitting[10] room are looking to buy a detached bungalow **in this**[20] area. The couple wish to move **as soon as possible**[30] **as their** bedsitting room is cold and damp. They realise[40] **it will not be** easy to find a bungalow **at**[50] **a** low price but, obviously, are **not able to** pay[60] **a lot of** money when they move. **They are looking**[70] **forward to the** challenge of finding a bungalow **at a**[80] good price. They say they still need to live within[90] five miles **of the city centre**[96].

Task 10.4

Read and write 'When spring has sprung!'

With spring on its way, the daylight hours are, **at**[10] **last**, lengthening. **We shall** soon **have the** opportunity to go[20] walking **in the** nearby hills or **along the** sandy beach[30] **in this** area, **as we** live near **to the** sea[40]. The views here are absolutely lovely and **it would** make[50] anyone happy **to see** them just **as the** sun is[60] setting. Everyone ought to take some time out of **each**[70] **day**, where they live, to take **in the** air **and**[80] **the** views. **Of course, if you** live within a busy[90] **city centre** you **may be able to** take your walk[100] in a park. **On the other hand**, you **may be**[110] **able to** escape by taking your car or catching a[120] bus out **of the** noisy city and going **somewhere else**[130] to enjoy the scenery, peace and quiet. Spring **is a**[140] good time to go **to the** seaside. The big waves[150] go crashing **into the** rocks. **We have** spent many a[160] happy time **watching them**, laughing loudly **and then** dashing away[170] from them so as not to get soaking wet[179].

Unit 11 – Extending vowel indicators as word endings and more new word beginnings

Task 11.1

Write the following sentences in neat Teeline outlines.

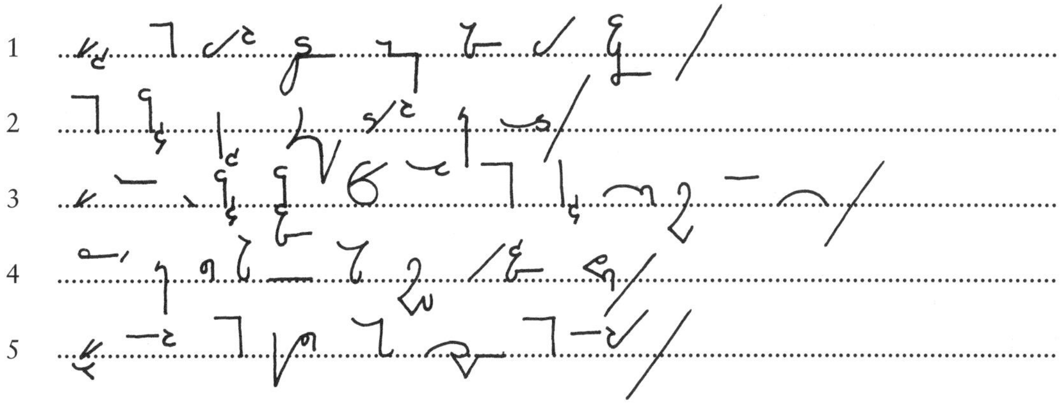

Task 11.2

Read and write the following sentences.

1 As they rowed near to the river bank they thought[10] the boat might sink because weeds had got tangled beneath[20] it[21].

2 You may incur huge bills if you do not insulate[10] your house. I would also encourage you to insure the[20] building[21].

3 The band had been encouraged to do an encore and[10] the lead singer, who was one chunky hunk, rose to[20] the challenge[22].

4 Why do you insist that you will not make your[10] will? It is not a good idea to die intestate[20].

5 Instead of sitting in the sun, I am inclined to[10] find some shade. Skin diseases caused by the sun are[20] increasing these days[23].

Task 11.3

Read and write 'Sheep'.

The sheep had been encouraged to go into the enclosure[10] by the intelligent dog. We have nothing but respect when[20] animals act in this way. We have been told the[30] sheep are put into the enclosure and are checked to[40] see if they have any diseases because they may need[50] to be seen by a vet[56].

Task 11.4

Read and write 'Tanker sinks in channel'.

A tanker sank in the English Channel last September. Do[10] you think the Italian man who was charged with acting[20] dangerously should have been charged? I believe that he will[30] challenge this offence as he thinks he has been wrongly[40] charged. There may be a language barrier, of course, but[50] I am inclined to think that if he has a[60] good lawyer this will help him to put across his[70] case. There has been a lot of talk lately about[80] this case in the local press. It will be a[90] good thing when it has been settled, as everyone needs[100] to move on[103].

Task 11.5

Read and write 'Disappearing jobs'.

In this day and age, there are a number of[10] jobs which we no longer hear about. The job of[20] a tinker is one that springs to mind. These days[30], if you need new pots and pans, you will usually[40] visit your local shop and buy just what you need[50] there and then, instead of waiting to have things mended[60]. In some ways it is a pity that these skills[70] will disappear, but changes will occur in everything in life[80].

Task 11.6

Transcribe the following special outlines.

1	begin	2	opportunity
3	too much	4	always
5	ladies and gentlemen	6	north
7	without	8	obviously
9	equivalent	10	respect

Unit 12 – Words ending -NCE, NCH and words beginning ANTI-, ANTE-, ANTA-

Task 12.1

Read and write the following sentences.

1. The announcer did not have to walk any long distance[10] to speak into the mike. He was very nervous and[20] had sweaty hands[23].
2. Sitting on the fence and dangling his legs in the[10] long grass below, the little boy was happier than he[20] had ever been[23].
3. The accountancy company announced that it would be financing a[10] new staff agency in the city centre which would only[20] be a little distance from their new offices[28].
4. Bouncy castles are often enjoyed by young boys and girls[10] as well as face painting. In adolescence they change quite[20] a lot and like going dancing[26].
5. Romance is in the air in this leap year. I[10] think Kate may pop the question to Paul. I really[20] think he needs a bit of a push[28].

Task 12.2

Read and write the following sentences.

1. Without his teeth, the old man was not able to[10] munch his lunch at the weekly luncheon club. He enjoyed[20] the company of the men and women there[28].

2 When launching her appeal to raise money in aid of[10] the local hospice, a very moving speech was made by[20] Lady Jane White[23].

3 Much has been said about the wrench caused when moving[10] schools, but I think it is not a bad thing[20] to branch out and make new acquaintances[27].

4 Judge John Dodds had sat on the bench many times[10], but had not had such a sad case to deal[20] with as this one seemed to be[27].

5 Things did not look good after the boy had punched[10] the old man. Think about what might happen to the[20] lives of both of them. They will both be changed[30].

Task 12.3

Read and write the following sentences.

1 We are told that if antibiotics are used too much[10], they will have no effect when we are really ill[20].

2 They waited in the ante-room at the old manor house[10]. The room had many antiquated chairs which belonged to the[20] Squire[21].

3 Her visit to the Antipodes had been a huge success[10]. We anticipate that she will wish to stay in New[20] South Wales a little longer[25].

4 As there was no antidote to the snake's bite, he[10] used antiseptic spray on her leg and hoped the young[20] girl would survive. He took her to the jungle hospital[30] as soon as he was able to[37].

5 This was supposed to be a once-in-a-lifetime[10] visit. The view he saw from the ship in the[20] Antarctic was absolutely amazing[24].

Task 12.4

Read and write 'Kite-making takes off at museum'.

A number of boys and girls, together with some adults[10], made kites at a museum in this village last Tuesday[20] afternoon. A spokesman said, 'We have all been very busy[30]. Everyone really enjoyed the afternoon and made their kites without[40] any difficulty. We could not take the kites out to[50] launch them that day because it was too cold and[60] there had been some snow.' There will be many different[70] types of kite to be made again at the museum[80] in a month's time, when we hope the cold snap[90] will be gone. Details from the museum by calling 2[100]63796[105].

Task 12.5

Read and write '"Enough of this rubbish" say locals'.

Men and women living in the West Way area have[10] told us, at *The Gazette*, that they are very unhappy[20] with the cleansing services they have received lately. Their dustbins[30] have not been emptied at all in the last three[40] weeks. All kinds of rubbish and an abundance of black[50] bin bags have been left in the passageways and against[60] the fences because there is no room left inside the[70] dustbins. Allowances have been made by the locals, but in[80] the circumstances they have had enough and will not put[90] up with this mess near to their homes any longer[100].

Unit 13 – Letter L

Task 13.1

Read and write the following sentences.

1 The paper is to launch an appeal after a youth[10] died last night. The young male had been with a[20] gang who had been glue-sniffing behind the village hall[30].

2 Those living near the village hall, where the young boy[10] was found, said hooligans increasingly met outside the hall because[20] there was nothing else going on in the village[29].

3 Ladies and gentlemen, it is appalling in this day and[10] age that the youth of this village have nowhere to[20] go at night. We must think of something that will[30] encourage them to stop sniffing glue[36].

Task 13.2

Read and write the following sentences.

1 With an increasing number of old men and women living[10] longer these days, it is vital that they have the[20] facilities that they need to help them enjoy their lives[30].

2 We should be thinking about quality of life as much[10] as length of life. Utilities, such as gas and electricity[20], should be cheaper so that they are able to heat[30] their houses easily[33].

3 They should be able to reach facilities easily by ambulance[10] if they need to visit their G.P. or the hospital[20] at any time of the day or night[28].

4 Many old gentlemen and ladies value their agility and mingle[10] at weekly luncheon clubs, etc. They help by serving the[20] meals and are often seen helping out at jumble sales[30] and the like[33].

Task 13.3

Read and write the following sentences.

1 That road is not my favourite route. My favoured route[10] is the road by the Court[16].

2 The child hurt her knee quite badly when she slipped[10] on the road last week[15].

3 They pulled the cord hard and then held on tightly[10], hoping they would not crash immediately[16].

Task 13.4

Read and write the following sentences.

1 The popularity of the company chairman could not be in[10] doubt after the prize-giving to staff which was held[20] last week[22].

2 Security was a priority when putting forward ideas about the[10] visit of the P.M. to the town centre[18].

3 Tickets have been issued on the basis of staff seniority[10] when deciding who should go to the charity ball[19].

Task 13.5

Read and write 'M.P. supports local swimming pool'.

An M.P. is to give his backing to local residents[10] who wish to save their swimming pool. The local authority[20], whilst remaining sympathetic, says the pool costs too much to[30] keep open all year. It does not wish to close[40] the pool just as a result of budgeting. It says[50] there are too many pools in the Borough and it[60] would obviously be best to keep just one leisure centre[70] open. The majority of residents say that they are not[80] satisfied and do not accept the local authority's sympathy. It[90] would cause them a lot of difficulty to go to[100] a different swimming pool. Most of them go swimming regularly[110], and do not wish to stop doing so[118].

Task 13.6

Read and write 'Ideas needed for Charity Ball'.

Ladies and gentlemen, this meeting has been arranged so that[10] we may discuss the Charity Ball to be held in[20] June. Although it is only January, we do have a[30] lot to discuss in this regard. I notice, as I[40] glance at you in this room, many eyes are looking[50] at your shoes. I hope you will put forward your[60] ideas and meet the challenge, so that it is not[70] left, as it usually is, to those of us who[80] regularly help. I assure you, we are a jolly lot[90] really! There has been a lack of ideas to raise[100] money to fund the Charity Ball. I know John Piers[110] has suggested a sponsored gunge tank, and I would be[120] happy to be dipped in it if you all agree[130] to pay a huge sum[135]!

Unit 14 – Letter F

Task 14.1

Read and write the following sentences.

1 It was tough, but he had to face the fact[10] that his football career had reached its end[18].

2 The car was defective and this had caused the fatal[10] accident on the busy road[15].

3 When the child asked if he could have a toffee[10], his mum answered no because he would not eat his[20] lunch that day[23].

4 The tough guy showed his fist in defiance, but seemed[10] less hard as he made his defence in the courtroom[20].

5 It was a fine day and she fiddled with a[10] tuft of grass which blew on to her face[19].

Task 14.2

Read and write the following sentences.

1 At first you may think surfing is fraught with danger[10], but follow the rules and you will be quite safe[20].

2 He reflected on the job offer and was thankful for[10] the influence of his referee[15].

3 It would be useful and helpful if you could refurbish[10] the flat as soon as possible. I am sure it[20] needs a fresh lick of paint[26].

Task 14.3

Read and write the following sentences.

1 There was a sense of helplessness among the family when[10] they got together at the funeral of John's wife. She[20] had been infected by a deadly disease whilst on a[30] long-haul holiday and died shortly afterwards[37].

2 Her self-esteem rose and she was laughing quietly to herself[10] as she finished half of the Teeline shorthand theory. She[20] was a resourceful girl and the fact that she was[30] self-taught made her feel really good about herself[39].
3 The boys seemed baffled by the thing flying through the[10] air and felt very afraid as they rushed back home[20] to tell their families. They thought it might have been[30] a U.F.O[32].
4 Although she was a hefty girl her family said she[10] looked feminine and that was enough to give her the[20] lift she needed so that she felt encouraged to carry[30] on with her latest faddy diet[36].

Task 14.4

Read and write 'New library books'.

A school building, which was deemed past its shelf life[10] by a local authority spokesman, has just announced it has[20] received a donation to enable it to buy new books[30] for its library. The Westgate Lane Junior School is due[40] to close when it joins with South Bank Road Junior[50] in a few months' time. The Westgate Lane School will[60] be demolished as a priority, because parts of it are[70] unsafe. A new school will be built on the South[80] Bank Road site. But, while Westgate Junior remains, younger pupils[90] will begin reading thanks to the donation, which was enough[100] to buy the new books for the library. A range[110] of big books has been bought which is aimed specifically[120] at two to five year olds in the nursery[129].

Task 14.5

Read and write 'Accident in the Alps'.

A family is suffering the grief of losing their youngest[10] son following a freak accident. We have been informed that[20] the seventeen year old, Carl Watson, died of serious injuries[30] whilst on holiday in the Alps. The accident happened on[40] 23 February, just three days before Carl's eighteenth birthday. The[50] holiday had been arranged so that his college class could[60] study the area as part of their A level course[70]. Carl had been to the Alps before with his family[80] and was used to snowboarding and skiing. On that fateful[90] day it appears that there had been some sort of[100] difficulty with the ski lift. Unfortunately Carl was delayed in[110] reaching the summit. The rest of his class had safely[120] reached the bottom of the hill, but it appears that[130] Carl was caught in an avalanche which had not been[140] forecast by the local radio that day[149].

Unit 15 – Words ending -MENT, -AVITY, -EVITY and -TIVITY

Task 15.1

Read and write the following sentences.

1 An agreement was made by the gangs for the shipment[10] of heroin to be sent separately[16].
2 The Parliamentary spokesman told the press that it was no[10] good being sentimental at this time[16].
3 Her appointment was fundamentally flawed, but it had been made[10] with the agreement of management[15].

Task 15.2

Read and write the following sentences.

1 The cavity caused by tooth decay was causing a lot[10] of pain and her cheek was definitely swollen[18].

2 The depth of the gravity of the case was too[10] amazing for them to deal with[16].

3 Longevity is something we shall have to deal with within[10] families and not rely on the state totally[18].

Task 15.3

Read and write the following sentences.

1 It was very nice to see your child take part[10] in the nativity scene at the village hall in December[20].

2 His tooth showed sensitivity when touched by the piece of[10] cold metal and he jumped in pain[17].

3 The baby loved the activity centre put in his cot[10] and did not feel ready to go to sleep[19].

Task 15.4

Read and write 'Youths speak out at forum'.

A youth service is hosting the North East Regional Assembly[10] for the first time this week. The Assembly meets once[20] every six to eight weeks to discuss issues affecting young[30] men and women. The Engaging Youth Study is hosting the[40] day at the City Studies Institute in the city centre[50]. Local youths will be represented at the forum. Local youths[60] will be required to represent this area at the forum[70] and meet a number of youths from outside the north[80]-east area. Katie Hillyard, Youth Development Officer said, 'The youth[90] assembly will be able to make a real difference. We[100] hope to have representatives from every school and college in[110] the area sitting on the borough's board. The assembly will[120] discuss the fundamental needs of youth today[127].'

Task 15.5

Read and write 'Educating families about healthy eating'.

Boys and girls from a local infant school have been[10] taught about healthy eating in a fun-filled day. With funding[20] from the Health Activity Zone, teachers joined pupils for a[30] host of activities as part of the school's, 'I feel[40] good about me' day. Making collages, games and, of course[50], food tasting had been included in the day. Each child[60] got a pencil, a fruit-shaped rubber and a sticker[70] to take home to show their family. Ben Collins, aged[80] six, said, 'Healthy eating means eating lots of fruit and[90] veg to keep you fit. I like carrots and have[100] them regularly.' Staff said, 'Hopefully, the boys and girls will[110] go home and tell their families how much they enjoyed[120] the fruit and veg and will ask to eat it[130] every day[132].'

UNIT 16 – Words ending -SHUN, -SHL, -SHIP and -SHUS and words beginning SUPER-

Task 16.1

Read and write the following sentences.

1 Although the musician was in possession of heroin he did[10] not mention this when questioned by the police[18].

2 The Member of Parliament for this ward was passionate about[10] his beliefs and occasionally his impatience could be felt by[20] those close to him[24].

3 We need additional support before the election in May to[10] help us get the new documentation ready[17].

4 She had difficulty showing her emotions in this situation and[10] there seemed to be no solution[16].

5 He was always efficient, showed proficiency on every occasion and[10] so the panel had no option but to appoint him[20].

Task 16.2

Read and write the following sentences.

1 The referee felt it was essential to check with the[10] fourth official. It was crucial he took impartial advice[19].

2 A judicial statement was made to the jury on the[10] final day of the racial abuse case[17].

3 The beautician said her speciality was the facial, but an[10] initial assessment would be needed[15].

4 She was told to write her initials in block capitals[10] on the official form before signing it[17].

5 A special visit was made by the Member of Parliament[10] for the official opening of his political party's social club[20].

Task 16.3

Read and write the following sentences.

1 The new headship had been fraught with difficult staff relationships[10], but the last week had been especially bad[18].

2 The couple visited the Social Services department to discuss the[10] amount they could claim from the hardship fund[18].

3 Initially the child enjoyed the game of battleships, but at[10] the crucial moment his dad beat him and he was[20] upset[21].

Task 16.4

Read and write the following sentences.

1 The supervisor said, 'Make a superhuman effort in the amount[10] you do, or you might be thought superfluous to the[20] company[21]'.

2 The final supersonic flight occurred in 2003 and there is[10] nothing to supersede it[14].

3 She showed superiority in her knowledge of the necessary superannuation[10] calculations and that was why she was the supervisor[19].

Task 16.5

Read and write the following sentences.

1 They seemed gracious and thanked their host for a delicious[10] meal, despite the vicious fish bone[16]!

2 They stepped cautiously into the room where they could smell[10] noxious fumes[12].

3 If you are superstitious, be cautious and look for a[10] rabbit's foot or a lucky black cat[17].

Task 16.6

Read and write 'Police station to open longer hours'.

A local police station has stated its intention to have[10] longer opening hours following demands from rural residents. The petition[20] was signed to highlight this need in view of the[30] increasingly anti-social attitude of many local youths. Those who live[40] on the edge of the Borough feel isolated and say[50] that police resources are being poured, in particular, into the[60] town centres. The police give these areas special attention, especially[70] on Friday nights, while rural areas are being ignored. Police[80] are anxious to allay residents' fears and have therefore decided[90] to open the police station for ten hours each day[100] of the week and at weekends from 5 January. They[110] hope this will be seen as a huge benefit for[120] the residents in the area. There will be a full[130]-time officer on duty instead of the usual part-time[140] officer. Response teams will also answer calls in the area[150]. For additional information, call P.C. Price[156].

Unit 17 – T and D blends

Task 17.1

Write the following words in Teeline.

travel  terminal  history 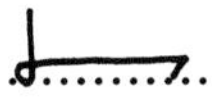 later  enter 

Madrid  drooping 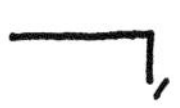 withdraw 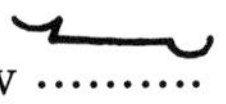 slander 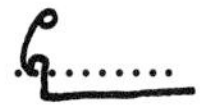 corridor 

Task 17.2

Read and write the following sentences.

1 The reporter met the pop star to interview him for[10] a feature she was writing for her magazine[18].

2 It was strange to think that the terrorist had been[10] trapped on this very terrace following the disturbance[18].

3 It had been an endurance test to have his child[10] sitting on his shoulders during the rugby match[18].

4 An elderly gentleman was discovered in the dark, dirty bedroom[10] of the house. It was difficult giving time of death[20].

5 Water started to fall on the door which had been[10] painted only two hours ago[15].

Task 17.3

Read and write the following sentences.

1 There has been a tendency for trendy young ladies and[10] men to stand in tanning booths but in the long[20] term it gives wrinkles[24].

2 The wooden chair was stained to retain its antique character[10] before being sold at the auction[16].

3 Entertainment was free at the modern Indian restaurant in the[10] centre of London[13].

4 They are usually forbidden to stand there because the digger[10] may return and they would be hidden[17].

5 The drainage system is in need of modernisation, although we[10] may be able to retain some of the pipes[19].

Task 17.4

Read and write 'A rewarding future in entertainment'.

Jobs in the entertainment and leisure industries have long suffered[10] because of their image. Many believed that such jobs did[20] not amount to being 'real jobs'. Across the U.K. today[30], according to the latest Government statistics, a staggering three million[40] have jobs in the leisure industry, and that number is[50] increasing all the time. There is an opportunity to forge[60] a career in this industry today. Belonging to the leisure[70] industry was once a euphemism for being a barman or[80] a barmaid and, thankfully, there are a lot of them[90] still in the job, but these days the term is[100] used for the entire tourist industry, sports, leisure and entertainment[110] sector. One of the beauties of the leisure industry is[120] that it tends to have open opportunities. There are few[130] rigid career structures to hamper the path of the ambitious[140] and able[142].

Unit 18 – THR, CTR and RN blends and words ending -NESS

Task 18.1

Read and write the following sentences.

1 A mother and father smothered their child with kisses and[10] love when she got home[15].

2 Other things had to be done, and they could not[10] be bothered cooking a meal that night[17].

3 A man who threatened a youth who had burgled his[10] house was arrested by the police on Thursday[18].

4 Sometimes it is difficult to gather information for feature material[10] for a newspaper[13].

5 The thrifty woman gathered fruit from the hedgerows to make[10] pies to sell at the jumble sale[17].

Task 18.2

Read and write the following sentences.

1 The lecturer in the catering department cooked a delicious meal[10] for the students[13].

2 Jobs at the factory are difficult to get for anyone[10] who is not skilled[14].

3 The author tried to write an interesting book at his[10] quiet cottage, but lacked inspiration[15].
4 Although the tractor on the farm was defective, he would[10] not dispose of it. In fact, he would throw nothing[20] away[21].
5 The caterer was rather reluctant to cater for children's birthday[10] parties and preferred lucrative weddings[15].

Task 18.3

Read and write the following sentences.

1 It was raining hard, but it did not stop the[10] runner from training for the race[16].
2 An asylum seeker was asked to surrender his passport at[10] the airport[12].
3 Children watched as the hay burned, and thought that the[10] farmhouse might also catch fire[15].
4 The coroner told the parents of the children who had[10] died in the house fire, that they had his sincere[20] sympathy[21].
5 After the epidemic of foot and mouth disease in this[10] area, many herds of cows had to be slaughtered and[20] burnt[21].

Task 18.4

Read and write 'Boost for tourism'.

A decision has been made to boost tourism in the[10] area. The local authority has devised a strategy to attract[20] visitors here and also hopes to attract funding from various[30] charities and local businesses. The authority believes that the superb[40] natural resources of the beach and rural areas will encourage[50] visitors to flock here. It agrees that a significant amount[60] still needs to be done, such as putting beach lifeguards[70] further along the coast and making better car parking facilities[80]. Some other ideas include attracting visitors with specific interests, such[90] as fishing, surfing and a skateboard park for younger visitors[100].

Task 18.5

Read and write 'Surfer thanks lifeguards'.

Anna Ford, a members' assistant at a local gym, has[10] praised two men who saved her life after she was[20] swept out to sea by a strong current while surfing[30] with a friend. Beach lifeguard, Paul Cook, aged nineteen, swam[40] into the choppy seas with a rescue board to try[50] to save her, but the rough sea knocked them both[60] off the board. Paul was in the water when a[70] lifeboat reached him. He was feared dead but, thankfully, only[80] suffered mild hypothermia. Meanwhile, another lifeguard, Nick White, used a[90] surfboard to go out to sea to bring Anna safely[100] back to shore. Anna, who was suffering from shock, had[110] to go to hospital, but later said the men had[120] been fantastic in putting their lives at risk to save[130] others[131].

Unit 19 – LR, MR and WR blends

Task 19.1

Read and write the following sentences.

1 A notorious drug dealer met the young female drug addict[10] and surreptitiously passed the heroin wrap to her before he[20] walked nonchalantly towards the city centre[26].

2 That man was once thought of as a pillar of[10] society and popular with local businessmen, but since his affair[20] with the mayor's wife he was thought of as nothing[30] but a flirt and a cad[36].

3 At sixteen years of age, the youth had already learned[10] his trade as a burglar. He had been taught by[20] young men not much older than himself[27].

4 Their monthly salary was paid into their bank accounts and[10] they drew half of it out straight away so that[20] they could go to the fashion clearance sale at the[30] large city-centre store[34].

5 He tried to act normally and appeared cool, but the[10] police knew that he was the killer as they had[20] gathered forensic evidence at the scene earlier that day[29].

Task 19.2

Read and write the following sentences.

1 Mr and Mrs Jones had marvellous memories of their holiday[10] in the Far East[14].

2 Many of us admire glamourous models as they strut along[10] the catwalk[12].

3 It is a marvellous moment when one's final mortgage payment[10] has been made[13].

4 The doctor carried out the post mortem at the scene[10] before taking the body to the mortuary[17].

5 The interview had gone well. His smarter appearance had helped[10] secure the job[13].

Task 19.3

Read and write the following sentences.

1 They were worried that the warm weather would harm the[10] flowers and watered them well[15].

2 The warden thought the lower floor might not be secure[10]. He put them on the upper floor[17].

3 The telescopic viewer at the top of the tower gave[10] a long-range view[14].

4 He reported it as the worst warfare he had ever[10] seen in all his years as a war correspondent[19].

5 Weariness showed in her face after the long illness, but[10] she was certainly a fighter[15].

Task 19.4

Read and write the following sentences.

1 After walking for twenty miles in the Lake District she[10] felt very weak indeed[14].

2 In his new workshop Paul was inspired, and carved the[10] wood with renewed zest[14].

3 Why do the weekends seem to go by so fast[10], whereas weekdays drag[13]?

4 His workmanship was terrific and he was thanked sincerely by[10] everyone at the hospice[14].

5 Tea pickers work very hard and receive quite low pay[10] for all their effort[14].

Task 19.5

Read and write 'Award for foster carer'.

A foster mum who offers round-the-clock support to[10] fellow carers has received a well deserved award. For more[20] than twenty-two years, Sue Fisher has cared for at[30] least fifty young children. Realising that foster carers themselves sometimes[40] need somewhere to turn and someone to talk to, Sue[50] set up a twenty-four hour telephone helpline for local[60] carers. The Local Authority's Social Services Department honoured Sue in[70] their first annual awards ceremony which was held at Newburn[80] Hall last week. Sue, who dreamed up the hotline idea[90], told our reporter that about fifty other carers have her[100] telephone number so that they are able to call her[110] if they have a crisis or just need someone to[120] talk to. She said new carers particularly tend to feel[130] a bit isolated. They might just need someone to tell[140] them they were quite right to make a particular decision[150].

Unit 20 – Colloquialisms, numbers, currencies and measurements

Task 20.1

Read and write the following sentences.

1 I'm about to buy a lottery ticket and I'm hoping[10] to be lucky and get the eight-million pound prize[20]. If I do, I shall change the money at the[30] bank and use one-thousand dollars to go to America[40].

2 He's had hundreds of opportunities to get his qualification. He[10] started the course in 2001. I think we should put[20] him on the spot and get him to finish the[30] course[31].

3 The diet had been successful. She had weighed seventy kilograms[10] at the start and had reached her target weight of[20] sixty kilograms after only six months[26].

4 The euro is the currency of Ireland, and I've to[10] go to the bank and withdraw about two-hundred euros[20] for my holiday during May[25].

5 The difference in their level of attendance was amazing. Six[10] students had a one-hundred per cent record, whereas seven[20] students had only eighty-two per cent[27].

Unit 21 – X blends

Task 21.1

Read and write the following sentences.

1 While exercising on the treadmill at the gym he exerted[10] a lot of energy. He then fell very awkwardly[19].

2 He badly hurt his ankle and had it examined at[10] the hospital. He was sent for an X-ray[18].

3 He could not drive home and telephoned for a taxi[10] to collect him. He will remember his expedition to the[20] gym[21].

4 The couple expressed an interest in the luxury bathrooms to[10] the demonstrator at the Ideal Homes Exhibition[17].

5 A luxury car had been exported from Japan and was[10] found to have excessive exhaust fumes when examined in the[20] UK[21].

6 They built an extension on the detached house and had[10] hoped to have it finished by Xmas 2005 but without[20] success[21].

7 The drunk was intoxicated with cheap gin and lived a[10] sad existence on the streets of London[17].

Task 21.2

Read and write the following sentences.

1 The excerpt of the music I heard was excellent and[10] I would like to buy the CD for my mother[20] as soon as possible[24].

2 A young journalist interviewed the famous actor and claimed an[10] exclusive story for her paper[15].

3 Students had to excavate the old Roman ruins as part[10] of the course and said it was very exciting[19].

4 The boxer flexed his muscles before going into the ring[10] for the championship fight, although he was rather frightened[19].

5 She made an excuse not to go on the excursion[10] with the old folk. At sixty-five she felt too[20] young[21].

Task 21.3

Read and write 'Help your local hospice'.

There are many exciting and extraordinary ways to help your[10] local hospice. Why not, for example, take part in one[20] of the regular fundraising activities in the area. Make a[30] donation of items to one of its excellent charity shops[40], or buy a hospice lottery ticket. By taking part in[50] the lottery, not only will you get the chance to[60] gain two-thousand pounds every week, but your one pound[70] will enable the hospice to carry on with its specialist[80] care. A more energetic way to raise money would be[90] to take part in a parachute jump, an abseil or[100] a sponsored five-mile walk. Local businesses may support the[110] cause at the summer ball or the golf tournament. Further[120] details from Sue Miller[124].

Task 21.4

Read and write 'Mistake with nail glue'.

A schoolgirl is extremely lucky that she will not lose[10] her sight, despite having glue put into her eye by[20] her mother, by mistake. Kate's right eye lid was glued[30] shut after her mum accidentally treated her daughter's eye infection[40] with drops of glue normally used for sticking false nails[50], instead of the eye drops. In the second it took[60] to realise what had happened, the damage was done. At[70] the hospital Kate's eye was checked and she was told[80] that it should heal in approximately six weeks. Her reflex[90] action of blinking could not be checked. Kate's mum was[100] very upset. She told us that the bottles of nail[110] glue and eye drops were exactly alike. Both were pink[120] with pointed nozzles. She asked parents to read the packaging[130] carefully before dispensing eye drops, as mistakes were easily made[140].

Task 21.5
Transcribe the following special outlines.

1 importance
2 perfectly
3 difficulty
4 unfortunately
5 establish
6 station
7 incident
8 first of all
9 absolutely
10 society
11 usually
12 tomorrow

Unit 22 – CM blends and words beginning RECOM-

Task 22.1
Write the following words in Teeline.

camper, competence, competition, comments, camber, chameleon, comparison, camouflage, composed, commuter, accompaniment, ecumenical

Task 22.2
Read and write the following sentences.

1 A campaign was launched to save the chemical company which[10] had come to the area a number of years ago[20].
2 The chemists said it would be difficult to find similar[10] jobs to accommodate their particular skills[16].
3 A chemical company spokesman said he welcomed the interest of[10] a cement factory which might buy the site[18].
4 The union said that gave little comfort and thought the[10] whole business was a scam[15].
5 The workers were only interested in securing their income and[10] backed a strike campaign[14].
6 As is common in these situations, nobody really gains. The[10] workers lost their income by striking[16].
7 The cement factory decided to go somewhere else and the[10] union's recommendation was a redundancy settlement[16].

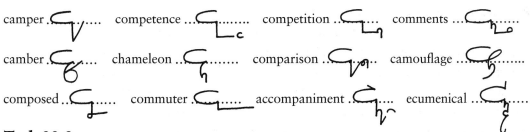

Task 22.3

Read and write the following sentences.

1 I have come to the conclusion that a residents' committee[10] should be set up to discuss the matter of speed[20] cameras and then report back with its recommendations[28].

2 The commercial companies became very competitive and began dropping their[10] prices to encourage customers to come back to them[19].

3 Vox pop is a Latin phrase meaning popular voice. Excellent[10] communication skills are needed by journalists who interview men and[20] women in the street[24].

4 The residents' association decided to set up a combination of[10] a finance and social committee in order to sort out[20] their affairs at the community centre[26].

5 Income tax bills may be paid using a computer. This[10] trend is welcomed by those who are computer literate, but[20] those who are less competent have difficulty[27].

Task 22.4

Read and write 'Speed cameras'.

A speed camera scheme was piloted in the Teesside area[10] in 2002 at a cost of nearly one million pounds[20]. The number of accidents fell dramatically by about fifty per[30] cent and approximately fifty-nine thousand motorists were caught speeding[40] in the first two years. Mobile speed cameras operate all[50] over the region these days and most motorists respect the[60] speed limits imposed when a camera is seen in operation[70].

Task 22.5

Read and write 'Hi-tech police force'.

A hi-tech police force will be able to keep tabs[10] on their day-to-day work while also training at[20] the police headquarters, thanks to the new computer kiosks which[30] have been installed. The first of five kiosks has been[40] installed so that visiting staff may monitor emails and keep[50] up-to date with the news from their particular patch[60]. The idea behind the five-thousand pound scheme is to[70] allow officers throughout the force area to access the full[80] range of computer facilities which they would normally have at[90] their desks. The Head of Information and Communications believed that[100] a lot of the officers who came to the police[110] headquarters for training courses would use the new facilities[119].

Unit 23 – N and V blends

Task 23.1

Read and write the following sentences.

1 November 5th is Guy Fawkes Night. Traditionally, fireworks are let[10] off and bonfires are lit, but it is a shame[20] that vandals sometimes spoil things for others[27].

2 A large amount of investment has been put into the[10] community centre. Toys have been bought for the children's scheme[20] and the kitchen facilities are much better than they were[30] before the refurbishment[33].

3 Sam Fox was one of the first voluptuous models to[10] appear on page three of the *Sun* newspaper. After that[20], the volume of male readership increased dramatically[27].

4 Their anniversary was marked by a walk along the river bank[10] where they first met. They never would have thought that[20] their relationship would last so long[26].
5 The judge summed up in the court case involving six[10] villains in the city centre. He invited the members of[20] the jury to give their verdict of guilty or not[30] guilty[31].

Task 23.2

Read and write the following sentences.

1 Nowadays, town twinning is common. Our town has been twinned[10] with a similar sized town in France and everyone is[20] excited about the event to be held here later in[30] the year[32].
2 Christmas Eve is wonderful for children whatever their age. The[10] younger ones never want to go to bed and sleep[20] because they are so excited about Santa Claus visiting[29].
3 The owner of the navy van was evasive about his[10] ownership of the vehicle so the police began to wonder[20] why he had left it in the town near the[30] government building[32].
4 The newt is classed as an endangered species. However, I[10] own a garden pond and have found two of them[20] there after clearing up after winter[26].
5 On that eventful day a World War II bomb was[10] found. We had to evacuate the building and everything calmed[20] down eventually. At the time, everybody was in high spirits[30].

Task 23.3

Read and write the following sentences.

1 If you have to interview somebody, make sure you know[10] exactly where you are going to meet them. Arrive several[20] minutes early for your appointment and keep calm[28].
2 Their new working environment was lovely. Everyone knows that if[10] your working environment is upside down then your work too[20] is likely to be chaotic[25].
3 In our opinion, there is no doubt that it is[10] an advantage to have experience of taking shorthand notes in[20] the courtroom before you have to do so as part[30] of your real job as a reporter[37].
4 The invention of the computer radically changed the working environment[10] in which journalists now work. Although many saw the disadvantages[20], in our opinion computers have been a welcome change[29].
5 There was a lively atmosphere in the nightclub, but the[10] landlord was worried about binge drinking by some youngsters because[20] he knew he could lose his licence[27].

Task 23.4

Read and write 'Police to stop rising tide of violence'.

There has been a rising tide of violence in the[10] town centre. It is thought that many of these violent[20] attacks and acts of vandalism are related to binge drinking[30] and alcohol abuse. Police chiefs have decided that they will[40] take tough measures to stamp this out here and now[50]. More officers will be seen on the beat, especially on[60] Friday and Saturday nights. They will arrest anyone on suspicion[70] of excess drinking and will not tolerate anti-social behaviour[80].

Task 23.5

Read and write 'Successful airline business'.

It is good to report that this new airline company[10] has been very successful during the current year. We have[20] managed to fight off fairly stiff competition to secure new[30] business. Our aim has always been to give our customers[40] a higher standard of comfort and service. Our airline fleet[50] has the highest standard of excellence and safety and we[60] have given passengers more space, comfort and leg room. We[70] have installed the most up-to-date equipment and systems[80] for our admin staff. In order to meet our aims[90], we knew that we would have to reduce our costs[100] or increase our fares and the figures in our accounts[110] reflect this[112].

Unit 24 – CN blends

Task 24.1

Read and write the following sentences.

1 Candidates taking their shorthand examination must stay calm, relaxed, and[10] listen to what the invigilator has to say before the[20] exam begins[22].

2 Candidates should enter the exam room with confidence and be[10] ready to listen carefully and concentrate. If successful they may[20] have the incentive of a pay rise[27].

3 If you encounter someone who has become ill, do not[10] move them because they may be unconscious. Phone for an[20] ambulance and try to keep the invalid warm[28].

4 Censorship of some films at the cinema continues to be[10] inconsistent or is it just that I am being cynical[20]?

5 I lost confidence in the accountant who was continually being[10] economical with the truth whenever I spoke to him. I[20] think it is scandalous and I am feeling extremely concerned[30].

Task 24.2

Read and write the following sentences.

1 Two colours merged as the canvas had not been allowed[10] to dry. The painting was spoiled[16].

2 The English convict was not conversant with the language spoken[10] in the Spanish jail[14].

3 It was a convivial atmosphere when we convened at the[10] jazz festival last June[14].

4 Our conversation convinced the woman to convey our thanks to[10] them[11].

Task 24.3

Read and write the following sentences.

1 At the recent Conservative Party Conference, Councillor Jones asked for[10] a vote of thanks to be given to the retiring[20] Chairman in recognition of his excellent work on behalf of[30] the Party at local level[35].

2 Councillor Smith said, 'I can tell you that council tax[10] payments for the majority of our senior citizens will be[20] lower because discounts will be given to those aged seventy[30]'.

3 I cannot tell you how relieved I am to see[10] so many of you here today from all over the[20] country. I am sure that you will be glad that[30] you have taken the time to come here today for[40] this conference[42].

4 Ladies and gentlemen, I can tell you that congratulations are[10] in order. The Town Council has recently decided to erect[20] a permanent memorial statue near to the conference facilities[29].

5 You can be sure that the County Council recognises that[10] this sort of thing cannot continue and we can congratulate[20] them for that[23].

Task 24.4

Read and write 'Fines for dropping litter'.

A Council has become the first in the region to[10] launch fixed-penalty fines for children as young as ten[20] who drop litter. The fifty pound fines are seen as[30] a last-ditch attempt to cut the amount of litter[40] dropped in the area. The authority says that the litter[50] includes sweet wrappers, chip wrappers and pop bottles dropped by[60] school children. Until now, the Council has been powerless to[70] punish such children. The Council's Environmental Health Department will also[80] issue fifty pound fixed-penalty fines to errant dog owners[90] who fail to clean up after their pets. Parents say[100] they are unable to watch their children twenty-four-hours[110]-a-day. On-the-spot fines for adults had gone[120] some way to cleaning up the streets, but this was[130] a step further by the Council who say they are[140] trying to educate youngsters through their schools not to drop[150] litter[151].

Task 24.5

Read and write 'Fake cash machines'.

Police have been hunting thieves who have recently robbed many[10] bank accounts in this county. Detectives say bank account holders[20] have lost many thousands of pounds to a fake cash[30] machine scam. Police claimed a major setback for the thieves[40] on Tuesday, following the recovery of a fake front for[50] a cash machine, including a mini-computer used for recording[60] card details. It seems that the mini-computer had become[70] dislodged in the hands of an inquisitive customer. It is[80] thought that thieves, watching from nearby, moved in quickly to[90] retrieve the mini-camera, which would also have been attached[100] to film numbers as they were typed in. Police say[110] the fake cash machine housings are an exact colour match[120] with the real machine, even down to the detail of[130] the bank's logo and typeface. There have been several victims[140], including one person whose account was emptied. The banking industry's[150] intelligence service suggests that the gangs who are harvesting millions[160] from accounts throughout the U.K. are not from this country[170].

Unit 25 – P blends

Task 25.1

Read and write the following sentences.

1 It is my pleasant duty to declare this splendid leisure[10] complex open and I invite you to join me in[20] the pavilion for a complimentary glass of champagne[28].

2 Placards complaining about the poverty in many parts of the[10] world were displayed, together with a plea for donations of[20] money to help supply plenty of food and warm clothing[30].

3 When considering the application, the representative from the planning department[10] was unhappy about the position of the pavements and complained[20] to the applicant who said he would change the plans[30] immediately[31].

4 At the Hallowe'en party, water was splattered all over the[10] place as the children excitedly splashed about in the kitchen[20] sink bobbing for apples[24].

5 As the troops became a little too complacent and relaxed[10], the enemy deployed some of its soldiers towards the front[20] line to pave the way for the ensuing battle[29].

Task 25.2

Read and write the following sentences.

1 The lecturer explained the complicated formula to the chemistry students[10].

2 Terrorists caused an explosion in the city centre but had[10] not been explicit when they phoned a warning[18].

3 Exploratory work was carried out by the scientist to try[10] to find a cure[14].

4 The expletives exploding from his mouth were appalling to listen[10] to[11].

5 He was explicit in his reply and explained exactly where[10] and when he would leave the appliance[17].

Task 25.3

Read and write the following sentences.

1 It is my pleasure to expel this myth for members[10] of the public gathered here today[16].

2 We are pleased to know that so many people are[10] interested in this complicated matter[15].

3 The publican gave publicity to the forthcoming social event to[10] be held in his pub in a simple leaflet he[20] had published[22].

Task 25.4

Read and write 'Riverside Festival success'.

After ten days of extremely varied weather, the Riverside Festival[10] finished with style. A spectacular firework display rounded off the[20] Festival on the river's banks. Tens of thousands of people[30] turned out to watch the explosive end to this annual[40] event. During the ten days, people have been sunburned and[50] drenched as scorching weather in the first few days changed[60] into a torrential storm. Despite the changing weather, not a[70] single show was withdrawn. Planning has already started for next[80] year's event. The Planning Director told us that the Festival[90] had been a wonderful success with visitors being treated to[100] world-class performances. He said that music, street theatre and[110] circus shows would be remembered for many years to come[120].

Task 25.5

Read and write 'Waste collection'.

A Council attempted to collect around fifty tons of waste[10] last weekend. It was an attempt to clear a backlog[20] of two-thousand-five-hundred jobs by the end of[30] this month. The Borough Council launched its free waste-collection[40] services in the nineties. They have been removing unwanted items[50] such as beds, three-piece suites and fridges for about[60] ten years. The service has been unable to keep pace[70] with demand. Hence the attempt last weekend when a fleet[80] of fourteen refuse vehicles began an operation to clear six[90]-hundred jobs. In future residents will be encouraged to recycle[100] more or use the two civic amenity tips. Another alternative[110], which is due to begin in April, is a ten[120] pound express service which will ensure pick up of unwanted[130] items within five working days[135].

Unit 26 – Full vowels used as word endings

Task 26.1

Write the following words in neat Teeline outlines.

available/availability ...... durable/durability ...... gables ...... lovable ...... nibbles ......

adaptable/adaptability ...... gullible/gullibility ...... horribly ...... flexible/flexibility ......

Task 26.2

Read and write the following sentences.

1 Information collected must be reliable and therefore it is terribly[10] important to doubly and trebly check it[17].
2 A bomb-disposal unit was dispatched to disable the device[10] which was barely visible and hardly accessible[17].
3 Jane Austen wrote *Sense and Sensibility* more than a century[10] ago, but it is a valuable novel recently made into[20] a film[22].
4 Sometimes gardeners remove pebbles from an accessible beach, but should[10] realise that this is illegal[15].
5 It can be fashionable for a man to have stubble[10] on his face rather than be clean shaven[18].
6 If stolen valuables are not labelled carefully by police officers[10], they will have trouble matching them with the owners[19].

Task 26.3

Read and write the following sentences.

1 Rebels find it impossible to accept another person's authority but[10] inevitably have to succumb[14].
2 Who is responsible for filling the bathroom with bubbles? It[10] has made me popping mad[15]!
3 The respectable couple decided they were compatible and think that[10] an engagement is possible[14].
4 Something insuperable is unconquerable, but not many things can be[10] so difficult that they cannot be sorted out[18].
5 It is impossible to be a responsible and a respectable[10] adult in this rebellious society[15].

Task 26.4

Read and write 'Disabled charity busker's parking ticket'.

A disabled man who has raised more than two-hundred[10]-and-fifty-thousand pounds for charity is likely to have[20] his parking fine cancelled. Last week the sixty-year-old[30] man, Mr James Noble, who has suffered from multiple sclerosis[40] since the age of sixteen, received a parking ticket from[50] a traffic warden. The musician gives up hours of time[60] each week in order to entertain people in the High[70] Street. He parked his specially adapted car in its usual[80] position, in a disabled parking bay, just metres away from[90] where he regularly sings and plays his accordion. However, he[100] failed to notice that his blue disabled parking badge was[110] out of date[113].

Mr Noble who is currently raising money for the holistic[10] cancer unit at the local university hospital said that he[20] was amazed by what had happened and felt absolutely terrible[30] about it. The traffic warden said that he was only[40] doing his job. Mr Noble said he realised that, but[50] thought that the traffic warden should have given him a[60] warning, not a thirty pound parking ticket. The council sent[70] a letter to Mr Noble last week saying that they[80] would consider a refund if he supplied them with further[90] evidence of his circumstances, as this was his first offence[100].

Unit 27 – More word beginnings and endings

Task 27.1

Read and write the following sentences.

1 I understand that they will undertake to put the oil[10] pipeline under the sea[14].
2 The ambulance transported the donor's heart for an emergency transplant[10] operation[11].
3 Did I overlook to let you know that I am[10] going overseas next week? My vacation is long overdue[19].
4 I know that you have a hangover today, so I[10] will take over and pick the children up from school[20].
5 We shall transform this garden, especially underneath the apple tree[10] which overlooks the pond. We will work all over[19].

Task 27.2

Read and write the following sentences.

1 The multi-national company had an excellent equal opportunities policy and[10] employed a multi-racial workforce[14].
2 At the semi-final of the rugby match, the player became[10] semi-conscious after being kicked in the head and had to[20] be carried off[23].
3 She objected to being given the injection by the doctor[10] and rejected the offer of pain relief[17].

4 Residents objected to the flyover being built near their semi-detached[10] houses. Transporter lorries would be too noisy[17].
5 She did not understand why the bank rejected the transfer[10] of money from her account in England to one overseas[20].

Task 27.3

Read and write the following sentences.

1 Over the past few months there has been trouble all[10] over the world because of terrorist activity[17].
2 All over the country people have been extra vigilant, but[10] especially on the Tube stations in London[17].
3 The trouble is that people hear about it over and[10] over again, become complacent and then it goes over their[20] heads[21].
4 I shall be glad when all this talk of terrorism[10] is over and done with[15].
5 Eventually, I hope that all over the world peace will[10] overcome the evil of these terrorists[16].

Task 27.4

Read and write 'Headteachers help police'.

A number of headteachers from all over the region are[10] joining the police on their weekend patrols in an attempt[20] to catch under-age drinkers. They have decided to help the[30] police to identify pupils, some as young as thirteen, who[40] are out on the streets at night, or even drinking[50] in pubs and clubs. The headteachers will be able to[60] help identify trouble makers and anti-social gang members who regularly[70] meet outside off licences and on housing estates. The heads[80] are keen to undertake this task in order to try[90] to cut the number of pupils at their schools who[100] arrive with hangovers. They also hope to transform the behaviour[110] of those pupils who are abusive to their teachers[119].

Unit 28 – More word beginnings and endings

Task 28.1

Read and write the following sentences.

1 Electrification of the railway line between London and the North[10] East has helped to speed up the service[18].
2 A magnificent effort was made by fundraisers for the local[10] hospice who held a sponsored abseil[16].
3 I remember reading a book called *Mr Magnolia* to my[10] young children and we loved it[16].
4 In the large theatre, without the aid of a microphone[10], the singer gave an electrifying performance[16].
5 Do not touch the microwave oven in this kitchen as[10] the wiring is unsafe and you might electrocute yourself[19].

Task 28.2

Read and write the following sentences.

1 It was a magnanimous gesture to supply the school with[10] microscopes for their new biology laboratory[16].

2 Microwave towers all over the country have assisted telecommunications technology[10].

3 People worry about the safety of atomic power stations even[10] though nuclear energy gives cheaper electricity[16].

4 The technical terminology was explained clearly by the lecturer at[10] the College of Technology[14].

5 Phrenology is the study of a skull's shape. Theory suggests[10] character and mental powers are indicated by the shape of[20] the skull[22].

Task 28.3

Read and write 'Rightful owners asked to come forward'.

Detectives have recovered an estimated one-thousand pound's worth of[10] stolen goods and are now appealing for the rightful owners[20] to come forward to claim them. Police officers collected more[30] than twenty-five pieces of equipment from a car which[40] they had stopped and searched, including a number of electronic[50] games, a sanding machine and a child's bicycle. Police have[60] said that the goods were being taken to a car[70] boot sale being held in the car park of a[80] nearby technical college. They said the haul had been significant[90] and appealed to members of the public to mark their[100] valuables[101].

Task 28.4

Read and write 'Appeal for new blood donors'.

An appeal is being made to try to avert a[10] crisis at the region's blood banks. The National Blood Service[20] will lose approximately fifty-thousand donors because of fears over[30] the human form of mad cow disease. Although the risk[40] of infection is said to be very small, everyone who[50] has had a blood transfusion since 1980 is being[60] barred from giving blood. Unless new donors come forward in[70] significant numbers, haematology departments will lose thousands of units of[80] blood every year. Therefore every healthy person between the ages[90] of seventeen and sixty should consider attending a blood donor[100] session[101].

Unit 29 – The R principle – BR, CR, GR and PR and words ending -GRAPH and -GRAM

Task 29.1

Read and write the following sentences.

1 The robber brandished a gun as he broke into the[10] bank on Broad Street last Friday afternoon[17].

2 To celebrate his twenty-first birthday, Lee went to a[10] brilliant new club under the bridge[16].

Task 29.2

Read and write the following sentences.

1 Detectives cracked the mystery of the criminal damage caused to[10] the concrete statue[13].

2 After the acrobatics display, an incredible amount of discomfort was[10] caused by cramp in his leg[16].

Task 29.3

Read and write the following sentences.

1 For a grown man he was very aggressive and needed[10] to get a grip of his emotions[17].

2 Flagrant flouting of the rules at the club aggravated the[10] situation so new ground rules were established and agreed by[20] the committee[22].

Task 29.4

Read and write the following sentences.

1 The gardener's speciality was to grow top-grade fragrant roses[10] in his greenhouse[13].

2 On the craft stall there were many beautiful embroidery kits[10] for sale at bargain prices[15].

3 Bribery and corruption were rife in the old Italian town[10] until the new police chief took over[17].

4 The pitch at the cricket club was ruined by moles[10] digging up the soft ground[15].

5 The undergraduate needed great self-discipline to stay and study[10] while his friends went to the pub[17].

6 Evidence of broken glass was shown to incriminate the thief[10] as his fingers had been all over it[18].

7 It is only a good idea to abbreviate Teeline outlines[10] that you can read easily or you will regret this[20] when transcribing[22]!

Task 29.5

Read and write the following sentences.

1 Crime prevention officers explained the merits of the neighbourhood watch[10] scheme to the members of the community association[18].

2 The judge proposed to place the prowler on probation for[10] a period of twelve months[15].

3 A Social Services Committee considered various child protection cases at[10] their weekly case conference[14].

4 When the precocious child was prevented from playing near the[10] riverbank, for his own safety, he protested[17].

5 The National Lottery promotes many good causes, but it is[10] difficult to predict the winning numbers[16].

6 Police issued a description of the man they wished to[10] interview. He had been wearing a brown jacket[18].

7 Bric-a-brac always sells well at jumble sales and antique fairs[10] in our village hall[14].

8 An unusual inscription on the grave helped them to trace[10] their ancestors[12].

9 Scrabble is a great word game which can be played[10] by people of all ages and helps to keep the[20] brain active[22].

10 She had been extremely discreet whilst talking to the journalist[10], who proposed to extract more information[16].

Task 29.6

Read and write the following sentences.

1 Youngsters waited outside the theatre in order to get the[10] star's autograph[12].
2 Photographers jostled with each other as they tried to grab[10] an impressive shot[13].
3 Her autobiography had recently been published in the national press[10] and that was why there was a lot of interest[20].
4 She had appeared on the television programme on Saturday night[10] to celebrate the occasion[14].
5 She craved the attention of the media and the public[10] and posed for photographers that evening[16].
6 Details of the secret location had been leaked, so the[10] press office produced a diagram for them[17].
7 She wore a black dress with a monogram embroidered in[10] white silk on the collar[15].
8 When questioned, she said her preferred newspaper was *The Telegraph*[10], but occasionally she read the *Sun*[16].

Task 29.7

Read and write 'Firefighter caught speeding'.

A firefighter has appeared in court having been charged with[10] speeding in a fire engine. Brian Green, aged forty-one[20], of Granville Terrace, was driving a fire engine down the[30] High Street when he was caught by a speed camera[40] in April last year. Magistrates were told, last Thursday, that[50] Brian plans to plead guilty to breaking the thirty miles[60] per hour speed limit, but claims that there was a[70] problem with the fire engine's speedometer. Craig Brown, defending Green[80], said that the Fire Brigade's vehicles do not give correct[90] readings, and that was why police speed cameras were regularly[100] clocking them. The engine in question is to be inspected[110] by police and an engineer from the Fire Service. Other[120] evidence from experts may be given at the next court[130] hearing, to be held on 21 May. Emergency services are[140] exempt from speed limits if they have their blue lights[150] flashing, are on an emergency and are driving with due[160] care and attention. But as soon as the emergency is[170] over, normal rules apply[174].

Unit 30 – The R principle – AR, OR, UR

Task 30.1

Read and write the following sentences.

1 The artist displayed his paintings on the craft stall and[10] members of the public asked if they were originals[19].
2 Oranges were grown in the orchard in the European sunshine[10] and sold for just a few euros per kilogram[19].
3 Urdu is the language spoken by Hindu people and is[10] a fascinating language to read[15].

4 At the flower show there was an interesting array of[10] ornamental grasses[12].

5 Shall we check that the arrangements have been made for[10] our forthcoming trip to European cities[16].

6 As the orchestra began to play I felt the urge[10] to cry as the music brought back sad memories[19].

7 The couple spoke to the vicar and the organist about[10] their order of service and the music for their wedding[20] ceremony[21].

8 The argument continued to get them nowhere, so the union[10] officials agreed to go to arbitration[16].

9 A sense of urgency struck her as she walked home[10] through the urban landscape late at night[17].

10 Journalists do not often fall foul of scandalising the court[10] but are more likely to be in contempt of publication[20], for example accidentally publishing a defendant's previous convictions[28].

Task 30.2

Read and write 'Revised plan for new homes'.

Plans for a housing development that attracted more than five[10]-hundred-and-forty objections have been modified and re-submitted. The[20] Housing Trust has now discarded its original plans for twenty[30], two-storey self-contained flats at Whitelands Farm Cottages. More than one[40]-hundred people turned out to protest against the original plans[50] in October. They were concerned that the flats would not[60] be in keeping with the surrounding area. The application was[70] amended but rejected by the planning committee in January. A[80] Trust spokesman said he could understand the residents' concerns and[90] their architect had designed new drawings accordingly[97].

Task 30.3

Read and write 'Church hit by vandalism'.

A vicar is calling for action against vandals damaging a[10] deteriorating churchyard. Tomb stones have been destroyed and the grounds[20] are plagued by drug users who frequently leave their needles[30]. This inevitably causes problems for people with children and pets[40] who walk through the grounds. The vicar said some of[50] the grave stones have been smashed to pieces. When confronted[60], one youth, who was rocking a grave stone which had[70] been there for more than two-hundred years, said he[80] was testing it to see if it was secure. The[90] vicar admitted that part of the problem was that the[100] graveyard was overgrown and had become a bit of an[110] eyesore. Thefts also recently occurred from the church vestry during[120] a choir practice[124].

Unit 1 – Common words

Outline	Words
	able able to ability after
	a
	at
	be been
	once offence
	local
	do day
	electric
	England
	ever every
	from
	go gentleman guilt
	guilty
	he
	I eye intelligent
	Ireland
	kind knowledge
	King
	like
	letter
	a lot a lot of
	me
	time
	million
	and new knew
	begin
	began
	begun
	or
	of
	page pence police
	equal

question

Queen

are
authority

south

Scotland

to

you

very
have
versus

evidence

above

we

Wales

accident
cross

accident black spot

your

Unit 1 – Common words listed alphabetically

a

a lot

a lot of

ability

able

able to

above

accident

accident black spot

after

and

are

at

authority

be

been

began

begin

begun

cross

day

do

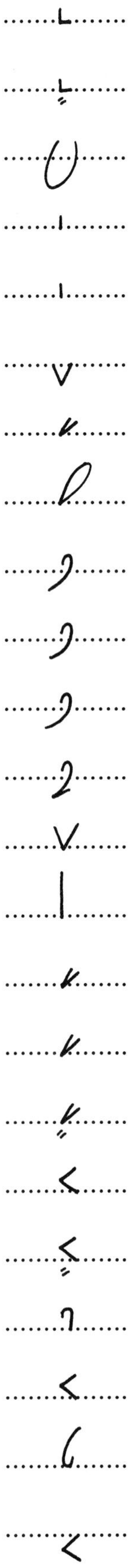

electric
England
equal
ever
every
evidence
eye
from
gentleman
go
guilt
guilty
have
he
I
intelligent
Ireland
kind
King
knew
knowledge
letter
like

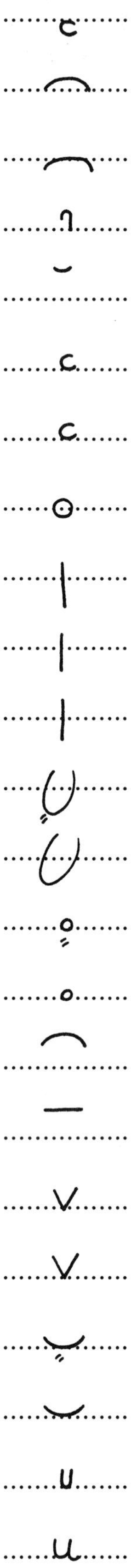

local
me
million
new
of
offence
once
or
page
pence
police
Queen
question
Scotland
south
time
to
versus
very
Wales
we
you
your

Special outlines

Unit 2

	account
	because
	company
	etcetera
	o'clock
	opportunity
	represent/ative
	they
	with

Unit 3

	chairman
	each
	English
	much
	shall
	such
	that
	the
	there/their
	to do/today
	too much
	what
	where
	which

Unit 4

	access
	also
	always
	business
	businesses
	city
	services
	success
	witnesses

Unit 5

	club
	hospital

job/jobs

Unit 6

blood

husband

nation

non(e)

north

number

number of

Unit 7

immediate

incident

together

within

without

Unit 8

absolute

absolutely

electricity

immediately

necessary

obvious

obviously

oil

Unit 9

Archbishop

area

equivalent

individual

only

ought

someone

Unit 10

anything

arrange

charge

language

nothing

respect

something

Unit 11

enclose

enclosed

enclosure

inability

Unit 12

circumstance

circumstances

difference

different

difficult

difficulty

importance

important

inch

inches

insurance

Unit 13

establish

major

majority

regularly

resident

satisfactory

satisfied

separately

sympathetic

sympathy

Unit 14

before

February

fortunate

frequent

inform

manufacture

perfect

perfectly

prefer

reference

respectful

successful

telephone

therefore

unfortunate

unfortunately

Unit 15

advert

advertisement

amount
category
department
development
government
member

Unit 16

anxious
application
attention
electrician
financial
identification
information
intention
particular
qualification
station
substantial
super
superb
supermarket

Unit 17

alternative
children
general
generally
identify
minimum
remember
yesterday

Unit 18

association
insignificant
residents' assn
significant
society

Unit 19

emergency
landlord
motorway
our
remarks
tomorrow

world

Unit 21

approximately

examination

exchange

expensive

experience

extra

extraordinary

inexpensive

inexperience

maximum

Unit 22

combination

commerce

commercial

communication

community

competitive

comprehensive

computer

recommendation

Unit 23

advantage

arrival

arrive

disadvantage

environment

however

several

Unit 24

conference

congratulate

congratulations

convenience

convenient

council

councillor

discontinue

discount

inconvenient

permanent

recent

recently

recognise

 taken

Unit 25

 employ

 employer

 employment

 people

 public

Unit 26

 impossible

 insuperable

 respectable

 responsible

Unit 28

 electronic

 technical

 technological

Unit 29

 agriculture

 appropriate

 improve

 improvement

 prejudice

 preliminary

 preparation

 prepare

 principle/ principal

 probable

 probably

 problem

 production

 profit

 prominent

 proportion

 prosecution

 subscriber

 subscription

Unit 30

 ordinarily

 ordinary

 organisation

Special outlines listed alphabetically

absolute
absolutely
access
account
advantage
advert
advertisement
agriculture
also
alternative
always
amount
anxious
anything
application
appropriate
approximately
Archbishop
area
arrange
arrival
arrive

association
attention
because
before
blood
business
businesses
category
chairman
charge
children
circumstance
circumstances
city
club
combination
commerce
commercial
communication
community
company
competitive
comprehensive

computer
conference
congratulate
congratulations
convenience
convenient
council
councillor
department
development
difference
different
difficult
difficulty
disadvantage
discontinue
discount
each
electrician
electricity
electronic
emergency
employ
employer
employment
enclose
enclosed
enclosure
English
environment
equivalent
establish
etcetera
examination
exchange
expensive
experience
extra
extraordinary
February
financial
fortunate
frequent
general
generally
government
hospital
however

husband
identification
identify
immediate
immediately
importance
important
impossible
improve
improvement
inability
inch
inches
incident
inconvenient
individual
inexpensive
inexperience
inform
information
insignificant
insuperable
insurance
intention

job
jobs
landlord
language
major
majority
manufacture
maximum
member
minimum
motorway
much
nation
necessary
non(e)
north
nothing
number
number of
o'clock
obvious
obviously
oil
only

opportunity
ordinarily
ordinary
organisation
ought
our
particular
people
perfect
perfectly
permanent
prefer
prejudice
preliminary
preparation
prepare
principle/principal
probable
probably
problem
production
profit
prominent
proportion

prosecution
public
qualification
recent
recently
recognise
recommendation
reference
regularly
remarks
remember
represent/ative
resident
residents' assn
respect
respectable
respectful
responsible
satisfactory
satisfied
separately
services
several
shall

significant
society
someone
something
station
subscriber
subscription
substantial
success
successful
such
super
superb
supermarket
sympathetic
sympathy
taken
technical
technological
telephone

that
the
there/their
therefore
they
to do/today
together
tomorrow
too much
unfortunate
unfortunately
what
where
which
with
within
without
witnesses
world
yesterday

Distinguishing outlines

Unit 3

 this

 these

 those

Unit 4

 has

 his

 amused

 amazed

 purpose

 perhaps

Unit 7

 in fact

 in effect

Unit 8

 behind

 beyond

 years ago

 years of age

Unit 9

 on

 one

 use

 ease

 usually

 easily

 easy

 easier

Unit 14

 firm

 form

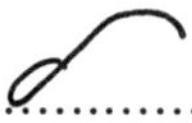 farm

Unit 16

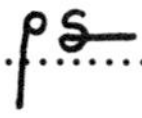 specialist

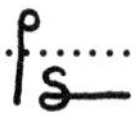 specialised

Unit 17

 industries

 industrious

Unit 18

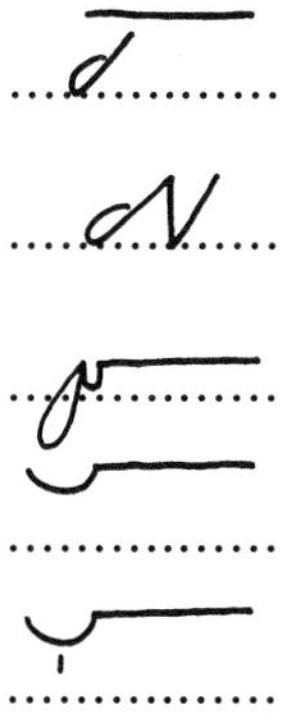

farther
further
future
water
weather
whether

Unit 19

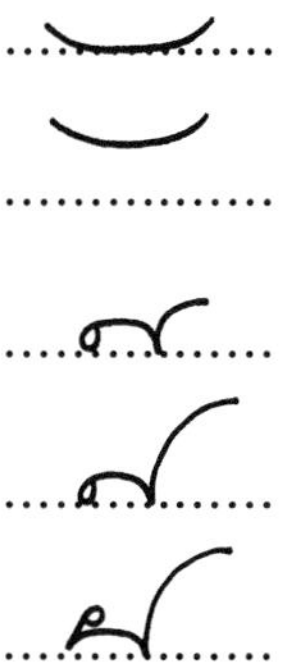

were
where
small
smaller
similar

Unit 21

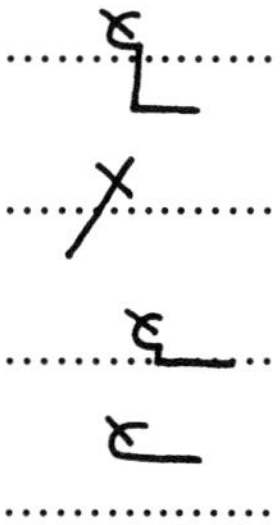

except
expect
exceed
exact

Unit 22

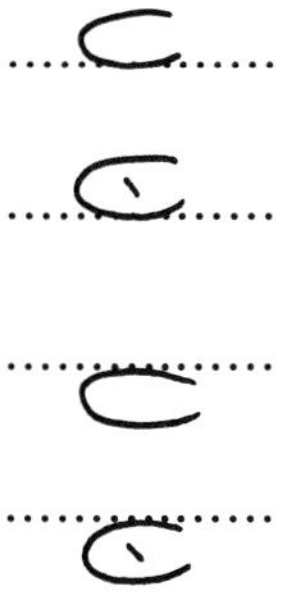

come
came
become
became

Unit 23

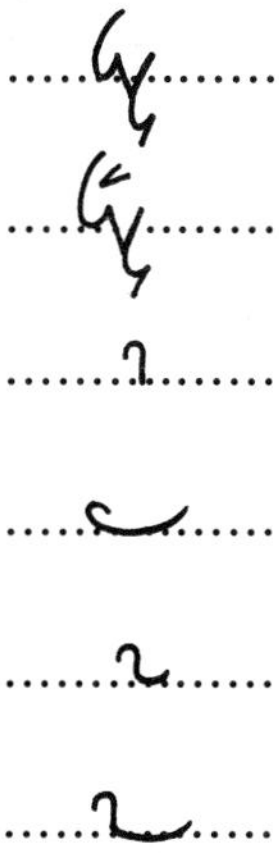

lovely
lively
new/knew
now
no
know

Unit 24

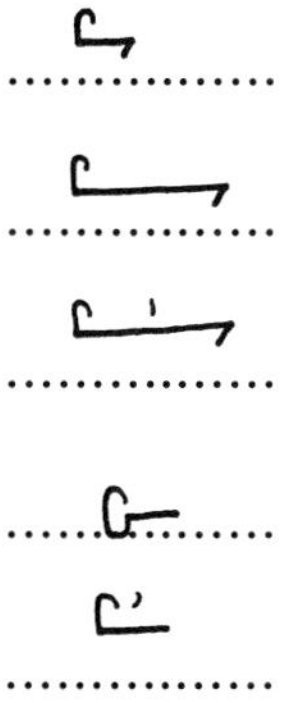

county
country
century
cannot
can't

Unit 25

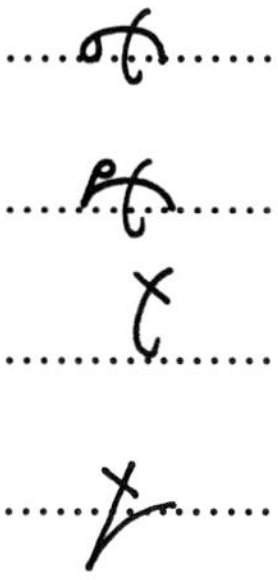

sample
simple
excel
expel

Unit 28

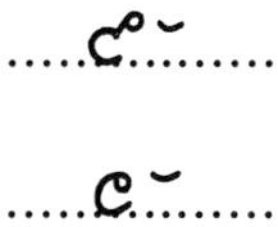

psychology
sociology

Word groupings

Unit 5

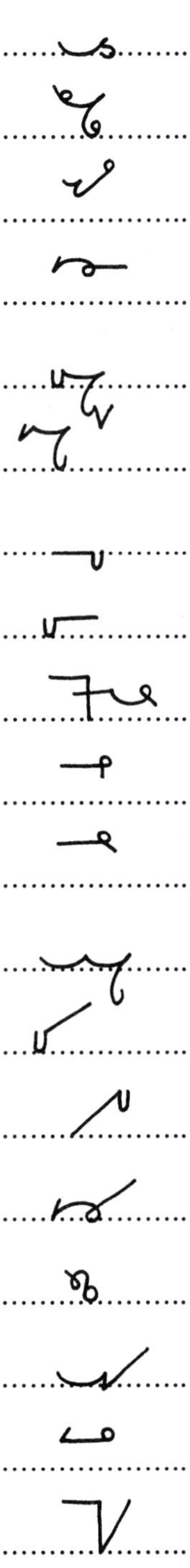

we shall
as well as
of course
I must
you will have
I will
do you
you do
that was a
to see
to say
we will
you are
are you
I am sure
as soon as
we are
it is
they are

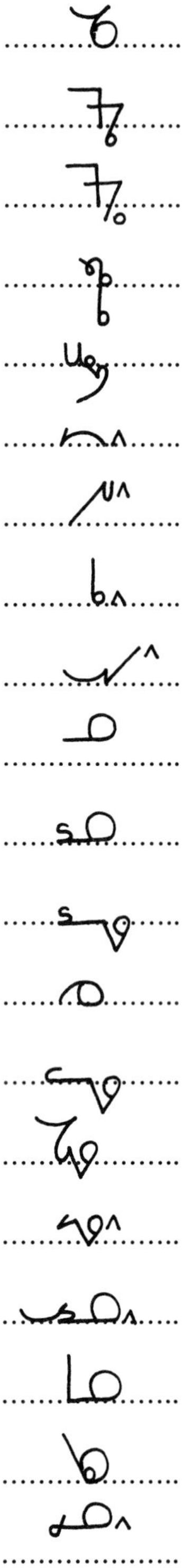

will be
that this
that this is
as soon as possible
years ago
I am able to
are you able to
he is able to
we are able to
to be
should be
should have been
may be
could have been
will have been
I have been able to
we should be able to
had been
has been
is to be able to

....	it has been
....	they have been
....	must be
....	I must be able to
....	that it has been able to
....	there is
....	there has been
....	is there a
....	there is no
....	there are
....	there is to be
....	have there been
....	is there/their
....	that there/their
....	we shall be there/their
....	all the
....	by the
....	from the
....	in the
....	we have the
....	is the
....	as the
....	at the
....	of the

....	across the
....	that the
....	and the
....	with the
....	to the
....	if the
....	be the
....	as soon as the
....	at the same time
....	was the
....	will have the
....	this is
....	this is the
....	that this is
....	if this is the
....	at the centre
....	from the centre
....	to the centre
....	leisure centre
....	town centre
....	at the middle
....	to the middle
....	from the middle
....	in the middle

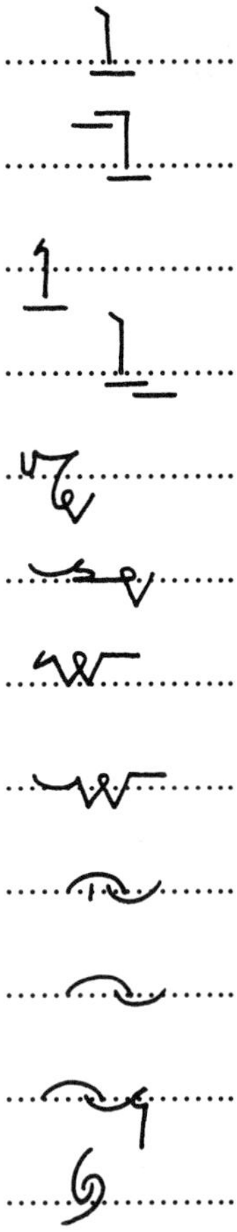

at the end

to the end

in the end

at the end of the day

you will receive

we should receive

I have received

we have received

men and women

man and woman

man, woman and child

ladies and gentlemen

Unit 6

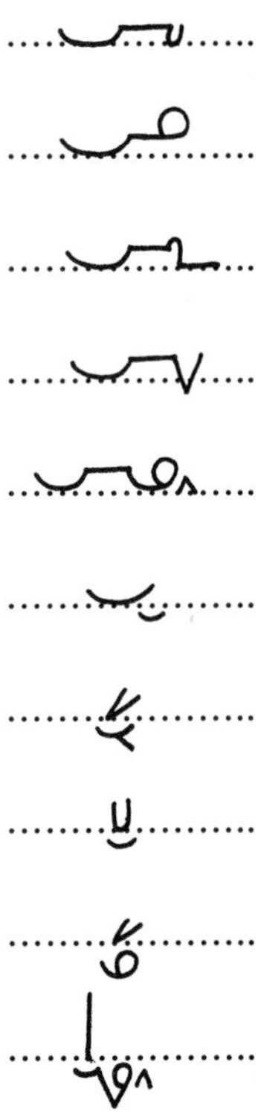

would you

would be

would not

would have

would we be able to

we would

I would like

you would

I would be

he would have been able to

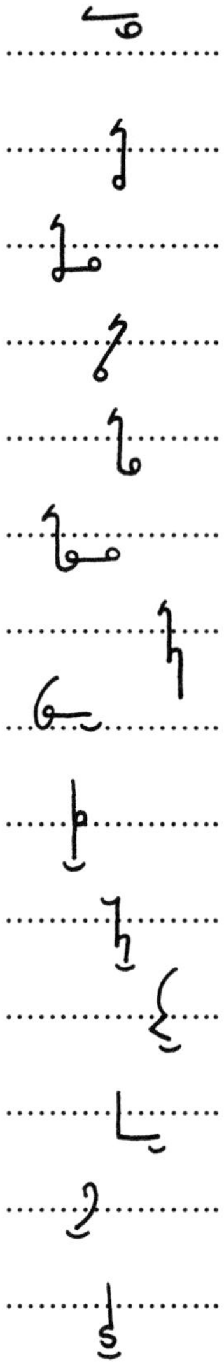

it would be

in these

in these days

in this

in those

in those days

in the north

last word

hospital ward

open wide

look forward

put forward

go forward

push forward

Unit 7

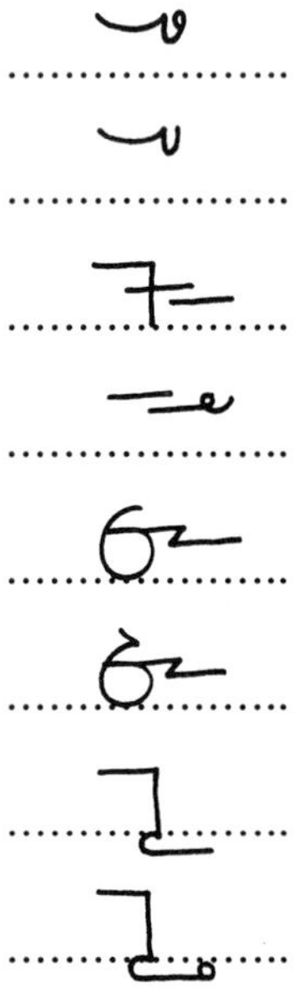

with us

with you

that day

to do so

but it

about it

the fact

the facts

the fact that

it is a fact that

Unit 8

I am sorry

in this day and age

last week

Unit 9

not only

on the other hand

no doubt

Unit 10

needing the

having the

making the

being the

doing the

meeting the

needing this

having these

making those

meeting them

hoping they

good thing

many things

all things

such a thing

such things

something else

charged with

Unit 11

to the bank

river banks

the banking hall

the bank manager

to thank

their thanks

I am thanking

they thanked

I think

we think

do you think

are you able to think

thank you

vote of thanks

we enclose

Unit 12

- at once
- in the circumstances
- circumstantial evidence
- it is important
- most important
- as much as
- such as

Unit 13

- the facility
- these facilities
- hospital facilities
- local authority
- health authority
- all sorts of things
- as a result

Unit 14

- for the
- far from
- first of all
- for ever and ever
- as far as
- so far as
- some sort of
- in accordance
- for instance

Unit 15

- do you require
- the required
- it is a requirement
- we required
- he requires
- we are requiring
- not guilty
- in favour
- last minute
- Houses of Parliament
- Member of Parliament
- M.P.

Unit 16

- Social Services

Unit 17

- high street
- as a matter of fact

as a matter of course

in order to

in order that

name and address

names and addresses

Unit 18

during their

whether or not

some other

car park

Unit 19

more than

older than

rather than

smaller than

later than

bigger than

worthwhile

this morning

smaller and smaller

larger and larger

more and more

more or less

more and more important

much more important

parts of the world

all parts of the world

sum of money

sums of money

worth considering

worse for wear

where were you

we were quite right

we were quite wrong

all over the world

all over the district

all over the shop

Unit 20

there were hundreds of

there were thousands of

there were hundreds and thousands of

straight to the point

on the spot

Unit 21

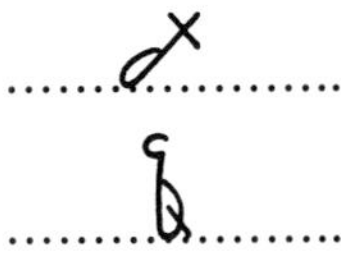

- for example
- chief executive

Unit 22

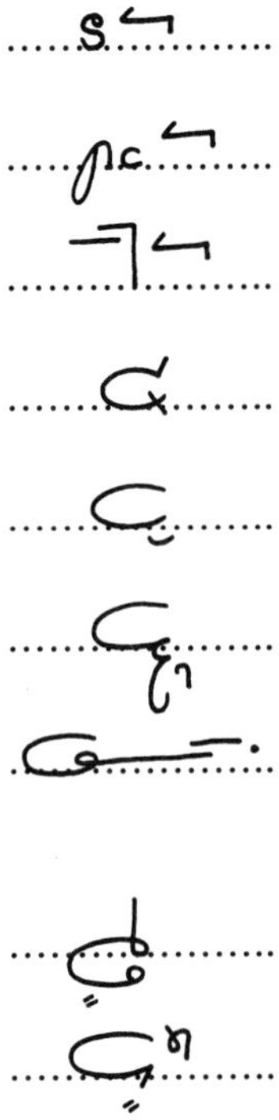

- social committee
- finance committee
- to the committee
- income tax
- come forward
- come to the conclusion
- come straight to the point
- House of Commons
- Community Association

Unit 23

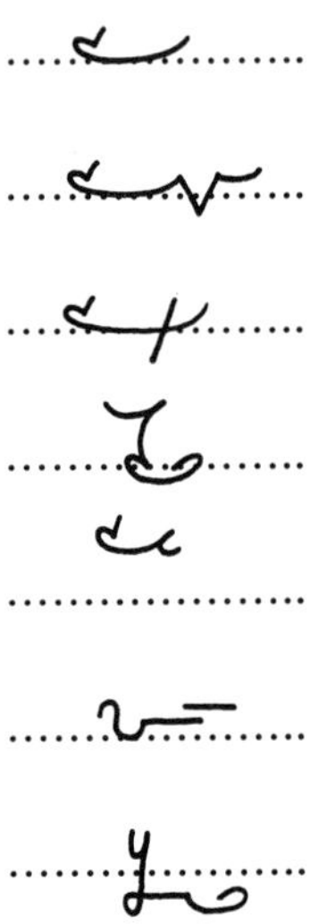

- in our
- in our view
- in our opinion
- well known
- in which
- no doubt
- upside down

Unit 24

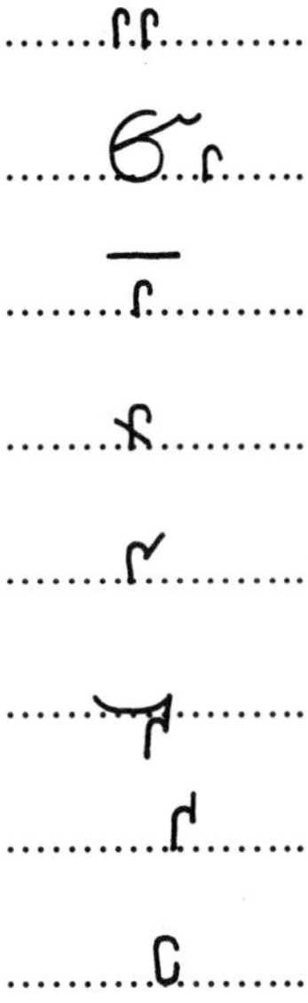

- county council
- borough council
- town council
- council tax
- I can
- we can
- you can
- can you

Unit 25

- members of the public
- we should be pleased
- we are pleased to know
- it is my pleasure
- I am pleased
- your reply

Unit 27

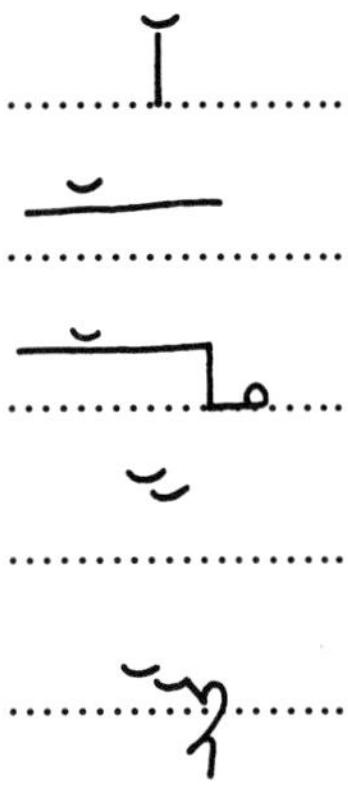

- over the
- over there/their
- over their heads
- over and over
- over and over again

 over and done with

 all over the country

 all over the district

 all over the place

 all over the world

 multi-storey car park

Unit 28

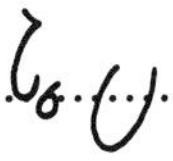 all things being equal

Unit 29

 credit card

 great deal

 at present

 at the present time

Unit 30

 at home and abroad

This page may be used to note additional or alternative Teeline outlines, shortcuts, word groupings etc.: